Psychology of Learning

PERGAMON GENERAL PSYCHOLOGY SERIES

Editors: Arnold P. Goldstein, *Syracuse University*
Leonard Krasner, *SUNY, Stony Brook*

The terms of our inspection copy service apply to all the above books. A complete catalogue of all books in the Pergamon International Library is available on request.

The Publisher will be pleased to receive suggestions for revised editions and new titles.

Psychology of Learning:
A Conceptual Analysis

Kenneth P. Hillner
South Dakota State University
Brookings, South Dakota

PERGAMON PRESS
Oxford / New York / Toronto / Sydney / Frankfurt / Paris

41437

Pergamon Press Offices:

U.S.A.	Pergamon Press Inc., Maxwell House, Fairview Park, Elmsford, New York 10523, U.S.A.
U.K.	Pergamon Press Ltd., Headington Hill Hall, Oxford OX3, OBW, England
CANADA	Pergamon of Canada, Ltd., 75 The East Mall, Toronto, Ontario M8Z 5W3, Canada
AUSTRALIA	Pergamon Press (Aust) Pty. Ltd., 19a Boundary Street, Rushcutters Bay, N.S.W. 2011, Australia
FRANCE	Pergamon Press SARL, 24 rue des Ecoles, 75240 Paris, Cedex 05, France
WEST GERMANY	Pergamon Press GmbH, 6242 Kronberg/Taunus, Pferdstrasse 1, West Germany

Copyright © 1978 Pergamon Press Inc.

Library of Congress Cataloging in Publication Data

Hillner, Kenneth P.
Learning psychology.

(Pergamon general psychology series)
1. Learning, Psychology of.   I.   Title.
LB1051.H527   1976   153.1'5   76-22696
ISBN 0-08-017864-2
ISBN 0-08-017865-0 pbk.

*All Rights Reserved. No part of this publication may
be reproduced, stored in a retrieval system or transmitted
in any form or by any means: electronic, electrostatic,
magnetic tape, mechanical, photocopying, recording or
otherwise, without permission in writing from the publishers.*

Printed in the United States of America

This book is formally dedicated to my sons, Paul and Andrew, and their grandparents. It is symbolically dedicated to Cookie Lavagetto.

Contents

41437

Preface

INTRODUCTION

Learning constitutes one of the classical areas of experimental psychology, both at the empirical and theoretical level. At one phase in its history (the macro-theoretical era: 1930s-1940s), learning served as the model area for the entire field of experimental psychology. The content and scope of contemporary experimental psychology is so immense and diverse that learning has devolved into merely one of a number of alternative approaches to the experimental analysis of behavior; however, the methodological techniques and theoretical mechanisms used by learning psychologists have become so sophisticated over the last two decades that the area of learning has undergone a virtual revolution. This revitalization of the core area of learning has sufficiently compensated (if not overcompensated) for its changed relationship to the overall field of experimental psychology.

Anyone who has been assigned the task of organizing a one-semester introductory course on learning knows that this revitalization has led to the publication of numerous excellent, but highly specialized, learning texts covering such topics as operant conditioning, punishment and aversive techniques, verbal learning, concept formation, human memory, mathematical models, information processing, language acquisition and behavior, etc. Unfortunately, the fragmentation of experimental learning psychology into a number of highly technical subareas has made the construction of a general conceptual introduction to the field a virtual intellectual and marketing impossibility. As a consequence, there is no up-to-date introductory learning text on the market to which the student can appeal for a presentation of learning as an organized set of operational and theoretical principles with a uniform set of terminology.

This book represents the author's attempt to partially fill this conceptual need. The book does not treat the many and diverse "facts" of learning as such; it does not review the myriad sets of experimental data generated by learning research. Rather, the book presents the conceptual framework in which most of the "facts" of learning have been generated. A conservative assessment of the volume is that it analyzes and classifies the various metatheoretical assumptions used by experimental psychologists to investigate the empirical phenomenon of learning. A more grandiose claim would be that the book codifies the area of experimental learning psychology.

The text is geared to the serious, professionally oriented experimental psychology student, either undergraduate or graduate, who desires a deductive presentation/analysis of learning psychology. Since the level of presentation minimally presumes prior exposure to an experimentally oriented introductory psychology course in which learning constituted one of the "selected topics," an introductory chapter, reviewing the nature and purpose of both experimental psychology and learning, is included in the text. Additional prerequisites depend upon the individual student's background and interests. The student with some philosophical and mathematical sophistication and a high interest level in learning can profit from the book without prior exposure to a rigorous, analytical learning psychology course. For other students, the contents of the book will be more meaningful if processed as part of a standard lecture or laboratory course on the psychology of learning.

OVERVIEW OF THE CONCEPTUAL ANALYSIS

Alternative conceptual frameworks for analyzing learning or alternative organizations for presenting the metatheoretical assumptions of learning exist. Somewhat arbitrarily, I have chosen to analyze the structure of learning psychology as opposed to the dynamics of learning psychology and I have divided the conceptual learning situation into three (not necessarily mutually exclusive or independent) structural units: (1) the input situation, (2) the output situation, and (3) the intervening situation. The first two structural units are assumed to refer to real, existential events in the universe — the input and output situations constitute essentially objective events in the universe which can be actively produced, controlled, and/or measured by the experimenter. As such, they constitute a descriptive level of reality, although their analysis requires many interpretive assumptions. The third structural unit is not assumed to refer to objective events in the universe — the intervening situation refers strictly to convenient or pragmatic postulations on the part of the experimenter relative to what goes on in the organism while learning. As such, the third structural unit constitutes a purely theoretical, nondescriptive level of reality.

Procedurally, each structural unit is defined and analyzed independent of its use in learning psychology; only later is it deductively related or applied to the learning situation. Analysis of the input situation covers such conceptual problems as the nature of a stimulus, the notion of an experimental operation, and the concept of experimental procedure. Application of the analytical input situation to the learning situation generates such problems as the nature of a reinforcing stimulus, the notion of a reinforcing operation, and the concept of a standard learning task. Analysis of the output situation includes such conceptual problems as the nature of a response, methods of response specification, and response measurement. Application of the analytical output situation to the learning situation generates such problems as the nature of a learned response, methods of learned response specification, and quantification of a learned response. Analysis of the intervening situation refers to such problems as the nature, origin, construction, and evaluation of a theory, and types of theories and theoretical constructs. Application of the analytical intervening situation to the learning situation generates such problems as the nature of the underlying learning process, the different theoretical approaches to learning, and the theoretical mechanisms underlying the procedural effects of reinforcement.

Figure 1 depicts the linear sequencing and logical structure of the conceptual analysis. The book consists of nine chapters and the essential content of each is indicated on the figure. The number associated with each chapter/topic on the diagram indicates its linear order of appearance in the text. The logical structure of the conceptual analysis is represented by a branching configuration. The spatial location of each topic cell in the branching configuration represents its position in the logical structure of the conceptual analysis. Both the vertical and horizontal dimensions of the figure have meaning. The three main vertical branches represent the structural input, intervening, and output situations, respectively — in a left to right direction. The three horizontal rows — from top to bottom — represent successively deeper levels of the conceptual analysis. Level One defines and analyzes the three structural units of the conceptual analysis and relates them to the learning situation in a preliminary way. Level Two represents the systematic and comprehensive application of the basic structural units to the conceptual learning situation. The content of Level Three overlaps quite heavily with the kind of material found in the typical introductory book on learning. Note that the last two topics (chapters) relate to more than one structural unit. As an example of interpretation of the figure, topic 5, "Learning and Extinction Tasks and Phenomena" (discussed in Chapter 5), concerns the input situation at the second level of analysis.

Mention should be made of the scope of the analysis contained in Level Three. Chapter 5 in Level Two formally distinguishes between learning tasks, extinction tasks, learning phenomena, and extinction phenomena. The last three terms constitute logical and/or procedural extensions of a learning task per se. But to delimit the scope of the conceptual analysis of the learning situation, Level Three focuses on learning exclusively as a property of a learning task per se and concentrates solely on the nature of the learning process and the nature of reinforcement associated with the acquisition or original learning phase (of a possible multiphase learning experiment). This means that extinction, extinction phenomena, and learning phenomena such as generalization, discrimination, memory, transfer of training, partial reinforcement, etc., although generated at the second level of analysis, are not analyzed in depth at Level Three.

The reader is invited to follow any one of the conceptual or logical branches of the analysis, instead of the linear sequence, depending upon specific interests and motivations; however, it is advisable to process the topics/chapters along a specific branch in sequence because of the deductive method of presentation and nested order of topical coverage.

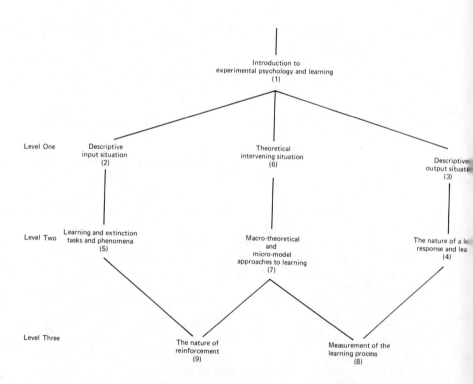

Fig. 1. Linear Sequencing and Logical Structure of the Conceptual Analysis

Acknowledgments

Many people contribute to the composition and production of a book. I would like to express appreciation to Gerald P. Deegan, formerly Managing Editor, and Mrs. Sylvia M. Halpern, Chief Manuscript Editor, of Pergamon Press. My friend and colleague, Al Branum, read and commented upon portions of the text. My wife Sally (nee Sarah) transcribed the initial 75 pages of the text from written to typed form. Recognition is extended to the South Dakota State Psychology Department and its Chairman, Richard Ritter, for providing Ms. Ronetta Blackburn who assiduously typed a ditto copy of the first seven chapters of the manuscript. The South Dakota State printing department performed miscellaneous duplication. Finally, mention should be made of a number of prominent learning psychologists who made me feel that learning psychology is the most fascinating topic in the world: Edward Green and John McCrary (Dartmouth College); William Estes (Rockefeller University); James Greeno (University of Michigan); Frank Restle, Irving Saltzman, Lloyd Peterson, and Donald Lauer (Indiana University).

Roger Brown once acknowledged a certain Boston radio station for providing him with appropriate background music for writing his book on social psychology. I wrote this book because it had to be written; at a more analytical level, I thank my parents for providing me with a need for achievement motive and an atmosphere in which scholarly endeavors were appreciated and reinforced.

Kenneth P. Hillner
Psychology Department
South Dakota State University
Brookings, South Dakota 57006
USA

1
Introduction to Experimental Psychology and Learning

INTRODUCTION

The Preface established the fact that learning is a subarea of experimental psychology. This chapter presents a rudimentary account of experimental psychology as well as an initial, low-level characterization of learning. A brief discussion of experimental psychology is necessary to demonstrate the explicit source of two of the structural units of analysis – the input and output situations. A brief description of learning affords the opportunity for each reader to develop the same essential or minimally consistent conception of learning from which the conceptual analysis can logically proceed. The topic of learning is considered first in the chapter so that certain aspects of experimental psychology can later be more meaningfully illustrated in a learning context. The chapter concludes with a transitional section in which the descriptive input and output situations are formally generated.

AN INITIAL CHARACTERIZATION OF LEARNING

The term "learning" is one of the few technical terms of experimental psychology that is also part of the general culture. Laymen use the term to refer to changes on the part of the organism occasioned by exposure to some sort of past experience or training condition(s). The layman's use of the term is certainly continuous with most operational definitions of learning put forward by learning psychologists; but the cultural use of the term in no way connotes all the diverse natural phenomena to which professional learning psychologists apply the term. The following listing attempts to present the general flavor of the diversity of learning and learning phenomena.

1. Learning encompasses all organismic behavior, both animal and human. It is also concerned with the adaptive behavior of inanimate conceptual systems such as machines, robots, computers, etc. Likewise, learning is not only applicable to the behavior of the intact or whole organism but also to the activity of an isolated response system.

2. Learning not only deals with the behavior of the average or statistical subject but also with individual differences (i.e., slow learners, fast learners, etc.).

3. Learning involves such diverse events as the occurrence of an isolated muscle twitch, the acquisition of a prejudice, the acquisition of an abstract, symbolic (often unverbalizable) concept or grammatical rule, the acquisition of a neurotic symptom, etc.

4. Learning is not limited to the external responses of the organism, which operate on the environment, but also relates to the many and diverse internal and strictly physiological responses of the organism.

5. Learning encompasses punishment and punishment phenomena as well as other aversive control techniques and mechanisms in addition to the more culturally visible reward or positive incentive control techniques and mechanisms.

6. Learning is not only concerned with the original acquisition of a learned response (the original acquisition phase of a learning experiment) but also with its later disappearance (extinction), its retention after a time-out interval (memory), and its possible value in the acquisition of a new, different response (transfer of training), etc.

7. Learning is related to such nonlearning operations and phenomena as motivation, perception, psychological development, personality structure, social and cultural factors, etc.

8. Learning has a physical or structural (i.e., physiological, biochemical, etc.) reality as well as a strictly psychological or operational (functional) reality.

9. Learning is not only associated with a long intellectual, theoretical, and aesthetic tradition but also serves as a source of practical application and implementable technology.

10. Learning and learning phenomena are continuous with and serve as a component of the more general linguistic, communicative, cognitive, information-processing, and decision-making activities of the organism.

Regardless of whether this listing has accomplished its intended purpose, it would be didactic at this point to formally characterize the nature of a learning psychologist's activities and interests. These are only limited by the dual restriction that the natural phenomena under investigation (1) possess some degree of permanence or potential irreversibility and (2) be related in some way to reinforcement or reinforced practice (these two conditions implicitly serving as a low-level characterization of a learning or learning-related event). It would not be too far amiss to describe the primary experimental task of a learning psychologist as the determination of just which experimental operations or naturally occurring events can serve as reinforcing operations or events and just which behaviors are learnable. The concept of reinforcement is the canonical aspect of learning and is continuous with the more general psychological notions of feedback, knowledge of results, servomechanical mechanisms of control and regulation, evolutionary selection mechanisms, etc. It is too soon to characterize the structural basis or potential irreversibility of a learned change in behavior.

In brief, learning psychology studies the permanent or potentially irreversible behavioral phenomena related to reinforced practice by using the same essential conceptual framework, theoretical assumptions, methodological techniques, etc. characteristic of the overall field of experimental psychology.

THE NATURE OF EXPERIMENTAL PSYCHOLOGY

INTRODUCTION

Probably no other academic discipline is more misunderstood than psychology. Misconceptions range from "Psychology studies the mind" to "Psychology is Freud." These misconceptions do not extinguish because the layman is only exposed to nonacademic psychology by the mass media and even individuals who have had the opportunity to study general, introductory psychology are not immune to the proactive and retroactive forces which lead to forgetting. The following discussion is intended either to correct what you now erroneously believe about psychology or to refresh your memory about what you once knew concerning psychology so that the source of the input and output situations can be adequately described.

DEFINITION, PURPOSE, AND CONTENT OF PSYCHOLOGY

Most American psychologists, since they operate in the tradition of Watsonian behaviorism, would argue that the primary focus of psychology is behavior — the behavior of living organisms, whether animal or human. This statement does not gainsay the existence of phenomenologically oriented psychologists. But they simply do not constitute a significant proportion of experimental, especially learning, psychologists. Other academic disciplines are also interested in behavior: art, literature, philosophy, theology, etc. What distinguishes psychology from them is its methodology. Psychology investigates behavior by means of the scientific method. Thus, psychology is often defined as the science of behavior. If the traditional methodology and techniques of science are applied to the study of behavior, the discipline of experimental psychology arises. It is the purpose of psychology to give behavior a scientific explanation. This fact has at least three major consequences for the subject matter and content of psychology:

1. The only behaviors explainable by psychology as a scientific discipline are those that can be brought into and studied in the experimental laboratory. As a consequence, psychologists usually investigate only limited or restricted forms of behavior at a given time.

2. Once a particular behavior has been given a scientific explanation, it should also be possible (in theory at least) to manipulate, control, and predict that behavior. This fact serves as a partial justification for analyzing behavior in scientific terms. No other kind of explanation allows the prediction and control of behavior. A more complete treatment of the notions of prediction and control in relation to scientific explanation is given in a later subsection.

3. A scientific explanation of behavior has a certain structure or form, which is derived from certain assumptions about the nature of scientific "truth," as dictated by the philosophy of science. Whatever constitutes a fact or "truth" in science has a certain structure or form. Psychology, as a branch of science, must use the same structure or form for its facts or "truths" about behavior. It is now necessary to describe the nature of scientific explanation in some detail.

THE NATURE OF SCIENTIFIC EXPLANATION

The nature of scientific explanation rests upon the assumption that every natural event in the universe has a cause; if the cause can be made to occur, the natural event must occur. Events in the natural world are lawful; they follow some causal law. So, behavior, as a natural event in the universe, is determined. It is not a random, unpredictable event, occurring in a vacuum. The causes of natural events, like behavior, are assumed to be other overt, physical, external, natural events.

The term "cause" is no longer used by most scientists because, for many reasons, the concept of causation is out of fashion in the philosophy of science. One of these reasons will be specified later in the chapter. The terms "external factors," "antecedent conditions," or "preceding events" are used instead of "cause(s)." When any one of these three terms is employed, the assumption underlying the nature of scientific explanation is stated somewhat differently: every natural event in the universe, like behavior, can be expressed as a function of certain external factors, antecedent conditions, or preceding events. This statement can be represented symbolically, as in Fig. 1-1. This sequence of symbols is usually read as "Y is a function of X_1, X_2, etc., up to X_N, where N is some finite number." With Y representing a piece of behavior and the Xs representing the antecedent conditions of which it is a function, the sequence can be interpreted as "A piece of behavior is a function of numerous, but finitely countable, antecedent conditions."

$$Y \qquad = f\,(X_1, X_2, X_3, X_4, \ldots X_N), \text{ where } N < \infty.$$

	Natural events
Natural Event	External factors
Behavior	Antecedent conditions

Fig. 1-1. Symbolic Representation of a Functional Relationship

Let us illustrate this rather abstract sequence of labels by reference to a specific kind of learned behavior and a specific set of appropriate antecedent conditions. For instance, the behavior in question could be the operant response of an organism (rat, pigeon, monkey, human, etc.) in an appropriately constructed "Skinner box". The term "response" is used here as a full equivalent for the word "behavior" to allow flexibility in exposition, although the notion of a response will not formally be introduced until later in the chapter. The specific response manipulandum varies with the species: a bar for a rat, a circular disc for a pigeon, a lever for a monkey, a button for a human, etc. The basic point is that the specific rate of operant responding exhibited by the organism depends upon a host of factors. Limiting ourselves to just one set of factors – the set generated by the reinforcement dimension or the nature of reinforced practice – the specific factors could include schedule of reinforcement, delay of reinforcement per response, quantity or amount of reinforcement per response, quality or hedonic value of reinforcement per response, the reinforcement criterion, etc. The nature of the physical reinforcing object itself varies with the species: a commercial food pellet for the rat, a few seconds exposure to a grain dish for the pigeon, a few licks of water for the monkey, a candy bar or some kind of symbolic token for the human, etc. So, operant responding, as a kind of learned response, is a function of various reinforcement factors such as schedule, delay, amount, etc.

Two characteristics of a $Y = f(X)$ relationship should be made explicit. Initially, do not make the mistake of inferring that the spatial order of symbols from left to right also represents the temporal order of symbols. The causes of a specific piece of behavior must either precede or be simultaneous with the behavior in time. The causes of a specific piece of behavior cannot follow the occurrence of that behavior in time. Secondly, the total number of causes for a piece of behavior must be assumed to be finite. In order for behavior to be determined, all of its causes must eventually be capable of being known or isolated. This is not possible under an assumption of infinite causation. One could start today, continue forever, and never isolate all the causes of a piece of behavior. So, in effect, infinite causation is equivalent to no causation (free will), and nondeterminism exists at either end of the numerical causal continuum (zero, infinity).

THE DEFINITION OF SCIENTIFIC EXPLANATION

The physical representation of a functional relationship in Fig. 1-1 is important because it also represents the structure of a scientific explanation. Scientific explanation is merely the specification of those factors that are related to the occurrence of a natural event. A piece of behavior Y has been scientifically explained once it has been placed in a specific $Y = f(X)$ relationship.

Let us refer to the operant responding example again. What constitutes a scientific explanation of operant responding? Operant responding has been scientifically explained once it has been related to different sets of external factors, such as reinforcement. Operant responding has been scientifically explained once it has been placed in a specific $Y = f(X)$ relationship.

THE SOURCE OR ORIGIN OF A SPECIFIC FUNCTIONAL RELATIONSHIP

Since it is the task of experimental psychology to scientifically explain a piece of behavior by placing it in a specific $Y = f(X)$ relationship, the question of the source or origin of a functional relationship naturally arises. How is a specific functional relationship set up? How do we know operant responding is a function of various reinforcement factors? The complete answer to these questions would represent the essential content of a course in experimental design and statistics. The process of establishing a functional relationship can be briefly characterized in terms of three summary steps — with specific reference to operant responding and amount of reinforcement per response as the representative antecedent condition. For the remainder of this subsection, operant responding will be abbreviated as OR and amount of reinforcement per response as ARpr.

1. Initially, the psychologist believes or thinks that the ARpr is a determinant of the rate of OR. At this stage, the belief that OR is a function of ARpr is often called a hypothesis. Note that a hypothesis has the same structure or form as a functional relationship: $Y = f(X)$. The only difference is in the truth value of the statement. You do not know that $Y = f(X)$; you simply believe that

$Y = f(X)$. In fact, the next step in the process is an explicit attempt to assess the actual truth value of the hypothesis.

Before proceeding to the second step, it is logical to discuss the source or origin of a hypothesis. Where does a specific hypothesis come from? Briefly, there are four common sources. (a) It can be formally derived from a theory; it is an explicit prediction of some theory. (b) It can result from an assiduous and conscientious search and review of the research literature by the psychologist; as such, the content of the hypothesis represents the most reasonable or logical summary generalization explaining all the experimental data reviewed. (c) It is simply an informal "hunch" on the part of the psychologist, which suddenly appears in the psychologist's head, usually while engaged in some activity unrelated to psychology, like bathing, lawn mowing, daydreaming, etc. (d) It results from systematic naturalistic observation of events occurring in the context of everyday life. With reference to OR and ARpr, the psychologist might notice that baseball fans seem to clap longer and louder each time a "home run" hitter is due at bat than when a "singles" hitter is due at the plate.

2. The truth value of a hypothesis is assessed through the physical process of experimentation — i.e., through designing and conducting an experiment. The purpose of experimentation is to generate "data" by which to evaluate the hypothesis. The simplest and most primitive experimental design by which to generate data is the two-group or two-condition experiment. With reference to the OR-ARpr hypothesis, the content of the two groups could be as follows. One group of subjects — group A — would have its rate of OR measured while receiving a large ARpr. The other group of subjects — group B — would have its rate of OR measured while receiving a small ARpr. An attempt must be made to keep every other aspect of the experiment constant or the same across the two groups of subjects (i.e., other reinforcement factors, experimental apparatus, instructions to the subjects, deprivation conditions, background of the subjects, etc.). This is necessary to implement the essential logic underlying the design of the experiment, a description of which follows.

The essential logic underlying the design of the experiment specifies that, if the two groups of subjects A and B differ in terms of their overt behavior, the behavioral difference must be due to the one specific input factor to which they are differentially exposed. Operationally, this inference of causation can only be

Groups	Constant or Equated Factors	The Varied Input Factor	Behavioral Output
A	a, b, c, d, ... q . .	Large amount of reinforcement per response	Rate of responding Q
B	a, b, c, d, ... q . .	Small amount of reinforcement per response	Rate of responding P

$$(Q \neq P)$$

∴ Amount of reinforcement per response (APpr) is the cause of the differential rate of operant responding (OR).

Fig. 1-2. The Logic Underlying the Design of a Simple Two-Group Experiment: John Stuart Mill's Method of Inductive Inference, the Method of Concomitant Variation

valid if the two groups of subjects A and B do in fact differ only with respect to the one crucial input factor. Figure 1-2 presents the underlying logic in structural form. It is a variant of one of John Stuart Mill's methods of inductive inference, specifically the method of concomitant variation. This reference to the underlying logic leads naturally to the third step — interpretation of the data.

3. The rate of responding data generated by the two groups of subjects are compared. Three different experimental outcomes are possible. Three possible quantitative relationships exist between the rate data of groups A and B: (a) A > B; (b) A < B; and (c) A = B. The meaning and significance of each outcome will be discussed in turn.

a. A > B: Group A performs "appreciably better" than group B in terms of the rate of responding data. With this outcome, we can safely infer that ARpr is a determinant of rate of OR. OR is a function of ARpr. OR increases as ARpr increases. The inference can be safely made because only one difference between the two groups was designed into the experiment — the difference in ARpr. The difference in the rate performance between the two groups must be due to the difference in ARpr. "Appreciably better" is given a statistical interpretation. Whether there is an appreciable difference between the two groups can only be determined on the basis of some appropriate statistical test applied to the data. Those with some degree of statistical sophistication will recognize the phrase "statistically significant difference." So, operationally, the large ARpr group being "appreciably better" than the small ARpr group means that there is a "statistically significant difference" between the two groups. Just what has been actually accomplished? We have validated the original hypothesis. We have established that the original hypothesis is true. The original hypothesis is now a causal law or functional relationship.

b. A < B: Group B performs "appreciably better" than group A in terms of the rate of responding data. With this outcome, we have also validated the original hypothesis and established the existence of a causal law — but here the relationship between OR and ARpr is in the opposite direction. OR increases as ARpr decreases.

c. A = B: The third possible outcome is the occurrence of "no appreciable difference" between the two groups A and B with respect to the rate of responding data. Statistically, the two groups are found to be equal in performance. More technically, there is no "statistically significant difference" between the performances of group A and group B. The hypothesis that OR is a function of ARpr is not supported. The hypothesis does not become a causal law. The hypothesis has not been validated. It has not been demonstrated as true. Note that it has not been explicitly proved false. The failure to validate the hypothesis does not demonstrate its falsity. The logic underlying the design of the experiment, as presented in Fig. 1-2, is mute when the behavioral outcome of one group (A: response rate Q) is equal to the behavioral outcome of the other group (B: response rate P). The logic underlying the design simply does not apply when the behavioral outcomes of the two groups are the same (Q = P) and nothing can be inferred about the actual truth value of the hypothesis.

THE NATURE OF TRUTH IN SCIENCE: THE TRUTH VALUE OF A HYPOTHESIS IN PERSPECTIVE

Introduction

Science does not deal with "absolutes" at any level of analysis — with the possible exception of the proposition that sense experience is the only source of "true or worthwhile knowledge." Consequently, science does not deal in absolute truth or falsity, interpreted as monolithic categories. Contexts in which absolute truth and falsity are meaningful notions include theology, logic, mathematics, etc. Theological, logical, and mathematical propositions can be absolutely true or false. But empirical propositions are not absolutely true or false. Rather they possess some probabilistic truth value. This is because the truth value of an empirical proposition is not established through the use of deductive logic or blind faith but rather by means of induction or inductive inference.

Hypothesis Testing and Induction

An experiment is a sophisticated form or type of inductive inference. Consequently, hypothesis testing through experimentation involves inductive inference. Because of this, no experiment demonstrates a hypothesis to be absolutely (logically) true or false. The results of an experiment merely increase or decrease the probabilistic truth value of the hypothesis it is evaluating. Whenever the results of an experiment support the hypothesis being tested, the hypothesis is increased in probabilistic truth value; analogously, whenever the results of an experiment do not support the hypothesis being tested, the hypothesis is decreased in probabilistic truth value.

Conventional Description of the Results of A Hypothesis-Testing Experiment

Scientists typically do not behave as if their discipline only involved probabilistic truth value. This is especially true at the level of reporting the results of hypothesis-testing experiments. Conventionally, the positive evaluation of a hypothesis is referred to as "the confirmation of the hypothesis," "the acceptance of the hypothesis," or even "the demonstration of the absolute truth of the hypothesis." Likewise, the negative evaluation of a hypothesis is conventionally referred to as "the disconfirmation of the hypothesis," "the rejection of the hypothesis," or even "the demonstration of the absolute falsity of the hypothesis." Thus, experimental results are reported as either establishing or not establishing causal laws or functional relationships in an all-or-none fashion.

This conventional description of the results of an experiment, although technically in error, is not harmful because the trained scientist knows and understands the ultimate nature and limitations of "scientific truth." (It does lead to trouble when reporting and interpreting research results to the general public.) Also, this conventionalization has great pragmatic value on many dimensions. The dimension of greatest relevance for our conceptual analysis is that of theory evaluation. The empirical evaluation of the truth value of a theory involves the use of deductive logic and the notions of valid and invalid argument forms. The logical truth value (absolute truth or falsity) of a hypothesis must appear as one of the premises in the valid and invalid deductive argument forms required to evaluate a theory empirically. A formal discussion of empirical theory evaluation appears later in the text as part of Chapter 6 on the nature of the theoretical situation, the third unit of analysis.

For the remainder of the conceptual analysis, the conventional description of the consequences of hypothesis evaluation will be used. It is absolutely necessary to keep this in mind to understand and appreciate the contents of Chapter 6.

SCIENTIFIC EXPLANATION IN RELATION TO PREDICTION AND CONTROL

Introduction

It will be instructive to describe why the nature of a scientific explanation of behavior allows the prediction and control of behavior. Recall that explaining a piece of behavior amounts to placing it in a specific $Y = f(X)$ relationship and that the appropriate Xs either must precede or be concurrent with the behavior in time.

Control

The notion of control of behavior is reducible to three operations: (1) creating the onset (initial appearance) of the behavior, (2) regulating and modulating its degree of intensity or rate of occurrence after its initial onset, and (3) causing the termination (eventual disappearance) of the behavior. The initial production of a piece of behavior can be done by instituting all the antecedent causal factors of which it is a function. In practice, many of the relevant antecedent conditions are already present in the situation and all that is necessary is the institution of the remaining factors (often only one — the key or crucial factor). To regulate the intensity or rate of ongoing behavior, all that is necessary is to change the value of one of the causal factors of which the behavior is a function. To terminate ongoing behavior, only one of the conditions of which it is a function need be removed from the situation.

It is difficult to present an example of all three aspects of control in the context of only one kind of learned response. The relevance or utility of each aspect of control varies with the specific type of learned response appealed to as an example. Let us refer to the operant response situation again. Most experimental applications of the principle of control to the operant response situation involve only the modulation aspect. The rate of operant responding can be increased or decreased by varying any one of the reinforcement factors of which it is a function. The nature of the operant response situation is such that the entire set of necessary and sufficient conditions for response occurrence is always present. The experimenter need do nothing to explicitly onset operant responding. Likewise, operant responding can never be permanently terminated under the usual set of circumstances in effect. The best example of creating the initial appearance of a learned response occurs in classical conditioning, where the experimenter exposes the subject to a specific sequence of environmental events explicitly to generate a so-called conditioned response. The best example of terminating a learned response involves the operation called "counter-conditioning," in which the organism is not only not reinforced for performing the undesired response but also is actively reinforced for performing another kind of response incompatible with the undesired one.

Prediction

The structure underlying control also applies to prediction; in a sense, the ability to predict underlies the ability to control. The distinction between prediction and control is merely one of intention. Once a piece of behavior has been scientifically explained, we have achieved all the relevant knowledge about it. Knowledge about a behavior's causal antecedents allows us to predict the occurrence (onset, regulation, termination) of the behavior, given the state of the antecedent conditions at the time. At the intention level, the psychologist does not interfere and actively try to manipulate or change the conditions and thus actually control the behavior. As such, "prediction" is simply another term for the knowledge of a specific causal law or functional relationship.

The relationship between rate of operant responding and amount of reinforcement per response serves as a good example here. Assume that an experimental subject is about to be switched from reinforcement level A to reinforcement level B. Given prior knowledge of the values of this antecedent condition, it is possible to predict ahead of time the new rate of responding to be exhibited by the subject once the switch in reinforcement level from A to B has actually occurred.

THE NOTION OF CAUSATION IN CONCEPTUAL PERSPECTIVE

Two explicit aspects of causation require discussion.

1. It was previously stated that the term "cause" is out of fashion among philosophers of science. This is primarily because the 18th-century British Empiricist David Hume successfully argued that causation per se does not exist "out there" among the environmental events themselves but rather exists only in the consciousness of the perceiver. Causation is not a property of the real world per se; "physical" causation does not exist. Rather, causation is a mere inference made by the individual when experiencing the events of the physical world around him; causation is really "psychological" or "symbolic." The phrase "functional relationship" is preferred by philosophers of science over the phrase "causal law" because the former does not imply the existence of actual, physical causation. Natural events in the universe can be regarded as covarying or being functionally related to each other — without the implication of physical causation.

2. The main point of this discussion of experimental psychology has been that natural events, such as behavior, are deterministic and predictable. Yet in other introductions to experimental psychology you are likely to encounter such statements as "Behavior is largely indeterminate and unpredictable" or "Behavior is probabilistic, not deterministic." Contrary to one's immediate impression, there is no contradiction involved here. The above two statements do not mean that behavior is not caused or is not related to other natural events or is not predictable. Rather, they mean that determination and predictability are relative concepts, not absolute concepts. The degree of determination and the precision of prediction in any one case of behavior is itself a function of numerous factors. Alternatively, experimental psychologists accept the principle that behavior is determined and predictable; but the notion of behavior itself is so complex and can be defined in so many different ways that its exact degree of determination and predictability varies from one situation to another.

Let us allude to the operant response situation again and refer explicitly to a rat pressing a bar in a "rat" Skinner box. The degree of determination and precision of prediction of the rat's responding depend both upon the definition of the response event and the specific experimental procedure in effect. Consider the following examples:

a. The rat's rate of responding will be quite variable if reinforced according to a continuous reinforcement schedule. Conversely, the rate will be quite stable if reinforced according to some partial reinforcement schedule, after much training on the schedule.

b. The probability that the rat will press the bar at least once during the experimental session under typical conditions is virtually one. Conversely, the probability that the rat will accumulate exactly k number of responses before satiating and falling asleep in the corner of the apparatus under typical conditions is essentially unknown, uncalculable.

c. The probability that the rat will press the bar with exactly 83 grams of pressure (force) on any one response occasion is essentially indeterminate under a reinforcement criterion of rewarding any bar press response occurrence above the apparatus minimum (say 40 grams of pressure). Conversely, the probability of this specific response event is high after much training under a reinforcement criterion of only rewarding bar press responses whose pressures range between 80 and 85 grams (as a "reinforcement band").

Illustrative statements such as these could be extended indefinitely. The basic point is that, under some circumstances, the behavioral event, as defined, is completely determined and highly predictable; under other circumstances, the behavioral event, as defined, is more probabilistic and less predictable, sometimes to the degree of virtual indeterminacy. The typical learning psychologist simply defines his behavioral events and conducts his experiments at a level of determinacy and precision which meets his own pragmatic and aesthetic needs or criteria.

SOME BASIC PSYCHOLOGICAL TERMINOLOGY

Introduction.

It is now necessary to introduce two different pairs of basic psychological terms. This can be accomplished quite easily in the context of the $Y = f(X)$ symbolization. Initially, the Y and Xs were interpreted as referring to any natural events in the universe which happened to be related to each other in a functional fashion. The natural events were then relabeled as "behavior" and "causal antecedents," respectively, once the $Y = f(X)$ structure was applied to psychology. But most experimental psychologists prefer to give a more technical specification to the X and Y terms. The $Y = f(X)$ relationship is referred to either as an independent variable-dependent variable relationship or as a stimulus-response relationship.

Independent Variable-Dependent Variable Relationship

Any natural event in the universe that can assume any one of a number of different values is a variable. For instance, amount of reinforcement per response, as an antecedent condition of operant responding, can exist at any one of a virtually infinite number of different values. In general, any piece of behavior can be described as a function of numerous variables. In particular, rate of operant responding is a function of variables such as schedule of reinforcement, delay of reinforcement, etc. But, behavior, as a natural event, can also exist at any one of a number of different values—low, medium, or high rates of operant responding, for example. Thus, behavior and rate of operant responding can appropriately be referred to as "variables." So, in a functional relationship, one variable (Y) is a function of one or more other variables (Xs). To distinguish the X and Y variables, the individual X variables are referred to as "independent" variables and the Y variable is referred to as a "dependent" variable. Thus, a dependent variable is a function of one or more independent variables. Operant responding, as a dependent variable, is a function of schedule of reinforcement, delay of reinforcement, etc., as independent variables.

This choice of terminology has its limitations for two reasons. Initially, students unfortunately impute the everyday denotative properties of "independent" and "dependent" to the two kinds of variables. Secondly, many unwary students confuse dependent with dependable and then generalize to the concepts of independable and dependable variables. Reference to the original $Y = f(X)$ notation shows that there are only two substantive differences between independent and dependent variables: (1) an independent variable must precede or be concurrent with the dependent variable to which it is related, and (2) the values that an independent variable can assume are under the direct control of the experimenter, while the values that a dependent variable can exhibit are only under the indirect control of the experimenter — that is, they are a property of the responding organism.

The independent-dependent variable language is primarily used in learning psychology to describe the structure and results of specific laboratory experiments; therefore, understanding this terminology is necessary in order to decode and interpret research-oriented journal articles and technical discussions. Referring back to the process of experimentation discussed earlier, the purpose of an experiment can now be restated as follows: to actively vary the levels of an independent variable to see what effect they will have on the value(s) exhibited by a dependent variable. In the illustrative experiment described earlier, group A received one level of the independent variable of amount of reinforcement per response (large) and group B received another level of the independent variable of amount of reinforcement per response (small). The dependent variable for both groups was the rate of operant responding. In the two experimental outcomes where $P \neq Q$, the independent variable did have an effect on the values exhibited by the dependent variable.

Stimulus-Response Relationship

The terms "stimulus" and "response" are the bread-and-butter terms of experimental psychology. Most learning psychologists ultimately reach a stage where they implicitly interpret every aspect of the external environment as a stimulus event, a response event, or both. At a technical level, these two event categories serve as the fundamental analytical units for describing psychological reality. The extensive denotative meanings of these two terms will be presented in later chapters. Only a set of low-level correspondences will be introduced now. The term "response" is grossly equivalent to the term "behavior"; it refers to the behavioral output or activity exhibited by the organism. Thus, operant behavior is a response exhibited by the organism. The term "stimulus" overlaps in large part with "an antecedent causal factor" and is usually a specific aspect of the experimental operation or laboratory procedure currently regulating the organism's behavior. Thus, reinforcing events, motivational conditions, instructions to the subject, physical features of the experimental apparatus, etc. are stimuli. Operant behavior, as a response, is a function of numerous factors, now interpreted as stimuli. Experimental psychology interprets the general $Y = f(X)$ relationship characteristic of science specifically to mean: "A response is a function of various stimuli." The subject matter of psychology can be restated in this way: Experimental psychology studies any measurable response on the part of an organism which can be related to preceding or concurrent stimuli.

TRANSITION TO THE NEXT TWO CHAPTERS: GENERATION OF THE DESCRIPTIVE INPUT AND OUTPUT SITUATIONS

The organism as a real-world event intervenes between two other kinds of real-world events: (1) environmental, experimental operations or conditions and (2) behavior. The environmental conditions could be termed "input." The behavior could be termed "output." The organism receives input and produces output. At a more technical level, the organism intervenes between a descriptive input situation and a descriptive output situation. The organism is merely an energy transduction device; it is stimulated by energy of one form and transmits energy of another form. Many psychologists prefer to deemphasize the act of transduction or the object performing the transduction and simply emphasize the input and output events. Other psychologists are only interested in the act of transduction as performed by some typical or average subject (usually statistically defined). This is why the stimulus input and response output situations are the two primary units of analysis of experimental psychology. This is why the psychologist can be interested in behavior per se or in external operations or conditions per se independent of the intervening organism.

It will be the primary task of the two successive chapters to analyze the descriptive input and output situations. Classification systems and sets of terminology will be developed for describing the input and output situations which can later be applied to the seemingly diverse phenomena and situations characteristic of learning.

At this point, it is necessary to note that under certain circumstances the same abstract environmental event can operate both as a stimulus and a response. For instance, the response of organism X can serve as a stimulus for organism Y at the same moment in time, and the response of an organism at time N can serve as the stimulus for the same organism at time N + 1. Consequently, the same abstract environmental event can be analyzed either as an element of the input situation or as an element of the output situation or both. In order to prevent all sorts of conceptual problems from arising, most experimental psychologists deny that any fundamental difference exists between a stimulus event and a response event at a relatively high level of abstraction. Because of the ultimate synonymity of a stimulus event and a response event, there will be certain correspondences and analogues between the classification systems and sets of terminology used to describe the input and output situations. But it is worthwhile to analyze the input and output situations separately because the operational problems associated with each are vastly different. The input situation essentially involves problems of production and control, while the output situation essentially involves problems of specification and measurement.

SUMMARY

Psychology is often defined as the science of behavior. The experimental psychologist seeks to relate the behavior of an organism to preceding and concurrent environmental events. This relationship constitutes scientific explanation and such explanation derives from hypothesis testing and/or experimentation. The primary advantage of scientific explanation is that it allows the prediction and/or control of behavior.

The semantics of scientific explanation should be briefly reviewed. Experimental investigation of behavior in the laboratory leads to the establishment of probabilistic (1) causal laws or (2) functional relationships. In the context of causal law terminology, behavior is more or less viewed as the mechanical effect of environmental causes. In the context of functional relationship terminology, both behavior and environmental events are treated as variables, and behavior (the dependent variable) exists in some kind of symbolic relationship with environmental events (independent variables).

Experimental psychologists prefer to equate behavior with the concept of response and environmental events with the concept of stimuli. Thus, the purpose of experimental psychology is to establish stimulus-response relationships. Stimuli and responses constitute real-space and real-time events and, from an analytical perspective, generate the descriptive input and output situations, respectively.

Learning is a subarea of experimental psychology. The learning psychologist studies responses which possess some degree of permanence or potential irreversibility in relation to reinforcing stimulus events or operations — by using the same essential conceptual framework, theoretical assumptions, methodological techniques, etc. characteristic of the overall field. Although the notion of learing has much "cultural visibility," learning phenomena are much more diverse and pervasive than the cultural use of the term generally implies.

2
The Nature of the Input Situation:
The first unit of analysis for learning psychology

INTRODUCTION

Chapter 1 established the fact that the input into an organism is a natural event with real-time and real-space properties. Although the stimulus inputs into the organism are continuous over time in the context of the organism's everyday existence (even a sleeping organism is behaving and is affected by environmental events), the different forms and sequencing of environmental stimulation are so numerous and diverse that they defy rational classification. To get a handle on all the specific stimulus inputs in the real world, it is necessary to bring the organism into the laboratory. In effect, it is necessary to set up the notions of experimental operation and experimental procedure, which in turn can serve as models or analogies for the stimulus events acting in the real world. In this new, more restrictive, laboratory context, stimuli and responses will serve as the underlying primitive building blocks out of which specific operations and procedures are formed.

Response units constitute a part of the input situation because they usually must be used to define and characterize specific experimental operations and procedures. No conceptual disparity about their inclusion should result if it is recalled from Chapter 1 that an organism's prior responding or the current responding of another organism can serve as part of the current stimulus input. Also, it will become evident later in the chapter that the operational specification of a stimulus event requires the inclusion of its effect on behavior and that the properties which a particular stimulus event possesses cannot be empirically determined without reference to its associated response events.

Heretofore, the following terms have been used more or less equivalently:
- natural or environmental event
- causal factor or antecedent condition
- independent variable
- stimulus
- input situation
- experimental operation
- experimental procedure

The last four terms on the list must now be used more selectively, with differentiated meanings. The term "input situation" is reserved for the overall structure to be analyzed — i.e., the independent variables in the more restrictive laboratory context. The input situation will be interpreted as directly divisible into one or more "experimental procedures." The experimental procedure in turn is regarded as composed of one or more "experimental operations." Finally, the experimental operations can be analyzed in terms of primitive "stimulus" and "response" units (See Fig. 2-1).

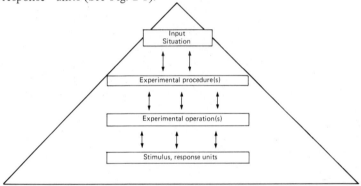

Fig. 2-1. The Hierarchical Structure of the Input Situation

The bidirectional arrows of Fig. 2-1 indicate that the hierarchical division of the input situation is meaningful in either direction: (1) any given input situation is divisible (analyzable) into its components and (2) any desired input situation can be constructed from a given set of stimulus-response units. The triangle configuration represents the fact that a higher order level is an integration of the contents of the adjoining lower order level.

Because the input situation essentially involves problems of production and control, it will be easier to define and describe the hierarchical levels of the input structure in the upward direction: stimulus units, experimental operation(s), procedure(s), and then the overall structure itself. Detailed analysis of response units will be deferred to the succeeding chapter on the nature of the output situation.

THE STIMULUS

INTRODUCTION

The concept of stimulus is one of the most ubiquitous in experimental psychology. The notion of a physical, external stimulus event is really only one aspect of a larger and more comprehensive stimulus processing system. The mechanics of this system at a physiological level have always been a matter of greater concern to sensory and perceptual psychologists than to learning psychologists. There has also been a tendency for most learning psychologists to take the concept of stimulus for granted at the conceptual level. Traditionally, the theoretical nature of the other unit of analysis — the response or learned response — commanded the attention of the learning psychologist. Only within the past 10 to 15 years has learning psychology explicitly begun to focus on such problems or processes as stimulus decoding, stimulus selection, pattern or object recognition, feature extraction, attention, etc. Conversely, at the operational level, the physical production and control of stimulus events has always been a matter of utmost concern to the experimental learning psychologist. Functionally, this concern is translated into problems of laboratory apparati and electronic instrumentation. The technical literature abounds with laboratory manuals and instrumentation handbooks describing the classic set of apparati used by learning psychologists as well as the newer applications of the computer to laboratory stimulus production and control.

This section presents a rudimentary description of a stimulus at the operational level and also assigns some denotative properties to a stimulus event at an informal interpretive level.

DEFINITION AND INITIAL CHARACTERIZATION

A stimulus is a change in some aspect of the environment (onset, termination, or modulation of amount) which can produce a reaction in the organism or to which the organism can react. If an environmental change results in a change in behavior, it is a stimulus. This definition of a stimulus is circular. A stimulus event cannot be isolated or defined independent of its effects on behavior. Philosophers of science frown upon such a definition and prefer to leave the primitive or ultimate terms of a discipline undefined — i.e., the notion of an undefined, primitive term. But such a circular definition of a stimulus is necessary to determine operationally which environmental changes can serve as stimuli and which cannot.

The list of environmental changes that affect behavior is descriptively infinite. Let us present a representative sample of stimuli that are of interest to learning psychology: the onset, termination, or change in amount (if defined) of

- a light
- an electric shock
- a piece of food
- a member of the opposite sex
- corrective information
- the word "good"
- a paycheck
- overt, external fear
- a sentence in a book
- a letter grade – for an exam

Two refinements of the notion of stimulus should be mentioned. First, a stimulus event need not originate from the physical, external environment itself. Events occurring in the organism's body can also serve as stimuli. These are called "internal" or "physiological stimuli" – for instance, hunger pangs. Secondly, when an organism's prior response or the current response of another organism serves as a stimulus for the organism, technically they are referred to as "response-produced stimuli" or "cues." For instance, your bet during a previous hand of poker and the flick of a female's eyebrow.

The above list contains some simple objects or events encountered in everyday life using the vernacular. But the basic point is that they are stimuli from the psychologist's viewpoint. Further subanalysis of any one of the listed stimulus events is unnecessary on a nonpsychological dimension. It is irrelevant that a light is an object of interest for physics, that food is an object of interest for chemistry, that "good" is an object of interest for linguistics, etc.

Actually, the concept of a stimulus is not as simplistic as it appears once the attempt is made to produce and/or control a stimulus event in the laboratory. The stimulus events under investigation can be quite esoteric and can require detailed technical specification and/or description: for instance, the ratio of the brightness levels of two different colors, the intensity of brain stimulation, the angle of a tree limb in a picture, the concentration of a sugar solution injection in the blood stream, the meaningfulness of a Chinese character, the clarity of dial readings, the emotional value of a facial photograph, the size of a texture gradient, etc.

At a technical level, a specific stimulus event possesses both a class membership (type) and a specific analogical value within that class. For instance, a shock, as an environmental event, is a type of stimulus but analogically it is mild, medium, or strong in intensity, short or long in duration, abrupt or gradual in its onset time, etc. A stimulus event has analogical reality because it consists of various attributes or dimensions: e.g., size, shape, color, emotionality, pleasantness, meaningfulness, etc. Quite often in the lab the crucial aspect of a stimulus event is not its class membership but rather its specific analogical value — a specific stimulus dimension or attribute of the stimulus event is used to represent or describe the entire stimulus event. For instance, a subject might say: "On the prior trial the stimulus event was 'large'; on this trial the stimulus event is 'small.'"

The concept of a stimulus is infinitely descriptive. Learning psychologists do not necessarily use the verbal categories and descriptions of objects characteristic of the English vernacular. When an experimental psychologist says an environmental event (like a shock) is a stimulus event, it is more than just a semantic label — it is more than assigning additional jargon of a psychological nature to an environmental event that has already probably been overdescribed and over-categorized by other disciplines anyway. What is necessary is further analysis at a psychologically relevant level — e.g., "Do environmental events possess any common characteristic that makes them stimuli" or "Do stimulus events possess any special set of properties?" These are theoretical questions, independent of the operational definition of stimulus as an environmental change resulting in a change in behavior.

STIMULUS PROPERTIES

At this point, it is only appropriate to make a rather low-level, functional analysis of stimulus properties. There is one property characteristic of all stimulus events — namely, that of information. The use of the term "information" in this context does not correspond exactly to its dictionary meaning. Information is not limited to verbal or language input with cognitive content. Rather, practically any kind of input physical energy form (light waves, sound waves, chemical stimuli, etc.) can carry information, at least in the mathematical, information theory sense, and practically any neuronal level of the organism's nervous system can decode input stimuli or signals of some kind. What is really meant by the term "information" here is a reduction in uncertainty about the nature of the external world. The specific stimulus input occurring at any moment X is just one input alternative from the entire set of N possible stimulus input alternatives, where N is some countably large number, and, as such, represents a reduction in uncertainty.

Other, more specialized properties of a stimulus are definable once the manner in which the information is presented to the organism is analyzed. Actually this dimension cannot be described or operationalized independent of the possible relationships existing between a stimulus event and a response event. Conceptually, there are at least four ways in which a stimulus can be related to a response: (1) the stimulus can inform the organism of the appropriateness or correctness of an immediate past response occurrence; (2) it can inform the organism of the appropriateness or correctness of an immediate future response event; (3) it can elicit a specific response event in and of itself; and (4) it can inform the organism of the appropriate general behavioral level at which to be functioning — i.e., it can arouse the organism and make it more active. Thus, a stimulus event is relatable to a specific past, present, or future response event and to the current activity level of the organism. Let us give a technical name to each kind of stimulus property.

1. A stimulus that either corrects or confirms the organism's immediate past behavior is called a "reinforcing stimulus." The information (uncertainty reduction) can be presented in such a way that it is reinforcing.

2. A stimulus that informs the organism of the future correct course of action to follow is called a "discriminative stimulus." The information (uncertainty reduction) can be presented in such a way that it is discriminative.

3. A stimulus that automatically leads to a specific response occurrence on the part of an organism is called an "eliciting stimulus" or simply an "elicitor." If the stimulus event is a biological elicitor of a response, the specific S-R connection or association is called a "biological reflex." If the stimulus event is a learned (conditioned) elicitor of a response, the specific S-R connection or association is called a "learned (conditioned) reflex." So the information (uncertainty reduction) can be presented in such a way that it is elicitive.

4. A stimulus that informs the organism of the correct or appropriate level of general behavioral activity at which to be operating is called a "motivational" or "motivating stimulus." The information (uncertainty reduction) can be presented in such a way that it is motivational.

A particular stimulus can possess only one of the specialized properties with respect to a particular response. A particular stimulus can possess more than one of the specialized properties at the same moment in time only with respect to more than one response. For instance, a particular stimulus event can be reinforcing for the preceding response and discriminative or eliciting for the succeeding response. An initial motivational stimulus often becomes an eliciting stimulus. Also, as will become apparent shortly, when an eliciting stimulus is used in a certain experimental operation, it becomes a reinforcing stimulus.

It should be finally noted that, in the context of a specific experimental manipulation, a stimulus is often given a specific name germane to the nature and purpose of the experimental manipulation — for instance, training stimulus, test stimulus, stimulus cue, generalized stimulus, conditioned stimulus, unconditioned stimulus, signal, S-delta, response-produced cue, etc. But it still is classifiable as one or more of the above four types of stimulus events.

THE NOTION OF AN EXPERIMENTAL OPERATION

INTRODUCTION

While participating in a laboratory experiment, the subject is exposed to some kind of restricted input situation which is assumed to represent a more general and less well-controlled input situation encountered in the everyday real world. The laboratory input situation more technically involves some kind of experimental operation. The independent variable(s) manipulated by the experimenter in a specific experimental study is (are) ultimately analyzable in terms of one or more experimental operations.

DEFINITION AND INITIAL CHARACTERIZATION

An experimental operation can be explicitly defined as any appropriate, meaningful, or pragmatic combination of stimulus and response units. Therefore, any specific input situation used in an experiment is analyzable in terms of stimulus and response units. More importantly, the input situation characteristic of learning experimentation is also divisible into stimulus and response units. Unfortunately, the typical introductory learning text regards the many and diverse experimental learning tasks as unrelated and independent and makes no attempt to analyze each task into the basic experimental operations out of which it is composed. As a consequence, the typical introductory learning text neither compares nor contrasts the experimental operations characteristic of each learning task in order to determine whether or not there is a unique or defining set of operations which differentiates between learning and nonlearning experimentation.

It is the purpose of the following subsection to assume such an analysis has already been made and to present the fundamental set of experimental operations characteristic of learning. It might seem that the author is putting the cart before the horse by making an analysis of different experimental learning tasks before the substantive nature of these tasks has even been discussed. But remember that one of the aims of the conceptual analysis is to develop a prior underlying structure in the context of which specific experimental learning tasks can be later introduced.

THE BASIC SET OF EXPERIMENTAL OPERATIONS CHARACTERISTIC OF LEARNING EXPERIMENTATION

There are four different experimental operations characteristic of learning experimentation. What is implied here is that any learning task can be broken down into one or more of these four fundamental operations. Initially the operations will be defined and specified solely in terms of stimulus and response units. Later, they will be labeled and given some denotative properties.

With S representing stimulus and R representing response, the four operations are as follows: (1) the S-S operation, (2) the S alone operation, (3) the S-R-S operation, and (4) the S-R operation. In the S-S operation, the subject is exposed to the successive or simultaneous presentation of two discrete stimulus events — e.g., a tone and a shock. A response is not part of the definition of this operation at all. The operation has been performed whenever the experimenter has presented the two stimuli, independent of and regardless of the subject's behavior. In the S alone operation, the subject is only exposed to one of the two stimuli, usually the first, of a corresponding S-S operation. Typically, the S alone operation is only meaningful for a subject subsequent to initial exposure to the S-S operation — e.g., exposure to tone alone, following exposure to tone paired with shock. Again, no reference to a response term is made in the definition of the S alone operation. In the S-R-S operation, the subject is presented with the succession of two stimulus events, but an active response on his part must intervene between them. Typically, the experimenter only has control over the second stimulus. If the R occurs, the experimenter presents the second S. If the R does not occur, the experimenter does not present the second S. For instance, a child upon entering the kitchen (S) requests a cookie from his mother (R) and she fulfills the request (S); or a rat in a Skinner box apparatus (S) presses a bar (R) and receives a pellet of food (S). In the S-R operation, the experimenter does not present the second S following occurrence of the R. Typically, the S-R operation is only meaningful for a subject subsequent to initial exposure to the S-R-S operation — e.g., the mother no longer presents a cookie upon request or the rat no longer receives a food pellet following a bar-press response.

COMPARISON OF THE FOUR OPERATIONS

The S alone operation is a subset of the S-S operation, and the S-R operation is a subset of the S-R-S operation. With somewhat less justification, the S-S operation can be interpreted as a subset of the S-R-S operation. The significance and meaning of this particular pattern of relationships depend upon the denotational properties assigned to the individual S-R terms.

DENOTATIONAL PROPERTIES OF THE FOUR OPERATIONS, BASED UPON A SPECIFIC INTERPRETATION OF THE SECOND STIMULUS

Introduction

There are many alternative ways of interpreting the symbols of the four operations. Our analysis will assign a specific label to the second stimulus and emphasize the presence or absence of the second stimulus in the operation. Specific denotational properties of the first S term and the R term are disregarded in the analysis.

The Reinforcement Operation

Learning psychologists typically interpret the second S as a reinforcing stimulus; the basic stimulus property characteristic of the second stimulus is that of reinforcement. Therefore, the S-S and S-R-S operations collectively are often called "reinforcement operations" or simply "the reinforcement operation." Since reinforcement is the canonical aspect of learning, the reinforcement operation is often termed "the learning operation." Two subsidiary terms also exist for the reinforcement operation: (1) the conditioning operation and (2) the acquisition operation.

Since the reinforcement operation can take two forms, what significance should be attached to their difference? What specific significance does the presence or absence of the R term possess? In the S-S operation, the reinforcing stimulus is presented whenever the experimenter exposes the subject to the paired stimuli. The presentation of the reinforcing stimulus is independent of the subject's behavior. Therefore, the occurrence of the reinforcing stimulus in the S-S reinforcement operation is termed "experimenter-contingent" or "non-response-contingent." In the S-R-S operation, the reinforcing stimulus is presented only after the prior occurrence of the response in question. (In many contexts, the R can appropriately be labeled an instrumental response.) The presentation of the reinforcing stimulus is not independent of the subject's behavior. Therefore, the occurrence of the reinforcing stimulus in the S-R-S reinforcement operation is called "subject-contingent" or "response-contingent." The basic distinction between experimenter-contingent and response-contingent reinforcing events is a critical one for our analysis and will reappear throughout the rest of the book.

The Extinction Operation

The S alone and S-R operations lack reinforcing stimuli (in the sense presented above). Therefore, the S alone and S-R operations collectively are nonreinforcement operations or simply the nonreinforcement operation. The technical term preferred by learning psychologists for the nonreinforcement operation is "the extinction operation." Two subsidiary terms also exist for the extinction operation: (1) the deconditioning operation and (2) the unlearning operation. The S alone extinction operation is appropriate following experimenter-contingent reinforcement; the S-R extinction operation is appropriate subsequent to response-contingent reinforcement.

ADDITIONAL CHARACTERIZATION OF THE REINFORCEMENT OPERATION

What is the crucial difference between the S-S and S-R-S reinforcement operations and on what basis was the S-S operation previously conceptualized as being a subset of the S-R-S operation?

To answer these questions requires a more functional analysis of the two operations. The events which both operations have in common are the simultaneous or successive presentation of two stimuli. This is a procedural definition of temporal contiguity. Two events are contiguous in time if their respective onset times are simultaneous or nearly simultaneous (successive=nearly simultaneous). (Note: In many experimental procedures, the two stimulus events can be spatially contiguous, besides being temporally contiguous — i.e., proximal in space as well as time.) The law of contiguity as a necessary condition for learning is ancient — but until the advent of experimental learning psychology it was usually stated in terms of "ideas" or "mental elements": contiguity of two or more ideas was an essential prerequisite for the learning of an association between two or more ideas. So the S-S reinforcement operation could be termed "the contiguity operation." The S-R-S reinforcement operation involves contiguity plus something else. This something else relates to the intervening response. This response leads to the second stimulus. The response and the second stimulus are also contiguous, either temporally or spatially or both. But most psychologists prefer to emphasize the fact that the response has an effect or a consequence. The law of effect as a necessary condition for learning is also ancient — but until the advent of behaviorism, the effect or consequence was usually interpreted in terms of subjective feeling states such as "pleasure," "pain," "satisfaction," or "dissatisfaction": response events resulting in pleasure or satisfaction tended to be strengthened; response events resulting in pain or dissatisfaction tended to be weakened. Since the S-R-S reinforcement operation involves not only contiguity but also effect, it could be termed "the effect operation."

Referring back to the two questions which introduced the section, it should now be apparent that the crucial difference between the S-S and S-R-S operations is the absence or presence of effect and that the S-S operation is a subset of the S-R-S operation because it involves only contiguity, and not effect.

FURTHER CHARACTERIZATION OF THE EXTINCTION OPERATION

The learning psychologist's use of the reinforcement operation to create a learned response is arbitrary and optional, especially in the laboratory context. It is just as meaningful for the learning psychologist to later discontinue the use of the reinforcement operation and see what effect this has on a learned response. But exposing the subject to the extinction operation is only meaningful following prior exposure to the reinforcement operation. As mentioned in Chapter 1, many learning experiments not only involve an original acquisition or learning phase but also a later extinction phase. Typically, the learned response which was acquired during the learning phase "disappears" (at least temporarily) during the extinction phase. (Since the experimenter arbitrarily "built in" the response, he can arbitrarily "build it out" also.) Because of this, extinction is often referred to as "the mirror image of learning." But interpreting extinction as the simple mirror image of learning is misleading, on at least three levels.

1. At the operational level, extinction is not the mere mirror image of learning because the reinforcing stimulus can only be deleted following prior exposure to the reinforcement operation. The extinction operation per se is not merely the use of the S alone operation or the S-R operation, but rather the use of the S alone operation following the use of the S-S operation, or the use of the S-R operation following the use of the S-R-S operation.

2. At the behavioral level, extinction is not the mere mirror image of learning. It typically takes only one session of exposure to the reinforcement operation to acquire a learned response; conversely, it typically takes many sessions of exposure to the extinction operation to make a learned response permanently "disappear."

3. At the interpretive or process level, extinction is not necessarily the mirror image of learning. During the learning phase, a response is acquired because it is learned in the context of the reinforcement operation; but not all learning psychologists interpret the "disappearance" of the learned response in the context of the extinction operation as being due to unlearning or deconditioning.

The above distinctions are much more than semantic. The basic point is that just because the extinction operation per se is derivable from the reinforcement operation per se, it does not follow that the effect of the extinction operation is the mirror image of the effect of the reinforcement operation, either at the behavioral level or at the interpretive level.

Customarily, learning psychology is characterized as being primarily concerned with the reinforcement operation and the acquisition of a learned response. The use of the extinction operation and the study of the "disappearance" of a learned response are subsidiary or derivative interests of the learning psychologist and, as such, do not constitute part of the typical public relations view of the learning psychologist. The present conceptual analysis adheres to the public relations view of learning in the sense that it focuses on the reinforcement operation and the original acquisition phase of a learning experiment. The extinction operation and its effects on behavior are only discussed to a degree that is necessary for putting the canonical reinforcement operation and its relation to learning in proper analytical perspective.

THE CONCEPT OF EXPERIMENTAL PROCEDURE

INTRODUCTION

Two reference points must be established in order to discuss the notion of experimental procedure. (1) The specific stimulus input situation or set of independent variables to which the subject is exposed in any particular experiment is directly describable in terms of some experimental procedure. The content, and sometimes even the ultimate purpose, of the experiment can be conveniently stated at the level of experimental procedure. (2) The experimental procedure used in any particular experimental study is ultimately analyzable into one or more experimental operations. A specific experimental procedure is generated by using one or more experimental operations in some appropriate, meaningful combination.

GENERATION OF ONE TYPE OF EXPERIMENTAL PROCEDURE: THE DISCRETE-TRIAL PROCEDURE

In the most common experimental procedure, the ultimate discrete event in time is the trial. A trial consists of a presentation of the specific stimulus input to the subject and the recording of the response (or lack of response) emitted by the subject. Thus, the content of a trial is an operation. The experimental procedure for an experimental study is a presentation of N successive trials. The experimental procedure is an application of an operation N times. Because successive trials occur in time and take time, there must also be a time period between successive trials – i.e., an intertrial interval between successive applications of an operation. An experimental procedure composed of N trials and N-1 intertrial intervals is technically called "a discrete-trial procedure." What the experimenter is usually interested in is a gross or selective change in responses over trials.

GENERATION OF A SECOND TYPE OF EXPERIMENTAL PROCEDURE: THE CONTINUOUS-TIME PROCEDURE

In this type of procedure, there are no trials and no intertrial intervals. The provision for the occurrence of the operation is continuously in effect. The subject can respond any time "he wants to." This is frequently referred to as "the free-responding situation" and can only be conveniently run in the context of the response-contingent reinforcement operation (or associated extinction operation). The subject generates N responses (i.e., the operation occurs N times) — but the specific moment in time when a response occurs and an operation is definable is determined by the subject. Natural terminology for this kind of procedure is "the continuous-time procedure." What the experimenter is usually interested in is a gross or selective change in responses over time.

DENOTATIVE TYPES OF EXPERIMENTAL PROCEDURES

There are two denotative kinds of experimental procedures: simple and complex. Simple procedures employ N occurrences of one operation type. Complex procedures minimally employ K occurrences of one operation type and N-K occurrences of another operation type. Since there are only four basic experimental operations, there are only four simple experimental procedures: the two kinds of reinforcement procedures and the two kinds of extinction procedures. It is meaningful to speak of a subject as undergoing the reinforcement or extinction procedure. The number of complex experimental procedures in theory is infinite — because there is an infinite number of ways four different operations can be combined or programed repetitively over time. But a basic set of about a dozen complex procedures has evolved over the years. Typically, each of these complex procedures is given a name, which does not include the terms "reinforcement" or "extinction." A representative list of complex experimental procedures includes the following: spontaneous recovery, stimulus generalization, stimulus discrimination, response generalization, response discrimination, relearning, re-extinction, retention, partial reinforcement, etc. Chapter 5 analyzes these and other complex procedures in greater detail.

THE OVERALL MACRO-INPUT SITUATION

INTRODUCTION

The input situation is the particular experimental procedure applied to the organism when serving as a subject in an experiment. As such, it is simply another term for causal antecedent conditions. The relationship of the input situation to two other notions should be made explicit.

BOUNDARY CONDITIONS AND STANDARD INPUT SITUATIONS

In a simple experiment one independent variable is manipulated (i.e., exists at two or more levels) and all the other potential independent variables should be kept constant at some level (not necessarily the same level). The levels at which these other nonmanipulated independent variables are kept constant are referred to as the "boundary conditions" of the experiment. Using the terminology of experimental procedure, it is the experimental procedure which is the focus of interest in an experiment and the background context in which it is introduced is kept constant (i.e., it exists at some value). The background context in which the experimental procedure is introduced constitutes the boundary conditions of the experiment.

The exact level of the boundary conditions used in an experiment is optional. There is no mathematical formula or theoretical rule that dictates at which level the boundary conditions should be fixed. But, on the other hand, the exact level at which the boundary conditions exist can tremendously influence the results of the experiment. Because of this, standard boundary condition values or a standard set of boundary conditions have evolved over the years in learning psychology such that boundary conditions are not emphasized and are often even left implicit. This gives rise to the notion of a standard input situation. When a specific procedure is introduced into a standard set of boundary conditions, a standard input situation results.

In effect, what the text analyzes are the standard input situations used in learning psychology. The substantive content of this book is organized around the standard input situations recognized by experimental learning psychologists.

STANDARD INPUT SITUATIONS AND LEARNING TASKS

The terms "standard input situation" and "learning task" are virtually synonymous. The former is the author's own private, analytical terminology. The latter is the more standard terminology characteristic of learning psychology in general. The preceding analysis of the nature of the input situation is in effect an analysis of the structure of a learning task.

Chapter 9 analyzes some of the most common learning tasks studied by experimental psychology. A classification system for the most common learning tasks constitutes the substantive content of Chapter 5.

SUMMARY

The descriptive input situation consists of hierarchically related analytical levels: (1) stimulus and response units, (2) experimental operations, and (3) experimental procedures. Stimulus and response events constitute the ultimate building blocks out of which experimental operations are constructed; experimental procedures are, in turn, composed of one or more experimental operations. When a specific experimental procedure is embedded in a standard set of boundary conditions, the notion of a standard input situation is generated and the current focus of interest is the set of standard input situations used to investigate learning. More conventional terminology for the latter is that of "learning tasks." The content of each analytical level should be briefly reviewed.

1. A stimulus is any discrete aspect of the environment (internal or external) to which behavior (or a response) can be related. Stimulus events possess the critical property of information or uncertainty reduction about the state of the environment. Specific categories of stimulus events include (a) reinforcing, (b) discriminative, (c) eliciting, and (d) motivational.

2. An experimental operation is any meaningful or pragmatic combination of stimulus and response units. There is a basic set of four experimental operations characteristic of learning experimentation: (a) S-S, (b) S-R-S, (c) S alone, and (d) S-R. The second S of the first two operations represents reinforcing events and the S-S and S-R-S operations collectively constitute reinforcement operations. The S alone and S-R operations lack a reinforcing event and collectively constitute extinction operations.

3. A specific experimental procedure is generated by using one or more experimental operations in some appropriate, meaningful combination and can be administered to a subject in a discrete-trial or continuous-time manner. Simple procedures involve the use of only one operation type, while complex procedures involve the use of both the reinforcement and extinction operations.

Thus, learning, extinction, and related learning and extinction phenomena are investigated in the laboratory by the use of standard input situations consisting of simple or complex experimental procedures involving reinforcement and/or extinction operations.

3
The Nature of the Output Situation:
The second unit of analysis for
learning psychology

INTRODUCTION

Chapter 1 established the fact that the output of an organism is a natural event with real-time and real-space properties. Although the response outputs of the organism are continuous over time in the context of its everyday existence, the different forms and sequencing of behavioral outputs are so numerous and diverse that they defy rational classification. To get a handle on all the specific response outputs in the real world, it is necessary to bring the organism into the laboratory. In effect, it is necessary to set up an analytical structure to serve as a model or analogy for the output situation in the real world.

The terms "reaction," "output situation," "behavior," "response," "dependent variable," etc. have been used more or less equivalently so far in referring to the natural events exhibited by the organism. Since it is now necessary to give a formal analytical structure to the output situation in the more restrictive laboratory context, differentiated meanings must be assigned to the last four of these terms. The term "output situation" is reserved for the overall structure to be analyzed — i.e., the natural events exhibited by the organism. The output situation will be interpreted as directly divisible into behavior. "Behavior" in turn is regarded as composed of one or more responses. Finally, "responses" will be treated as quantifiable or measurable by one or more dependent variables or response measures (See Fig. 3-1).

The triangular configuration and bidirectional arrows have functions analogous to those depicted in Fig. 2-1 of the input situation. But an important difference between the two hierarchical representations should be noted. The experimenter has direct control over the input situation, such that the input hierarchy represents successive levels of production or control. The output situation is only directly under the control of the subject in an experiment, such that the output hierarchy represents successive levels of measurement or

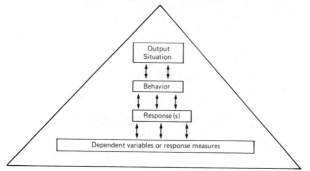

Fig. 3-1. The Hierarchical Structure of the Output Situation

representation. The immediate effect of this crucial difference is to change the order of discussion of the hierarchical levels. It will be easier to define and describe the level of behavior first, followed by the response level second, and then the response measure level third. The overall macro-level of the output situation itself can be more meaningfully discussed at the end.

BEHAVIOR

INTRODUCTION

Behavior became the focus of concern for psychology when John Watson revolted against its preoccupation with conscious experience (consciousness) — both in a structuralist content sense and a functionalist utility sense. The concept of behavior is just as ubiquitous and infinitely descriptive as that of stimulus. A physical, external behavioral event is just one part or aspect of a larger and more comprehensive behavioral production system. Most psychologists regard behavior as the final end product of the workings of this system.

The immediate reality level of a natural event labeled "behavior" is physiological. Buts its physiological reality is irrelevant. Physiologists simply are not interested in the physiological natural events that are called "behavior" by psychologists. The physical events that psychologists call "behavior" must possess some unique property which makes them appropriate objects of study for psychology. It is very difficult to verbalize exactly what this unique property is. The problem is compounded by the fact that many psychologists use behavior to infer what processes are occurring inside the organism. These processes are their real focus of concern and they use behavior as an indirect means of studying them.

Perhaps the most neutral way of characterizing the unique property of behavior is by regarding behavior as the specific event during which the transformation of the input energy into output energy occurs. It is the final link of the process transforming input energy into output energy. At a much lower level of description, we usually say that the organism is "doing something" or "affecting the environment" or "simply reacting to the environment." The point is that these acts or events of energy transduction have a meaning and significance which only psychologists are willing to regard as proper objects of concern and analysis.

This section considers and evaluates a rather low-level "working" definition of behavior.

A DEFINITION OF BEHAVIOR

Behavior can be defined as any directly measurable (observable and quantifiable) or indirectly measurable (nonobservable, but quantifiable) activity on the part of an organism which can be related to a preceding or concurrent stimulus. Thus, for a natural event exhibited by an organism to be classified as behavior, it must clear each of three interrelated hurdles: (1) initially, it must be activity; (2) secondly, it must be measurable activity; (3) thirdly, it must be measurable activity relatable to a stimulus event. Let us analyze the three conditions in turn.

Activity

Introduction and definition. While the author would prefer to treat "activity" as a primitive, undefined term, a characterization of it can be given at a physiological level. Activity is any kind of physiological event which affects (changes) either the external physical environment or the internal environment of the organism. Most, but not all, instances of activity occur whenever one or more of the physiological effectors of the organism is (are) activated. The physiological effectors, at a very informal level, are the muscles and the glands. Noneffector-related physiological events such as brain waves, blood pressure level, stomach acid secretions, various nerve potentials, etc. are also regarded as activity.

Noneffector-related activities only directly affect the internal environment of the organism and do not directly affect the physical, external environment. What effector-related activity directly affects depends upon the specific kind of effector involved. Activities of only one type of muscle necessarily lead directly or immediately to a change in the external environment. Activation of the other types of muscles or of the glands only leads directly or immediately to internal changes in the organism. So, only one type of activity (one kind of muscular movement) invariably consists of external events, resolvable by the naked eye. But, as will become apparent shortly, the ability to perceive a physiological event externally is not a prerequisite for such physiological activity to be classified as a behavioral event.

A more technical discussion of effector-related activity follows.

Types of muscles and glands. Let us be more specific about the different types of muscles and glands.

There are three basic types of muscles in the human organism which, as effectors, regulate the operation of other "meaningful" parts of the body (e.g., leg, heart, mouth, toe, internal viscera, etc.). Skeletal or striated muscles underlie limb and position movements of the body. Smooth or nonstriated muscles underlie the functioning of the internal viscera. Cardiac muscle underlies the operation of the heart. So, technically, only skeletal or striated muscles can lead directly to physical changes in the environment.

There are two types of glands in the human organism which, as effectors, secrete chemical substances for the maintenance of biological life. The duct or exocrine glands secrete chemicals directly into a specific body cavity or tract. The ductless or endocrine glands secrete chemicals, called hormones, directly into the bloodstream. Thus, neither type of gland directly affects the external environment.

Application of this definition of activity to some representative events. While this definition of activity might seem clear-cut and unambiguous, let us actually apply it to some representative events to see just what is meant by activity and what is not meant by activity.

    A.   Initially, consider the following set of events:
       1)   human being chopping wood (by axe in the hands);
       2)   rat pressing a bar (with its left front paw);
       3)   monkey manipulating a lever (with its right front paw);
       4)   pigeon pecking a colored disc (with its beak).
Clearly, these are activities; each of the events involves a muscular movement, although stated in such a way as to focus attention on the effect the movement has on the environment.

    B.   Secondly, consider these events:
       1)   dog salivating in the mouth;
       2)   sheep raising its right hind foot;
       3)   human being closing an eyelid.
Clearly, these are also activities; each of the events is a muscular movement or a

glandular secretion (salivation is the secretion of salivary glands), with the effect on the environment (if any) left unstated.

    C. Thirdly, assume this set of events:
        1) human being standing at attention;
        2) stationary human being carrying a knapsack.

These are activities because they involve muscular or postural "steady states."

    D. Fourthly, imagine a human being
        1) marking the "yes" alternative on a questionnaire item;
        2) saying "I love you"; or
        3) reading a book aloud.

These are activities because they involve muscular movements, although the symbolic or verbal significance of the movements far surpasses their physical significance.

    E. Now, for the first instance of possible ambiguity: what if the human being were reading silently to himself, instead of aloud? The initial interpretation might be one of nonactivity, until it is realized that eye movements must be occurring.

    F. As a variation of the preceding example, imagine the individual listening to someone else reading aloud. A strict effector-related interpretation of activity would require the event of listening to be nonactivity. But this is conceptually disastrous because both the events of reading silently and listening to an external source reading aloud can eventually have the same consequence for the organism! What difference does it make if the organism reads silently to himself or listens to someone else doing the reading aloud? There are two nonmutually exclusive ways out of this dilemma:
        1) Postulate the existence of some perceptual, or observing, or orienting activity on the part of the organism, existing independent of muscular movement or glandular secretion. Listening would then be perceptual activity.
        2) Regard listening as a noneffector-related physiological event. Thus, listening might result in or be associated with characteristic brain waves or characteristic blood pressure levels. The problem with these kinds of physiological events is that they are not directly observable with the naked eye in the way that overt muscular movements are.

    G. Consider a human being
        1) daydreaming about his girl friend; or
        2) thinking about creation.

Clearly, these are nonactivities according to the strict effector-related interpretation of an activity. But they are activities if viewed from the broader noneffector-related interpretation of any physiological event on the part of the organism, assuming daydreaming and thinking result in or are associated with characteristic physiological events, like brain waves, etc.

    H.   Now, for another class of ambiguous events: a human being feeling sick, tired, happy, etc. The organism describes himself as being sick, tired, happy, etc.; he is labeling his current "mental or emotional state." These are nonactivities according to the strict effector-related interpretation. But they become activities according to the broad noneffector-related interpretation if they have any kind of characteristic physiological events correlated with them. For instance, the feeling of happiness is activity if it is accompanied by a specific pattern of autonomic nervous system activity.

    I.   Next, assume an individual is describing the content of his current conscious sensory experience:

    1) "I see a bright-green color";

    2) "I hear a loud, high-pitched sound"; or

    3) "I feel a hot sensation in my arm."

Customarily, these are regarded as activities in the broad noneffector-related sense — they have physiological referents — but not as behavior. The reason for this cannot be presented until the next section.

    Thus, the effector-related characterization of activity in terms of directly observable physiological muscular movements or steady states does not exhaust all the events psychologists regard as activity. Any kind of physiological event exhibited by the organism must be regarded as activity. But many of the latter events tend to be nonobservable and this leads to the second aspect of the definition of behavior to be discussed.

The Notion of Measurable Activity

    Not all activity is measurable; therefore, not all activity is ipso facto classifiable as behavior. Measurable means quantifiable. An activity is quantifiable if it can be assigned some number on a numerical scale or if it can be assigned some label on a rating scale. For instance, a specific occurrence of eyelid closure activity might take .05 seconds to accomplish. It can be assigned the number .05 on the numerical time scale (with seconds as the unit of measurement). Analogously, a specific occurrence of eyelid closure activity might be assigned the label "fast" on a gross rating scale of speed composed of three categories: slow, medium, fast. More technical aspects of measurement will be introduced later.

    Quantifiable activities that are directly observable with the naked eye (i.e., gross muscular movements) are termed "directly measurable." A human being can serve as the measuring device. Quantifiable activities that are not directly observable with the naked eye (i.e., brian waves, GSRs, blood pressure level, etc.) are termed "indirectly measurable." A machine or physical device must perform the measurement. The significance of this distinction relates back to the initial discussion of activity. Activity includes many physiological events that are not discernible to the naked eye. Internal physiological events therefore have the possibility of being ultimately classified as behavior, if they can be appropriately measured, and one of the prime problems facing experimental psychology is the indirect measurement of internal physiological events.

At first thought, it might seem that there is no such thing as an unmeasurable activity. If the organism can point to an occurrence or existence of a specific activity, it, ipso facto, can be measured. Existence and quantification are the same thing. This is true at a very low level of analysis. Once you have pointed to an occurrence of a specific kind of activity, you have implicitly assigned it to the "yes" category on a two-category existence scale containing the slots "yes" and "no." But the technical aspects of measurement go far beyond the simple question of existence or occurrence.

When the technical aspects of measurement are taken into account, activities that occur or exist are not necessarily measurable. These technical aspects of measurement refer to the characteristics that a measuring device must possess. Briefly, a measuring device must be both reliable and valid. A measuring device is reliable if it yields approximately the same value or number for the same event on successive measuring occasions. For example, a ruler is reliable because it yields approximately the same length reading for the same object on successive measuring trials. A measuring device is valid if it truly measures what it is supposed to measure. For example, a ruler is a valid measuring instrument for length or extension. It is not valid for volume, weight, etc. − unless length can be mathematically transformed into volume, weight etc. Thus, a given instance of activity is only measurable in the sophisticated sense if a reliable and valid measuring device can be applied to it. If a given activity cannot be assigned a number or label by a reliable and valid measuring device, it is unmeasurable.

Unfortunately, reliability and validity are not absolute properties of measuring devices. They are only relative, statistical properties of measuring devices − i.e., reliability and validity exist in degrees less than "100%." For instance, even a metal ruler can expand or contract, depending on the heat level in a room. So a given activity is measurable only to the extent that it can be quantified by a measuring device possessing some minimal degree of reliability and validity. What constitutes a minimal degree of reliability and validity varies from psychologist to psychologist; so what constitutes measurable and unmeasurable activity varies from psychologist to psychologist.

Let us apply the notion of variable degrees of reliability and validity to examples (A) to (I) of the preceding subsection.

1. Practically every experimental psychologist would agree that the activities referred to in examples (A) to (E) are measurable. A rat pressing a bar, a dog

salivating in the mouth, a human being standing at attention, or reading aloud or silently are measurable activities. All these activities are subject to direct measurement. There are no serious problems of reliability or validity with the measuring devices employed to quantify these activities.

2. There would be little agreement among psychologists with respect to measurability concerning the activities referred to in examples (F) to (H): human being listening, daydreaming, thinking, or feeling. All these activities are only subject to indirect measurement. There are many serious problems of reliability and validity with the measuring devices used to quantify these activities. "Hard-core" behaviorists do not regard "listening," "thinking," "daydreaming," "feeling," etc. as quantifiable activities. Functionally oriented psychologists are more inclined to treat these activities as measurable. Humanistically or phenomenologically oriented psychologists do not necessarily make measurability a condition of behavior and therefore can easily treat these activities as proper events of concern for psychology.

3. Practically no contemporary psychologist, except for some latter-day structuralists, would treat the activities referenced in example (I) as measurable. Accepting verbal reports of current conscious sensory experience (introspection) has gone out of style – basically because the reliability and validity of such verbal reports cannot be assessed.

Let us illustrate with the statement: "I see a green color." There is no way to check the validity of this statement. There is no way another organism, as observer, can get inside the introspector's brain to check whether the introspector's green is the same color as the observer's green. Thus, there is no way to assess whether person X's green is the same color sensation as person Y's green. There is also no way of assessing the reliability of this statement. Sensory experience, besides being private, is also unique. There is no way to replicate the exact same color sensation twice, thrice, etc. Checking whether or not the first green is the same as the second green is the same as the third green, etc. is a meaningless operation.

In summary, practically all psychologists regard the content of subjective experience as private, unique, nonreplicable, etc. and therefore not amenable to measurement. Therefore, it fails the second hurdle and can never be conceptualized as behavior.

Example (I) concerning the verbal report of current conscious sensory experience should not be construed to mean that psychologists never accept verbal report as measurable activity. Verbal report simply cannot be reliably and validly used to quantify aspects of conscious experience in the introspective sense. Verbal report can be reliably and validly used to quantify other aspects or characteristics of the organism.

Verbal report is essentially speech. Speech is a type of physiological effector activity. An instance of verbal report is an effector-related physiological event having an effect on the external environment that can be reliably and validly observed (quantified) by an independent external observer (measuring device). A speech sound is an objective discriminative event in the universe just like leg flexion, eyelid closure, button pushing, bar pressing, etc. and, as such, constitutes measurable activity.

The vast majority of human learning experiments involve verbal report as measurable activity, simply because language is the most convenient type of human physiological effector activity to quantify. For instance, the human subject can say "yes" instead of pushing a button or pointing to a stimulus object; he can learn and verbalize a specific verbal stimulus-response association (like COW-SIX) instead of having eyelid closure conditioned to the onset of a light; he can perform an abstract verbal or symbolic puzzle instead of performing a cumbersome physical or motor puzzle, etc.

The acquisition and development of the language system itself is a focus of interest of learning psychology. This would not be possible if speech sounds did not satisfy the criteria for measurable activity.

Measurable Activity Relatable to a Stimulus Event

For the second time, the author is guilty of using a circular definition. This definition of behavior is circular because an occurrence of a piece of behavior cannot be isolated or determined independent of the stimulus condition which caused it. If a stimulus event precedes or concurs with the measurable activity, it is behavior. If no stimulus event precedes or concurs with the measurable activity, it is not behavior.

This restriction derives from the fact that behavior, as a natural event in the universe, cannot occur in a vacuum and must have another natural event as its cause. (Recall, using psychological terminology, that these other natural events are called "stimuli.") In order to guarantee that behavior possesses real-time and real-space properties, it is necessary to specify just what it is a function of in its definition. Or, from a slightly different perspective, this restriction derives from the fact that behavior was previously characterized as the final link in a chain transforming input energy into output energy. Only those measurable activities that are involved in the transformation of input energy into output energy constitute behavior.

Finally, as will become apparent later, it is impossible to evaluate the correctness or appropriateness of a behavior independent of its related stimulus event.

THE NOTION OF RESPONSE

INTRODUCTION

We have now reached the point where analysis of the second primitive unit, the response, is appropriate. The response unit is the second kind of primitive building block (in addition to the stimulus unit) out of which specific experimental operations are constructed. Since R units are only directly under the control of the subject in an experiment, the basic problems faced in their analysis are specification and measurement.

DEFINITION OF RESPONSE; THE NOTION OF RESPONSE VERSUS THE NOTION OF BEHAVIOR

Behavior refers to the totality of the ongoing measurable activity of the organism relatable to the stimulus event(s) at any time. Conceptually, N different behavior types could be occurring concurrently, where $1 \leq N < \infty$. The experimental psychologist procedurally cannot record the totality of ongoing behavior in the lab; he must be selective and can only record a few aspects of the total behavior displayed by the subject. Those specific aspects of behavior that are selected for recording in an experiment are what is meant by responses. Thus, a response is the specific aspect of the totality of behavior or the specific piece of behavior currently under investigation in the lab. For instance, let us refer to a specific learning situation. During the classical conditioning of salivation in the dog, the specific piece of behavior of interest is salivation. It is recorded and is referred to as the response under investigation. Other aspects of the totality of ongoing behavior — ear pricking, eye movements, head waving, tail wagging, leg movement, general body movement, barking, etc. — are suppressed and neglected. Although behavior, they are not responses.

The distinction between behavior and response is basically semantic, having no real conceptual significance. But the term "response" has become so ingrained in the cognitive structure of the typical experimental psychologist that he regards the concept of response as "psychologically" equivalent to the total behavioral output situation itself. It is conceptually incorrect to regard the totality of behavior as composed of or divisible into N responses — because of the way response is defined. (The totality of behavior is divisible into N responses only if each individual aspect of behavior is being recorded, an impossibility when N is very large.)

RESPONSE SPECIFICATION

Introduction

Response specification concerns how (on what basis) the occurrence of a specific piece of behavior is isolated from the totality of ongoing behavior and recorded as the occurrence of a response. There must be some underlying decision rule which, when applied to the totality of ongoing behavior, recognizes occurrences of the response of interest. In the context of learning psychology, there are basically two different, but not necessarily mutually exclusive, methods of response specification: (1) physiological or indirect response specification and (2) functional or direct response specification.

Physiological or Indirect Response Specification.

This method employs one of the aspects of the previously discussed definition of activity (specifically, any physiological event on the part of the organism) to achieve response specification. Whenever a specific effector is activated or whenever some kind of noneffector-related physiological event is quantified, a response has occurred. In effect, this method of response specification usually takes a meaningful physiological effector system and gives it a psychological interpretation as a response system. So, a psychologist can take practically any measurable physiological activity of the organism and call it a response. Since the response is mere physiological activity — or more specifically the by-product of physiological activity — it is recorded as physiological activity, usually by the blip of an inked pen on a moving sheet of recording paper.

A physiologically specified response has two major characteristics: (1) It is not an overt act of intention on the part of the organism and any consequences it has for either the external environment or internal environment of the organism is incidental and irrelevant. (2) It has a shape or topography or form — this is an immediate given of the way in which it is recorded. Often the shape of the physiologically specified response is more important than the fact that it has occurred. These two characteristics can be rephrased as follows: The most important aspect of a physiologically specified response is how it is formed or what it looks like, not any consequences it might have.

The activities described in (B) of the activity discussion subsection (salivation, leg flexion, eyelid closure) are physiologically specified responses. Let us illustrate with specific reference to salivation. The salivary response occurs whenever the salivary glands secrete saliva. The salivary response is nothing more than the by-product of the activities of the salivary glands, as effectors. Many physiologists are interested in salivation as a dependent variable — but only as a function of physiological independent variables. Psychologists study the activity of the salivary glands as a function of certain psychological or environmental conditions (i.e., stimulus events) and in so doing conceptualize that physiological activity as a response.

Physiological specification is often labeled as indirect specification because many physiological events are only subject to indirect measurement. Finally, it should be noted that responses associated with the S-S operation and its corresponding S alone operation must be specified physiologically.

Functional or Direct Response Specification.

This method emphasizes another aspect of the previously discussed definition of activity (specifically, change in the external environment) to achieve response specification. The occurrence of a specific piece of behavior can function so as to act on the environment and have consequences for the organism. This property of behavior can be exploited for purposes of functional response specification. Thus, if a specific piece of behavior acts on the environment and produces consequence X for the organism, it is a response X. If a specific piece of behavior acts on the environment and does not produce X for the organism, it is not a response X (but could be a response Y). Functional response specification divides the totality of behavior into two different responses: those that achieve X and those that do not achieve X. Thus, the occurrence of a specific piece of behavior from the totality of behavior must be assignable to or resolvable in terms of one of two types of responses.

In functional specification, a piece of behavior is classified according to its effects, not in terms of what specific physiological events (effectors, etc.) are involved in its production. Therefore, the two major characteristics of a functionally specified response are the reverse of a physiologically specified response: (1) It is an overt act of intention on the part of the organism having definite consequences for the organism or explicitly operating on the environment. (2) It does not have one specific shape, form, or topography – in fact, the form of a functionally specified response is rarely recorded. The fact that it occurred is more important than any shape it might possess. These two characteristics can be rephrased as follows: The most important aspect of a functionally specified response is its occurrence, not how it was formed or what it looks like. It should be emphasized that many differently formed or shaped behaviors can be occurrences of the same response. The physiological or physical manner in which the behavioral act is committed is irrelevant.

The activities described in (A) of the activity discussion subsection (chopping wood, pressing a bar, manipulating a lever, pecking a disc) are functionally specified responses. The specific aspect of the environment which is manipulated by the organism is specified in the description of the behavior. (The physiological effectors employed are indicated in parentheses merely to indicate one way in which such an act might be accomplished.) The consequence of the act is left unstated in the examples − but at this point we can assume that all four of the behaviors listed lead to presentation of food to the organism.

Let us illustrate with specific reference to bar pressing by a rat. Bar-press behavior leads to food. Performing any other behavior (nonbar pressing) does not lead to food. Therefore, bar pressing (X) is one response. Nonbar pressing (Y) is another response. The rat can be engaged in only one of two responses at any one time: bar pressing or nonbar pressing. It is irrelevant how the bar is pressed down: with front left paw, with front right paw, with head, with tail, with "whole body," etc. Any behavior that gets the bar down is a bar-press response. Likewise, any behavior that does not result in depression of the bar is a nonbar-press response: sleeping, climbing the walls of the experimental apparatus, exploring the bar, etc.

Functional specification is often labeled as direct specification because overt behaviors acting on the environment and producing consequences are readily subject to direct measurement. Finally, it should be noted that the responses involved in the S-R-S and S-R operations must be at least partially specified functionally.

Combination Physiological-Functional Response Specification or Functional Response Specification with a Physiological Limitation

It is also possible to combine functional and physiological specification in such a way that the response is primarily functionally specified with an attendant physiological limitation. The essential notions can best be introduced in the context of the bar-press example. Assume that the parentheses surrounding the phrase "with left front paw" are removed from the bar-press example described above; the bar-press behavior must be performed by the rat with the left front paw. Bar pressing and nonbar pressing are no longer the two responses in the total behavioral situation. Now, bar pressing with the left front paw is one response and bar pressing any other way or nonbar pressing constitute the other response. Thus, with the attendant physiological limitation, a more restricted number of behaviors constitute response X and an increased number of behaviors constitute response Y.

This third method of response specification is only applicable to the S-R-S and S-R operations.

Response Specification of Strictly Verbal, Linguistic, or Symbolic Responses

Introduction. In the context of human learning experimentation, typically the verbal, linguistic, or symbolic significance of a learned response far surpasses its existential status as physiological activity or as a functional event having a specific effect on the environment. Only in such tasks as perceptual-motor-skills learning or classical conditioning is the learned response a motor or glandular response, with no symbolic significance of any kind attached or superimposed.

Definition of verbal, linguistic, or symbolic responses. A symbolic response is any response whose interpretive significance or meaning is given by some higher order cognitive or semantic system. Verbal and linguistic responses are subkinds of symbolic responses. A verbal response involves speech sounds, although they need not have linguistic or natural language reality. A linguistic response possesses linguistic reality and quite often is a natural language response. Consider the following examples:

(1) In probability learning the response of pressing a button is in and of itself irrelevant − it is simply the means by which the subject operates on the environment and informs the experimenter of his current state of knowledge about the predictive task in question. The situation is analogous in problem-solving and concept-formation research. The physical form of the response itself is irrelevant. They are merely referential or symbolic responses which indicate how the subject is progressing in the experiment.

2. In verbal learning the response events are strictly verbal, but not necessarily linguistic, in nature − namely, words, nonsense syllables, numbers, paralogs, etc.

3. Quite often in information-processing tasks and language-learning tasks the response events are strictly linguistic.

Symbolic Response Specification

Introduction. Verbal, linguistic, or symbolic responses pose no real problems of specification and, in effect, symbolic response specification is continuous with physical response specification. Symbolic response specification involves physical response specification as a proper subset. Symbolic response specification simply requires additional evaluative dimensions − the number and nature of which depend upon the specific learning task. The logic and decision rules of symbolic response identification are analogous to those of the simple physical identification case. Let us illustrate this by extending the notions of (1) indirect physical response specification and (2) direct physical response specification to the symbolic case.

Indirect Symbolic Response Specification. Indirect symbolic response specification involves more than just physiological effector activation — this alone is not sufficient to distinguish between different responses — because all verbal and most linguistic responses involve the same essential set of articulators. New evaluative dimensions must be used to distinguish between the different symbolic events generated by the same set of effectors: e.g., phonetic, phonemic, acoustic features, grammatical or form class features, semantic features, etc. For instance, the symbolic response events in a verbal learning experiment are indirectly specified — a specific word, as a symbolic response event, is a combination of specific acoustic, form class, and semantic features. Also, the symbolic response events in a language-learning experiment are "natural language responses" and are indirectly specified with grammatical, syntactical, linguistic rules serving as the essential criterion dimensions.

Direct Symbolic Response Specification. Direct symbolic response specification does not literally transform a specific piece of physical behavior having an effect on the environment into a symbolic response X. Rather, direct symbolic response specification is applied to specific pieces of behavior, already classified as symbolic responses, and determines which symbolic events lead to consequence X and which do not lead to consequence X, according to some conceptual criterion rule. As such, direct symbolic response specification assumes prior indirect symbolic response specification. Physiological activity (articulation per se) is given a symbolic interpretation by some indirect symbolic response specification mechanism and this symbolic event is then assigned by some direct symbolic response specification scheme into one of two response classes: X or non-X.

Operationally, what direct symbolic response specification establishes is two classes of symbolic response events: (a) those in one class result in consequence X and (b) those in the other class result in consequence non-X. In effect, direct symbolic response specification determines which symbolic behaviors in the whole population of possible symbolic behaviors are equivalent to each other. For instance, in a problem-solving task, usually the correct or appropriate solution (response) can assume many different, but equivalent, symbolic forms. Although prior indirect symbolic response specification can distinguish between all the possible symbolic output events (solutions) exhibited by the subject, the specific conceptual rule defining the correct solution, associated with direct symbolic response specification, must assign the specific symbolic event to response X (correct solution) or response non-X (incorrect solution). Likewise, in a concept-formation experiment, usually the correct or appropriate defining characteristic of the concept can be stated in many different, but equivalent, symbolic ways. Although prior indirect symbolic response specification can distinguish between all the possible symbolic output events (verbalizations of concept definition) exhibited by the subject, the specific conceptual rule identifying the nature of the concept, associated with direct symbolic response specification, must assign the specific symbolic event to response X (correct verbalization) or response non-X (incorrect verbalization).

INTERNAL RESPONSES VERSUS EXTERNAL RESPONSES

Introduction

Recall that at the level of behavior, certain physiological events, invisible to the naked eye but subject to indirect measurement, are regarded as behavior. The experimental psychologist's use of the term "behavior" need not correspond to the layman's view that behavior only occurs when the organism is acting on the external environment. This distinction also extends to the level of response. A dichotomy must be set up between "external response" and "internal response."

External Responses

External responses are responses that can be seen with the naked eye and that are subject to direct measurement. The method by which the response is originally specified is irrelevant. All the examples of functionally specified responses and most of the examples of physiologically specified responses presented so far are external responses.

Internal Responses

Internal responses are responses that cannot be seen with the naked eye and that are only subject to indirect measurement. Again, the method by which the response is originally specified is irrelevant. Since the only examples of internal responses presented so far are physiologically specified responses, it might seem that internal responses are limited to physiologically specified responses. But functionally specified responses can be internal responses. There is much current experimental evidence that indicates that the R term in the S-R-S learning operation can in fact be an internal response. The presentation of the reinforcing stimulus to the organism can be made contingent upon the prior occurrence of such physiological events as a specific brain wave, a specific GSR reading, a specific pattern of autonomic neuronal firing, secretion of a specific acid in the stomach, etc.

Significance of the Distinction

This dichotomy between internal and external response is significant because what the experimental psychologist means by a learned response is not limited to external responses. As we shall see, the characteristics of a learned response are independent of how the response is specified and how the response is measured.

THE NOTION OF RESPONSE CLASS VERSUS THE NOTION OF RESPONSE INSTANCE

Once the transition from the behavioral level to the response level is made, there are two aspects of the notion of response which must be technically distinguished.

Initially, what the response specification rule establishes is a conceptual response class. For instance, eyelid closure, as physiologically specified, is a response class. Bar pressing, as functionally specified, is a response class and nonbar pressing is another response class; thus, the typical functional response specification sets up two response classes.

Secondly, the physical occurrence of any specific response event during an experimental trial or moment in time is a response instance. Thus, the actual occurrence of an eyelid closure is a response instance; likewise, the rat's actual pressing of the bar is a response instance.

A response instance is a member of a response class; and a response class is composed of many different response instances. Thus, the notion of response class corresponds to the notion of response type and the notion of response instance corresponds to the actual physical occurrence of a particular response type. Previously, the single term "response" was used to refer either to the response type or to the actual response occurrence, depending on the interpretive context.

The technical distinction is more than semantic. The notion of response, as response class, is intimately related to initial response specification or definition. The notion of response, as response instance, is more related to the trial-by-trial variation in the occurrence of the physical response itself. What the experimental psychologist means by a learned response is a response class. What the experimental psychologist investigates in a learning experiment are systematic changes over trials or time in the response instances (variants) of a response class. The next section on response properties presumes this technical distinction between response instance and response class.

RESPONSE PROPERTIES

Introduction

Since the input situation involves active production and control on the part of the experimenter, the notion of stimulus properties was basically analyzed in terms of stimulus functions. Since the output situation is under the direct control of the subject, the notion of response properties is best analyzable in terms of measurable response characteristics.

The notion of measurable response characteristics is really a complex notion composed of two subparts: (1) response characteristics can be defined, independent of their later measurement, and (2) alternate ways of measuring a given response characteristic can be defined. (Remember that existence and measurement are independent concepts at the sophisticated level.) The notion of response characteristics is really a property of the response class as a whole — i.e., what characteristics does a particular response class possess? The notion of response measurement is really a property of the response instance(s) — i.e., how is a particular response instance measured? Response characteristics will be discussed first, followed by response measurement.

RESPONSE CHARACTERISTICS

Introduction

Initially, a distinction must be made as to whether one or more than one response class is definable or meaningful in the context of the specific learning task. If only one response is definable or meaningful, it will be referred to as a single or unitary response situation. If more than one response is definable or meaningful, it will be referred to as a multiple response situation. In a unitary response situation, during any trial or at any one moment in time, the single response of interest either does or does not occur. In the multiple response situation, during any trial or at any one moment in time, one of the responses from the set of N available responses always occurs. (The unitary case is a subset of the multiple case, in which $N = 2$, and one of the responses is simply "the lack of responding.") This distinction is necessary because the response characteristics of interest depend heavily on whether the learning task is a single or multiple response situation.

The Single or Unitary Response Situation

Since a unitary response has real-time and real-space properties, the following constitute the meaningful spatial and/or temporal characteristics of a response:

1) onset or initial appearance of a response;
2) termination or cessation of a response;
3) response duration;
4) response latency or interresponse time;
5) response size, magnitude, or amplitude;
6) response shape, form, or topography.

These six characteristics can best be defined implicitly, in the context of a figure (See Fig. 3-2).

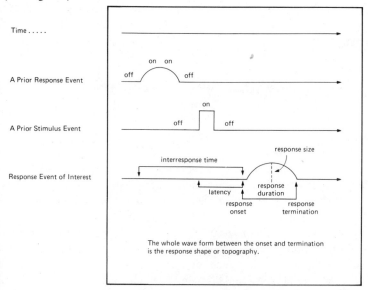

Fig. 3-2. The Characteristics of a Unitary Response. The Record of a Unitary Response Occurrence Over Time

The Multiple Response Situation

The above six characteristics are meaningful and definable for each response of the multiple situation. But they are not the response characteristics of primary interest. The response characteristic of primary interest in the multiple response situation is which of the N responses actually occurs during a trial or at a specific moment in time. This primary characteristic can be labeled "the characteristic of response occurrence." This property of a set of N responses is a measurement characteristic. What is really the focus of concern is which kind of response instance occurs, not any of the six response characteristics of one of the N response classes. Since the characteristic of response occurrence is a measurement characteristic, it will be discussed in detail later.

Some Conceptual Perspective

Physiologically specified responses have shape as a factor of importance and are primarily associated with S-S and S alone operations; functionally specified responses have occurrence as the factor of importance and are primarily associated with S-R-S and S-R operations. If we now assume that shape is merely representative of the other five response characteristics, it becomes apparent that unitary or single response learning situations tend to be S-S or S alone operation-associated, physiologically specified response situations. It should likewise be apparent that multiple response learning situations tend to be S-R-S or S-R operation-associated, functionally specified response situations.

RESPONSE MEASUREMENT; THE CONCEPT OF
DEPENDENT VARIABLE OR RESPONSE MEASURE

INTRODUCTION

It was previously stated in the introduction to the chapter that a response is quantifiable or measurable by one or more dependent variables or response measures. Using more recently introduced terminology, the experimenter must decide how to measure any one or more of the six characteristics of a unitary response or the characteristic of response occurrence in the multiple situation. Different measuring devices can be applied to the response characteristics of a response class or the response instances of a certain response class. We shall use the terms "dependent variable" and "response measure" equivalently to refer to the manner in which a specific response characteristic or a specific response instance is measured.

Before proceeding to the typical response measures of learning psychology, it is necessary to present the two rather broad methods of response measurement. A response characteristic or a response instance can be measured digitally or analogically.

DIGITAL RESPONSE MEASUREMENT

Digital response measurement corresponds to the more or less low-level interpretation of measurement discussed previously — where existence entailed measurement and there were no problems of reliability and validity. Digital response measurement presumes a qualitative scale of existence or occurrence with two categories: existence or occurrence and nonexistence or nonoccurrence. At any one time or during a specific trial, the response instance either is or is not occurring — i.e., the response instance is in one of the two categories.

Digital response measurement is the only kind of measurement that can be applied to naturally occurring binary-category variables like pregnancy (yes, no), sex (male, female), marital state (married, single), etc. It is so easy to apply that it is often employed to quantify any kind of variable even though the variable exists in degrees. For instance, response instances vary in magnitude across trials or time; but the exact magnitude values can be repressed and never recorded. Instead, the digital measuring scale sums across all the different values of magnitude and measures mere occurrence (if magnitude > 0) or nonoccurrence (if magnitude $= 0$). The characteristic of response occurrence, as a measuring characteristic, is digitally measured.

ANALOGICAL RESPONSE MEASUREMENT

Analogical response measurement corresponds to the more or less sophisticated interpretation of measurement discussed previously — where existence did not necessarily entail measurement and where reliability and validity were of concern. Analogical response measurement is the natural way to quantify any one of the six response characteristics of a response class. Analogical response measurement is only meaningful if the variable or response instance of interest actually does occur. (A nonoccurring response possesses no response characteristics.) Analogical response measurement presumes that some scale of N ($N \geq 2$) categories is applicable to the variable or response characteristic of interest. Thus, at any time or during a specific trial, the various response characteristics of a response instance are in one of the N categories of some measuring scale. For instance, if a response occurs, it has some value of magnitude, shape, duration, latency, etc. Thus, the response characteristics of a unitary response could be referred to as "analogical response characteristics."

Unlike the digital response measurement of response instance occurrence or nonoccurrence, there are many different analogical measuring scales and devices, of differing power and resolvability, applicable to each of the six analogical response characteristics of a response class. One commonly accepted hierarchical classification system of analogical measuring devices postulates four kinds of analogical scales: (1) nominal, (2) ordinal, (3) interval, and (4) ratio. Briefly, a nominal scale is composed of unordered, unrelated categories. For instance, a basket of fruit is divisible into N types of fruit. (Note: a digital scale is a nominal scale composed of two categories.) An ordinal scale is composed of ordered, related categories. For instance, a group of men can be arranged in order by height (smallest → largest). An interval scale is an ordinal scale with a quantitative unit of measurement, but without an absolute zero starting point. For instance, the centigrade and Fahrenheit temperature scales are interval scales (both possess arbitrary "0" or starting points). A ratio scale is an interval scale with an absolute "0" or starting point. Virtually every physical measuring scale or device is ratio — i.e., a ruler for length, stopwatch for time, etc.

The higher up a particular scale is in the analogical measurement classification system, the greater the probability that the scale possesses some minimal degree of reliability and validity. So it is important to measure a specific analogical characteristic of a response class with the most powerful (highest) analogical measuring scale possible. For instance, response magnitude (height of response wave) can be expressed in actual inches (ratio scale) — why bother expressing it on an ordinal scale: say small, medium, large.

RESPONSE MEASUREMENT OF UNITARY RESPONSE CHARACTERISTICS

Introduction

At the level of response measurement, the six analogical response characteristics of a unitary response reduce to only four independent, mutually exclusive measurable characteristics: (1) latency or interresponse time, (2) duration, (3) magnitude, and (4) topography. (Response onset and response cessation are completely derivable from response latency [or interresponse time] and response duration; or latency [or interresponse time] and duration are completely derivable from response onset and response cessation readings.)

Response Latency and Interresponse Time

Response latency is the time between the onset of the stimulus event (typically coinciding with the onset of a trial) and the onset of the response following it. The characteristic of response latency is indigenous to the discrete-trial procedure. Interresponse time is the time between the onset of the Nth response (where $N > 0$) and the onset of the $N + 1st$ response in an experimental session. The characteristic of interresponse time is more meaningful in a continuous-time procedure. Time can and should be measured on a ratio scale: stopwatch, automatic clock timer, etc. in terms of some convenient unit of measurement: milliseconds, seconds, minutes, etc.

Response Duration

Response duration is the time between the onset and the termination of a specific response instance. The comments about the measurement of time presented above are equally applicable here.

Response Magnitude

Response magnitude is . . . . . . There is no one way of specifying or quantifying what response magnitude is! Usually, it is quantified in terms of the maximal height of the response wave in the vertical direction (See Fig. 3-2). It could also be quantified in terms of the maximal width of the response wave in the horizontal direction. (Be careful — because this dependent variable of response measure covaries "100%" with response duration.) It could also be quantified in terms of some weighted average of the maximal degrees of displacement in the vertical and horizontal directions, yielding virtually an infinite number of possible magnitude values because the coefficient values can vary. It could also be quantified in terms of the area encompassed by the response wave form. Other response measures or dependent variables for response magnitude could be listed ad infinitum. No matter which dependent variable or response measure is chosen to quantify magnitude, the ideal measuring scale to use is ratio. Length or extension is readily quantifiable in terms of millimeters, centimeters, inches, etc.

Response Topography

Response shape is . . . . . . There is no one way of quantifying response shape either! Response shape is not readily measurable by interval or ratio scaling, unless the experimenter redefines shape in terms of characteristics like rise time or speed of the wave form, down time or speed of the wave form, or level time or stationary speed of the wave form, etc. In the absence of a sophisticated measuring model for shape, it is a response characteristic which possesses at most ordinal scale properties. For instance, various response instances can be rated in terms of their roundness or squareness, or in terms of their sharpness or abruptness, or in terms of their completeness or incompleteness — each response instance is assigned to one of an ordered class of gross descriptive categories.

RESPONSE MEASUREMENT OF MULTIPLE RESPONSE OCCURRENCE

Since the characteristic of response occurrence is digitally measured, the measuring procedure "simply" amounts to the experimenter or some automated response recording apparatus deciding and recording which response class of the N response classes occurs during a trial or at any moment in time. Let us assume a two-response situation for expostulatory purposes: response class A and response class B. Thus, the measuring device would output on any particular trial or moment in time the equivalent of either "A occurs" or "B occurs."

Because more than one response class is available for occurrence on a trial or moment in time and because the response class that actually does occur can be evaluated with respect to the specific learning operation or procedure in effect, there can be interpretive significance to the response that does occur beyond the fact that it merely occurs. Specifically, once the stimulus input situation is taken into account, a judgment concerning the appropriateness or correctness of the response can be made. Thus, the individual A and B response occurrences can be relabeled as correct (C) or incorrect (I) and the measuring device, given stimulus input information, can be programmed to output on any particular trial or moment in time the equivalent of either "C occurs" or "I occurs." It must be emphasized that response appropriateness or correctness is not a measurable characteristic of a response class per se in isolation — it only becomes a meaningful response characteristic of the multiple response situation if the input situation is taken into account.

DIGITAL MEASUREMENT OF RESPONSE OCCURRENCE IN THE UNITARY RESPONSE SITUATION

The option is open to digitally measure the mere occurrence (or nonoccurrence) of the one definable response class of a unitary response situation. In fact, the digital response characteristic of occurrence of a unitary response is measured more often than one or more of its analogical response characteristics because it is simply more convenient to do so. Assuming response class A represents the unitary response, the measuring device would output the equivalent of either "A occurs" or "A does not occur" on any particular trial or moment in time. In the unitary response situation, "A occurs" is always equivalent to "C occurs" and "A does not occur" is always equivalent to "I occurs." so no additional, second order evaluative judgment is necessary.

ANALOGICAL MEASUREMENT OF UNITARY RESPONSE CHARACTERISTICS IN THE MULTIPLE RESPONSE SITUATION

The option is open to analogically measure one or more of the response characteristics of the specific response class (A or B) which does occur on a particular trial or moment in time in the multiple response situation. All the comments made in the context of the response measurement of unitary response characteristics are equally applicable here.

MEASUREMENT CHARACTERISTICS OF STRICTLY VERBAL, LINGUISTIC, OR SYMBOLIC RESPONSES

Human learning tasks involving symbolic responses are almost invariably multiple response situations and, therefore, the response characteristic of primary interest is the digital measurement characteristic of response instance occurrence. Quite often, the second order or evaluative significance of the occurring response — whether it is correct (C) or incorrect (I) — is more important than its content — the specification of its response class. Therefore, in many human learning tasks, the measuring device is set up to output "C occurs" or "I occurs" directly on any one trial or during any one response occurrence.

The analogical measurement characteristics of a single or unitary response class — i.e., latency, magnitude, duration, shape, etc. — are definable and meaningful response characteristics of a verbal, linguistic, or symbolic response class. But they are rarely recorded during a human learning experiment. For instance, the response SIX emitted orally by a subject to the stimulus XFT during a paired-associate verbal learning experiment has a latency, an intensity on the auditory dimension, a duration, a specific phonetic or phonemic shape, etc. Yet these are not recorded unless the specific experimental hypothesis being tested or the specific theoretical relevance of the paired-associate learning study requires such quantification.

RESPONSE MEASUREMENT IN RELATION TO THE EXPERIMENTAL PROCEDURE: SHORT-TERM AND LONG-TERM CHARACTERISTICS OF RESPONSES

The preceding discussion of response measurement applies only to the quantification of an individual response during one trial or at one moment in time. Since a specific experimental session involves N discrete trials or a continuous-time procedure (free responding over N minutes), the results of individual response measurement must eventually be presented in such a way as to adequately represent how the subject(s) performed over the entire course of the experimental session. As a logical extension of this, sometimes the focus of interest is how the subject(s) performed over many different experimental sessions (i.e., over many successive independent applications of the experimental procedure). The former situation quantifies short-term characteristics of a learned response, while the latter situation quantifies long-term characteristics of a learned response. In addition, the short-term phase of experimentation involving the initial application of a specific experimental procedure is often subdivided into three temporal phases: (1) the initial phase of responding, (2) the transition phase of responding, and (3) the maintenance or asymptotic phase of responding.

Quantification of short-term and long-term characteristics of learned responses is a matter of statistical analysis, both descriptive and inferential, and, in part, is contingent upon one's theoretical approach to learning. Because of this and because it is the purpose of this section to only analyze the nature of the individual R term, it will be more didactic to analyze short- and long-term aspects of response measurement later in Chapters 7 and 8.

THE NOTION OF A MACROMOLAR RESPONSE CLASS VERSUS THE NOTION OF A MICROMOLAR RESPONSE CLASS

If a particular response class is defined solely by functional specification, it is commonly referred to as a macromolar response class. For instance, bar pressing by a rat is a macromolar response class. If a particular response class is defined by a functional specification plus an additional analogical response characteristic limitation, it is usually labeled as a micromolar response class. Any one of the four measurably independent analogical response characteristics can be appended to the initial functional response specification. For instance, bar-pressing behavior is only a bar-pressing response if it possesses a certain magnitude, or a certain shape, or a certain duration, or a certain interresponse time, or any combination of the above. "Certain" is usually specified in terms of a "reinforcement band or range." For example, in order for a bar-press occurrence to constitute a bar-press response, the bar press must occur with a response pressure between 40 and 80 grams (magnitude), or with the paws placed on the extreme left-end side of the bar (shape), or with a bar depression lasting between two and four seconds (duration), or with an interresponse time between 30 seconds and one minute. Illustrating pressure in depth, bar-press occurrences with response pressures lower than 40 grams or higher than 80 grams are not bar-press responses. They are members of the other response class — nonbar press responding.

A micromolar response class differs from a functionally specified response class with a physiological limitation. In the former, the additional analogical limitation is made without reference to the underlying effector or effector system involved; in the latter, the additional physiological effector limitation is made without reference to the effects it might have on the analogical characteristics of the response. There is one potential area of overlap. It is possible to characterize the analogical characteristic of shape in physiological effector terms. For instance, a response class defined as "bar pressing with the left front paw" involves both analogical (shape) specification and physiological (left paw) specification. In effect, here, the notion of shape is physiologically defined; the response characteristic of shape is measured by using a scale composed of categories specifying which physiological effector is involved.

At a conceptual level, any macromolar response class is divisible into practically an infinite number of different sets of mutually exclusive and exhaustive micromolar response classes. Here are two examples: (1) The macromolar response class of bar pressing is composed of the micromolar response class of bar pressing with response magnitude between "0" and five grams, the micromolar response class of bar pressing with response magnitude between six and 10 grams, the micromolar response class of bar pressing with response magnitude between 11 and 15 grams, etc. up to the normal physiological limit of about 250 grams. (2) The macromolar response class of bar pressing is divisible into bar pressing with the left paw alone, bar pressing with the right paw alone, bar pressing with both paws, bar pressing with the nose, bar pressing with the tail, bar pressing with the mouth, etc. until every conceivable physiologically shaped response is provided for.

The distinction between macromolar and micromolar response classes has great theoretical import for learning psychology. As we shall see in Chapter 7, how response classes are initially defined or set up can determine how a specific learning theory or learning approach is constructed to account for the learning or acquisition of those response classes. Also this distinction has relevance for the measurement of the learning process discussion of Chapter 8.

THE OVERALL MACRO-OUTPUT SITUATION

The output situation, as a real-space and real-time event, has just been analyzed in terms of successive hierarchical levels of representation or measurement. Since the output situation is never interpreted independent of the associated input situation, the specific output situation of interest to us is the one associated with the standard input situations used by learning psychology — i.e., the common learning tasks studied by experimental psychology. The output situation of interest to us must have its behavior and response levels composed of learned behavior and learned responses. Using these terms loosely, the standard output situation of concern in this book is learned behavior or learned responses.

Although the structure of behavior and/or responses in general has just been presented, it is still necessary to analyze the notion of learned behavior and/or learned responses. What the characteristics of learned responses exactly are and how they differ from the characteristics of unlearned or nonlearned responses, etc. constitute the substantive content of the next chapter.

SUMMARY

The descriptive output situation consists of hierarchically related analytical levels: (1) behavior, (2) responses, and (3) measurable response characteristics. The output situation is usually interpreted as directly divisible into behavior, which in turn is composed of one or more responses that are quantifiable by one or more dependent variables or response measures. The specific output situation of current concern is the one associated with the standard input situations used by learning psychology and consequently has its behavior/response levels composed of learned behavior/responses — i.e., the standard output situation is learned behavior/responses. The content of each analytical level should be briefly reviewed.

1. Behavior can be defined as any directly or indirectly measurable activity on the part of an organism that can be related to a preceding or concurrent stimulus. Activity is usually characterized as any kind of physiological event that affects (changes) the environment (internal or external) of the organism. Measurable activity only consists of those consequential physiological events that are quantifiable by some kind of measuring device or scale.

2. Responses refer to those specific aspects of the totality of ongoing behavior that are selected by the experimenter for actual recording (observation) during a given experiment. (The distinction between behavior and responses is more semantic than conceptual.) Responses can be specified physiologically (indirectly), functionally (directly), or by a combination of the two methods. The notion of response is both internally and externally resolvable and can be approached from the perspective of either "instance" or "class."

3. A response possesses certain measurable response characteristics, of which there are two primary types: digital and analogical. The basic digital measurement characteristic is that of response occurrence or nonoccurrence. The analogical measurement characteristics include latency or interresponse time, duration, magnitude, and topography. The results of individual response measurement must eventually be presented (accumulated) in such a way as to adequately represent how a subject performed over the course of the entire experimental session.

4
A Characterization of "Learning" and "Conditioning"; The Characteristics of a Learned Response and a Conditioned Response

INTRODUCTION

This chapter has four interrelated purposes:
1) to present the characteristics of a learned response;
2) to define learning as the process which leads to the acquisition of a learned response;
3) to characterize conditioning as a specific type of learning; and
4) to characterize a conditioned response as a specific type of learned response.

THE CHARACTERISTICS OF A LEARNED RESPONSE

INTRODUCTION

There are two characteristics of a learned response which distinguish it from a nonlearned response: (1) the measurable characteristics of the response must have undergone a permanent change, (2) but only as a result of or as a function of reinforced practice. Thus, the specification of a learned response involves reference to both the structural properties of the response and the specific, associated input condition. If the change in the measurable characteristics of the response is not permanent or if the change in the measurable characteristics of the response is permanent but not due to reinforced practice, it is not a learned response. Let us analyze the meaning and significance of these two characteristics in detail.

A PERMANENT CHANGE IN THE MEASURABLE CHARACTERISTICS
OF THE RESPONSE

What is Meant by Change in the Measurable
Characteristics of a Response?

For the rest of this section, the word "response" will be used to refer to "measurable characteristics of a response." The notion of a change of a response only has meaning over trials or over time. More specifically, the response must jump from an initial or preliminary state of occurrence (S_1) to a second state of occurrence (S_2). This jump from S_1 to S_2 is the specific denotation of the notion of change. In this context, there are five types of changes that are applicable to learning psychology:

1) The onset or initial appearance of the response. Here S_1 = nonoccurrence; S_2 = occurrence.
2) The final disappearance or termination of the response. Here S_1 = occurrence; S_2 = nonoccurrence.
3) The increase of the response above some initial baseline level. Here S_1 = a level of occurrence; S_2 = a higher level of occurrence.
4) The decrease of the response back down to a lower or initial baseline level. Here S_1 = a level of occurrence; S_2 = a lower level of occurrence.
5) Cyclic variations in the response. Here S_1 and S_2 represent two different levels of occurrence and the response alternates between them systematically or randomly.

Changes (1) and (2) are only meaningful in the context of the digital measurement characteristic of response occurrence. Changes (3), (4), and (5) are meaningful for either the digital measurement characteristic of response occurrence or any of the analogical measurement characteristics of a unitary response. As a property of digital measurement, the last three kinds of changes are usually represented by the percentage of response instance occurrence across trials (blocks of trials) or by the rate or response instance occurrence across time. As a property of analogical measurement, the last three kinds of changes are usually represented by mean or average latency or amplitude readings of the response class across trials (blocks of trials).

Before the five types of changes can be more fully related to the characterization of a learned response, it is necessary to discuss certain relationships among the types of changes and certain correspondences with the four operations presented in Chapter 2.

Change (1) is a subset of change (3) in the context of digital measurement of response occurrence. Change (3) reduces to change (1) if the initial level of occurrence is zero. Change (2) is a subset of change (4) in the context of digital measurement of response occurrence. Change (4) reduces to change (2) if the terminal level of occurrence is zero. Change (1) and change (2) are mirror-image changes in the digital context. Change (3) and change (4) are also mirror-image changes in both the digital and analogical contexts. Change (5) is a judicious combination of change (3) and change (4) either in the digital or analogical context.

Changes (1) and (3) are primarily associated with the reinforcement operation. Change (1) is usually associated with the S-S reinforcement operation, while change (3) is usually associated with the S-R-S reinforcement operation. The S-S operation is primarily used to create the initial appearance or onset of a response. The S-R-S operation can only be applied if the response to be reinforced already occurs at some initial baseline level of occurrence. Changes (2) and (4) are primarily associated with the extinction operation. Change (2) is more meaningful in the context of the S alone operation, while change (4) is more meaningful in the context of the S-R operation. The specific correspondences here in the context of the extinction operation are mirror-image analogies to those of the reinforcement operation. Responding in an S alone extinction operation situation can eventually disappear. Responding in an S-R extinction operation situation just decreases to the initial baseline level of occurrence. No specific correspondence will be indicated for change (5) at this point because it is primarily associated with various types of complex procedures.

Changes (1) and (3) are the types of changes usually associated with the acquisition of a response deemed to be learned — i.e., the learning or acquisition phase of a learning experiment. Changes (2) and (4) are the types of changes usually associated with the extinction of a response originally deemed to be learned — i.e., the extinction phase of a learning experiment. The above statement might seem to contradict the qualification of permanent that is applied to change. How can a learned response, once acquired, extinguish if it is permanent? This seeming contradiction will be resolved once the exact meaning of "permanent" is presented.

Thus, functionally, if a specific response is to be classified as learned, it must have undergone a type (1) or type (3) change as a result of reinforced practice some time in its past response history. But, since many experimental learning psychologists are interested primarily in the extinction of a learned response (for instance, getting rid of an undesirable "habit") and never have observed the actual acquisition of it — type (1) or type (3) change — under conditions of reinforced practice, the fact that a response is observed as undergoing a change (2) or change (4) following the introduction of the extinction operation is considered sufficient evidence to establish that it is a bona fide learned response. The notion of change in measurable characteristics is a required denotative property of a learned response — but which aspect of the change — change to (acquisition) or change from (extinction) — is irrelevant. These only become relevant when characterizing the process of learning itself (changing to) or the process of extinction itself (changing from).

Significance of the Lack of a Normative, Prescriptive, or Evaluative Adjective Modifying the Word "Change"

There is no specification that the change in response necessarily be good, desirable, appropriate, or beneficial for the organism. This lack of specification is significant because most educators and teachers, particularly with respect to classroom learning, and even some psychologists, state that the change involved in a learned response must be an improvement. But all the learned responses that an organism acquires need not be improvements — for instance, the cigarette "habit," a prejudice against a specific racial or minority group, or a simple, low-level neurotic symptom. It is best to leave the characterization of a learned response neutral or noncommittal with respect to the ultimate worth or benefit of the change involved; and it is certainly not justifiable to limit the changes underlying a learned response only to those that are deemed evaluatively beneficial.

What is Meant by a Permanent Change in the Measurable Characteristics of a Response?

Typically, the term "permanent" is given a temporal specification by the layman: "permanent" means long-lasting, long-term, even eternal. But the experimental learning psychologist does not use "permanent" in its temporal sense. The notion of "eternal" has no real empirical meaning. "Permanent" is used as an equivalent of functionally irreversible. Once the change in the measurable characteristics of the response has occurred from one state (S_1) to the other (S_2), the change does not spontaneously revert back to S_1. The change is irreversible unless the experimenter institutes specific means by which to cause a reversion.

The basic experimental condition leading to reversion of the change has already been analyzed in the text: introduction or use of the extinction operation or procedure. Any complex procedure that has the extinction operation as one of its constituent elements can also lead to reversion of the change. For instance, very often the complex procedure used to measure forgetting and usually the complex procedure used to create a stimulus discrimination involve the extinction operation and can lead to the reversion of the change. So it should not seem too surprising that some permanent changes only last for five or 10 minutes in the context of some learning experiments.

Significance of Qualifying "Change" with the Term "Permanent"

Qualification of the term "change" with "permanent" automatically excludes from consideration as a learned response any response whose measurable characteristics can only undergo a reversible change. There are many input conditions that can only generate a reversible change in measurable response characteristics. Two specific independent variables that act in this way are motivation (drive level) and certain activating drugs. These variables generate a type (1) or type (3) change in measurable response characteristics when they become part of the input situation. At this time, their associated type (1) or type (3) changes are indistinguishable from those of a learned response. It is only after drive level decreases or drug effects wear off that the measurable characteristics of the response can be observed reverting back to the initial state or level. Thus, this reversibility after the input situation is eliminated is the only way to distinguish these kinds of type (1) and type (3) changes from the type (1) and type (3) changes characteristic of learned responses.

Also, depending on exactly how they are measured, independent variables such as sensory adaptation, fatigue, and depressant drugs generate type (2) or type (4) changes in the measurable characteristics of a response. Their reversibility after sensory adaptation diminishes or fatigue dissipates or drug depression wears off is the only thing that distinguishes them from responses deemed learned through observing a type (2) or type (4) change following introduction of the extinction operation or procedure.

The Conceptual Locus of the Term "Permanent"

Introduction. The term "permanent" was just discussed as a property of the overt learned response itself — i.e., at the behavioral level. This locus of the term "permanent" has at least two conceptual drawbacks associated with it.

1. You might be wondering why the original characterization of a learned response did not contain the term "functionally irreversible" instead of the term "permanent." Actually, nothing would be gained by doing this. Functional irreversibility would have to be characterized as permanence, but not in the layman's temporal sense, etc., and the same circle would result, but from the opposite direction. A resolution of the contingent arbitrariness or ambiguity associated with the use of "permanence" or "functional irreversibility" is not possible at the behavioral level.

2. For many learning psychologists, locating the term "permanent" at the behavioral level assigns very unrealistic and ultrastrict operational or empirical requirements to a response deemed to be learned — requirements that are not satisfied by the actual response data in every learning experiment (namely, *consistent* response occurrence and *indefinite* response occurrence). In other words, once a specific response has been learned (i.e., the switch from S_1 to S_2 has occurred), the response does not occur consistently or indefinitely, even though the change itself from S_1 to S_2 is characterized as permanent or

functionally irreversible. With respect to consistency, depending on the specific experimental conditions in effect and the response measure being used, it is possible for overt responding to vary all over the place from trial to trial or from one measuring occasion to the next. With respect to indefiniteness (or persistence), overt responding eventually ceases, especially in the context of animal learning studies, even though reinforced practice, as the input condition, is still in effect — due to the influence of nonlearning variables such as fatigue, satiation, etc. (In much human learning research, the actual cessation of responding is a "cognitive" event contingent upon the specific requirements of the experiment as specified by the instructions and is independent of the fact that reinforced practice is in effect as the input condition.)

Because of the above two drawbacks, many learning psychologists prefer to assign the property of permanence to the underlying physiological, structural, or process level — so the merits of this locus of the term "permanent" must also be discussed.

The physiological, structural, or process level. (The following comments presume that the reader is already aware of the event of learning conceptualized as a process — an entity residing in the individual resulting from reinforced practice and leading to the performance of learned responses — a topic to be discussed later in the chapter.) In this approach to the notion of "permanent," reinforced practice results in a permanent structural or physiological change in the organism which in turn leads to the appearance of learned responses. This physiological change has been variously interpreted as consolidated memory traces, altered paths or patterns of neuronal synaptic transmission, additional protein synthesis and coding, etc.

In this approach, it is possible for overt responding to vary "all over the place," depending upon the specific experimental procedures and variables in effect, although the structural representation or residue of reinforced practice has not been changed. Also the permanence of learning (in the layman's temporal sense) in this approach becomes a theoretical issue or question. It is no longer an operational problem associated with the level of overt behavior occurrence and the actual longevity or persistence of a response in a specific experimental context is not a crucial defining characteristic or empirical criterion determining whether the behavior can properly be labeled a "learned piece of behavior."

REINFORCED PRACTICE

What is Meant by Practice?

Practice is grossly equivalent to the phrases "past experience" or "training." The author prefers the term "practice" over the other two because it is more easily modifiable by the term "reinforced" — a necessary restriction soon to be discussed, and it is more easily translatable into what the experimenter actually exposes the subject to in the context of the laboratory — i.e., the notion of practice trials.

Significance of Inclusion of the Term "Practice" in the Specification of a Learned Response

Inclusion of the term "practice" in the specification of a learned response is absolutely essential. Only a permanent or functionally irreversible change in a response as a result of or function of practice can be classified as a learned change. There are other nonpractice (basically physiologically based) input situations that lead to permanent changes in the measurable characteristics of a response. For instance, the onset of maturation, the onset of senescence, and the occurrence of an accidental or unexpected physiological event such as brain damage, severed spinal cord, etc. result in permanent changes, just as practice does.

There is one basic difference between practice as the input condition and maturation, senescence, or an accidental physiological event as the input condition. In the latter case, the input conditions can never be eliminated once onset has begun — i.e., maturation or senescence can never cease after onset; a severed spinal cord is never correctible; only a few kinds of brain damage are correctible and then only to a partial degree. In the former case (practice), the input condition can be eliminated or can even be actively replaced by the extinction operation or procedure. Thus, the organism can leave the practice situation and discontinue practice or be actively exposed to the extinction procedure. This difference is reflected in the type or degree of irreversibility exhibited at the level of change in measurable response characteristics: while a change in the context of practice is merely functionally irreversible, a change in the context of one of the physiological variables is truly irreversible — i.e., "permanent," in the layman's temporal sense.

Significance of Qualifying Practice With the Term "Reinforced"

Most introductory learning texts refer to the standard learning input situation as involving merely practice, training, or past experience. The term "practice" by itself is too general and misleading — for instance, it is not sufficient to distinguish the standard learning input situation from other input situations used by learning psychologists (primarily the extinction situation). Analysis of what practice means, specifically in the laboratory context, always leads to the notion of reinforcement. So it is technically desirable to specify that the standard learning input situation involves reinforcement at the definitional level. This can best be accomplished by modifying "practice" with "reinforced," such that the standard learning input situation is regarded as consisting of reinforced practice.

What is Meant by Reinforced Practice?

It will be easy to define "reinforced practice" in terms of the reinforcement operations introduced in Chapter 2: experimenter-contingent (S-S) and response-contingent (S-R-S), where the second stimulus in each representation is the reinforcing stimulus. Whenever the subject is exposed to a reinforcing stimulus during the occurrence of a reinforcement operation, he is said to be reinforced. Each occurrence of reinforcement constitutes a reinforced trial or reinforcing event for the subject. Exposure to a series of N successive reinforced trials or N successive reinforcing events (where $0 < N < \infty$) constitutes reinforced practice. Using other terminology introduced in Chapter 2, reinforced practice is a specific kind of experimental procedure – namely, one composed of N successive reinforced trials or N continuous-time reinforcing events.

A DEFINITION OF LEARNING

INTRODUCTION

Learning is the process that results in the acquisition of a learned response. To avoid circularity, let us substitute the denotative properties of a learned response for the phrase "acquisition of a learned response." A new temporal qualification of the term "change" must also be included. Thus, the following constitutes an acceptable definition of learning. Learning is the process by which the measurable characteristics of a response undergo a permanent change, either immediate or delayed, as a result or function of reinforced practice.

While many of the above terms have been previously analyzed in conjunction with the characteristics of a learned response, four aspects of the definition require discussion: (1) the significance of qualifying change with the phrase "either immediate or delayed," (2) the structure of the definition, (3) the type of definition, and (4) the notion of a process – i.e., what is learning exactly? Also, the definition, as a whole, will be put in further perspective by evaluating it on some relevant dimensions.

SIGNIFICANCE OF QUALIFYING CHANGE WITH THE PHRASE "IMMEDIATE OR DELAYED"

If no temporal qualification of change were included, it would automatically be interpreted that the change is always immediate — i.e., cotemporaneous with the initial onset of reinforced practice or certainly concurrent with the occurrence of the initial reinforced practice session itself. But the fact is that learned changes in response characteristics need not appear immediately. There are many conditions under which the initial appearance of a learned change does not occur until the extreme end of the initial reinforced practice session or the beginning of a second reinforced practice session (or test session) which follows the initial reinforced practice session after an intervening time-out period.

There are two primary reasons for a delayed appearance of changes in the measurable characteristics of a response: (1) conditions associated with the way in which the reinforced practice is administered and (2) the methodological or procedural impossibility of assessing whether a learned change has in fact occurred during the initial reinforced practice session itself. The most common example of (1) occurs when reinforced practice is administered in a "massed-practice fashion" — i.e., with very short or no intertrial intervals. The consequent build-up of fatigue or some fatigue-related construct associated with massed practice prevents the changes in response characteristics from immediately appearing. After the fatigue or fatigue-related construct is allowed to dissipate, the anticipated learned changes will occur if they are appropriately tested for. With reference to (2), imagine an individual memorizing the blueprints for a specific house (i.e., initial reinforced practice). It would be impossible to assess whether he has learned anything until he either draws the blueprint from memory or recognizes it in a set of similar blueprints or builds a scale model of the house or actually builds the "real" house, etc.

In the context of simple learning experimentation, most learned changes are exhibited immediately; on the other hand, in the context of more complex learning experimentation, there is a tendency for learned changes to be delayed. The distinction between an immediate and delayed change in response characteristics is technically labeled by learning psychologists as "the learning-performance distinction." Performance refers to the state of the response characteristics currently; performance may (immediate change) or may not (delayed, later change) be indicating that actual learning is occurring in the context of current, ongoing reinforced practice.

THE STRUCTURE OF THE DEFINITION

The structure of the definition corresponds in form to what was previously referred to as a functional relationship or causal law. Permanent changes in measurable response characteristics constitute the Y. Reinforced practice is the X. The definition of learning relates changes in the measurable characteristics of a response to prior or concurrent reinforcing stimuli. The definition of learning relates change in behavior, as a dependent variable, to reinforced practice, as the independent variable. Since experimental psychology is nothing but a collection of stimulus-response relationships or independent variable-dependent variable relationships, learning psychology is merely that subset of psychology which deals with reinforced practice as the independent variable and permanent changes in response characteristics as the dependent variable.

Since permanent changes in response characteristics are definitionally related to reinforced practice, it is not the focus of learning psychology to establish whether in fact learned responses are a function of reinforced practice. Rather, learning psychology is concerned with a series of sophisticated experimental and/or theoretical questions that derive from the fact that learned responses are related to reinforced practice in a functional relationship form. The key theoretical questions facing learning psychology are indicated in Chapter 7. The primary experimental question facing learning psychology can be conveniently discussed at this point.

The primary experimental question facing learning psychology is: What specific operations on the part of the experimenter constitute reinforced practice for the organism? This question is not as vacuous as it appears. For instance, will the onset of a light following the occurrence of a response by a rat constitute a reinforcing event? Will the occurrence of brain stimulation following the occurrence of a response by a monkey constitute a reinforcing event? Will the occurrence of the words "I agree" following the emission of a "belief" by a human constitute a reinforcing event? Will the accumulation of symbolic points by an institutionalized schizophrenic earned by getting out of bed on time constitute a reinforcing event? Will the stimulation of a planarian by a light in conjunction with an electric shock serve as the basis of a permanent change in the measurable characteristics of a response? These are substantive, content questions which in effect give meaning or specific application to the two abstract reinforcement operations introduced in Chapter 2. (The first four examples are instances of the S-R-S operation with initial S unspecified, while the fifth is an instance of the S-S operation.)

THE TYPE OF DEFINITION

This is an operational definition of learning. An operational definition of a concept such as learning is stated in terms that reduce the concept to observations which can be made on the physical world and manipulations which can be performed on the physical world. Operational definition defines a concept in terms of the operations used to measure that concept. More specifically, the entities "permanent changes in the measurable characteristics of a response" and "reinforced practice," the constituent terms of the definition, possess real-time and real-space properties and, as such, can be measured, manipulated, and investigated.

The primary advantage of an operational definition is that it ipso facto specifies just what has to be done to measure the concept being defined and bring it into the laboratory. A second advantage of operational definition is that it leads to very little misunderstanding or misinterpretation, assuming the individual knows the meaning of its constituent terms.

THEORETICAL DEFINITIONS OF LEARNING

There are other ways of defining learning. Another prominent class of definitional types is theoretical. There are as many theoretical definitions of learning as there are learning theorists. At this point, we need not be overly concerned with the various theoretical definitions of learning because the notion of theory will not be presented until Chapter 6. Suffice it to say that a particular theoretical definition of learning does not necessarily specify how learning should be quantified in the laboratory nor is it readily understandable or interpretable. For instance, let us consider a typical theoretical definition of learning — one that could be constructed by virtually any perceptually oriented or cognitively oriented psychologist: "Learning is a reorganization of the perceptual world of the learner." What is "reorganization" and what is "perceptual world"? How are "reorganization" and "perceptual world" measured and brought into the lab? Also, there is no reference in the definition to what the "reorganization" is a function of. Assuming "reorganization" and "perceptual world" are measurable, etc., with what input situations are they associated?

THE NOTION OF A PROCESS — i.e., WHAT IS LEARNING EXACTLY?

So far only external physical events have been explicitly referred to and described in detail: the input situation (stimulus events) and the output situation (response events). The environmental entity connecting the two is the organism. Something must go on inside the organism in order to transduce the stimulus energy into response energy. This "something" can be referred to as a process. When reinforced practice is the input situation and permanent changes in the measurable characteristics of a response constitute the output situation, the connecting process is called learning.

A process possesses two interrelated characteristics: (1) with respect to time, it intervenes between a stimulus event and a response event, and (2) it is unobservable. Since a process intervenes, it is commonly referred to as an intervening variable — to provide continuity with the notions of independent and dependent variables. Thus, learning is an intervening variable. Since a process is unobservable, its existence can only be inferred from behavior exhibited in a specific stimulus situation. The existence of learning can only be inferred from permanent changes in response characteristics in the context of reinforced practice. Assuming reinforced practice is in effect, learning may or may not be currently exhibited in behavior. Recall the learning-performance distinction.

Since a process is an inferred entity, a process is often referred to as a theoretical construct. Thus, learning is a theoretical construct. The functions and properties of a theoretical construct (theory) are so important, that the notion of a theoretical construct is regarded as the third unit of analysis and constitutes the substantive content of Chapter 6. At this point, let us merely relate the process of learning as a theoretical construct to two aspects of the prior discussion on how learning is defined.

1. You can now see why there are as many theoretical definitions of learning as there are learning theorists. Since learning is a theoretical construct, a psychologist can assign any properties or functions to it that he desires and at any level of reality he desires. The specific theoretical definition referred to previously (perceptual reorganization) gives learning a "psychological" reality; more specifically, it is a perceptual psychological construct. Other psychologists prefer to give learning a physiological, neurophysiological, chemical, bio-chemical, biophysical, or mechanical, etc. "reality." For example, you could define learning theoretically as "a permanent change in the synaptic connections among a group or sequence of neurons." Also, it is possible to deny the existence of learning as a process or theoretical construct. The approach taken by Skinner to the psychology of learning is the primary contemporary example of this denial. Skinner's view is often referred to as the "empty organism" or "empty black box" approach: the only things that exist are the physical overt stimulus and response events. There is no learning-performance distinction. Everything is performance.

2. You can now see why it is necessary to give learning an operational definition. Since learning is unobservable, it must be defined in terms of observables (change in response, reinforced practice) so that it can be quantified and empirically investigated.

EVALUATION OF THE DEFINITION

Let us evaluate this characterization of learning with respect to (1) its representativeness, (2) the layman's conception of learning, (3) its open-endedness in regard to the notion of change or learned response, and (4) its suitability for complex human learning and cognitive phenomena, especially language phenomena.

Representativeness

Every operational definition of learning ever devised is some variant of all those that preceded it in time. This one is no exception. It is representative of all other attempts of characterizing learning operationally. In terms of the actual language used, it bears its closest resemblance to Gregory Kimble's classic operational definition of learning.

The Layman's Conception of Learning

"Learning" is one of the few technical terms of psychology that is also part of the English vernacular. In fact, the term "learning" is so culturally pervasive that it would be disconcerting if the nontechnical and operational uses of the term differed significantly. Fortunately, such is not the case. Consider the following nontechnical statements about learning, as a subset representative of all the remarks you have ever heard about learning emitted at your corner bar.

"We learn on the basis of past experience."

"Learning is an adjustment in the face of a change in circumstances."

"Learning is simply an adaptation to the conditions around you."

"A person learns to do X in order to get Y."

"Stay away from that crowd or you might pick up some bad habits."

Granted that the above examples differ in their degree of approximation to our formal definition, none of them contradict it. Actually, the middle three statements constitute implicit functional relationships if we make a liberal interpretation of adjustment and adaptation as behavior and repress the existential status of learning implied in the statements (i.e., as something *not* intervening). In effect, most laymen regard learning as a pragmatic adaptability in the face of changing environmental circumstances and this conception is certainly not beyond the denotation of our operational definition of learning.

Open-Endedness of the Notion of Change or Learned Response

We described a learned response in part as involving a permanent (functionally irreversible) change in one or more of its measurable response characteristics. All that was connoted by change was a jump from one level of occurrence (S_1) to another level of occurrence (S_2) over trials or time. This characterization of change is essentially open-ended — basically because it puts no constrictions on the origin or existential status of a learned response. For illustrative purposes, let us present two kinds of questions which this notion of change avoids.

1. Does a learned response appear out of nothing (nowhere), or is it constructed out of components (parts), or is it a transformation of another response class, or is it a response class that has transferred (generalized) from another stimulus situation? This is basically a theoretical or philosophical question, which can be important in the context of a specific learning task or manipulation being run in the laboratory. But, it is not relevant for the initial definition or characterization of a learned response.

2. Is a learned response a completely new response, or is a learned response an old response, or is a learned response a combination of both old and new elements? This is a structural or logical question, which has meaning in the context of a specific learning task, as ultimately relatable to the type of reinforcement operation being used. But, again it is a type of question that is not relevant for the initial definition or characterization of a learned response.

Definitionally limiting a learned response to any one of the above alternatives with respect to its origin or existential status would be too restrictive. More specifically, characterizing a learned response as strictly new and appearing out of nowhere would exclude much significant learning phenomena and research from learning psychology.

Suitability for Complex Human Learning and Cognitive Phenomena, Especially Language Phenomena

The original operational definitions of learning were constructed by animal and/or conditioning psychologists who did not seriously intend their formalizations to be applied beyond the animal and/or conditioning context. (The current conceptualization of learning is not original and is representative of these past definitional attempts.) But, the current formalization of learning is perfectly adequate for every kind of learning phenomenon and task described in the text. This is because the other two key aspects of the definition — reinforced practice and the learning process — besides the permanent changes in measurable response characteristics, are also open-ended. As an illustration, consider the following.

1. Granted that reinforced practice is primarily explicit and physical in animal learning and/or conditioning, while it is primarily implicit and verbal or symbolic in complex human learning and cognition — our definition is open-ended with respect to the nature or content of reinforced practice.

2. Granted that learned responses in animal learning and/or conditioning are motor or physical, while they are primarily verbal or symbolic in complex human learning and cognition — our definition is open-ended with respect to the nature or content of the learned response.

3. Granted that the learning process underlying classical conditioning can be conceptualized as quite simple and primitive and, at the neuronal level might only involve a simple shift in neuronal pathways, while the learning process underlying the acquisition of the content of one's natural language can be conceptualized as exceedingly complex, involving a sophisticated inductive or information-processing model or system having some physiological reality in the brain as a whole — our conceptualization of learning as a process leaves it open-ended and it can cover any denotative type of learning. Thus, there is nothing in our operational definition of learning that precludes the learning process from being interpreted as involving complex cognitive structures, complex mathematical or logical structures, or complex decision or inductive rules, etc.

The essence of the argument is this: If there is a key or crucial difference between simple and complex learning or between animal and human learning, it is extradefinitional — it exists outside the bounds of one's original operational characterization of learning.

A CHARACTERIZATION OF CONDITIONING

INTRODUCTION

Because many students confuse the notions of "learning" and "conditioning" and even use the terms equivalently, it is necessary to differentiate between the two before going on to Chapter 5, where the common learning tasks of interest to experimental psychology are listed. "Learning" is the more general term and is used to refer to the entire domain of learning phenomena. Any situation in which reinforced practice and permanent changes in measurable response characteristics are co-occuring can be properly labeled "a learning situation." Like the concept of learning, "conditioning" can be given an operational definition or a theoretical specification. There are no problems associated with characterizing conditioning operationally; it is simply a specific kind of learning procedure or task. As such, the conditioning procedure is simply a subset of the domain of extant learning procedures. There are problems associated with characterizing conditioning theoretically because there are many different ways to give conditioning a theoretical specification. The specific theoretical characterization that a psychologist chooses to represent conditioning is crucial because this in part determines how he also conceptualizes the relationship between conditioning and learning at the theoretical level. One assumption which almost all theoretical conceptions of conditioning have in common is that conditioning is the simplest form of learning. So, the minimal interpretation of conditioning at the theoretical level makes it the simplest form of learning in the universe of learning phenomena.

Because theoretical notions are not discussed until Chapter 6, this section only describes conditioning as an operational phenomenon — i.e., as a specific kind of learning task. How conditioning can be variously related to learning at the theoretical level will be a focus of concern in Chapter 7.

OPERATIONAL SPECIFICATION OF CONDITIONING

Introduction

Operationally, the term "conditioning" is used to collectively refer to two different types of reinforced practice situations: (1) classical conditioning and (2) instrumental conditioning. Classical conditioning is often referred to as "Pavlovian conditioning," in deference to the Russian physiologist who popularized it. Since Skinner stresses the fact that classical conditioning involves the conditioning of respondents, as opposed to operants, many operantly oriented psychologists currently refer to classical conditioning as respondent conditioning. Instrumental conditioning has no valid descriptive equivalents, although it is often referred to as selective learning or trial-and-error learning. Also, the reader is warned that many psychologists use the terms "operant conditioning" and "Skinnerian conditioning" as full, true equivalents of instrumental conditioning. As will become evident in the next chapter, this author prefers to characterize operant or Skinnerian conditioning as a subtype of instrumental conditioning.

Classical Conditioning

In classical conditioning the subject is exposed to N successive trials of the S-S reinforcement operation. The second or reinforcing stimulus is a biological elicitor of a response or an already learned (conditioned) elicitor of a response and is termed the unconditioned stimulus, or UCS. The response which the UCS automatically elicits during each of its presentations is called the unconditioned response, or UCR. The first stimulus is an originally neutral stimulus in the sense that it does not elicit a response of the same response class as the UCR at the beginning of the session. As a result of contiguous pairing with the UCS (i.e., successive S-S occurrences), the first stimulus eventually achieves the capability of eliciting a response instance from the same response class as the UCR. This latter response is referred to as the conditioned response, or CR; once the first stimulus begins to elicit the CR, it is referred to as the conditioned stimulus, or CS. The substance of the learning involved in the classical conditioning situation is the elicitation of the CR by the CS.

As an example of classical conditioning, let us refer to a variant of Pavlov's "classic" study of classical conditioning of salivation in the dog. Meat or meat powder placed directly in the dog's mouth is used as the UCS to elicit the UCR of salivation. An auditory tone serves as a convenient originally neutral stimulus and is presented to the dog in conjunction with the UCS for many trials. Eventually, the tone itself, having achieved CS properties, elicits salivation as a CR.

Instrumental Conditioning

In instrumental conditioning the subject is exposed to N successive trials or N successive continuous-time occurrences of the S-R-S reinforcement operation. The initial stimulus, if specified and actively manipulated by the experimenter, is called a discriminative stimulus. The response is the instrumental response, which eventually gets conditioned. The second stimulus is some kind of reinforcing event. Since reinforcement is response-contingent in this type of reinforcement operation, the reinforcement is only presented following occurrences of response instances from the instrumental response class of interest. Thus, the instrumental conditioning procedure involves the selective reinforcement of response instances from a predetermined instrumental response class. Continued reinforcement of the instrumental response leads to an increase in its percentage or rate of occurrence above the initial prereinforcement level of occurrence; and the instrumental response is said to be conditioned or learned once it has reached this new, higher level of occurrence. Note that an instrumental response is already part of the organism's repertoire at the outset and already occurs as part of its natural activity. Reinforcement merely causes it to occur more frequently. So, conditioning of an instrumental response amounts merely to increasing its frequency of occurrence.

As an example of instrumental conditioning, let us refer to operant conditioning of the bar-press response in the rat Skinner box apparatus. The initial stimulus is usually left unspecified. The instrumental response is the bar-press response. The reinforcing stimulus is a rat food pellet. Every time the rat presses the bar, it is reinforced with a presentation of a food pellet.

Continued reinforcement of the bar-press response over time leads to an increase in its rate of occurrence above the initial prereinforcement rate of responding — i.e., the bar-press response is conditioned.

CHARACTERIZATION OF A CONDITIONED RESPONSE

A conditioned response is simply the learned response that is generated by using either of the conditioning procedures. The learned response acquired in the context of classical conditioning is called a classically conditioned response, or CR. The learned response acquired in the context of instrumental conditioning is called an instrumentally conditioned response (sometimes symbolized as CR). Since conditioning is usually conceptualized as the simplest form of learning, a conditioned response is likewise usually regarded as the simplest kind of learned response. To further extend the analogy of conditioning as a subset of learning, conditioned responses are a subset of the entire set of learned responses.

TRANSITION TO CHAPTER 5

This chapter has established reinforced practice as the major condition leading to the acquisition of a learned response and has presented an analytical, operational definition of learning. The next chapter lists the many different forms that reinforced practice can take — i.e., the different tasks characteristic of learning psychology. Such a description of the common learning tasks of interest to experimental psychology is a prerequisite for analyzing just what constitutes the nature of reinforced practice associated with some of these tasks — the substantive content of Chapter 9.

SUMMARY

There are two characteristics of a learned response: (1) its measurable characteristics must have undergone a permanent change, (2) but only as a result or function of reinforced practice. The notion of change entails a jump from some initial level of occurrence to a later, different level of occurrence. The change need not necessarily be normatively evaluated as beneficial. "Permanent" simply means "functionally irreversible" — the change does not "spontaneously revert." The requirement of functional irreversibility eliminates transient, short-term behavioral changes due to such factors as drugs, motivation, fatigue, and sensory adaptation from being treated as learned behavioral changes. The notion of practice is grossly equivalent to that of training and its inclusion is necessary to differentiate a learned response from a long-term change in behavior due to underlying structural/physiological changes in the organism. Practice must be modified by the term "reinforced" in order to distinguish it from the extinction procedure; exposure to a series of reinforced trials or reinforcing events in time technically constitutes reinforced practice.

Learning is the process by which the measurable characteristics of a response undergo a permanent change (either immediate or delayed) as a result or function of reinforced practice. The new temporal (parenthetical) qualification of change allows the definition, as stated, to absorb the technical distinction between learning and performance. This definition is an operational one, expressed in implicit causal law or functional relationship form, and can be contrasted with various theoretical approaches to defining learning. In the context of this definition, learning itself is a process — an inferred theoretical entity or construct, whose ultimate existential reality level is arbitrary. This definition is representative of all other (previous) attempts of characterizing learning operationally, is continuous with the layman's conception of learning, and treats the notions of process, learned change, and reinforced practice as open-ended constructs.

The notion of "conditioning" can be given an operational or theoretical specification. Operationally, it is used to collectively refer to two different types of learning tasks: classical conditioning and instrumental conditioning. Classical conditioning exclusively involves the S-S reinforcement operation and instrumental conditioning minimally involves some form of the S-R-S reinforcement operation. The minimal interpretation of conditioning at the theoretical level makes it the simplest form of learning in the universe of learning phenomena.

A conditioned response is simply the learned response that is generated by using either of the two conditioning procedures and is usually regarded as the simplest or most primitive kind of learned response.

5
A Taxonomy (Classification System) for Learning Tasks, Extinction Tasks, and Related Learning Phenomena: A listing of the laboratory tasks and phenomena studied by learning psychology

GENERATION OF THE CHAPTER CONTENT

INTRODUCTION

This chapter will present various classification systems based upon (1) the four experimental operations discussed in Chapter 2, (2) the notion of an operational learning (extinction) continuum ranging from simple to complex, and (3) the distinction between animal and human learning.

THE NOTION OF A LEARNING TASK, AN EXTINCTION TASK, AND A LEARNING PHENOMENON

Chapter 2 presented two kinds of simple operations: the reinforcement operation and the extinction operation. Any experiment composed of the reinforcement procedure (N trials or N occurrences in continuous time of the reinforcement operation) will be referred to as a learning task. Any experiment composed of the extinction procedure (N trials or N occurrences in continuous time of the extinction operation) will be referred to as an extinction task. Chapter 2 also introduced the notion that the reinforcement operation and extinction operation could be combined to form numerous, meaningful complex procedures. Any experiment composed of a complex procedure (N trials or N occurrences in continuous time of K reinforcement operations and N-K extinction operations) will be referred to as investigating a learning phenomenon – not as a complex learning or complex extinction task.

Although the distinction between the term "task" and the term "phenomenon" is largely semantic, they emphasize different aspects of the situation. When the experimental procedure is exclusively composed of one of the two simple operations, the usual classificatory focus is on the nature of the procedure itself (i.e., a specific learning or extinction task). When the simple operations are combined to form a specific complex procedure, usually in one of many possible alternative ways, the focal point of classificatory interest is the specific effect that the particular complex procedure has on behavior (i.e., a specific learning phenomenon). The primary use of a complex procedure is to measure a specific learning phenomenon. For example, forgetting is a phenomenon to be measured, rather than a complex learning task to be investigated. Another way of stating the distinction between a task and phenomenon is by emphasizing that a specific learning phenomenon can be investigated in the context of many different learning tasks, while the converse of this makes no semantic sense at all. For instance, forgetting can be investigated in classical conditioning, verbal learning, concept formation, perceptual-motor learning, etc.

This chapter will present three different learning taxonomies or classification systems: one for learning tasks, another for extinction tasks, and a third for learning phenomena.

THE DICHOTOMY BETWEEN EXPERIMENTER-CONTINGENT AND RESPONSE-CONTINGENT PROCEDURES AS A KEY ANALYTICAL CLASSIFICATORY DIMENSION

Chapter 2 divided the reinforcement operation and its associated extinction operation into two types: experimenter-contingent and response-contingent. Constructive use can be made of this distinction in the context of learning and extinction tasks. A specific learning task can be assigned to one of these two types; likewise, a specific extinction task can be assigned to one of these two types. In experimenter-contingent procedures, the learned response tends to be given to, presented to, or elicited from the organism, more or less automatically. On the other hand, in response-contingent procedures, the learned response tends to be selected from a number of response alternatives by, or actively constructed by, or actively discovered by the organism. For example, in classical conditioning, the CR is determined by the UCR used (ultimately, the UCS used). In instrumental conditioning, the instrumentally conditioned response must be selected, constructed, or discovered by the organism.

Thus, the learning task and extinction task classification systems will employ this dichotomy as a key, analytical subclassification dimension.

THE NOTION OF AN OPERATIONAL LEARNING (EXTINCTION) CONTINUUM RANGING FROM SIMPLE TO COMPLEX AS A KEY ANALYTICAL CLASSIFICATORY DIMENSION

Introduction

Learning and extinction tasks are assumed to exist along a physical continuum ranging from simple to complex. Simple and complex are merely the two extreme end points of the continuum, not two dichotomous categories separated by empty space (nonexistent tasks). The notion of a physical continuum implies that there is only a quantitative difference between simple and complex tasks at the input-output level. The notion of a discontinuous dichotomy could in addition imply that there is a qualitative difference between simple and complex tasks at the input-output level. Also note that intermediate tasks exist along the physical continuum and are not meaningful in a discontinuous dichotomy. Thus, the learning and extinction task classification systems will employ the notion of an operational continuum ranging from simple to complex as another key, analytical subclassification dimension.

Denotative Properties of "Simple" and "Complex"

Introduction. What are the denotative properties of the terms "simple" and "complex" in this context? (Simple and complex do not refer to the underlying operations employed.) The notion of a learning (extinction) continuum is descriptively infinite, so the terms "simple" and "complex" are really multi-dimensional in nature. The distinction between a simple learning (extinction) task and a complex learning (extinction) task exists at many different levels. Five specific differences will be presented here, as an illustrative subset of the total population of differences.

1. *The number of stimulus and response units involved.* Simple tasks are usually composed of one S unit and one learned R unit. Complex tasks are usually composed of many individual S and learned R units (occurring in a temporal sequence) or of physically complex macro-S and learned macro-R units (existing at the same moment in time) or of both.

2. *The nature of the stimulus (input) situation.* The stimulus events in simple tasks are usually readily detectable physical changes in the external environment − e.g., the onset, termination, or modulation in amount of a tone, buzzer, light, shock, piece of food, etc. Viewed from another angle, the stimulus situation in most simple tasks is regarded strictly as a matter of sensation or sensory

reactivity, not as a matter of complex perception or perceptual decoding or information processing. The stimulus events in complex tasks usually have a symbolic (verbal or linguistic) significance beyond their existence as mere physical environmental changes — e.g., words, nonsense syllables, pictures, sentences, etc. Analogously, the stimulus situation in most complex tasks is a matter of perceptual decoding or information processing.

3. *The nature of the response (output) situation.* The learned response in simple tasks is usually motor and/or physical. More specifically, the learned response is strictly some kind of physiological activity having no symbolic significance. On the other hand, the learned response in complex tasks usually has symbolic or cognitive significance beyond the fact that it is some kind of physiological activity. (Refer back to Chapter 3 for a detailed discussion of the distinction between a physical and symbolic response.)

4. *The nature of the reinforcing event or stimulus.* The notion of reinforcement is descriptively infinite, and the nature of reinforcement in simple and complex tasks can be compared on many different dimensions. Suffice it to say that in a simple task the reinforcing event is usually a discrete physical change in the external environment and, as such, is a primary positive or negative reinforcing stimulus. In a complex task, the reinforcing event is usually a symbolic event, often internally sourced, and, as such, is a secondary positive reinforcing stimulus. Chapter 9 analyzes the nature of reinforcement in simple and complex tasks in greater detail.

5. *The nature of the underlying theoretical learning process.* Recall that Chapter 4 established learning as a process or theoretical construct. The nature of the underlying learning process in a simple task is usually regarded as "simple" and the nature of the underlying learning process in a complex task is usually regarded as "complex." "Simple" is usually interpreted to mean the formation of an association, either an S-R association or an S-S association, where the S and/or R terms refer to the external, discrete, operational events of the experiment or task. "Complex" is usually interpreted as the formation of some kind of cognitive structure of some degree of complexity or organization, and this structure is not typically regarded as reducible to one simple association or even a linear series of multiple associations. Chapters 7 and 8 put the nature of the underlying learning process in greater perspective.

THE DISTINCTION BETWEEN ANIMAL AND HUMAN LEARNING

No functional classificatory significance will be assigned to the distinction between animal and human learning, other than indicating for which of the two subject types the particular task is applicable. Basically, tasks applicable to the human subject extend the entire length of the physical continuum, while tasks applicable to the animal subject do not extend beyond the intermediate area of the physical continuum. The tasks at the extreme right end of the continuum presuppose that the subject possesses either the language function or a sophisticated set of highly manipulable effectors (e.g., hands).

A TAXONOMY FOR LEARNING TASKS

THE LEARNING TASK TAXONOMY

Figure 5-1 lists the common learning tasks studied by experimental psychology. The dichotomy between S-S reinforcement operation tasks and S-R-S reinforcement operation tasks is represented on the row dimension. The learning continuum from simple to complex is represented by the column dimension. The applicability of the individual tasks to human and animal learning is indicated by a horizontal line running parallel to the learning continuum representation. Classical conditioning, instrumental conditioning, and verbal learning constitute major subtask categories and are bounded by closed lines. Note that verbal learning, concept formation, and natural language learning tasks appear in both macro-rows of the taxonomy. These tasks are so flexible they can be operationalized in either the S-S or S-R-S reinforcement context. Chapter 9 will demonstrate this explicitly for paired-associate verbal learning and concept formation.

EVALUATION

Since no classification system can be all-inclusive, exhaustive, and entirely logically consistent, the three inadequacies of this particular taxonomic system should be pointed out.

1. Avoidance conditioning and conditioned suppression involve both the S-S and S-R-S reinforcement operations. They are classified under the S-R-S operation because most psychologists are primarily concerned with their response-contingent reinforcement aspects — i.e., their instrumentally conditioned response aspects.

2. S-R-S reinforcement operation verbal learning tasks often employ the S-S reinforcement operation on the first trial of the experimental session.

3. The testing of the acquisition of a learned response during the course of reinforced practice often requires the use of the S alone extinction operation — i.e., the use of test trials interspersed among reinforced trials. This is especially true for classical conditioning and S-S reinforcement operation verbal learning

tasks. The taxonomy makes no reference to these interspersed or "occult" extinction trials.

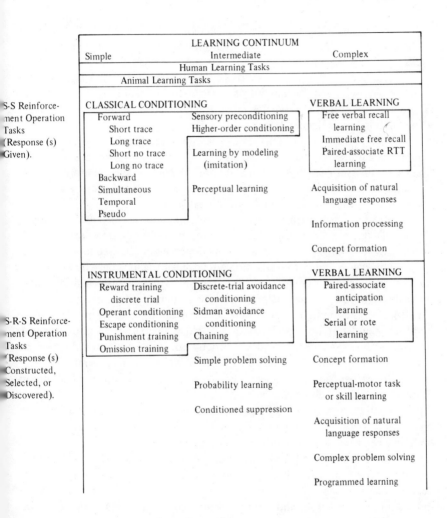

Fig. 5-1. A Taxonomy of Learning Tasks

A TAXONOMY FOR EXTINCTION TASKS

INTRODUCTION

Constructing a taxonomy for extinction tasks involves two sources of difficulty not encountered in establishing a classification system for learning tasks.

1. The use of the extinction procedure following a period of reinforced practice simply is not meaningful or relevant for a number of learning tasks. There are at least four classes of learning situations in which the additional phase of extinction is meaningless or irrelevant.

a. The original acquisition session is not carried out to a criterion of complete learning so that the response(s) is (are) never completely learned. Exposing the subject to only one reinforced trial or one reinforcement in continuous time is a subset of this. Immediate free verbal recall and paired-associate RTT learning are examples of this category.

b. Learning tasks such as pseudoconditioning and sensory preconditioning are rarely, if ever, followed by the extinction procedure because they are only variants of the straightforward reinforcement procedure. In pseudoconditioning, if the subject is exposed to a traditional reinforced trial it is only by accident or chance. Pseudoconditioning is of interest only as a methodological control procedure for the definitional classical conditioning procedure. Sensory preconditioning is a multiphase procedure which involves two different kinds of S-S reinforcement operations and one test S alone operation. It is of primarily theoretical interest and it would be difficult to decide which of the two S-S reinforcement operations should be switched to the extinction operation.

c. Perceptual learning and learning by modeling are examples of laboratory learning procedures whose analogues in the real world are rarely, if ever, followed by the extinction procedure. The primary perceptual aspects of one's environment tend to be consistent or stable and the stimulus source of an organism's imitative behavior rarely exhibits spontaneous changes.

d. There is a class of learning tasks that is regarded as so socially desirable or privately beneficial that it is considered "ethically wrong" to actively undo any learning that has accrued from them. Simple and complex problem-solving tasks, programmed instruction, and information-processing tasks are examples of this category. Once an organism has learned how to solve a particular problem, it is considered dirty pool to make the original solution or class of solutions inappropriate. Note that this restriction does not preclude switching to an easier or more efficient solution. The whole purpose of programmed instruction is to facilitate learning or make learning easier and any attempt to extinguish such learning is frowned upon. Analogous comments apply to information-processing tasks.

So, in summary, it cannot be implicitly assumed that the extinction procedure associated with each learning task is meaningful or relevant. The specific learning tasks referred to above will be excluded from the extinction taxonomy.

2. Although the extinction procedure definitionally leads to reversion in the change of measurable response characteristics, there are actually two different ways to effect the extinction operation for an already learned response. Explicit reference to only one of these has so far been made — namely, switching the S-S or S-R-S operation to the S alone or S-R operation. Here the subject continues to be exposed to the original stimulus situation but occurrences of the original learned response class cease to be reinforced.

There is a second way to effect the extinction operation: switch the original S-S or S-R-S operation to a new S-S or S-R-S operation. A new S-S operation would entail a new second stimulus (reinforcing stimulus); a new S-R-S operation would entail minimally a new R term (i.e., a new response gets reinforced). Again the subject continues to be exposed to the original stimulus situation and occurrences of the original learned response class cease to be reinforced. But, in addition, the subject is actively reinforced for exhibiting occurrences of another response class. The extinction of response class X is achieved procedurally by the active reinforcement of response class Y in the context of the same stimulus situation. Technically, this operation (procedure) is called the counterconditioning operation (procedure).

Although this second way of implementing extinction is applicable to any learning task, it is more meaningful for the multiple or compound symbolic and motor responses of the complex end of the learning continuum — i.e., strictly human learning tasks. The pure definitional extinction operation itself is most often associated with the simple end of the learning continuum, where only one response (usually a motor response) is learned.

Therefore, the input condition underlying a particular extinction task cannot be assumed to automatically involve either of the definitional extinction operations per se. This necessitates the inclusion of the two reinforcement operations in the extinction taxonomy, particularly with reference to complex extinction tasks.

THE EXTINCTION TASK TAXONOMY

Figure 5-2 lists the common extinction tasks studied by experimental psychology. The structure of the figure is analogous to that used for Fig. 5-1, except for the inclusion of additional counterconditioning categories on the input dimension. The content of the figure is reduced somewhat due to the exclusion of nonmeaningful or irrelevant extinction tasks. Note that discrete-trial avoidance and conditioned suppression extinction occur in both the S alone operation and S-R operation rows, a reflection of the fact that both the S-S reinforcement operation and S-R-S reinforcement operation are required for their original acquisition. The extinction taxonomy need not be formally evaluated because it is a simple derivative of the learning classification system.

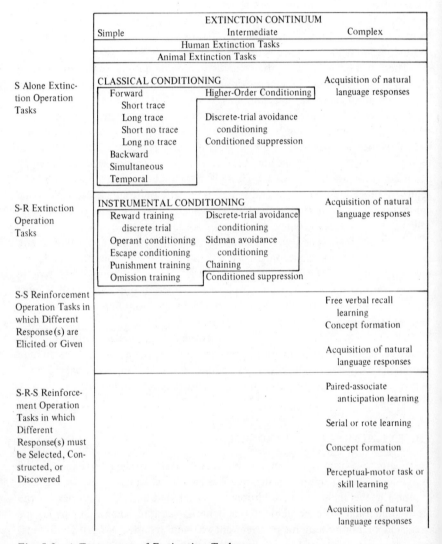

Fig. 5-2. A Taxonomy of Extinction Tasks

A TAXONOMY FOR LEARNING PHENOMENA

INTRODUCTION

A learning phenomenon is investigated by using both the reinforcement operation and the extinction operation in some meaningful combination. Thus, the input condition for a learning phenomenon is a complex procedure. The specific complex procedure associated with each learning phenomenon will not be represented by the classification system. The various learning phenomena are definable across the entire range of the learning continuum. This means a specific learning phenomenon can be investigated in the context of or by using virtually any one of the tasks listed in the learning task taxonomy. In effect, the basic taxonomy for learning tasks can be applied to each learning phenomenon or, conversely, each learning phenomenon is describable in terms of the basic learning task taxonomy. But a specific learning phenomenon is usually more meaningful and relevant over a restricted portion of the continuum — i.e., it is primarily actively investigated only by tasks located in that portion of the continuum. In order for the learning phenomenon taxonomy to represent this last fact, it will not employ the learning continuum as an analytical dimension. Rather, only three specific portions of the continuum will be used and they will be represented by specific learning tasks: (1) conditioning tasks, (2) intermediate tasks, and (3) verbal, symbolic, or complex motor tasks. The applicability of the various learning phenomena to animal and human learning is again an appropriate descriptive dimension and carries over intact in the learning phenomena taxonomy.

THE LEARNING PHENOMENA TAXONOMY

Figure 5-3 lists the common learning phenomena studied by experimental psychology. The input situation of complex procedures is represented on the row dimension. The three reference learning tasks are represented by the column dimension. The applicability of the individual learning phenomena to human and animal learning is indicated by horizontal lines running parallel to the tripartite learning task classification.

EVALUATION

Let us evaluate this learning phenomena taxonomy and thereby put it in greater perspective. There are four crucial points which require discussion.

1. The taxonomy cannot accommodate or makes no provision for at least three other kinds of "traditional" learning phenomena which can be investigated

in the context of virtually any kind of learning task: (a) learning phenomena which do not arise from reinforcement-related manipulations, such as the effect of motivation, drive level, or arousal on learning; the effect of physiological manipulations on learning; the effect of instructions on learning, etc.; (b) learning phenomena which arise from procedural or structural variations in the conditions of delivering reinforcement, such as incidental versus intentional

	Conditioning Tasks	LEARNING TASKS Intermediate Tasks	Verbal, Symbolic or Complex Motor Tasks
		Human Learning Phenomena	
	Animal Learning Phenomena		
C	Relearning	Relearning	Relearning
O	Re-extinction		
M	Partial reinforcement	Partial reinforcement	Partial reinforcement
P	Spontaneous recovery		Spontaneous recovery
L	Stimulus generalization	Stimulus generalization	Stimulus generalization
E	Response generalization	Response generalization	Response generalization
X	Stimulus discrimination	Stimulus discrimination	Stimulus discrimination
	Response discrimination (instrumental conditioning only)	Response discrimination	Response discrimination
P			Transfer of training
R			(under special circum-
O		Perceptual memory	stances: see text.)
C			
E			Forgetting, retention
D			Short-term memory
			Long-term memory
U			Proactive inter-
			ference
R			Retroactive
E			interference
S			

Fig. 5-3. A Taxonomy for Learning Phenomena

learning, distributed (spaced) versus massed (continuous) practice, whole versus part learning, overlearning, etc.; and (c) learning phenomena which arise from exposure to successive learning tasks, such as transfer of training and mediation experiments. But note that certain instances of transfer of training are derivable as learning phenomena from the current classification system under a very restrictive condition. When the second learning task is composed of the strict counterconditioning operation (i.e., the subject is exposed to a task with the same stimulus events, but different response events), transfer of training is a strictly derived learning phenomenon because the counterconditioning operation functionally operates as an extinction operation.

Thus, complex procedures result in learning phenomena, but not all learning phenomena are the result of complex procedures. The current classification system only taps some of all the learning phenomena in existence.

2. There is some arbitrariness as to whether a particular experimental procedure gets classified as a learning task or a learning phenomenon. Recall, by definition, that a learning phenomenon arises from using both the reinforcement and extinction operation in combination. As pointed out previously, many of the so-called learning tasks also use the extinction operation as a test operation interspersed with reinforced trials during the original acquisition session. The crucial difference for classification purposes is the significance and degree of use of the extinction operation. If it is used merely to test for the course of learning and is not part of the underlying definitional procedure, the resultant procedure is a learning task. If it is used on 30% to 50% of the trials and is part of the underlying definitional procedure (i.e., the particular behavioral effect could not occur without it), the resultant procedure is a learning phenomenon. For example, the sensory preconditioning procedure is classified as a learning task according to this criterion. The extinction operation is not necessary in creating the response associated with sensory preconditioning; it is needed merely to assess whether a sensory preconditioned response has been acquired. On the other hand, the stimulus discrimination procedure is an example of a learning phenomenon according to this classificatory approach. The extinction operation is necessary in creating the discriminative stimulus; it is not needed merely to assess whether a discriminative stimulus has been set up.

3. The notion of learning phenomena, as currently defined, precludes the existence of extinction phenomena. When the reinforcement operation and the extinction operation are combined to form a complex procedure, it is the learning notation or reference that survives to label the resulting phenomenon. Stating it from another angle, the phenomena resulting from complex procedures are related to or classified in terms of learning tasks, not in terms of extinction tasks. The reason for this is simple: the reinforcement operation is the ultimate reference or defining operation; the extinction operation is merely a derivative of it, as demonstrated in Chapter 2. There is one exception to the

above statement — the phenomenon of generalization of extinction. Both the reinforcement and extinction operations are used, but the extinction operation survives to label the phenomenon. Other extinction phenomena exist, which do not arise from the use of complex procedures and are meaningful over the entire range of the extinction continuum. Some examples are latent extinction, extinction under massed practice, extinction under excessive effort, etc. The situation here is analogous to that faced in the context of learning phenomena, except that the macroclassification system taps none of the extinction phenomena in existence.

4. The classification system for learning phenomena is merely a first-order taxonomy. It presents the initial level of common complex procedures studied by experimental psychology. Two or more complex procedures can be combined to form "combination complex procedures" or "macro-complex procedures." For instance, both stimulus and response discrimination can be investigated in an experimental study; partial reinforcement procedures and measurement of retention procedures can be combined in the context of the same experiment; or the successive re-extinction and relearning of the same learned response can be investigated. Formal construction of a second-, third-, or fourth-, etc. order taxonomy for learning phenomena would carry us to the point of diminishing returns because an infinite number of macro-complex procedure learning phenomena are definable. It is sufficient to merely point out that the higher order taxonomies are completely generatable from the initial, first-order taxonomy.

SUMMARY

It is meaningful to distinguish between a learning task, an extinction task, and a learning phenomenon. Any experiment composed exclusively of the reinforcement procedure can be referred to as a learning task. Any experiment composed of the extinction procedure can be regarded as an extinction task. Any experiment composed of a complex procedure (use of both the reinforcement and extinction operations is necessary) can be viewed as investigating a learning phenomenon.

It is possible to construct a taxonomy for each of the above — in terms of two orthogonal analytical classificatory dimensions. One dimension relates to the type of experimental operation used, in which context the dichotomy between experimenter-contingent and response-contingent procedures serves as a key element. The second dimension consists of an operational learning (extinction) continuum, ranging from simple to complex, in which context a trichotomy between conditioning tasks, intermediate tasks, and verbal, symbolic, or complex motor tasks serves as a convenient analytical device. A third possible dimension — one related to the distinction between animal and human learning — is treated as correlated with (or redundant to) the operational learning (extinction) continuum. The content of the three taxonomies is presented in Figs. 5-1, 5-2, and 5-3 respectively.

The process of constructing the three taxonomies made a number of relevant classificatory points explicit.

1. Some learning tasks involve the use of both types of reinforcement operations and many learning tasks involve the implicit use of the extinction operation as a test trial. Thus, the distinction between a learning task and a learning phenomenon is not all that clear-cut.

2. The use of the extinction procedure following a period of reinforced practice is not meaningful or relevant for many learning tasks and the extinction procedure can also be implemented by what is technically called the counter-conditioning procedure.

3. The current classificatory approach does not generate all the extant empirical phenomena traditionally regarded as learning phenomena and it precludes the existence of extinction phenomena.

6
The Nature of the Theoretical Situation:
The third unit of analysis for learning psychology

THE CONTEXT IN WHICH THE THEORETICAL SITUATION ARISES: GENERATION OF THE THEORETICAL LEVEL OF ANALYSIS

The basic point of Chapter 1 was that psychology relates behavior, as a natural event, to other natural events in the universe. In this context, the concept of a causal law or functional relation was introduced. A particular piece of behavior was regarded as scientifically explained once it was placed in a particular $Y = f(X)$ relationship. Thus, using the notions of stimulus and response, the two units of analysis discussed so far, scientific explanation structurally amounts to an S-R law or $R = f(S)$ relationship.

Now, let us assume that one of the functions of a theory is to explain. Therefore, once a particular piece of behavior has been scientifically explained by placing it in a particular $R = f(S)$ relationship (i.e., by describing it in stimulus and response terms), in a sense, a theory exists for that behavior. But, most psychologists prefer to characterize the notion of theory as involving more than simply the two descriptive units of analysis. A theory is supposed to encompass a series of interrelated hierarchical levels, in the context of which the functional relation is merely the initial level of the hierarchy. Thus, the use of S, R terminology is only a low-level or first-order explanation. This fact is usually expressed as follows: A functional relation is a descriptive explanation. Once a particular piece of behavior has been described in S, R terms, it has been descriptively explained. So the analysis of behavior in terms of the two fundamental units of analysis merely amounts to descriptive explanation and the latter is not completely equivalent to the notion of theory.

Chapter 4 introduced the notion of an unobservable, inferred theoretical construct which intervenes between a particular S term and a particular R term or which "lies behind" a particular functional relation. If we assume that a theory is composed of one or more hierarchically interrelated theoretical constructs, then theory provides an interpretation of a particular descriptive explanation; as such, it constitutes an entirely separate and independent unit of analysis. Thus, the notion of theory, as an analytical unit, is necessary to provide behavior with a higher order theoretical interpretation.

Let us apply the above comments to the concept of "learned behavior." Learned behavior is given a descriptive explanation by relating it definitionally to reinforced practice – using S, R or input, output terminology. But this constitutes mere first-order explanation. Higher order theoretical explanation is not achieved until the underlying learning process is given some properties as a theoretical construct. Different theories of learning assign different properties to learning as a theoretical construct and use different numbers and kinds of interrelated, higher order levels.

THE NATURE OF THE THEORETICAL SITUATION

INTRODUCTION

To provide continuity with the way in which the first two units of analysis were analyzed, the theoretical situation will also be represented as a triangular-shaped structure composed of hierarchical levels (See Fig. 6-1).

The overall, macro-theoretical situation is immediately divisible into one or more specific theories, which in turn are regarded as composed of one or more interrelated theoretical constructs. Collectively, the top three levels constitute higher order explanation. The theoretical constructs ultimately apply to, but are not divisible into, stimulus and response units, either individually or in combination. Thus, theories not only are designed to interpret causal laws but also the input situation alone or the output situation alone, although the latter use has not been emphasized previously. So, theories of the stimulus and of the response also exist. The descriptive level of analysis, comprising the two fundamental units of analysis, either individually or in combination, is not continuous with the higher levels. These two characteristics of nondivisibility and discontinuity are indicated pictorially by using unidirectional arrows and by enclosing the descriptive level with a dotted-line rectangle.

Since the higher order levels of the theoretical situation are not necessarily composed of real-time and real-space events, neither the production and control of events nor the measurement of events is the focus of concern. Rather, because a particular theory or higher order theoretical explanation is tentatively and cautiously postulated to interpret a set of one or more S, R, or S-R laws, the critical aspects of a theory are its origin, active construction, and eventual evaluation.

Since the level of descriptive explanation was analyzed in the first three chapters, it need not be formally treated here. The hierarchical levels of higher order explanation will be defined and characterized according to the following sequence: (1) the level of theory, (2) the theoretical-construct level, and (3) the macro-theoretical situation itself. The three critical aspects of the theoretical situation, as the third unit of analysis, will be treated in detail as properties of the overall macro-theoretical level of analysis.

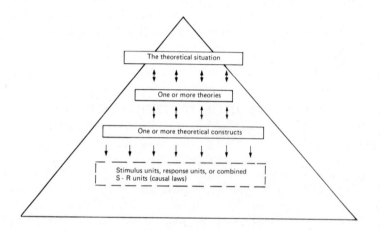

Fig. 6-1. The Hierarchical Structure of the Theoretical Situation

THEORY

Introduction

The preceding discussion has implicitly assumed that a theory serves as an explanation. But, defining a theory as an explanation would amount to defining it in terms of one of its functions and one which not every philosopher of science regards as the primary function of theory. Unfortunately, most psychologists define a theory in terms of what they want it to accomplish and, as such, many different "theoretical" definitions of a theory exist. We need an initial characterization of a theory which is independent of the functions that can later be assigned to it. Hopefully, characterizing a theory in terms of *generation* will solve this problem.

Definition

A theory is a set of verbal statements (blueprints, rules, etc.) which, if explicitly followed or actualized, would generate an aspect of the descriptive level of analysis (S alone, R alone, or both). Any set of verbal statements, regardless of its content, form, length, formality, degree of empirical validation, etc., constitutes a theory if it can generate an aspect of the descriptive level of analysis. Also, whether or not the set of verbal statements is actually followed or physically actualized to generate a descriptive level aspect (i.e., constructing a physical model or replica, using equations to derive predictions, etc.) is irrelevant for the definition. Only the potentiality for such generation need exist.

How generation is interpreted in this context will determine the adequacy of the definition. The most neutral approach is to interpret generation as production. The set of verbal statements specifies how the S, or R, or both can be produced. A theory is a description of what underlies the S situation, R situation, or both at a deeper level of analysis.

For instance, a theory of learning is a set of verbal statements which specifies the necessary and sufficient conditions under which learning occurs (i.e., how reinforced practice leads to learned changes in behavior). The specific denotative content, form, etc. of the set of verbal statements describing learning and whether in fact it has been used to generate (produce) an empirical aspect of learning are irrelevant for classifying it as a theory of learning.

Functions of a Theory

Introduction. There are five widely recognized functions which can be attributed to a theory: (1) explanation, (2) prediction, (3) integration, (4) classification, and (5) summarization. They are not mutually exclusive functions. Explanation and prediction tend to be grouped together in one subset and are the functions stressed by highly formal and precise theorists. The latter three are of subsidiary importance and tend to be emphasized by theorists who are interested in theory in a low-level or informal sense. Let us now analyze each of the functions in turn.

Explanation. A theory serves as a higher order explanation for an aspect of the descriptive level of analysis, usually the causal law or functional relation aspect. More succinctly, a theory is an explanation for an already empirically validated causal law. A causal law is explained by a theory specifically in the sense that it is derivable from the theory. The fact that the theory can generate or produce the causal law is now interpreted as explaining the causal law. Whether the validated causal law comes first, followed by construction of the theory, or whether the theory is constructed first, followed by causal law validation, is irrelevant. The temporal order of origination of a theory and a causal law is an irrelevant dimension when theory is assumed to be performing its explanatory function. Typically, a theory is never designed to explain just one causal law. The theory should be general enough to explain a series of related causal laws.

Prediction. A theory can generate aspects of the descriptive level of analysis which have never before been empirically investigated. A theory can generate statements in causal law form whose validity has not yet been tested. These were referred to in Chapter 1 as hypotheses. Thus, hypotheses are derivable from a theory and, as such, are termed predictions.

The predictive function of a theory is important because it is the only way in which the appropriateness of the theory can be empirically assessed. In order for a theory to be empirically testable, it must yield predictions (hypotheses) that can be directly evaluated by laboratory experimentation. Why a theory need be tested at all might be puzzling because it has been previously characterized as being capable of generating an aspect of the S situation, R situation, or both. The basic point is that more than one theory can be postulated to generate any specific descriptive level situation and one of the methods used to evaluate the appropriateness of the respective theories is to test their predictions experimentally in the laboratory.

The temporal order of origination of a theory and its theoretical derivation is fixed — the theory must precede the prediction. Also, as in the case of explanation, a good theory must be capable of yielding more than one prediction.

Explanation versus prediction. Since both explanation and prediction involve derivation, the logic underlying them is the same. Whether a theory is performing its explanatory or predictive function at any moment in time depends solely on the truth value of the derived statement. If the derivation is an already validated causal law, the theory is performing the explanatory function. If the derivation is as yet an unvalidated causal law (hypothesis), the theory is performing the predictive function.

Integration. If a theory is explicitly constructed to explain all the functional relationships already validated in a given input-output situation, it is commonly referred to as performing an integrative function with respect to that situation. Some theorists prefer to emphasize the fact that a theory can be designed to explain all the facts already accumulated in a given psychological subarea and they call this function "integration."

There is no real difference between explanation and integration. The theoretical explanation of a specific psychological subarea is simply semantically referred to as integration. For instance, a theory of learning is integrative with respect to the specific aspect of learning or learning task for which it is explanatory. Typically, the more general and more abstract (higher level) a theory is, the more integrative it is — i.e., it encompasses more empirical data and lower level theory.

Use of the term "integration" instead of "explanation" does lead to one operational consequence. The theorist who emphasizes the integrative aspect of theory as opposed to the explanatory aspect of theory is much less inclined to use theory in its predictive sense. The fact that a given theory integrates a given area of knowledge is sufficient justification for its existence. There is no additional compulsion for empirical assessment of the theory.

Classification. The notion that theory possesses a classificatory function can be viewed from two different angles: (1) a given classification system is a theory (i.e., it can explain and predict) and (2) once a theory has been applied to a given input-output situation, that situation has been classified. Illustrative of (1), the content of Chapter 5 constitutes one theoretical approach to a systematic or comprehensive description of the learning and extinction tasks and learning phenomena that are characteristic of learning psychology. With respect to (2), for instance, a specific theory of learning tends to classify the learning input-output situation in such a way that its classificatory description can be compared with those of other theories of learning or with those of theories of nonlearning input-output situations (namely, perception theory, social psychology theory, etc.).

The importance that one attaches to the classificatory function of theory depends upon how one evaluates the significance of classification. Although it is one of the primary functions of science to classify empirical phenomena, the resulting classification systems that are generated are rarely, if ever, actively evaluated. The typical working scientist represses the fact that a classification system is a theory or a theory is a classification system. Because of this, the classificatory function of theory is usually deemphasized and the appropriateness of a specific theory is rarely evaluated on this dimension.

Summarization. There are some theorists who claim that a theory has no surplus meaning over and above the aspects of the descriptive level, usually causal laws, which it is supposed to generate. The theory is simply a restatement of the myriad facts inherent in the causal laws themselves in terms of simpler, more precise, summary statements. As such, theory is not explanatory in the same sense as discussed previously (higher order interpretation). Theory is merely more precise or codified descriptive explanation. Also, since a theory possesses no surplus meaning over and above the S-R level of analysis, it cannot predict. Thus, the predictive function of a theory is not even an option in this interpretation. The only function that a theory can possess is a summary function. The causal laws must occur first in time and the verbal statements constituting the theory are mere redescriptions of the laws. For instance, in the context of learning psychology, the descriptive, or inductive, or "nontheoretical" approach of B.F. Skinner is the prime example of this interpretation of a theory. The justification of this approach to theory is ultimately philosophical — i.e., does the summarization characterization of theory lead to more positive benefits and less negative drawbacks than the more typical interpretation of theory as a higher order explanatory and predictive system?

The goal function of theory versus the means function of theory. Abstracting from the five possible functions of a theory described above, the experimental psychologist is interested in theory usually for one of two reasons, which happen to be related to the two general ways in which a theory can be evaluated.

The goal function. Many psychologists are concerned with the form, structure, content, etc. of the theory as an end in itself. They construct elaborate, formalized theories that can be compared with other theoretical endeavors and that can be analyzed (as theory) by the criteria for acceptable theory as dictated by the philosophy of science. In a later section, this will be defined as "heuristic evaluation." Since the formation of a philosophically acceptable theory is an end in itself, any empirical value or justification the theory might possess is a secondary consideration (i.e., a pleasant by-product). No experimental psychologist designs a theory independent of the known facts about behavior; it is just that the goal-oriented psychologist deemphasizes this aspect of a theory. In the face of conflicting experimental evidence, the goal-oriented psychologist is less likely to reject his elaborate theoretical structure and is more likely to retain its basic features or assumptions by making the minimally necessary revisions or adjustments.

The means function. Other psychologists use theory merely or solely as a guide to research. The fact that a theory is a source of hypotheses is stressed in the means function. The form, structure, and content of the theory is never fully developed; it is kept informal and tentative. Since the theory is never fully formalized, it is difficult to evaluate heuristically. Rather, it is continually being empirically assessed. Once the theory ceases to suggest further research or once it has been confronted with conflicting empirical evidence, it is dropped and the theorist goes on to constructing an entirely new informal theory.

Some perspective. The goal and means function of a theory can complement each other. There are a few experimental psychologists who do not emphasize one to the exclusion of the other and who do actively experimentally assess their elaborately constructed, formalized theories. It is these theorists who, in the context of learning psychology, have provided the primary historical impetus to the development of learning theory as a distinct formal subarea of learning psychology.

THE NATURE OF A THEORETICAL CONSTRUCT

Introduction

The set of verbal statements constituting a theory must contain or make reference to at least one theoretical construct. In substance, a theory is composed of one or more theoretical constructs.

Definition

A theoretical construct is a conceptual entity, assumed to reside at some level of reality, which allows the generation of an aspect of the descriptive level of analysis. (The notion of "level of reality" is discussed presently.) Thus, the theoretical construct is the conceptual entity to which the S input situation, the R output situation, or the causal law can be ultimately related for explanation, prediction, classification, etc. For instance, in the context of learning psychology, the S input situation is often conceived of as a population of many elements out of which random samples can be drawn by the subject; the R output situation is frequently regarded as a performance vector; and the underlying learning construct relating the external S to the learned R is often called habit strength.

Although this characterization of theoretical construct amounts to a mere reverbalization of the description of a theory, it does specify the elements of a theory that perform the actual generation. Theoretical constructs constitute the essential content of the higher order level of analysis. When reference is made to the content of a theory, what is meant is the theoretical constructs used by that theory, not the fact that the theory is a set of verbal statements. Not only are the characteristics of a theoretical construct independent of the functions of a theory, but also, while the evaluation of a theory necessarily entails the evaluation of its component theoretical constructs, the theoretical constructs can be evaluated according to certain criteria independently of the theory as a whole. The following subsection analyzes the possible characteristics of a theoretical construct in depth.

Characteristics of a Theoretical Construct

The characteristics of a given theoretical construct can conveniently be analyzed along three different dimensions: (1) level of reality, (2) area or range of applicability, and (3) existence status.

Level of reality. The level of reality refers to essentially the type of technical language used to describe the construct. Grossly, two levels of reality exist: the constructive and the reductive. Approximate equivalents of constructive and reductive are "behavioral" and "physiological" respectively. Thus, assuming that the descriptive level of analysis of concern for us is psychological or behavioral facts, a constructive theoretical construct is stated on the same level of reality as the fact to be explained, while a reductive theoretical construct is stated on some level of reality lower than the fact to be explained. Constructive theoretical constructs have only psychological or behavioral reality. Reductive theoretical constructs are essentially physiological constructs, which can appear at virtually any level of reality below that of behavior: neuronal, chemical, electrical, biochemical, bioelectrical, biophysical, etc.

Let us illustrate this fundamental dichotomy with reference to a key learning construct introduced above: habit strength. If the theoretical construct of habit is assumed to represent merely the degree of associative bond between a given S and R at the psychological level, it is a constructive construct. On the other hand, if the theoretical construct of habit refers to functional changes in synaptic connections, or altered concentrations of certain chemicals in the brain, or increased neuronal excitability (measured electrically), etc., it is being given a neuronal, or chemical, or electrical, etc. specification and, as such, is a reductive theoretical construct.

At one time in the history of the philosophy of science, the reductive level was considered to be a "better" (more basic, primitive, elemental, etc.) level of specification because it mimicked the mode of higher order explanation used by the natural sciences (i.e., the reduction of natural phenomena to purely physical, chemical terms). Most theorists in the social sciences have come to realize that in order for social science as a whole or experimental psychology in particular to survive as independent disciplines, effective, appropriate theoretical constructs must eventually be isolated at the constructive level of analysis. Ultimately, to explain behavior properly, theories composed exclusively of constructive theoretical constructs should be developed. Currently, theorists typically give their constructs constructive reality (i.e., that level of reality is minimally assumed) and further specification at an appropriate reductive level is kept open as a viable option.

Area or range of applicability. The area or range of applicability refers to the explicit aspect of the descriptive level of analysis which the construct is supposed to generate. A specific theoretical construct can be designed to cover one or more of the following: the S term, the R term, or combined S, R terms (causal laws). Stimulus constructs are explicitly designed to generate the input situation. Response constructs are explicitly designed to generate the output situation. The third kind of construct is designed to mediate between the input and output situations — i.e., generate causal laws or functional relationships. It is the latter kind of construct which is the denotation of the term "theoretical construct" when it appears unmodified in the literature. A naive interpretation of the notion of theoretical construct does not even consider the existence of S or R constructs.

Every major learning theory contains all three kinds of constructs. But, stimulus constructs and response constructs have been historically deemphasized by learning theorists and they are merely implicit in many learning theories. The constructs of primary concern to traditional learning theorists have been those that intervene or mediate between the input and output situations. Recall that learning itself, as a process intervening between reinforced practice and permanent changes in the measurable characteristics of a response, is this latter kind of construct. Until recently, S or R constructs were never used to explicate the nature of learning itself. But many of the contemporary theoretical approaches to learning have revitalized the notions of S or R at the theoretical construct level and appeal to them as the key constructs underlying the learning process.

Existence status. The existence status refers to whether or not the denotation of the theoretical construct really exists. Although every theoretical construct is postulated, this does not necessarily mean that the denotation of the theoretical construct really exists. By "existence" is meant that the theoretical construct not only generates the empirical phenomena of concern but also physically exists somewhere in the environment or the organism (i.e., it is a physical part of its structure) and as such possesses surplus meaning. By "nonexistence" is meant that the theoretical construct merely generates the empirical phenomena of concern but is not assumed in addition to be an actual physical part of the environment or the organism and as such possesses no surplus meaning beyond its function of generation.

The property of existence status has been basically developed in the context of S, R combined theoretical constructs. Mediating constructs that possess the existence property (surplus meaning) are called hypothetical constructs; mediating constructs that do not possess the existence property (surplus meaning) are called intervening variables. For instance, let us refer to the theoretical construct of habit again. It can be interpreted either as a hypothetical construct or intervening variable depending on whether the learning theorist assigns it existence status or not.

The functional significance of whether a theoretical construct is given existence status or not lies primarily on how the construct is evaluated. An intervening variable can only be evaluated in the context of how well it performs its generation function. A hypothetical construct can in addition be evaluated as a possible natural event in the universe — i.e., it is often possible to test whether in fact it physically exists. Once a hypothetical construct has been demonstrated to exist, naturally it is no longer "hypothetical" or theoretical. It assumes the status of an independent or dependent variable depending upon the context in which it is used.

Level of reality versus existence status. The characteristics of level of reality and existence status specification do not necessarily covary. Level of reality specifications are made independently of existence status postulations. But, the surplus meaning of a hypothetical construct is often interpreted to reside at some physiological level and, as such, it is a reductive construct. Analogously, since an intervening variable possesses no surplus meaning, its level of reality is often left implicit and, as such, it is automatically a constructive construct.

THE OVERALL MACRO-THEORETICAL SITUATION

Introduction

Learning theory, composed of the myriad, different theoretical approaches to learning, constitutes the specific macro-theoretical situation of concern for us. Prior to formal consideration of this topic in the next chapter, it is still necessary to discuss the three critical aspects of the postulated macro-theoretical situation: its origin, construction, and evaluation. Origin refers to why a theorist created the specific theory he did and no other. Construction covers the physical procedure of grinding out the theory. Evaluation refers to the process of testing the theory.

The Origin of a Theory

It has only been in recent years that a distinction has been made between the origin and construction of a theory. Traditionally, origin was either left as an implicit dimension or, if explicit, was regarded as synonymous with construction. What was meant by the origin of a theory was its actual construction. It eventually became apparent that construction only covered the physical procedure of grinding out a theory after certain basic structural and content decisions concerning the theory had already been made. The notion of theory construction neglected aspects of theory origination such as the source and type of assumptions used by the theorist, the source and type of theoretical constructs used by the theorist, the level of generality at which the theory was developed by the theorist (i.e., how much of the descriptive level of analysis it was set up to generate), the compatability of the theory with its historical precursors, etc.

So, the origin of a theory has become an area of empirical concern in its own right — i.e., it has become another natural event (another kind of behavior) in the universe requiring analysis and explanation. Unfortunately, very little is known about theory origination at a formal, scientific level of analysis. The current state of affairs can best be summarized in the context of three macro-statements.

1. Actual theory origination behavior is not directly amenable to laboratory investigation; very little reliable and valid correlational data exist describing the theoretical attempts of various psychological theorists; and experimental psychology has not yet isolated the specific independent variables of which theory origination behavior is a function.

2. The little data that do exist are primarily of the case study or self-report variety in which a specific theorist attempts to relate his efforts at theorizing to ostensive factors such as his specific graduate training and research experience, his specific beliefs or attitudes toward psychology, the content of his thought processes when his theory was created, etc. These make interesting reading; but, of course, such anecdotal reports do not constitute scientific analysis.

3. At a higher order theoretical level of analysis, most psychologists classify theory origination behavior as a subkind of complex problem-solving, information-processing, or decision-making behavior. Theories for such behaviors — specifically the variants already investigated in the laboratory — exist; but, no psychologist has as yet applied a general problem-solving, information-processing, or decision-making model to theory-origination behavior per se.

The Construction of a Theory

Introduction. There are three methods of theory construction employed by psychologists: deductive, functional, and inductive.

The deductive approach is the ideal, prescriptive approach. It is the way in which theory should be constructed. Analytical accounts in the technical literature on theory construction are almost invariably prescriptive. Philosophers of science use the way in which theory is constructed in the natural sciences, specifically physics and chemistry, as the model for the prescriptive approach. Thus, the way in which physicists and chemists construct theory is the ideal, prescriptive way.

The functional approach is the actual, descriptive approach. It refers to the many different ways in which a theory is actually constructed on a day-to-day practice level. Very few theorists, especially in the social sciences, employ the prescriptive, deductive approach to theory construction. Rather, they use variants or corruptions of the basic prescriptive approach. Note how the prescriptive, deductive approach is still used as the reference point of the description here. Collectively, all the descriptive variants of the prescriptive approach constitute functional theory construction.

The inductive approach is the approach to theory construction taken by those theorists who emphasize the summary function of a theory. They deny the relevance of both the deductive, prescriptive approach and any descriptive, functional variant of it. So, the method of theory construction indigenous to the summary function interpretation of a theory is induction.

It should be noted that when the word "type" is used to describe a theory, it is usually reserved for how the theory is constructed — i.e., there are three types of theory: deductive, functional, and inductive. Let us analyze and evaluate each of these in turn.

Theory Construction by Deduction

Introduction. In the deductive-construction approach, a theory is a formal set of postulates or axioms (in mathematical equation, symbolic logic, or verbal statement form), composed of primitive, derived, and logical terms, from which aspects of the descriptive level of analysis (called theorems) are logically derivable. Although the prescriptive mode of theory construction involves a set of formal rules which must be followed to grind out both the postulate set and the logical deductions from it, only the latter phase of the total construction process is strictly logical or mechanical in nature. The initial construction of the postulate set itself is really a matter of theory origination, although philosophers of science deemphasize this fact. It is appropriate at this point to present and analyze a brief, abstracted set of five formal construction rules, concurrently relating each to the aspects of theory already discussed.

An abstracted set of formal rules for constructing a deductive theory.
Rule 1. Postulate a set of one or more primitive, undefined terms. A primitive, undefined term is one which should be understood in a root, gut, emotional manner without formal clarification. These terms constitute the ultimate building blocks of the theory. The denotation of these terms constitute the fundamental assumptions and/or most abstract theoretical constructs of the theorist. The number, source, names, etc. of the primitive terms are a matter of theory origination — i.e., they are strictly psychological matters. No justification for or evaluation of the primitive term set need ever be given.
Rule 2. Define a set of one or more complex, derived terms in terms of the primitives and also assume a set of logical terms (connectors, quantifiers,

etc.). In this phase, the theorist not only creates a new set of terms defined in terms of the primitives, but also carries over a predefined set of terms from logic. The latter is merely mechanical, while the former is again basically a psychological process. The denotation of these derived, complex terms are theoretical constructs, but less abstract ones, which directly correspond to the notion of theoretical construct as discussed previously.

Rule 3. Using the primitive terms, derived terms, and logical terms, construct a set of axioms or postulates. An axiom or postulate is typically a statement (usually verbal) specifying a relationship between two or more terms (theoretical constructs). For all practical purposes, an axiom or postulate has the same form or structure as a hypothesis or functional relation, except that the theoretical constructs which it relates together are so high-order and abstract that the relation could never be directly interpreted or tested at the descriptive level of analysis. The content of each axiom (i.e., each relation) is assumed to be true. The set of axioms or postulates and how they are hierarchically interrelated serves as the physical denotation of the word "theory" as it was previously defined. Postulate construction is a psychological, not a logical, process. Given the same input set of terms (constructs), different output (axiomatic) structures are generatable. Ideally, in the deductive approach, postulates should be constructed in a vacuum — i.e., without reference to what is already known about behavior or independent of already established psychological facts.

Rule 4. Derive a set of theorems or consequences from the postulate set. This is the only phase in the total construction process that is strictly logical. Active, logical deductions are made from the essential structure of the postulate set and the activity involved in this step obviously serves as the name for this type of theory construction.

The means of deduction depend upon the well-accepted logical rules of deductive inference; but the form of the deduction depends upon the form of the original postulate set. If the postulate set is stated in math-equation form, then deductions can be easily accomplished by using math equations. If the postulate set is stated in symbolic-logic form, then deduction can be easily accomplished by directly using the language and symbolization of symbolic logic. If the postulate set is stated in verbal form, then deductions can only be accomplished by using logically related verbal statements.

The deductions from the postulate set are technically referred to as "theorems." Although the postulate set logically implies the theorem, the preciseness of the theorem varies with the form of the deduction. A theorem expressed in math-equation form is typically much more precise than one stated in the English vernacular.

The form of a postulate and a theorem is essentially the same — they express a relationship between two or more terms. The crucial difference is that a theorem is stated in descriptive S and R language. The terms contained in a theorem usually admit of easy operational definition/quantification and can be set in correspondence to aspects of the descriptive level of analysis.

Rule 5. Evaluate the significance of the individual theorems. The significance of a derived theorem depends upon whether the stated relationship has already been experimentally verified or not. If it has *not* already been verified, the theorem constitutes a prediction of the theory (postulate set) in the sense of the term used previously when describing the functions of a theory. This interpretation of a theorem is not a strict part of the total construction process and will not be described in detail until theory evaluation is discussed in a later section. If it *has* already been verified, the theorem constitutes a causal law or functional relationship. Since it has been explicitly derived from the theory (postulate set), the postulate set constitutes a sufficient explanation of the theorem in the sense of the term used previously when describing the functions of a theory.

Deductive theory and the functions of a theory. A deductively constructed theory by its very nature makes explanation and prediction the two key functions of a theory. Since the deductive approach emphasizes explanation, integration is also a relevant function for deductive theory, although integrative, deductive theory is far less common in psychology than it is in the physical sciences. Although a deductive theory can classify, this is rarely emphasized. Also, it should be obvious why a deductive theory precludes the very existence of the summary function of a theory. Finally, a deductively constructed theory possesses both the goal function and the means function. More specifically, it is the only one of the three types of theory that can be realistically evaluated along the goal-aspect dimension. So the psychological theorist who emphasizes both these aspects of a theory tends to be a deductive theorist.

Evaluation of Deductive Theory

Introduction. Although the deductive approach to theory construction is prescriptive, it is still the focus of much criticism. A comprehensive, systematic evaluation of the deductive approach is beyond the scope of this book. But some of the more common criticisms of the deductive approach should be indicated because these in large part have served as the genesis of the other two types of theories. Most of the criticisms to be listed derive from the fact that many deductive theorists either fail to recognize the theory origination aspects of the deductive approach — i.e., it is not that automatic or logical in its generation of an explanation and/or prediction — or become overly preoccupied with the goal function of deductive theory to the exclusion of the means function.

Criticisms. The following constitute legitimate criticisms of the deductive approach:

1. The primitive terms used by the deductive theorist are subjective and arbitrary.

2. The derived terms used by the deductive theorist are subjective and arbitrary.

3. The content of the postulates or axioms (i.e., the axiomatic structure) of a deductive theory is arbitrary.

4. The form of the axiomatic structure (and therefore the theorems) is arbitrary.

5. It is never possible to make all the assumptions used by the deductive theorist explicit. Thus, many hidden, implicit assumptions are actually used in the logical derivations.

6. The generality of a deductive theory is a matter of crucial importance. Since no deductive theory can cover or generate all empirical phenomena, the specific area or degree of empirical coverage of a specific deductive theory can pose a serious evaluative problem.

7. Since deductive theory possesses the goal function, the deductive theorist can become enamored of this and never actually evaluate his theory empirically.

8. Analogously, a deductive theory, which is actually evaluated empirically and is faced with contradictory evidence (i.e., a prediction that is demonstrated to be false in the lab), is rarely completely discarded because of its goal function.

9. A specific deductive theory is often constructed without regard to currently accepted psychological terminology and currently known psychological facts — i.e., the deductive theorist is often viewed either as stupid or contemptuous by knowledgeable nontheorists.

10. A deductive theory is very difficult, if not impossible, to understand by the layman and even by the professional not specializing in the specific area of the discipline to which it is applicable.

The notion of a deductively constructed theory versus the notion of a model

Introduction. The essence of a theory is to generate (usually explain and/or predict) aspects of the descriptive level of analysis. Deduction has been characterized as the prescriptive mode for accomplishing this and the axiomatic structure embodied by a specific deductive theory serves as the crucial element of the generation process. It now will be easy to discuss the notion of a model in the context of the two primary functions of a theory and the characteristics of a deductively constructed theory.

The context in which the notion of a model arises. The situation in which the notion of a model is definable can be structurally analyzed into four parts.

1. Some aspect of the descriptive level of analysis or the empirical situation requires generation.

2. Some elaborately constructed deductive system — complete with primitive, derived, and logical terms, an axiom set, and specific logical derivations — exists at some abstract level. Note that the word "system" is now used instead of the word "theory." The initial construction of this deductive system is irrelevant and of no concern whatsoever; in a sense, "it was always there."

3. Certain similarities are assumed to exist between the deductive system and the empirical situation to be generated.

4. Then, by analogy, the properties, functions, etc. of the deductive system are assumed to be also characteristic of the empirical situation to be generated. We can employ the deductive system as a model (a generative device) for the empirical situation.

Definition of a model. A model can be defined as an abstract, conceptual analogue, usually existing in the form of a completed deductive system, whose function it is to generate some aspect of the empirical situation.

An illustration of the above situation. Since the above description is quite abstract, let us reintroduce the notion of a model in the context of a specific example. Suppose that the aspect of the empirical world requiring generation is the human brain. How does one explain or predict the activity of the human brain? Well, it can be modeled — that is, we can find some other thing whose functions we already know and understand (a deductive system) which is similar to the human brain and declare that the brain acts analogously. A likely thing possessing such properties is the computer. Thus, the thing to be modeled is the brain, and the model is the computer. We do not know how the brain works. We do know how the computer works — after all, we constructed the computer. We say that the brain and computer are similar and then, by analogy, infer processes in the brain that are characteristic of the computer. The brain is assumed to act as if it were a computer. As such, the deductive system underlying the workings of the computer serves as a sufficient explanation of (a model for) the workings of the brain.

The brain-computer example can be presented structurally.

1. The brain (thing to be modeled) requires generation (A).

2. The computer is a deductive system, all of whose properties and functions are known and understood (B→a, b, c, etc.).

3. The brain and computer are similar (A s B).

4. Therefore, by analogy, the properties and functions of the computer (model) are also characteristic of the brain (A→a, b, c, etc.).

A deductive system as theory versus a deductive system as model. Since a deductive system, both as a theory and as a model, generates aspects of the descriptive level of analysis and also possesses the identical structure, content, etc., how do the two uses differ? There are at least four essential points of difference.

1. When a deductive system is used as a model, it has already been constructed and is currently brought in from some other area of application. The creative aspect of the process is the postulation of the similarity between the thing to be modeled and the deductive system to be used as the model. When a deductive system is used as a theory, it is initially constructed for the first time in the specific context of the empirical situation it is supposed to generate. The creative aspect of the construction is the deductive system itself.

2. When a deductive system is used as a model, it is merely a conceptual analogue. The thing to be modeled is merely assumed to act like the model. It is not equivalent to the model itself. For instance, no presumption is made that the brain is a computer. When a deductive system is used as a theory, it is supposed to be a true representation or higher order description of exactly how and why the descriptive level of analysis is such as it is. In this interpretation, if the deductive system underlying the computer were used as a theory for the brain, the brain would be a computer (i.e., another kind of computer).

3. When a deductive system is used as a model, it is assumed to be only an approximate description of the thing to be modeled. A model, only being an analogy, cannot be a completely accurate description of the thing to be explained. When a deductive system is used as a theory, it is assumed to be exhaustively descriptive of the thing to be explained. A theory, being a true representation, must be a completely accurate higher order description of the thing to be explained.

4. When a deductive system is used as a model, it can tolerate conflicting evidence that clearly is not in accord with it. After all, the model is not a complete description of the thing to be modeled. For instance, the brain can function in certain ways that are not characteristic of the computer; but the general computer-brain analogy still holds. When a deductive system is used as a theory, it cannot tolerate conflicting empirical evidence that clearly is not in accord with it. A theory is supposed to be a complete higher order description of the thing to be explained. For instance, if the brain functions in a certain way not predicted by the deductive system underlying a computer, then that deductive system is eliminated as a viable theory for the brain. So, basically the fourth point of difference reduces to the degree to which the notion of empirical verification is applicable to the deductive system.

Evaluation of a Model

Positive aspects. On the positive side, the use of a deductive system as a model answers practically all of the criticisms of the use of a deductive system as a theory.

1. Since a model is brought in from another area of application, the initial four criticisms related to the origination of a deductive sytem (i.e., arbitrariness and subjectivity of the primitive terms, derived terms, and form and content of the axiomatic structure) no longer apply.

2. The fifth criticism, concerning the use of hidden or implicit assumptions, disappears because a model is regarded as a nonexhaustive description of the thing to be modeled.

3. The problem of generality is now deemphasized. The focus of concern is the thing to be modeled, not the model itself. The generality of the deductive system, as a model, is not at issue vis-à-vis the empirical situation it is applied to. Remember it is merely a conceptual analogue. The generality of the deductive system underlying the model is strictly limited by the number of empirical situations to which it can be regarded as similar.

4. The fact that the application of a model is impervious to some degree of conflicting empirical evidence removes the seventh and eighth criticisms (emphasis on goal function and deemphasis of the means function) from consideration. Related to this is the fact that the deductive system embodying a model is already known as "true" — i.e., the deductive system is true for the model. What is at issue is the applicability of the model to the thing to be modeled. For instance, the deductive system underlying a computer is true for the computer. Possible empirical justification merely applies to the applicability of the same deductive system to the brain.

5. The ninth criticism (disregard of current psychological terminology and facts) is largely taken care of because a model is preconstructed and is merely a conceptual analogue. No presumption is made that a model actually represents the underlying psychological reality.

As will be seen in the next chapter, the use of a deductive system as a model has just about completely supplanted the use of a deductive system as a theory in the context of the overall macro-theoretical learning situation. Modeling has become the primary mode of formal explanation and/or prediction.

Negative aspects. On the negative side, the use of a model does not answer the tenth criticism — it is still difficult to understand. But there is a more serious criticism associated with the use of a model. It derives from the fact that a model is a conceptual analogue. Logicians have long realized that argument by analogy is dangerous. Specifically, just because system or object A is similar in many respects to system or object B, it does not logically follow that the properties, functions, etc. of one are also characteristic of the other. Arguments by analogy are encountered in wholesale lots in the context of everyday life but in a disguised form. They are not usually stated in such a formal manner and they usually use the word "same" instead of "similar." So the fourth aspect of the context in which a model arises requires a considerable degree of presumption; in many ways, it constitutes the source of subjectivity and arbitrariness associated with the use of a model.

Functional Theory

Introduction. Functional theory was previously characterized as any descriptive variant of the prescriptive mode of theory construction. There is no one positive attribute of functional theory other than the fact that it is nondeductive. Thus, there are many ways in which a functional theory can be constructed. (1) Theory construction in the prescriptive mode can break down at the level of any one of the first four rules and ipso facto yield functional theory. (2) A specific theorist can construct a theory in ignorance of the prescriptive mode and, by default, it is functional. (3) An active researcher, in reviewing the results of a series of related experiments, can construct the minimal number of low-level or informal explanatory statements or theoretical constructs necessary to generate the experimental results. (4) Etc. Thus, it is impossible to analyze functional theory construction in terms of an ordered set of rules.

Definition and description. The technical literature defines functional theory as consisting of more or less informal explanatory propositions in verbal-statement form that are closely related to the data and that are without fixed logical form. These informal explanatory propositions are analogous to the formal axiom set of deductive theory, but they are not derived from underlying primitive terms, nor are theorems formally, logically derived from them. Rather, the content of the informal explanatory propositions is usually suggested by current research findings which the theorist feels requires low-level, immediate, almost common-sense explanation, and they are usually stated in such a form that no valid logical inferences can be deduced from them − i.e., prediction is done piecemeal, at random, virtually at a pure verbal level.

Since functional theory usually arises in a specific experimental context (i.e., a specific kind of learning task or experiment), it typically does not employ ultra-abstract theoretical constructs nor is there any question regarding its essential generality. The goal function of a theory is irrelevant for a functional theory. It cannot be evaluated as a theory with respect to form and structure by the philosophy of science nor can it be meaningfully compared with other functional theories. The sole significance of a functional theory lies in its tool function − as a guide to future research. Once a specific functional theory can no longer perform this function, it can be quickly and easily discarded because it was not prescriptively constructed.

The value of functional theory is immediate and "short-term" − it meets the pragmatic need for some kind of underlying theoretical explanation on a day-to-day basis. The content of a functional theory cannot serve as the basis of long-range, comprehensive, high-level explanation. Functional theory is usually easily understood by the layman or professional nonspecialist because of its virtual anecdotal, common-sense form and language. Functional theory possesses face validity because of the way it structures psychological reality.

Functional theory and the functions of a theory. Functional theory explains — but by fiat or custom, not prescriptively. Likewise functional theory predicts — verbally, anecdotally, at a common-sense level, not logically. It is difficult for a functional theory to be integrative with respect to a large area of psychology because of the way it is constructed. Likewise, the informal nature of its structure and content vitiates much of its potential use as a classification system. Functional theory does not summarize in the strict sense that inductive theory does; but because it is constructed close to the data, summarization is not a wholly irrelevant function as it is in the deductive approach. Finally, as stated previously, functional theory only has value for the means function of a theory.

Evaluation of functional theory. Both the nonprescriptive aspects of functional theory and the discussion so far have implicitly evaluated functional theory negatively. Basically, the crucial question should be why functional theory continues to exist. There are two classes of reasons for this.

1. Functional theory is a formalization of what the typical theorist does on a day-to-day basis. In a sense, it is pre-theoretical (i.e., pre-deductive theory). It provides the groundwork in a practice sense for later, formal deductive theory. Most experimental psychologists are functional theorists in the context of their everyday behavior, but few psychologists possess enough creativity and intellectual background to actively construct a deductive system (theory or model).

2. Functional theory also survives because of what it is associated with rather than because of any inherent philosophical strengths. Historically, the term "functionalism" applied to a specific school of experimental psychology — the school that chronologically and intellectually intervened between strict stiucturalism and hard-core behaviorism. Functionalism was a transition school combining aspects of both structuralism and behaviorism. The legacy of functionalism is a contemporary eclecticism. Functional theorists tend to be eclectic, open-minded, easily changeable, pragmatic, etc. For many observers of the psychological scene, these constitute the positive characteristics of functional theory rather than its mode of construction (or nonconstruction).

The Inductive Approach to Theory Construction

Introduction. A theorist who emphasizes the summary function of a theory to the exclusion of the other functions was previously labeled an "inductive theorist." Inductive theory is not theory in the same sense of the term as used by either the deductive or functional approach. In fact, many psychologists regard it as a nontheoretical or even an antitheoretical approach. The theoretical statements embodied by an inductive theory are not constructed so as to either explain or predict. All the inductive theorist does is to redescribe ("summarize") the salient facts, features, functional relationships, etc. that are already known about the descriptive level of analysis. Thus, the method of theory construction in the inductive approach is quite explicit. Faced with a series of research findings, the theorist "induces" the minimal number of statements and/or constructs which can generate (summarize) them. The statements and constructs usually possess high operational specificity — i.e., they do not refer to abstract, postulated processes or events; rather they refer to explicit operations performed by the experimenter.

Definition and description. An inductive theory can be defined as a loosely organized set of descriptive statements, which merely summarize clusters of empirical facts or laws, with a minimum of inferential commitment. The set of descriptive statements is not analogous to either the axiom set of deductive theory or the set of informal explanatory propositions characteristic of functional theory. A descriptive statement is merely a summary kind of generalization based on a series of related facts or similar empirical phenomena.

There is very little confusion between deductive theory and inductive theory because the former always "starts at the top and works down," while the latter always "begins at the bottom and works up." But the set of descriptive statements characteristic of inductive theory is sometimes confused with the set of informal explanatory propositions embodied by the functional approach because both are "close to the data" and their mode of construction often overlaps.

There are two primary differences between the theoretical statements contained in an inductive and functional theory. Initially, an inductively constructed descriptive statement can neither explain nor predict, while a functionally constructed explanatory proposition can explain and/or predict, albeit at a low level. Secondly, the theoretical constructs of inductive theory usually refer to mere operational events, while those of functional theory do possess some degree of abstraction (i.e., are postulated as existing between the S and the R). The theoretical constructs used in an inductive theory typically are not as anecdotal or anthropomorphic as those employed in the functional

116 Psychology of Learning

approach. The layman or nonspecialist professional would have difficulty understanding a rigorously constructed inductive theory. The inductive theorist tends to structure psychological reality in terms of the strictest and most hard-core operational terms in current use.

Neither the goal function nor the tool function of a theory is relevant for the inductive mode of theory construction. Thus, with respect to the latter function, inductive theory can never be empirically evaluated — after all, it makes no predictions and is merely a cogent redescription of what is already known about behavior in a specific situation. Evaluation has meaning solely in a definitional or descriptive sense — i.e., is the theorist using the most appropriate term or statement to describe a certain research result? Because of this, the inductive approach is commonly referred to as the ultrapositivistic approach. Also, the notion of generality of a particular inductive theory is a meaningless concept.

Inductive theory and the functions of a theory. The only function of a theory that an inductively constructed theory can perform is summarization. Explanation, prediction, integration, and classification are all meaningless in the context of inductive theory. Recall that the goal and tool aspects of a theory are likewise irrelevant for inductive theory. Summarization is such a focal point of inductive theory that the previous discussion of the summary function of a theory (in the functions of a theory section) constitutes a virtual descriptive summary of inductive theory.

Evaluation of inductive theory. As already indicated during the discussion of the summary function of a theory, the justification for the inductive approach is ultimately philosophical. Inductive theorists believe that more is gained and less is lost by using inductively derived theoretical constructs than by going the deductive or functional route. Operant conditioning psychologists in general and B.F. Skinner and his associates in particular are the primary adherents of this view in the context of learning psychology.

Skinner's view is quite reasonable and has many advantages if it is evaluated solely in the context of what he is trying to accomplish. His basic concern is behavioral control and in the operant situation this can be achieved at the strict descriptive level of analysis. The behavioral data obtained in operant conditioning is so stable that the variation in the input situation itself can account for practically all the variation in the output situation without postulating the existence of intervening, higher order theoretical constructs. So in the context of behavioral control in the operant situation, the descriptive level of analysis (inductive theory) does serve as a sufficient and adequate explanation of behavior.

But beyond the confines of behavioral control in operant psychology, strict application of the inductive approach is regarded as unjustifiable by most learning psychologists. After all, the learning process itself is a higher order, intervening theoretical construct; and learning theory, in its functions of explanation and prediction, would be impossible in the context of the strict inductive approach.

It should be noted that deductive and functional theorists have been influenced by the intent of inductive theory. Formal theorists have come to realize that it is ridiculous to theorize about a particular piece of behavior until it has been subjected to sufficient experimentation (i.e., theory is no substitute for reliable, valid data), that the form of and interrelationships among theoretical constructs should be kept as "conservative" or simple as possible (for clear-cut derivation purposes), that specific theories must be designed so that they can be ultimately evaluatable, primarily at the empirical level (i.e., theoretical constructs must ultimately be reducible to operational terms), etc.

The Evaluation of a Theory

Introduction. Let us assume that a theory has been deductively or functionally constructed to cover some aspect of the descriptive level of analysis. Since the content of the theory is a tentative set of explanatory statements and since the theoretical constructs are only assumed to exist, the appropriateness of the theory for that aspect of the empirical situation must be assessed. There is the need to confirm (verify) or reject (falsify) the theory — i.e., there is the need to evaluate the theory. Two types of evaluation have already been mentioned in the text: empirical and heuristic. These two types of evaluation will now be discussed and analyzed in turn.

Empirical evaluation

Definition and initial distinctions. Empirical evaluation is related to the predictive function of a theory. A deductive theory produces one or more theorems from its axiom or postulate set, formally through the rules of deductive logic. A functional theory generates one or more predictions less rigorously from its set of informal explanatory propositions. Either type of prediction has the form of a postulated functional relation and possesses constituent terms which admit of easy operational definition. One of the terms is "behavior," a response term, the dependent variable and the other major term is an "antecedent condition," a stimulus factor, the independent variable. The content of the prediction is that behavior is a (or certain) function of the stimulus condition.

A postulated functional relation whose truth value has not yet been assessed is called a "hypothesis." So the prediction from a theory can also be labeled an hypothesis. The truth value of an hypothesis is established by an experiment, the results of which either statistically (probabilistically) accept or reject the hypothesis. Now for the main point: Evaluation of a hypothesis (prediction) directly in an experiment serves as an indirect evaluation of the theory from which it was derived. So, empirical evaluation of a theory procedurally amounts to evaluating one or more of its predictions in the laboratory.

The effect of the direct empirical evaluation of the hypothesis on the truth value of the theory depends on many factors. Two will be emphasized here: (1) whether the hypothesis is evaluated positively (accepted) or negatively (rejected) and (2) whether the theory is "simple" or "complex." Chapter 1 discussed the exact meaning or interpretation to be assigned to the notions of "positive evaluation" and "negative evaluation" of a hypothesis. The distinction between a simple theory and a complex theory is artificial in actual practice, but this distinction is absolutely necessary for current didactic purposes. By a simple theory is meant one whose set of explanatory statements contains only one member — i.e., the prediction is directly implied by that one statement. On the other hand, a complex theory is one whose set of explanatory statements contains numerous members — i.e., the prediction is obtained only through the use of a long chain of deductions involving many intermediate steps.

In effect, two binary-valued dimensions have been introduced which orthogonally generate a 2 x 2 table, involving four cells, each of which represents a different evaluation situation (See Fig. 6-2).

| | | Type of Theory Being Evaluated | |
		Simple	Complex
Empirical Evaluation of a Hypothesis	Accepted (True)	I	III
(Truth Value of Prediction)	Rejected (False)	II	IV

Fig. 6-2. Four Empirical Evaluation Situations

The content of each cell, as yet unspecified, represents how a theory is evaluated given the particular input conditions associated with it on the figure. Each of the four empirical evaluation situations will be discussed in turn.

The reader should be warned at this point that each empirical evaluation situation involves the use of logic and the notions of valid and invalid argument forms. The relevant underlying logical concepts will be introduced in the course of the presentation as the need arises. Also, the words "true" and "false" have been used rather loosely up to now. Henceforth, "true" means logically true and "false" means logically false.

I. Simple theory; Prediction confirmed. Theory A implies hypothesis B. If A is true, then B must be true. B is found to be true by an experiment. What can be logically inferred about the truth value of A? Nothing! More specifically, the confirmation of B does not prove that A is also true. Why not? Because the argument form implied in the above is not a valid argument form. Structurally:

(1)   A→B (A implies B).
(2)   B is true.
(3)   ∴ A is true.

(1) and (2) are premises; (3) is technically a conclusion. The above is an invalid argument form. If you do infer that A is true, you have committed a fallacy – specifically, the fallacy of affirming the antecedent.

To see exactly why the above is an invalid argument form, it is necessary to present the logical "truth table" associated with it. The truth table is as follows.

	A → B	B	A
(1)	T	T	T
(2)	T	T	Ⓕ←
(3)	F	F	T
(4)	T	F	F

A truth table is a two-dimensional array, composed of columns and rows. The columns represent the statements (both premises and conclusion) appearing in the argument. It is customary to assign a given statement to a column according to its ordinal position in the argument – e.g., the first premise is represented by the first column, the conclusion is represented by the last column, etc. Since the current argument has three statements, the above truth table has three columns. The rows represent all the possible logical truth value combinations associated with the statements of the argument. In the table, T means true and F means false. The current argument has two "simple" statements A and B. Since each individual simple statement can be either true or false, there are only four pairwise combinations of truth values possible for the simple statements when taken in combination: TT, TF, FT, and FF. Thus, the above truth table possesses four rows. The "compound" implicative statement A ———▶B has a truth value (T or F), depending on the specific truth value of its constituent simple statements. As the truth table indicates, the implication A ———▶B is true under every combination, except when B is false and A is true. The specific defining rule determining the truth value of A ———▶B, contingent upon the truth value of its constituent statements, is too complex to discuss here.

Now it is possible to explicitly state why this argument form is invalid. By definition, a valid argument form is one that has a T appearing in the conclusion column for each row in which every premise is also T in the truth table associated with it. Such is not the case here. Only the first two rows of the truth table are of relevance for us: (1) It is true that A implies B and (2) B has been shown to be true by experiment. But note that A is only true in the first row; it is not true in the second row. Thus, this argument form is invalid. A, the conclusion, does not necessarily have to be true just because A ———▶B and B are true; it is also possible for A to be false.

Just what has been accomplished with respect to the truth value of theory A? Nothing, with respect to the logical truth value of A. But on a psychological credibility level, the mere fact that a prediction of theory A has been borne out increases the emotional credibility of theory A. So, if we now introduce the notion of a psychological continuum of credibility extending from completely incredible to completely credible (the two end points of which could conceivably correspond to absolute logical falsity and truth), what we have in effect accomplished is to move theory A a little bit to the right on the continuum of credibility. Let us physicalize this in terms of a diagram (See Fig. 6-3).

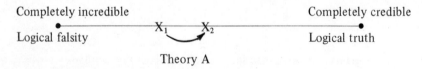

Completely incredible   Completely credible

Logical falsity X_1 X_2 Logical truth

Theory A

Fig. 6-3. The Psychological Continuum of Credibility

The initial degree of credibility of theory A lies at some amorphous point X_1 on the continuum. As a result of hypothesis B being demonstrated as true by experiment, theory A moves to the right some finite amount. Each additional prediction (C, D, E, etc.) which is confirmed would also move theory A farther to the right. But the extreme right end point can never be reached no matter how many different, individual predictions are confirmed. Remember, we are dealing with an invalid argument form and there is no way to demonstrate the absolute logical truth of theory A in this empirical evaluation situation. It should be made explicit that theory A can never reach the extreme left end point (logical falsity) either in this empirical evaluation situation. No valid conclusion of either kind (T or F) can be made in the context of the argument form associated with this empirical evaluation situation.

In actual practice, experimental psychologists continue for years to demonstrate that the myriad, different predictions of a simple theory A are true in the lab. Each successive demonstration moves theory A farther to the right. But the point of absolute logical truth is never reached and this is a prime reason why so much empirical research is done to evaluate a single, specific theory. Appreciable positive evidence must be accumulated before theory A achieves a respectable or considerable degree of credibility.

II. Simple theory; Prediction disconfirmed. Theory A implies hypothesis B. If A is true, then B must be true. B is found to be false by an experiment. What can be logically inferred about the truth value of A? Theory A has been demonstrated to be logically false. So the fact that hypothesis B has been disconfirmed in the lab does prove that theory A is also false. This is so because the argument form implied in the above is a valid argument form. Structurally:

(1)   A→B (A implies B).
(2)   B is false.
(3)   ∴ A is false.

Again (1) and (2) are premises and (3) is a conclusion. Here (3) is a valid conclusion. The above is a valid argument form — specifically, the valid deductive argument form called *modus tollens*.

To see exactly why the above is a valid argument form, let us refer to the logical "truth table" associated with it. The truth table is as follows.

	A → B	∿ B	∿ A
(1)	T	F	F
(2)	T	F	T
(3)	F	T	F
→ (4)	T	T	T

The nature and structure of this truth table is analogous to the one described in the context of case I. Again T and F mean true and false respectively. To represent the fact that both B and A are false in this argument, not B and not A constitute the second and third columns of the truth table (i.e., not B is true and not A is true). "Not" is symbolized as $\sim$ in the truth table. Functionally, this reverses the notation and truth value entries of the B and A columns of the previous (case I) truth table.

Now only the fourth row of this truth table is relevant for us: (1) It is true that A implies B and (2) B has been shown to be false by experiment (i.e., $\sim$ B is T). Note that with this input, A must necessarily be false ($\sim$ A is T). Whenever a T appears in the first two columns, there is never a $\sim$ A is F in the third column. So, *modus tollens* is a valid argument form and whenever A $\longrightarrow$ B is T and $\sim$ B is T, $\sim$ A also must be T.

Just what has been accomplished with respect to the truth value of theory A? Theory A has been demonstrated to be logically false. Or, it has been placed at the extreme left end point of the psychological credibility continuum. It cannot be the appropriate generation device for the specific aspect of the descriptive level of analysis for which it was designed or to which it was applied. (Note: The empirical evaluation is moot with respect to any other aspect of the descriptive level of analysis to which theory A might conceivably be applied.) Physically, in the context of Fig. 6-3, X_1 is some amorphous point on the credibility continuum and X_2 would be located at the extreme left end point.

Functionally, only one negative instance (disconfirmed prediction) is required to logically falsify a theory. It makes no difference how many prior positive instances (confirmed predictions) have occurred, if any. For instance, theory A could have moved closer and closer to the right end of the credibility continuum as an unattainable limit over a series of numerous confirmed predictions. But the occurrence of the initial disconfirmed prediction automatically shunts the theory to the logically false point no matter how far to the right the theory has already progressed.

In actual practice, the typical experimental psychologist does not accept the logical prescriptions just presented. (1) He is influenced by the number of prior confirmed predictions. If these are appreciable, then he is likely to regard the first negative instance as due to a "quirk," or unstable data, or "chance," or faulty physical experimentation (i.e., apparatus, instructions, execution, etc.). In effect, the experiment is replicated (performed again under as similar conditions as possible). If the replication confirms the prediction, the wise psychologist is then likely to discontinue the experiment and call the initial result a definite "quirk," etc. On the other hand, if the replication disconfirms the prediction, whether or not the psychologist proceeds to a second replication depends in large part on "emotional," psychological factors.

There is no rational, logical decision rule as to when successive negative-result replications should be terminated. (2) Even if the very first empirical evaluation of a theory is a negative instance and the psychologist dutifully refrains from performing further experimental evaluation, he is not likely to reject the entire original theory per se. Rather, he merely revises it and tries again with the main features of the original theory still intact.

III. Complex theory; Prediction confirmed. A complex theory was defined as one involving an explanatory set composed of more than one theoretical statement. Again, theory A eventually implies hypothesis B − but not directly in terms of one-step implication. As an illustration, let us suppose that theory A contains four explanatory statements C, D, E, and F. Taken together, C and D might imply Q. Q, although in functional relationship form, does not contain operational terms − i.e., it is still composed of theoretical constructs. E in conjunction with Q might imply R, another directly untestable relation. Finally, R and F might conjointly imply B, a prediction that is directly evaluatable empirically. B is found to be true by an experiment. What can be logically inferred about the truth value of theory A? Nothing! The argument form implied in the above is not a valid argument form. Structurally:

(1)   Theory $A \doteq C * D * E * F$

(2) $C * D \rightarrow Q$
(3) $Q * E \rightarrow R$
(4) $R * F \rightarrow B$

(5) $\therefore A \rightarrow B$
(6)   B is true.

(7) $\therefore$ A is true.

Note: * means "and" or "the conjunction of." $\doteq$ means "equivalent to."

If you do infer that A is true you have again committed the fallacy of affirming the antecedent. There is no need to demonstrate why the above form is an invalid argument − it is an extension of case I.

Just what has been accomplished with respect to the truth value of theory A? The situation is analogous to case I. The psychological credibility of theory A as a whole could be increased somewhat along the credibility continuum. On the other hand, the increase in credibility can be partitioned in any proportion desired among the individual statements C, D, E, F, Q, and R. Conceivably, the increase in credibility could be assigned exclusively to Q or R or Q and R and this would leave the truth value of theory A at its original point along the continuum.

In actual practice, there is no real difference between how experimental psychologists behave in the context of case I and case III, except that case III is much more frequent than case I because it is the more realistic evaluation situation (complex theory).

IV. Complex theory; Prediction disconfirmed. Again theory A eventually implies hypothesis B — but not through one-step implication. Let us suppose the same theory composition and derivation sequence as in case III, but now B is found to be false by an experiment. What can be logically inferred about the truth value of theory A? At least one of the theoretical statements must be logically false. Structurally:

(1)   Theory $A \doteq C * D * E * F$
_____

(2) $C * D \rightarrow Q$
(3) $Q * E \rightarrow R$
(4) $R * F \rightarrow B$
_____

(5) $\therefore$ $A \rightarrow B$
(6)   B is false.
_____

(7) $\therefore$ C, D, E, F, R or Q or any combination is (are) false.

NOTE: *means "and" or "the conjunction of." $\doteq$ means "equivalent to."

The above is a valid argument form — again a variant or extension of the *modus tollens* and no truth table need be appealed to in order to demonstrate the essential validity of the argument.

Just what has been accomplished with respect to the truth value of theory A? The situation is indeterminate, indecisive. The logical falsification could be assigned to theory A as a whole, or to C, D, E, or F individually, or even to Q or R or Q and R. The latter option, of course, leaves the original truth value of theory A unchanged. So, in the case of a complex theory, a disconfirmed prediction need not logically affect the truth value of the theory at all.

In actual practice, case IV is analogous to case II. The occurrence of a disconfirmed prediction is likely to be tempered by the psychologist by the number of prior confirmed predictions, by the possibility of slipshod or inappropriate physical experimentation, by the option of revising the theory, etc. But, in addition, the indeterminacy of case IV makes it a procedural horror. Faced with a disconfirmed prediction, a "friend" of theory A can assign the logical falsification to Q or R or at most to one of the statements composing theory A, while an "enemy" of theory A is more likely to assign the logical falsification to the entire theory A. So, in the current evaluation situation, the psychologist can "have his cake and eat it too," a thoroughly unacceptable conceptual situation.

Evaluation of empirical evaluation. Although it is a virtual truism among philosophers of science that a specific theory must yield predictions directly testable in the lab in order to be treated as a serious or viable theoretical construction, empirical evaluation itself must be given a negative evaluation.

At the logical or conceptual level, there are no circumstances under which a theory can be demonstrated to be absolutely (logically) true; and there is only one circumstance under which it can be demonstrated to be absolutely (logically) false — namely, a simple theoretical situation in which the disconfirmed prediction is a one-step implication of the main body of theory.

At the procedural or psychological level, even the logical restrictions of empirical evaluation are vitiated or violated. Successive confirmed predictions are interpreted as increasing the credibility of a theory in a psychological sense. The desire to perform that additional or next positive instance is an important causal factor regulating the day-to-day behavior of many experimental psychologists. The occurrence of a negative instance (or the first negative instance) is generally not reacted to according to its strict logical implications. Replication, theoretical revision, unjustifiable partitioning of the logical falsification among less crucial statements, etc. are common ways in which to circumvent the direct logical implication of a falsification.

So, it should not seem too surprising that empirical evaluation never realistically leads to the eventual complete acceptance or rejection of a theory. The reason a particular theory survives or does not survive is not solely related to its extent of empirical evaluation at all. Rather there are also other factors that determine the historical longevity and relevance of a theory. These factors can be lumped together and termed heuristic factors; they will be discussed and analyzed under the topic of heuristic evaluation. But, prior to consideration of heuristic evaluation, it is necessary to discuss the empirical evaluation of two or more theories simultaneously.

Empirical Evaluation of Two or More Theories Simultaneously

Introduction. Rarely is a single theory empirically evaluated in isolation, independent of other theories. A particular experiment is usually performed to arbitrate between two or more theories simultaneously. The notion of empirical evaluation was introduced in the context of a single theory merely as a didactic device — i.e., it was easier to present the logic and principles underlying empirical evaluation in that context. To simplify the following discussion, let us assume that just two theories are being simultaneously considered and that both theories involve one-step implicative predictions.

Empirical evaluation of two simple theories simultaneously

Introduction. Suppose simple theory K and simple theory L have been constructed to generate the same aspect of the descriptive level of analysis. The ultimate evaluation depends chiefly on whether theories K and L make the same or a different prediction with respect to the empirical situation to which they have been applied.

Same prediction case. Assume that both theories K and L predict B with respect to the empirical situation. Then that specific aspect of the descriptive level of analysis cannot empirically arbitrate between the two theories in the sense of logically rejecting one of them and implicitly adding to the credibility of the other. Some other empirical situation must be found in which the two theories make differential predictions. Assume that such an empirical situation does not exist and the current empirical situation is the only one in which the two theories can be empirically evaluated. Both theories can be evaluated — but they will always be given the same evaluation: both theories either will be made more credible (prediction B is confirmed) or both theories will be logically falsified (prediction B is disconfirmed). If both theories are made more credible, some distinction can then be made between them by appealing to one or more heuristic factors. For instance, although theories K and L are both evaluated positively on the empirical-evaluation level, theory L might be preferred on a heuristic basis. So, in summary, empirical evaluation in the same prediction case cannot arbitrate between two simple theories; it merely logically rejects both or adds to the credibility of both.

Different prediction case. Assume theory K predicts 16 and theory L predicts 19 with respect to the empirical situation. The use of numbers instead of letters to represent the respective predictions is necessary here in order to make all the possible evaluation outcomes explicit. Three classes of outcomes exist, one of which definitively arbitrates between the two theories.

    Arbitration outcome. One theory is logically rejected, the other theory is incremented in credibility. There are two ways for this to happen. (1) If the experimental data yields 16, then the prediction of theory K is confirmed and that of theory L is not confirmed — theory K is incremented in credibility and theory L is logically falsified. (2) If the experimental data yields 19, then the prediction of theory L is confirmed and that of theory K is not confirmed — theory L is incremented in credibility and theory K is explicitly rejected.

    Double rejection outcome. Both theories are logically rejected. This happens when neither prediction is confirmed. Many different numerical outcomes in the experimental data can do this. For instance, if the data yields 8, 12, 14, 23, 25, etc., neither prediction is confirmed and both theories must be rejected.

Inconclusive (unstable data) outcome. Neither theory can be empirically evaluated on the basis of the experimental results. This occurs when the data outcome is close to or approaches either or both of the theoretical predictions. For instance, assume the experimental data yielded 15 or 20 (or 17 or 18). Seventeen and 18 are right in between both predictions. Fifteen and 20 are adjacent to one of the two predictions. In an absolute sense, both theories must be rejected; but, the typical experimenter feels justified in labeling the experimental data unstable, inconclusive, etc. and proceeds to replicate the experiment with the hope of achieving a definitive 16 or 19 on the second attempt. Inconclusive data is very common in actual practice. "I need to run more subjects" is a common statement heard in an experimental psychologist's quarters.

Some perspective. Note that in the differential prediction case it is impossible for both theories to increment in credibility. The single numerical result of an experiment can never agree with or match the two different theoretical predictions. This is why the differential prediction case is the realistic empirical evaluation situation. This is why experimental psychologists are constantly striving to construct theories with differential predictions with respect to the same aspect of the empirical situation.

Heuristic Evaluation

Definition and initial description. Whether or not a specific theory has been empirically evaluated or the degree to which it has been empirically evaluated is just one of the factors which inputs into the overall evaluation of a theory. This overall evaluation of a theory can be referred to as heuristic evaluation. Assuming a theory has not already been rejected outright empirically, it possesses some degree of heuristic truth value. This can be defined as the degree of formal acceptance which a theory has achieved at any specific moment in time from the group of professionals most interested in the theory.

Since a theory can never be proven absolutely true in the context of empirical evaluation, heuristic truth serves as the primary dimension along which a theory is evaluated. We can assume the existence of a continuum of heuristic truth value ranging from zero to infinity, to some point along which any theory is assignable. A theory possessing a high degree of heuristic truth continues to survive; a theory possessing a low degree of heuristic truth slowly but surely fades from the scene and loses historical relevance. It has never been logically falsified; it has simply been replaced by one or more other theories possessing a higher degree of heuristic truth. The factors that determine the heuristic truth value of a theory are endless; but five of the more prominent ones will be singled out for discussion.

Five Factors Determining the Heuristic Truth Value of a Theory

1. The degree of empirical truth value already possessed by the theory. This essentially refers to the total number of predictions of the theory which have already been confirmed in the sense of case I and case III of empirical evaluation. The degree of empirical truth value possessed by a theory is the extent to which the theory has been moved to the right along the psychological credibility continuum. Heuristic truth value covaries positively, as opposed to negatively, with degree of empirical truth value.

2. The ease of subjecting the theory to empirical evaluation. This refers to how precise the prediction(s) of the theory is (are). Very specific, exact predictions are easier to disconfirm in the laboratory than more general, loosely stated predictions. For instance, it is easier to disconfirm a prediction of 16.333 in the lab than it is to disconfirm a prediction of "somewhere between 15 and 20." The easier it is to subject a theory to empirical evaluation, the higher the heuristic truth value it possesses. The more precise, explicit, formal, etc. a theory is, the higher its initial degree of heuristic truth value. For instance, prescriptively constructed theory tends to be more precise and formal than functionally constructed theory so it tends to possess a higher degree of initial heuristic truth value.

3. The extent of compatibility of the theory to previously constructed, related theories designed to cover the same empirical area. The more similar a theory is to previously accepted theory, the higher will be its initial heuristic truth value evaluation. Completely novel theoretical approaches, unrelated to prior theory, possess a low degree of immediate heuristic truth value. While this situation might seem ridiculous because it amounts to an automatic penalty for new, creative theory construction, it should be realized that this factor is the only reasonable criterion in existence for condemning the bizarre theories of obvious "quacks" and "nonexperts." The essence of scientific theoretical progress is a succession of slow, continuous, historically related developments. So-called "breakthroughs" or "novel approaches" (i.e., discontinuous developments) require a lot of time and effort before they become accepted by the everyday practitioner in a given empirical area.

4. The degree of generality of the theory. Generality refers to the amount/extent of the descriptive level of analysis which the theory is sup-

posed to generate. The heuristic truth value of a theory is positively related to its degree of generality. While there is nothing innately advantageous to an exceedingly general theory in an absolute sense because the degree of generality of a theory is usually not the focal point of interest or is even unknown at the moment of its initial construction, the degree of generality does serve as a key evaluative factor in a relative sense. Faced with two specific theories, both of which can adequately generate empirical area A, but only one of which can also sufficiently cover empirical area B, philosophers of science would prefer the more general one and it would possess the higher degree of heuristic truth value, assuming everything else is constant. The history of natural science is characterized by less general theories being replaced by more general theories. (Einsteinian relativistic physics replaced Newtonian absolutistic physics essentially because it was/is more general.) Some scientists envision the goal of science to be the eventual development of the most comprehensive theories possible for a given empirical area.

5. The simplicity of the theory. This term is customarily used to describe the size, design, configuration, etc. of the postulate set or set of explanatory statements associated with a theory. Simplicity is inversely related to heuristic truth value. The simpler a theory is, the more heuristic truth value it possesses. Again, this is a situation which seems anti-intuitive, at least in an absolute sense. But consider the case of two theories that adequately explain the same aspect of the descriptive level of analysis. Assuming everything else is constant, the simpler of the two theories is preferred and is assigned a higher degree of heuristic truth value. Expressed from a slightly different angle, the individual theoretical statement in the simpler of the two theories is more powerful (it generates more) than the individual theoretical statement in the less simple theory. (The Copernican view of the solar system overthrew the Ptolemaic view of the solar system simply because it was simpler.)

No significance should be attached to the order in which the five factors were presented above. There is no necessary hierarchical relationship among them such that one factor becomes relevant only after a decision has been made with respect to a prior factor. Likewise, it is currently unrealistic to differentially weigh each of the factors and mathematically combine them to calculate an actual global heuristic truth value score. This is not to say that hierarchical or combination models cannot be constructed in the future to perform these tasks. The list of five factors in the current context should be interpreted solely as a representative subsample of the population of factors contributing to the formal acceptance of a theory.

SUMMARY

The purpose of higher order (nondescriptive) interpretation is the generation (usually explanation and/or prediction) of aspects of the descriptive level of analysis or empirical situation (S alone, R alone, or S-R relationships). Deduction is usually characterized as the prescriptive mode for accomplishing this and the axiomatic structure (replete with postulated theoretical constructs and their interrelationships) embodied by a specific higher order interpretation serves as the crucial element of the generation process. Higher order interpretation is so important for learning psychology, the conceptual analysis treats it as a separate unit of analysis. Higher order interpretation can be accomplished through the use of either a theory or a model − i.e., the deductive system underlying a given higher order interpretation can be viewed either as a theory or a model; and a brief review of the four primary differences between a theory and a model constitutes the best way of summarizing the overall macro-theoretical situation.

1. Locus of the creative activity. When a deductive system is used as a theory, it is constructed for the first time in the specific context of the empirical situation it is supposed to generate. When a deductive system is used as a model, it has already been constructed and is currently brought in from some other context or area of application.

2. Manner of representation of the descriptive level. A theory is supposed to be a precise account of exactly how and why the descriptive level is such as it is. A model merely serves as a didactic device (conceptual analogue) to which the empirical situation can be compared for clarification, analysis, etc.

3. Exhaustiveness of representation of the descriptive level. A theory is assumed to be exhaustively descriptive of the empirical phenomenon to be generated. A model is assumed to be only an approximate description of the empirical phenomenon to be generated.

4. Extent of amenability to empirical evaluation. A theory cannot tolerate conflicting empirical evidence which is clearly not in accord with it. A model can tolerate conflicting empirical evidence which is clearly not in accord with it.

Two other aspects of higher order interpretation are worth reviewing.

1. The ultimate source of the deductive system underlying a theory or model is personalistic and the creator of a system has a choice concerning the (a) reality level, (b) area or range of applicability, and (c) existence status with respect to the higher order constructs embodied by the system.

2. The current relevance/viability and historical longevity of a specific higher order interpretive construction is more realistically related to a series of heuristic factors than to its state or extent of empirical evaluation.

7
An Introduction to Learning Theory; The Relationship Between Conditioning and Learning at the Theoretical Level

INTRODUCTION

This chapter has two interrelated purposes: (1) to analyze the nature of the overall macro-theoretical situation as it exists in learning psychology — i.e., the different theoretical approaches to learning, and (2) to relate conditioning to learning at the theoretical level.

OVERVIEW OF LEARNING THEORY

INTRODUCTION

An attempt will be made in this chapter to analyze the topic of learning theory along two different dimensions: (1) what it is supposed to generate and (2) how it actually goes about accomplishing this. These two dimensions are interrelated and have roughly undergone two different historical phases. Prior to 1950, learning constructs were designed to generate the entire area of learning as a whole through the use of very general, comprehensive theories. This can be referred to as the macro-theoretical era of learning psychology. Subsequent to 1950 and continuing into the present, learning constructs were (and are) designed to generate only a very limited area of learning (i.e., a specific learning task or phenomenon, etc.) through the use of highly specific and limited models. This can be referred to as the micro-model era of learning psychology. The next two sections descriptively summarize these two broad historical phases, using the two dimensions as the basis of the organizational structure. Subsequent to the discussion of the macro-theoretical and micro-model approaches (eras), other approaches to learning theory will be derived and a more detailed historical overview of learning theory will be presented.

THE MACRO-THEORETICAL APPROACH TO LEARNING PSYCHOLOGY

What Macro-Theory is Supposed to Generate

Introduction. The best way to introduce the notion of learning macro-theory is by reference to common-sense psychology. The typical layman is a macro-theorist in the sense that he often utters very low-level, semi-theoretical statements that are supposed to be characteristic of the underlying mediating learning process as a whole. For instance: "You learn by living (or by doing)." "A person cannot learn unless he is highly driven." "A person cannot learn unless he experiences satisfaction for his efforts." At this juncture, both the truth value and loose language of the above statements are irrelevant, although it would be easy to put them in hypothesis form employing technical language. The important point about the statements is that the underlying mediating learning process itself serves as the implicit denotation of the word learning.

The professional macro-theorist begins where the layman "leaves off" with the explicit assumption that the most appropriate way to theorize about learning is by regarding it as an absolute, all-pervasive, monolithic concept — i.e., the learning process has a meaning over and above the specific laboratory setting in which it is physicalized and investigated. Learning macro-theory is an explicit attempt to postulate the absolute set of properties underlying the learning process or the absolute set of conditions under which learning occurs. This explicit assumption and/or attempt has at least three major consequences for what learning theory is supposed to generate: (1) It determines just what aspects of the descriptive level of analysis are emphasized. (2) It determines just what constitutes the proper form of learning data (i.e., response measurement, statistical analysis, and learning experimentation). (3) It determines what is considered to be the key set of theoretical questions in learning psychology.

The Descriptive Level of Analysis as Interpreted by
Macro-Learning Theory

Background and initial description. Prior discussion has established the three structural parts of the descriptive level of reality: the input (S) situation, the output (R) situation, and the combined input-output (S-R) situation (i.e., functional relationships). Although every formal macro-theory has provision for all three aspects of the descriptive level of reality, the focal point of the typical macro-theory is the combined (S-R) descriptive situation. A large percentage of the content of a formal macro-theory directly concerns the intermediate process or theoretical construct of learning itself. Also, virtually every major macro-theorist prefers to state the content of his theory primarily in terms of combined S-R theoretical constructs.

More importantly, macro-learning theory explicitly attempts to represent the structure underlying the learning process, while only implicitly attempting to specify the dynamics underlying the learning process. The distinction between structure and dynamics will be explicated presently in the context of a simple example. In effect, macro-learning theory treats the structure of the combined input-output (S-R) situation as the most significant aspect of the descriptive level of analysis. For all practical purposes, macro-learning theory can be formally defined as the use of combined S-R theoretical constructs to generate the structure of the combined input-output (S-R) descriptive situation. Since macro-learning theory leaves the dynamics of the learning process implicit, the significant, viable generations (explanations/predictions) of macro-theory depend almost exclusively on its underlying structure. This fact is so crucial that it must be illustrated in the context of a simple example.

An Example of a Simple Macro-Theory

Description. Suppose a particular macro-learning theory postulates the existence of two theoretical constructs — A and B — as the structural components underlying or mediating the learning process. The two components, A and B, must interact in some fashion to generate learning. Four possible types of interaction exist at the mathematical level: (1) addition, (2) subtraction, (3) multiplication, and (4) division. For many reasons, the assumption of a subtractive or divisive interaction between A and B is not a reasonable one for generating learning. So, let us formally assume that A and B either interact in an additive manner — i.e., $A + B$ — or interact in a multiplicative manner — i.e., $A \times B$.

At the beginning of a learning experiment, each of the structural components is assumed equal to zero. This means that their sum or product is also zero. Functionally, this represents the fact that the subject has not yet acquired the response to be ultimately learned in the experiment and, in effect, is in the unlearned state. Now, as a result of exposure to a learning trial, either one or both of the two structural components is assumed to increment by some amount (i.e., any positive number). As the number of learning trials accumulates, the sum $A + B$ or the product $A \times B$ not only becomes a positive number but also continues to increment at some unspecified rate.

At this point, we must introduce the concept of a learning criterion, C, a positive number which when attained indicates that the subject has learned. Let us suppose that C = F in the context of this example. Thus, when the value of A + B or A x B finally attains the value F after many learning trials, the subject can be described as having learned the required response. Incidentally, the course of learning would be slower and the attainment of the criterion value would occur later in the context of the additive process than under the assumption of a multiplicative process — but this has no effect on the didactic features of the example. For instance, it could be argued that the value of the learning criterion C is always lower (i.e., F is a smaller positive number) in the context of an additive process than in the context of a multiplicative process (i.e., learning criterion value covaries with type of interaction).

So, in summary, the subject is in the unlearned state initially when A + B or A x B = 0 and has finally achieved learning once A + B or A x B has incremented to F and the various values of A + B or A x B during the intervening learning trials represent the learning process.

Interpretation: Structure versus dynamics. Basically, what does this simple macro-theory predict? It merely predicts that the subject will eventually learn, given enough learning trials. The reason the subject learns is because the value of A + B or A x B must eventually increment to F. The learning process is represented by the cumulative, additive interaction or cumulative, multiplicative interaction of two theoretical structural components. But the subject learns because of the inherent structure of the theory, not because of the dynamics implicit in the theory. This is because the prediction that the subject will eventually learn is completely independent of the postulation of any exact details of the incrementing process and the specific types of interaction relating the structural components A and B.

Examples of exact details of the incrementing process include the following:

1) which particular component (A or B or both) increments on any one learning trial;

2) the value of the increment on each learning trial;

3) whether the increment on each trial is a constant or varying value; and

4) whether the two components A and B are differentially weighted. (Above they are implicitly weighted equally — each has a coefficient value of one.)

Assuming that the additive and multiplicative processes exhaust the reasonable set of interactions that can relate the two theoretical components underlying or mediating the learning process, attainment of eventual learning is guaranteed (predicted) regardless of the specific relationship assumed between A and B. It makes no difference how A and B dynamically interact — learning is guaranteed in either case.

The full significance of the structure in macro-learning theory will become apparent over the next two subsections.

The form of learning data generated by macro-learning theory.

Introduction. The way in which a response class is measured, the way in which the response data is organized and statistically analyzed, as well as the way in which the experiment is designed and physically conducted depend in large part on the type of theory (i.e., prediction) that is being evaluated by the experiment. The fact that macro-learning theory primarily involves structural predictions about the intervening learning process basically determines the form of the learning data generated by the typical macro-learning theory experiment. Although the topics of statistical analysis and experimental design have not been formally discussed in the text, summary statements can be presented to give the general flavor of the form of learning data in the context of macro-learning theory experimentation.

Response measurement. Macro-learning theory typically regards all the different response measures discussed in Chapter 3 as being equivalent. For the macro-theorist, it ostensibly makes no difference how a particular response class is measured in an experiment because the measurable characteristics of a learned response are incidental to the learning process. Macro-theory uses such primitive R constructs that it cannot assign any differential significance or importance to the different response measures in any meaningful way. More specifically, in the context of macro-theory, one does not need a different theory to account for learned changes in each kind of response measure. Learned changes in all the different measurable characteristics of a response should be derivable from the same basic set of macro-theoretical statements. This has the effect of allowing mere physical convenience or the availability of specific kinds of recording apparati to dictate what the only or primary response measure(s) is (are) going to be in any specific macro-theory experiment.

Statistical analysis of response data. Recall from Chapter 4 that most learned changes in behavior involve a transition from one state (S_1) to another state (S_2). (With reference to the illustrative simple macro-theory presented above, A + B or A x B = 0 corresponds to S_1 and A + B or A x B = F corresponds to S_2.) Now, macro-learning theory is primarily concerned with measuring S_2 and deemphasizes the measurement of S_1 and the quantitative details of the transition from S_1 to S_2. Remember all that macro-theory can meaningfully predict is that the transition to S_2 ultimately occurs, not any specific details of the transition process itself. So the response data is usually statistically analyzed to quantify different aspects of the state S_2 — i.e., the number of trials or amount of time required to achieve S_2 (i.e., to learn), the strength of S_2 once achieved (i.e., the strength of the learned response at asymptote), etc.

The learning curve itself (i.e., the dynamics of the transition from S_1 to S_2) is frequently constructed — but only its general shape is predictable from macro-theory. Even in multiple response situations, where the learned response is the correct or appropriate response, macro-theory cannot predict the trial-by-trial appearance of the various response classes until the correct response occurs 100% of the time – so again basic quantification is only made of the state S_2.

Stated from a different angle, macro-theory only attempts to summarize how a specific subject performs in a learning experiment – i.e., how long it took him to learn, the extent of learning once achieved, etc. Trial-by-trial quantification of the actual development of the learned response is not a useful calculation because it cannot be predicted. As we shall soon see, this concern with the end state S_2 is reflected in the structure of the typical macro-learning theory experiment.

Learning experimentation. Since only some kind of summary statistic value is typically assignable to a subject to represent his performance in a macro-theory learning experiment, comparison among subjects (or groups of subjects) only has meaning if they have learned under a different set of input conditions. The typical macro-theory learning experiment must vary the conditions of learning or variables associated with the conditions of learning – i.e., it must employ a between-group experimental design such that each group of subjects is exposed to the learning task under a different level of the independent variable, whatever it is. In this context, macro-learning theory can then predict the rank order of occurrence of learning attainment among the individual groups. Procedurally, all that must be calculated and statistically compared at the level of response data is the mean number (and variability) of the trials to learning criterion of each group (an aspect of S_2).

For illustrative purposes, let us suppose that a particular macro-theorist is interested in the effects of the amount of reinforcement that is presented following the occurrence of a member of the response class of interest on the process of learning that response class. Continuing the simple macro-theory example from before, the theorist might postulate that the amount of reinforcement per response occurrence determines the size of the increment in A or B or both on each learning trial. An obvious prediction from this assumption is that the speed of reaching the learning criterion will be positively related to the amount of reinforcement per response. But this prediction cannot be evaluated in the context of only one group of subjects exposed to only one value of amount of reinforcement per response. It would require a minimum of two groups of subjects, each one of which is exposed to a different level of amount of reinforcement per response (i.e., small, medium, or large, etc.), so that their respective mean time or trials to learning criterion can be statistically compared.

The key set of theoretical questions in the context of macro-learning theory

Introduction. Macro-learning theorists have generated countless theoretical questions about the nature of the underlying learning process. Five basic questions stand out from the rest because they are the concern of all macro-learning theorists and can be interpreted as constituting the key set of theoretical questions. (No formal presentation will be made here of the numerous theoretical questions which are unique to a specific macro-theory or which are associated with at most two or three macro-theories.) The initial two questions directly concern reinforcement: its nature and its role in learning. The third question is related to the analytical units or building blocks which underlie the learning process — i.e., the nature of the structure underlying learning. The fourth question deals with the theoretical relationship between conditioning and learning and the theoretical relationship between classical and instrumental conditioning. The fifth question covers the essential conditions under which learning occurs.

The five questions. The key theoretical questions specifically are as follows.

1. What is the theoretical mechanism(s) underlying the procedural effects of reinforcement? Why does reinforced practice allow or cause permanent changes in the measurable characteristics of a response class? Every major macro-learning theorist has his own theory or interpretation of reinforcement and how a particular macro-theorist conceptualizes reinforcement at the theoretical level goes a long way in determining how he conceptualizes the nature of the underlying learning process itself.

2. Is reinforcement in the theoretical sense necessary for learning? Is the activation of the theoretical mechanism underlying the procedural effects of reinforcement necessary for a response to be learned? Although this is overtly a YES or NO answer kind of question, how a particular macro-theorist responds to it is typically not independent of the mechanism which he postulates to account for the procedural effects of reinforcement.

These two questions concerning the nature and role of reinforcement at the theoretical level are so crucial that they will comprise a major portion of Chapter 9 on the "concept of reinforcement."

3. What is learned in any specific learning situation at the theoretical level or what is the nature of the structure underlying learning? This query reduces to two more basic questions: (a) what are the ultimate components underlying the learned response, and (b) what is the nature of the connections which relate the individual components together? Since this theoretical question has lost much of its historical relevance — i.e., it has been virtually reduced to a question of semantics or "verbal gymnastics" — it will not be formally treated by a separate chapter; but variants of it will appear time and again throughout the remainder of the text.

4. What is the relationship between conditioning and learning at the theoretical level; and what is the relationship between classical conditioning and instrumental conditioning at the theoretical level? (Chapter 4 distinguished

between learning and conditioning only in a cursory manner and distinguished between classical and instrumental conditioning merely at the operational level.) This set of questions is more abstract and "philosophical" than the others. The questions are interrelated and are important because the way in which a particular macro-learning theorist answers them primarily determines the intended degree of generality or range of applicability of his particular learning theory. The range of answers put forth by various macro-theorists is quite extensive. An attempt will be made later in the chapter to create a classification system in terms of which any given macro-theoretical approach to these questions is resolvable.

5. What is the more-or-less absolute set of theoretical input conditions necessary for learning? This question is related to number two; but, the content of that question merely specifies one presumed condition necessary for learning – namely, the occurrence of reinforcement in the theoretical sense. The denotative content of this question can be interpreted as meaning that there are more. Sometimes this question is posed in terms of principles. What constitutes the fundamental principles of learning at the theoretical level? This question taps the very essence of macro-learning theory – namely, the generation of the underlying learning process. But, unfortunately, very few macro-learning theorists even attempt to define or interpret what this question explicitly means or entails. So the question is not consistently dealt with across the wide spectrum of macro-theorists. The next subsection will include a minimal (consistent) interpretation of this question and present some representative answers in the context of deriving the major types of macro-learning theory.

How Macro-Theory Accomplishes its Generation Objectives

Introduction. Ideally, we should examine in detail just how the macro-theoretical approach to learning actually accomplishes its generation objectives by conducting a representative sampling of specific macro-learning theorists and their approaches to learning theory. But a detailed presentation of the substantive content of the most influential classical theories of learning would be equivalent to cycling through a virtual textbook on classical learning theory, a task which extends far beyond the confines of a general conceptual analysis of learning psychology.

Pursuant to the primary objective of the text, an acceptable, compromise course of action to follow would be the development of a conceptual framework by which virtually all the major macro-learning theories can be generated. In effect, a viable classification system must be constructed in terms of which any macro-theory of learning can be resolved. The content of this classification system can then be used as the input for other kinds of analyses in the remainder of the book.

Let us call such a classification system a generative system. The fundamental problem associated with such a generative system relates to how much resolvability the system should possess. The notion of resolvability is essentially equivalent to that of discriminability. How discriminable should the generative system be, as a "measuring" or classification device, for distinguishing between the major macro-theories of learning? The two ends of the resolvability continuum — no resolvability and complete resolvability — are uninteresting cases. A generative system which would distinguish between no macro-learning theories — i.e., assign them all to the same category — is no resolving system at all; a generative system which would distinguish between every macro-learning theory — i.e., assign each one to its own unique category — would require a description of virtually the entire content of each theory. Rather, some intermediate degree of resolvability would constitute a highly desirable goal — i.e., some compromise value which would divide up all the macro-theories in existence into a dozen or so rather broad categories of theories that have historical or functional significance. The author's attempt to construct such a generative system follows.

A Generative System for the Macro-Theories of Learning Psychology

Introduction. A generative system can be characterized as a complex decision structure which, when applied to a specific input, "analyzes" the input and assigns it to a specific output category. In the context of macro-learning theory, any given input instance must be one of N different macro-learning theories, the output structure must be composed of linearly independent categories each of which represents a specific type of learning theory, and the generative system itself must consist of an internal decision structure involving analytical dimensions of relevance to learning theory.

The validity of the generative system depends almost wholly on the nature of the postulated internal decision structure. The input is already empirically given — it is the population of macro-learning theories already created. A specific output category is simply the termination point of a specific pathway through the network of internal structure and as such the only problem involved is that of naming the category — and this can usually be done in terms of a major nodal point of the internal structure. So, the pivotal aspect of a generative system for macro-learning theory is its postulated internal decision structure.

The Internal Decision Structure

Introduction. For all practical purposes, the internal decision structure can be regarded as a complex decision tree, consisting of hierarchically interrelated nodal points which represent significant analytical dimensions for learning theory and branches extending from each nodal point which exhaustively specify the category values associated with each analytical dimension. Refer to Fig. 7-1 or Fig. 7-2 at this point for a physical representation of a decision tree structure with nodal points and category branches. The nature of a generative system for macro-learning theory largely depends upon the total number (and denotations) of analytical dimensions that is used, the number of category values associated with each analytical dimension, and the specific hierarchical order in which the analytical dimensions appear. The specific decision structure to be described below employs five hierarchically ordered nodal points (analytical dimensions), each of which is assumed divisible into at most three categories (binary- or ternary-valued categories).

The five analytical dimensions and their associated values.
1. The method of construction of the macro-theory. Chapter 6 has already established this as essentially a binary-valued dimension: (a) a prescriptive, deductive category, and (b) a descriptive, functional category.
2. The level of reality of the primary theoretical constructs of the macro-theory. This has also been previously characterized in Chapter 6 as a two-category dimension: (a) the constructive, behavioral level, and (b) the reductive, physiological level.
3. The denotative reference of the primary theoretical constructs of the macro-theory. This dimension specifies just what kind of theoretical constructs are assumed to underlie the learning process. This has previously been established as a ternary-valued dimension in Chapter 6: (a) combined input-output construct, (b) input construct, and (c) output construct.
4. The units of learning postulated by the macro-theory. This dimension absorbs the essential content of the third question of the set of key theoretical questions as discussed in the immediately preceding subsection. It will by and large be treated as a binary-valued dimension, but the content (meaning) of the specific categories will not be independent of the categories associated with the third analytical dimension.
5. The fundamental principles of learning postulated by the macro-theory. This dimension is related to the second and fifth questions of the key theoretical set discussed in the prior subsection. Only a minimal interpretation of this dimension will be made, so only two fundamental principles of learning will be covered by the decision structure — namely, contiguity and effect. In essence, each of these principles operates as a separate subdimension and each one is binary-valued: (a) YES, the theory uses the principle; or (b) NO, the theory does not use the principle. Contiguity and effect were discussed as operational terms in the second chapter; but, they are used in a theoretical sense here. Contiguity means different things for different theorists but essentially refers to the crucial

arrangement of environmental events necessary for learning to occur. Effect is essentially a one-word equivalent for the content of the second key theoretical question: "Is reinforcement in the theoretical sense necessary for learning?" More will be said about contiguity and effect, as theoretical terms, in Chapter 9.

The denotation of the five dimensions and their hierarchical order. The initial three analytical dimensions use concepts and distinctions which can be regarded as abstract properties of a theory per se, independent of the fact that the theory at issue is a macro-theory of learning, and were discussed in detail as integral parts of Chapter 6. The last two analytical dimensions derive from the set of key theoretical questions of macro-theory and are necessary to make the decision structure uniquely applicable to classical learning theory. Although this specific set of five analytical dimensions constitutes only a small sample of the total population of analytical dimensions which could be used in the decision structure, it does adequately generate the traditional, historically relevant types of macro-learning theory.

The order in which the five analytical dimensions will appear in the decision structure corresponds to the sequence in which they were initially introduced above. It seems to be the most "natural" or "logical" order for this specific set of analytical dimensions — i.e., the decision structure proceeds from general, abstract, strictly theory-related analytical dimensions to more specific, psychologically relevant analytical dimensions.

A physical representation of the internal decision structure. Figure 7-1 presents a structural diagram of the generative system in such a way as to emphasize the content of the internal decision structure. In order to describe just how the diagram should be interpreted, let us follow the course of a typical macro-learning theory through the decision system. The basic processing pattern is such that the theory is evaluated on each successive dimension and is shunted down one of the branches extending from each of the successive evaluative modal points (small circles). Eventually, the theory is "deposited" into one of the terminal output categories.

The first dimension on which the theory is evaluated is its method of construction. More than likely, it will be sent down the descriptive, functional branch. Then it is evaluated with respect to the level of reality of its primary theoretical constructs and will more than likely be shunted down the constructive, behavioral path. So few macro-theories of learning are seriously postulated at the reductive, physiological level that further continuation on the path is only represented by a symbolic dotted-line arrow. (The author can only think of two serious physiologically stated macro-theories of learning: Pavlov's approach to learning and Hebb's approach to memory.)

Evaluation at the third dimension will send the theory down either of the first two paths, although the first path has a higher probability of occurrence associated with it. Most classical, macro-learning theories employ combined input-output theoretical constructs to generate the learning process. The output branch is so rare that the physical representation again terminates with

INPUT: A SPECIFIC, CLASSICAL MACRO-LEARNING THEORY

THE INTERNAL DECISION STRUCTURE: The Hierarchical, Analytical Dimensions

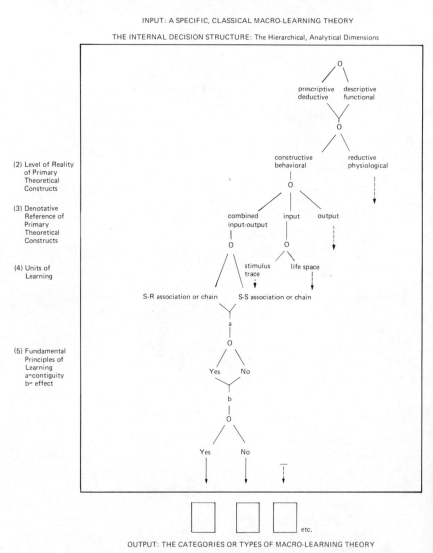

OUTPUT: THE CATEGORIES OR TYPES OF MACRO-LEARNING THEORY

Fig. 7-1. A Generative System for Macro-Learning Theory

a symbolic dotted-line arrow. (There is one macro-theoretical approach which could conceivably be shunted down this path — the micromolar response approach of Logan, who is a neo-Hullian.)

The third dimension is particularly significant because it delimits the possible values which the theory can assume on the succeeding dimension, that of units of learning. If the theory came down the input branch, then two appropriate categories for the units of learning would be (1) stimulus (memory) traces and (2) the life space. If the stimulus (memory) trace branch were extended to an output category it would yield the Gestalt approach to learning, as popularized by Wertheimer, Koffka, and Köhler. If the life space branch were extended to an output category it would yield the field theory approach characteristic of Lewin. Assuming that the theory is more likely to be coming down the combined input-output path, then the two traditional categories for the units of learning would be (1) S-R association (habit) and (2) S-S association (expectancy, hypothesis, cognitive map, etc.). This dichotomy between S-R learning theory and cognitive learning theory represents a distinction of primary historical importance.

The set of fundamental principles of learning is equally applicable to both the S-R and S-S approaches to learning. So, regardless of which units of learning branch the theory travels down, it will then be evaluated by the same minimally interpreted set of fundamental principles of learning. The probability is virtually one that it will be shunted down the YES branch on the contiguity subdimension. Finally, the probability that it will be sent down the YES path on the effect subdimension is about one-half.

Now, at this point, depending upon the exact route taken through the decision tree, the theory will fall into an output category box — i.e., it will be classified as to type. The meaning and significance of the output categories associated with the branches extending from the combined input-output category will be detailed in a later section because they in effect constitute the major types of classical macro-learning theory.

The nature of the input: The possibility of recycling through the internal decision structure. Although it has been previously stated that a specific macro-learning theory constitutes any given instance of input, it should not be inferred that a specific theory can only be evaluated by the decision structure once or a specific theorist can only be evaluated by the decision structure once.

A given theorist can change his basic theoretical formulation over time and successive evaluations can be performed and more than likely they will be deposited in different output categories. The possibility of successive recyclings of a specific theorist's macro-theory provides a mechanism for generating a theorist's "old" and "new" theories or for generating the distinct historical phases in the development of his theory.

A given theorist can have a different macro-theory for different subareas of learning (e.g., classical conditioning, instrumental conditioning, verbal learning, etc.) at the same moment in time. These must be individually evaluated and more than likely will be deposited in different output categories.

The possibility of multicyclings associated with a specific theorist is the way in which the generative system represents the analytical dimension of "generality" of the macro-theory. Not all macro-learning theorists construct a theory which is supposed to seriously generate the whole gamut of learning tasks and phenomena. Not all macro-learning theorists assume that the underlying learning process is the same for every kind of learning task or procedure. So, the number of times a specific theorist must be cycled through the decision structure is related to the generality of his approach to learning.

The generality of a theory in the context of the macro-theoretical approach to learning: Uniprocess versus multiprocess macro-theories. The notion of generality of a theory is usually discussed with different terminology in the context of macro-learning theory. Most macro-learning theorists intend their formulations to have complete generality – i.e., to account for the underlying learning process regardless of the specific learning task or phenomenon involved. These macro-theorists are usually called single process or uniprocess theorists. But, there is an appreciable number of macro-theorists who do not intend their formulations to possess complete generality – i.e., there are at least two kinds of learning at the level of underlying process. These macro-theorists are called multiprocess theorists, of which duoprocess is by far the most frequently occurring case. So, in effect, the current generative system represents the distinction between uniprocess and multiprocess macro-theories by allowing the possiblity of recycling through its internal decision structure.

The Output Structure

The total number of output categories. Using some assumptions that have not been made explicit in presenting the physical diagram of the internal structure, the decision tree will generate 96 output categories. Although this is appreciably more than the dozen or so previously specified as desirable, note that not all the 96 categories will be filled. Only about eight output categories will have any appreciable accumulation of specific theories and/or theorists; and, as implied in the physical diagram of the internal decision structure, those with the most accumulation appear under the combined input-output category value.

The major types of classical macro-learning theory. Refer to Fig. 7-2, which represents the area under the combined input-output category in microscopic detail. The branches extending from the combined input-output category are presented as a series of mutually exclusive pathways so that each output category is associated with a unique route through the decision structure. This is necessary for the full denotative significance and meaning of each output category to be unambiguously indicated. The category boxes are numbered one through eight from left to right.

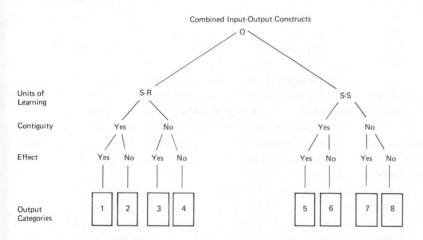

Fig. 7-2. The Major Types or Categories of Classical Macro-Learning Theory

Category numbers 3, 4, 7, and 8 will be empty because no macro-theorist making primary use of combined constructs denies contiguity as a fundamental principle underlying the learning process. Category number 5 will also be empty because no cognitive theorist bases his overall approach on the necessity of effect as a fundamental learning principle. This leaves categories 1, 2, and 6 as the major summary categories of classical macro-learning theory.

Each of the eight routes in Fig. 7-2 have passed through the constructive, behavioral value on the level of reality of theoretical constructs dimension. But, no exclusive univalue shunting through of the method of construction dimension can be assumed. Therefore, it should be realized that output categories 1, 2, and 6 can be terminations associated with either prescriptively or descriptively constructed theory. This does not lead to any severe classification problems because only one major classical macro-theory of learning can be regarded as even approaching categorization as a prescriptive, deductive theory.

So, disregarding the dimension of method of construction, there are three predominant types of classical macro-learning theory:

Category 1: Constructive, S-R, effect theory.

Category 2: Constructive, S-R, contiguity theory.

Category 6: Constructive, cognitive, contiguity theory.

These three types of classical macro-learning theory will be put in greater perspective when they serve as the necessary input into various conceptual analyses which will appear throughout the remainder of the text. A later section of the current chapter relates them to the issue of the theoretical relationship between conditioning and learning. Chapter 8 analyzes their methodological consequences for learning psychology. Chapter 9 relates them to the theoretical issues of the nature and role of reinforcement.

There follows a representative sampling of the theorists associated with each of these three types of macro-theory.

Macro-theorists associated with category 1: Hull (deductive approach), Spence (classical conditioning), Mowrer (old, instrumental conditioning), Thorndike (instrumental conditioning), Konorski, Miller (instrumental conditioning).

Macro-theorists associated with category 2: Miller (classical conditioning), Spence (instrumental conditioning), Mowrer (old, classical conditioning), Mowrer (new), Thorndike (classical conditioning), Guthrie, Sheffield, Watson, Seward, Osgood, Melton, Postman, Underwood.

Macro-theorists associated with category 6: Tolman, Krech, Harlow.

Chapter 9 will focus on how the specific macro-theoretical approaches of Hull, Guthrie, and Tolman interpret the S-R-S response-contingent reinforcement operation.

THE MICRO-MODEL APPROACH TO LEARNING PSYCHOLOGY

What a Micro-Model is Supposed to Generate

Introduction. Chapter 6 established the fact that an aspect of the descriptive level of analysis is modeled by stating its essential similarity to some other object, event, etc. in the natural world and postulating that the deductive system which generates the other object, event, etc. also underlies that aspect of the descriptive level of analysis. A model is a deductive system brought in from another area (oftentimes it was a theory originally constructed to generate that other area) in order to generate an aspect of the descriptive level of analysis of current concern. (Chapter 6 exemplified this by modeling the human brain in terms of the deductive system underlying the computer.)

Since an analogy must be drawn between the model and the thing to be modeled, the primary objective of the macro-theoretical approach — accounting for the underlying learning process — cannot transfer over to the micro-model approach. There is simply no one reference task or phenomenon which can be used to represent all learning situations and thus serve as the specific aspect of the descriptive level of analysis to be modeled. So micro-modelers make no pretense about generating a monolithic account of the underlying learning process. Rather, their focus of concern is the specific learning task, extinction task, or learning phenomenon itself. Their primary objective is to model a specific learning or extinction task or a specific learning phenomenon. Different micro-models are even constructed for the same generic task or phenomenon depending upon how it is explicitly investigated in the lab.

To prevent the development of some conceptual confusion later on, it should be pointed out that a micro-model can actually be constructed by a modeler for the first time and need not literally be preconstructed and brought in from another area. The principle behind modeling remains the same — only a temporal reversal in the order of events occurs. A specific learning experiment is still assumed to be similar to some other aspect of the natural world and the latter serves as a model for the former. It is just that the deductive system underlying the other aspect of the natural world has not been made explicit or been constructed yet. So the micro-modeler himself constructs the deductive system for the first time and refers to it as the model for the learning experiment. Thus, an analogy is still drawn and the nature of the analogy still determines the content of the model (deductive system). (Otherwise the deductive system would be a theory!)

The functional or pragmatic value associated with micro-modeling derives from the fact that if a specific learning experiment has been modeled "correctly," the values of one or more of the measurable characteristics of the learned response class generated in the experiment are predicted by the model — i.e., the "correct" model makes predictions which later agree with or "fit" the response data obtained in the experiment. Since a macro-theory was previously characterized as performing the same function, it must be realized that the nature of the predictions and response data is vastly different in the context of a micro-model. To see exactly how the micro-model approach differs from macro-theory, let us analyze micro-models along the same three dimensions: (1) the aspects of the descriptive level of analysis which are emphasized, (2) the proper form of learning data, and (3) the notion of a key set of theoretical questions.

The Descriptive Level of Analysis as Interpreted by
the Micro-Model Approach to Learning Psychology

Background and initial description. A micro-modeler does not profess an intrinsic interest in any one of the three structural aspects of the descriptive level of analysis per se. The descriptive level of analysis is never considered independent of the specific learning task or experiment which the psychologist is attempting to model. A specific modeler will focus on whatever aspect of the descriptive level he considers most appropriate to model in order to predict the response data obtained in the experiment. More often than not it is not the combined input-output descriptive situation, but rather the descriptive input situation or the descriptive output situation. The combined input-output descriptive situation can be of interest and modeled — but the modeling of the underlying learning process in this context is strictly experiment- or task-specific. Recall that macro-theory was not particularly concerned with theorizing about the descriptive input situation or the descriptive output situation per se. Many of the micro-models of learning contain explicit, if not elaborate, interpretations of the stimulus or response.

Correlative with the micro-model deemphasis of the combined input-output descriptive situation is its increased frequency of use of input and output theoretical constructs. The best way to model the descriptive input situation is with an input theoretical construct and the best way to model the descriptive output situation is with an output theoretical construct; but, the micro-model approach even models the combined input-output descriptive situation associated with a specific learning task or experiment with theoretical input and output constructs. This is probably a reflection of the fact that the aspect of the descriptive level of analysis which tends to be "more constant" across different learning tasks or experiments is the descriptive stimulus situation or the descriptive response situation, not the descriptive combined situation (i.e., the learning process underlying it).

For macro-theory, providing a theoretical interpretation of the structure underlying the combined input-output descriptive situation constituted an end in itself and the later evaluation of the theoretical attempt was somewhat incidental; on the other hand, the modeling of any one of the three aspects of the descriptive level of analysis by a micro-modeler is not an end in itself. A model, unlike a theory, is not supposed to be an account of the actual structure underlying the descriptive level. The modeling of an aspect of the descriptive level of analysis has instrumental value only — it is the means by which the response data obtained in the experiment is predicted. So, a micro-model can be more formally characterized as a predictive device which just incidentally represents one or more aspects of the descriptive level of analysis.

Since a micro-model does not emphasize any one of the aspects of the descriptive level of analysis independent of the specific experimental learning situation it is applied to and further since it does not even provide an account of the actual structure underlying the aspect(s) of the descriptive level of analysis that it does model, we must analyze the nature of the predictions the typical micro-model makes in order to establish why micro-models are constructed in the first place. The deductive system encompassed by a model is so detailed and specific that it can generate the trial-by-trial or moment-to-moment variability of the response data yielded by the experiment. Contrasted with the macro-theoretical approach, the predictions of a micro-model are not exclusively determined by the structure of the model. The significant predictions of a micro-model are dynamic in nature, usually derived with the use of one or more predictive math equations. Just as we did in the case of macro-learning theory, let us illustrate the above statement with a rather simple example.

An example of a simple micro-model. We shall basically model the input situation in order to predict the learned response data. Let us assume that the input situation is analogous to a barrel, which contains N - 1 white balls and one black ball, from which an organism can draw one ball at a time with replacement, the sampling process ending once the black ball is drawn.

Assuming that each of the N balls has an equiprobability of being chosen on any one draw, the probability of various events can easily be stated. The probability of choosing a white ball on any one draw is $\frac{N-1}{N}$, while the probability of choosing a black ball on any one draw is $\frac{1}{N}$. The probability that the black ball has not been chosen by draw number k is $(1 - \frac{1}{N})^{k-1}$. The probability that the black ball will be chosen on draw number k for the first time is $\frac{1}{N}(1 - \frac{1}{N})^{k-1}$.

Now we are in the learning micro-model business if we set up some correspondences between the process of sampling from this barrel and what the subject does during a learning experiment. Let us assume that the subject is exposed to a stimulus input situation interpreted as a stimulus population composed of N elements and that at the beginning of each learning trial the subject selects a sample of size one (i.e., one element) from the population. There are two kinds of elements: N - 1 elements which do not lead to learning (nonlearning elements) and one element which does lead to learning (the learning element). The subject is assumed to sample with replacement so that if a nonlearning element is chosen on a trial it is returned to the population at the end of the trial. (This way the size of the population stays constant over trials and makes predictions easier.) Sampling from the population continues over successive trials until the subject chooses the learning element, after which no additional samplings need be made, although successive learning trials may still be run. The selection of the learning element on a particular trial is interpreted as the moment in time when the subject actually learns the response to be acquired.

Again assuming that each of the N elements has an equiprobability of being selected on any one trial, the probability of various events can easily be stated. The probability of choosing a nonlearning element on any one trial is $\frac{N-1}{N}$, while the probability of choosing the learning element on any one trial is $\frac{1}{N}$. The probability that the subject has not learned by trial number k is $(1 - \frac{1}{N})^{k-1}$. The probability that the subject learns on trial k is $\frac{1}{N}(1 - \frac{1}{N})^{k-1}$.

The content of the above analogy (that the subject behaves during the learning experiment as if he were successively drawing balls from a barrel) is still incomplete for predicting the overt (obtained) response data. Specifically, some response rule axioms must be postulated so that the underlying sampling process can be tied down to the actual response data itself. So, let us assume that when a white ball is chosen, the organism says "gee whiz" with probability g and says "shucks" with probability 1 - g and that when a black ball is chosen, the organism says "gee whiz" with probability one and that the content of any further vocal emissions following the initial draw of the black ball is "gee whiz" with probability one.

Analogously, in the context of a learning experiment, if the subject selects a nonlearning element on a trial, the probability of occurrence of the learned response or correct response on that trial is g and the probability of occurrence of any other response on that trial is 1 - g; likewise if the subject selects the learning element on a trial, the probability of occurrence of the learned response or correct response on that trial is one; and the probability of occurrence of the learned response or correct response is one on any trial following the trial on which the learning element was selected.

We are now in a position to state the probability of occurrence of many different response events, of which only two will be presented here.

1. The probability of occurrence of the learned response or the correct response on trial k. This is functionally a "learning curve." It is equivalent to one minus the probability of occurrence of any other response on trial k. The probability of occurrence of any other response on trial k is $(1 - g)(1 - \frac{1}{N})^k$.

So the probability of occurrence of the learned response or the correct response on trial k is $1 - (1 - g)(1 - \frac{1}{N})^k$.

2. The probability that trial k is the trial of last error (i.e., the trial of last occurrence of any other response). This is equal to the probability of occurrence of any other response on trial k multiplied by the probability that no error response ever follows. So the probability that trial k is the trial of last error is
$$(1 - g)(1 - \tfrac{1}{N})^k \; \tfrac{1}{N} \left(\frac{1}{1 - g(1 - \frac{1}{N})} \right) .$$

Each of the above predictive equations is really the equation of a (different) probability distribution and is technically referred to as a "statistic." So the learning curve and the trial of last error (TLE) are statistics. As such, they each possess a mean and variance, although the exact formulae for such will not be presented here.

The importance of these equations lies in the fact that once the parameters are given specific values they can be used to attempt to predict the values of the corresponding statistics in the actual response data. The parameters are g and $\frac{1}{N}$ (or simply N); g must be some probability value bounded by 0 and 1: $0 < g < 1$. If g were 0, the learned response or correct response would not occur prior to selection of the learning element; if g were 1, the learned response or correct response would occur on every trial of the experiment. N can be practically any finite number greater than one and less than infinity: $1 < N < \infty$. If N were 1, all learning would occur on the first trial of the experiment; if N were ∞, functionally learning would never occur. The exact values which are given to g and N depend on many factors. Usually they are estimated from the data. Let us assume that g has been estimated to be .5 in value and N has been estimated to be equal to 4. Then, the two predictive equations become

(1) Learning Curve: $1 - (.5)(.75)^k$.

(2) TLE: $(.5)(.75)^k(.25) \left(\dfrac{1}{1 - (.5)(.75)} \right) = (.2)(.75)^k$.

Now, if the successive values of k were substituted in the equations (i.e., k = 1, 2, 3, 4, 5, etc.) the actual predicted probability distributions would be generated. (The reader is invited to generate the predicted distributions himself not only with the parameter values as currently given but also with any other set of reasonable parameter values to see exactly how the predictions will vary with the presumed parameter values.) The crucial part comes in "comparing" the predicted probability distributions with the obtained probability distributions. The latter are calculated from the response data actually yielded by the experiment. In the context of this example, it would merely be a matter of calculating the empirical frequency of learned or correct response occurrences across trials and the empirical frequency of trials of last error occurrences. By "comparing" is meant statistical comparison – the use of inferential statistics. The inferential statistical test itself actually decides whether the predicted distributions actually "fit" the obtained distributions.

The example in perspective. This simple example illustrates quite nicely what is meant by modeling of a learning experiment in order to predict certain aspects of the obtained response data. No one seriously believes that the subject is drawing balls from a barrel over the course of the learning session; but if he is assumed to be behaving as if he were drawing balls from a barrel (interpreted as sampling elements from the stimulus population), then specific predictions about obtained response events can be made. These predictions were previously characterized as dynamic in nature, being generated with the use of one or more predictive equations. They are dynamic because the specific predictions generated by the equations depend upon the exact values assigned to the parameters and any other way of characterizing the sampling process (i.e., without replacement or without equiprobability of sampling) or any other way of stating the response rule axioms (i.e., g is equal to 0 or 1 or an error response could be emitted following selection of the learning element) would yield a vastly different set of predictions.

Recall that the predictions made by the simple macro-learning theory example did not depend upon any specific values of or details concerning the two structural theoretical constructs and did not really depend on the exact nature of the interaction between the two theoretical constructs. These predictions were termed structural predictions and did not account for trial-to-trial variability in actual response data. Structural predictions are only low-level predictions, such as the subject eventually must learn, the speed of learning is related to the amount of reinforcement per trial (response), etc. Micro-models also yield structural predictions. For instance, the current sampling model does predict that the subject eventually must learn — i.e., the probability that the subject eventually samples the learning element is one. Because:

$$\frac{1}{N} + \frac{1}{N}(1 - \frac{1}{N}) + \frac{1}{N}(1 - \frac{1}{N})^2 + \frac{1}{N}(1 - \frac{1}{N})^3 + \ldots + \frac{1}{N}(1 - \frac{1}{N})^k$$

goes to one as k approaches infinity. But the focal point of micro-models is that they are capable of making dynamic predictions over and above mere low-level structural predictions.

The Form of Learning Data Generated by the Micro-Model Approach to Learning

Introduction. Just as in the case of macro-learning theory, the way in which a response class is measured, the way in which the response data is organized and statistically analyzed, as well as the way in which the experiment is designed and physically conducted depend in large part on the type of prediction which is being evaluated by the experiment. The fact that micro-models of learning primarily involve dynamic predictions of the trial-to-trial or moment-to-moment response events basically determines the form of the learning data generated by the typical micro-model learning experiment. The following comments will present the general flavor of the form of learning data in the context of micro-model learning experimentation.

Response measurement. Since the primary function of a micro-learning model is to predict the change in one or more of the measurable characteristics of a response class, the way in which the learned response is measured in an experiment is of crucial importance. The only measurable characteristics of a response actually worth recording in a specific experiment are those which the micro-model can predict. For instance, refer back to the simple model just presented. The simple model was stated in such a way that it can only predict the probability of occurrence of response events, either of the learned response (correct response) or other responses. The model was only designed to generate the digital aspects of the learned response. The analogical characteristics — latency, magnitude, shape, etc. — are beyond the bounds of the model and would not be recorded in an experiment designed to test the appropriateness of the model. In order for the simple model to predict one or more of the analogical measurement characteristics of the learned response, it must be supplemented by additional response axioms or theoretical response constructs.

So, the micro-model approach to learning does not treat all the different response measures discussed in Chapter 3 as ipso facto equivalent. The only condition under which they could be regarded as equivalent (i.e., mutually substitutable) is when the micro-model can generate them from the same set of underlying assumptions (i.e., deductive system). The author knows of no current micro-model of learning which possesses this property. Most micro-models (90%-95%) are explicitly designed to generate only the digital response characteristic of occurrence. In fact, if the model is designed to generate one or more analogical aspects of the learned response, this is usually stated in the title of the model itself — e.g., X's model for the latency of classically conditioned responses.

Statistical analysis of response data. Recall from Chapter 4 that most learned changes in behavior involve a transition from one state (S_1) to another state (S_2). (With reference to the illustrative micro-model just presented, S_1 corresponds to any trial during which a nonlearning element is sampled and S_2 corresponds to the trial on which the learning element is sampled.) Unlike macro-theory, the micro-model approach is primarily concerned with the quantitative details of the transition from S_1 to S_2 and not with measuring S_2 per se. The primary objective of the micro-model learning approach is the prediction of the subject's overt responses emitted during the transition from S_1 to S_2. There are many different kinds of statistics that can be calculated from the obtained response data to reflect this transition process — i.e., there are many different ways in which the trial-to-trial response events can be accumulated, two of which were alluded to before: the learning curve itself and the trial of last error distribution. Ordinarily, none of these statistics is meaningful in the context of only one subject's response data. The experimental testing of a micro-model requires a voluminous amount of data. So, the value of these various statistics are determined from group data — i.e., the responses of every subject run in the experiment are used in the calculation of each statistic. As we shall soon see, the ability of a micro-model to analyze the quantitative details of the transition process from S_1 to S_2 is reflected in the structure of the typical micro-learning model experiment.

Learning experimentation. In the typical micro-model learning experiment all subjects learn under the same set of learning conditions — namely, that specific set of conditions which the micro-model was explicitly designed to generate. Since many different sets of learning conditions exist in the context of the same learning or extinction task or learning phenomenon, that specific set chosen for modeling and actual physical experimentation must be a representative one. For instance, construction of a micro-model for classical conditioning would more than likely assume the following set of learning conditions: CS, UCS presentation is the forward order, CS-UCS interval of .5 seconds, medium CS and UCS intensities, neutral instructions given to the (human) subjects, 100% reinforcement schedule, etc. Again, as in the case of response measurement, if a specific micro-model is designed to model an unusual value of a member of the set of learning conditions, it will be stated in the title of the model — e.g., X's model for classical conditioning under conditions of partial reinforcement.

Thus, micro-model learning experimentation usually does not employ an independent variable, with a different group of subjects associated with each level of the independent variable, a la the macro-theory approach. This violates the basic dictum of traditional experimental methodology that a minimum of two groups of subjects (or two conditions) must be employed in an experiment. But criticism of the micro-model approach on this point would not be justified. The structural, ordinal predictions of macro-learning theory require traditional experimental methodology for their evaluation. The dynamic, ratio predictions of the micro-model approach allow for the fine-grain analysis of the response data generated by only one group of subjects. To require a minimum of two groups of subjects, each learning under a different set of learning conditions, in a micro-model learning experiment would lead to hardships on the conceptual and procedural levels.

Conceptually, varying the set of learning conditions or manipulating an independent variable in a micro-model learning experiment would minimally require different parameter values in the predictive equations for each variation or maximally require a totally different model (i.e., set of predictive equations) for each variation.

Procedurally, the micro-model approach requires a voluminous amount of response data. As a conservative estimate, the number of subjects run under the one condition in a micro-model learning experiment would be five or six times the number of subjects run in one group of a multigroup macro-learning theory experiment. So, a two-group micro-model learning experiment would require up to six times the number of subjects of a two-group macro-learning theory experiment.

For illustrative purposes, let us continue the example introduced previously in the context of macro-learning theory experimentation. Let us suppose that a particular micro-modeler is interested in the effects of the amount of reinforcement that is presented following the occurrence of a member of the response class of interest on the process of learning that response class. Extending the simple micro-model example introduced previously, the micro-modeler might assume that the amount of reinforcement per response occurrence affects the probability of sampling each kind of stimulus element. Previously this was covered by the blanket assumption that the probability of choosing a non-learning element on any trial was $\frac{N-1}{N}$ and the probability of choosing the learning element on any trial was $\frac{1}{N}$. Now let us assume that such is true only in the context of a small or unit amount of reinforcement per response occurrence. Under the condition of a medium amount of reinforcement per response occurrence, the respective probabilities might become $\frac{N-2}{N}$ and $\frac{2}{N}$ (assuming N $\geqslant 5$); and under the condition of a large amount of reinforcement per response occurrence, the respective probabilities might become $\frac{N-4}{N}$ and $\frac{4}{N}$ (assuming N $\geqslant 5$).

But the crucial point is that this particular assumption about how amount of reinforcement per response occurrence affects the learning of that response class does not have to be evaluated in the context of a three-group design in which each group of subjects is exposed to a different value of amount of reinforcement per response. Only one group of subjects, under one condition of reward, need be run because the model affords detailed quantitative predictions of trial-to-trial response events for that one group or condition. The reward condition that will actually be run in the experiment should be the one that is regarded as most representative — here, more than likely the unit reward condition. If the model does not predict the obtained data at this particular reward level, it would not predict the others either.

Implicit in the above is the assumption that N will be the same (equal) in all three reward conditions. Functionally, this means that N must be at least 5 in all three conditions. So, generalization of the previous model beyond the unit reward case also delimits further the values N can assume.

The Key Set of Theoretical Questions in the Context
of the Micro-Model Approach to Learning: Two Interpretations

Introduction. The micro-model approach has not generated its own set of key theoretical questions, in the macro-theory sense of the term, for two reasons: (1) a model is not a theory and does not necessarily represent underlying reality; (2) a micro-model is designed to generate only a highly specific, "isolated" task or experiment, while virtually all macro-theories are designed to generate the same thing — namely, the underlying learning process. So existing micro-models have not been designed to cover the same empirical phenomena and therefore cannot be compared on a common set of analytical dimensions.

The notion of a key set of theoretical questions is still meaningful in the context of the micro-model approach, in at least two other senses: (1) Most of the key set of theoretical questions engendered by the macro-theory approach transfer to micro-models either because the model must take a specific position with respect to the theoretical issue or because the model provides a sophisticated methodological tool by which the theoretical question could be evaluated. (2) Micro-models can be regarded as having engendered its own set of "current controversies" or "current issues" — ones that could only have arisen in the context of the highly sophisticated, analytical methodology inherent in the micro-model approach. Let us discuss each of these interpretations of the notion of a key set in turn.

The two interpretations. 1. The general transferability of the macro-theory set of key theoretical questions to micro-models can best be summarized by a figure (See Fig. 7-3). The extreme left-hand column lists the five theoretical questions. The second column indicates whether or not the typical micro-model must take a position with respect to each theoretical question. The third column

Macro-Theory Question	Theoretical Relevance	Methodological Relevance
The nature of reinforcement	No	Yes
The role of reinforcement in learning	Yes	Yes
The units of learning	Yes	Yes
The relationship between conditioning and learning, etc.	No	Yes
The fundamental principles of learning	No	No

Fig. 7-3. The Transferability of the Key Set of Macro-Theory Theoretical Questions to Micro-Models

indicates whether or not the typical micro-model could be used to methodologically arbitrate between the various theoretical approaches taken with respect to each theoretical question. Only one question does not transfer at all: "What is the more-or-less absolute set of theoretical conditions necessary for learning?"

2. The current issues engendered by micro-models consist of local and general ones.

Countless local issues have arisen as a by-product of the application of micro-models to the learning and extinction tasks and learning phenomena of traditional learning psychology. By local is meant task-specific, phenomenon-specific, or experiment-specific. For instance:

What is the effect of "blank trials" in probability learning?

What is the nature of the effective stimulus (pattern or element) in stimulus generalization and stimulus discrimination studies?

Is concept identification best modeled as a conditioning process or as a strategy-selection process?

Is the assumption of a short-term memory store necessary to account for paired-associate learning?

The micro-model approach has also generated a series of general issues which extend beyond the bounds of a specific task or phenomenon — although each issue must be evaluated in the context of each kind of task or phenomenon. For instance:

Does a subject learn exclusively on error trials, or exclusively on correct trials, or on either kind of trial?

What is the optimal sequencing of a list of verbal materials or items which the subject must learn?

Are the pre-solution responses in a learning experiment constant or stationary? Is the probability of an error response constant prior to reaching the S_2 state?

Is the process of transition from S_1 to S_2 all-or-none (sudden) or incremental (gradual)? This is commonly referred to as the all-or-none or one-trial learning issue, and it has become the key controversy in the context of micro-learning models. This issue gives rise to many related questions. For instance, under what conditions do you get all-or-none learning? Or, relabeling all-or-none learning as one-stage learning and relabeling incremental learning as infinite-stage (linear) learning, is the process of transition from S_1 to S_2 ever a multistage process (i.e., two, three, four, etc. stages); and, under what conditions do you get two- or three- or four-stage learning? The notion of all-or-none versus incremental learning reappears in Chapters 8 and 9.

How the Micro-Model Accomplishes its Prediction Objectives

Introduction. Ideally, we should examine in detail just how the micro-model approach to learning accomplishes its prediction objectives by presenting a representative sample of specific micro-models in the context of specific learning and extinction tasks and learning phenomena. But, for reasons analogous to those in the macro-theoretical case, this subsection will merely present the major types of micro-learning models. No attempt will be made to derive these types from some underlying generative system — again because the typical micro-model is situation (task)-specific and does not necessarily represent reality. As will soon become apparent, it is somewhat difficult to uniquely characterize the word "type" in the context of micro-learning models.

Types of Micro-Learning Models

Introduction. Whenever a modeler constructs a model for some specific aspect of the descriptive level of analysis, ordinarily he has a choice about the object, event, system, etc. in the natural world which serves as the source of the model and the expressive form of the deductive system encompassed by the model. But currently the deductive system encompassed by virtually every sophisticated micro-learning model is either directly expressed in mathematical form (i.e., the axiomatic structure and predictions of the model are stated in mathematical terms) or is implicitly expressed in mathematical form (i.e., so-called computer models whose deductive systems exist in the form of computer programs written in some kind of computer language). Therefore, it would not be worthwhile to attempt to differentiate among various micro-learning models at this level. Rather, it is much more meaningful to define the notion of *type* of micro-learning model in terms of what can serve as the source of a model.

The Possible Sources of a Micro-Learning Model

Introduction. It is impossible to present a mutually exclusive set of sources. This is because any event X in the natural world that is used as a model exists on many different levels concurrently. For instance, referring back to the computer-human brain analogy of Chapter 6, many different aspects of the computer could be employed as the actual content of the analogy. The computer is a logical device, an electrical system, an information processor, a huge memory bank, a heat generator, a physical machine, a conceptual system, etc. Keeping this limitation in mind, the following constitutes a fairly exhaustive set of sources — i.e., just about every micro-learning model in existence is assignable to at least one of these categories: (1) macro-learning theory, (2) mathematics, (3) physical machines, (4) physiology, (5) micro-psychological content stages.

Macro-learning theory. It might be surprising that a specific macro-learning theory can serve as the source of a micro-learning model. The modeler simply assumes that the subject behaves as if the theoretical constructs and principles espoused by the macro-theory were indeed actually true. Naturally, the theoretical constructs and principles of the old macro-theory must be tightened and refined, adapted to each individual learning task or experiment they will be applied to, and expressed and related in mathematical terms in order to create the micro-model. Essentially, there are two ways of viewing the finished product of this process: (1) The micro-model is regarded as completely new with the old macro-theory simply serving as the germ for the essential content (assumptions) of the model, or (2) the micro-model is regarded as the mere formalization (quantification) of the informal, loosely stated macro-theory.

The most historically significant micro-learning model derived in this fashion is Estes' "Stimulus Sampling Theory" or "Statistical Learning Theory." Working within the framework of Guthrie's contiguity approach to learning, Estes developed a broad set of assumptions about the nature of the stimulus, the conditioning process, and the response such that with specific interpretations of all three virtually any learning task can be modeled. Stimulus sampling theory dominated micro-learning models during the 1950s and through the first part of the 1960s. It is stated in such a way that the newer "smaller element and pattern" approaches of Bower, Atkinson, Suppes, and others are subsets of stimulus sampling theory. Another micro-model approach with roots in macro-theory is the general strategy-selection or hypothesis-selection approach of Restle, Overall, et al., developed in the cognitive tradition characteristic of Tolman Krech, et al.

Mathematics. While nearly all micro-models express the transition process between S_1 and S_2 mathematically, micro-models with mathematics as their source do so directly because the trial-to-trial behavior exhibited by a subject in the typical learning experiment is regarded as reflecting some standard mathematical operation or process. The basic operations or axioms of a certain subkind of mathematics is given a direct psychological interpretation. For instance, the subject is behaving as if he were a linear operator, or as if he were a random event generator, or as if he were maximizing expected utility, etc. So, it is the mathematical system itself, not the mathematical system assumed to be underlying some other object or event X, which serves as the source of the model.

Most of the micro-learning models constructed in this framework treat learning as a statistical or probabilistic process. Thus, they are often confused with the statistical models generated by stimulus sampling theory. For instance, the most historically significant math-oriented learning model is that of the statisticians Bush and Mosteller. Their approach is about as general as stimulus sampling theory; it coexisted and competed with stimulus sampling theory during the 1950s; and depending on the values of certain parameters and the inclusion or exclusion of certain assumptions, its basic learning curve is equivalent to that of Estes. To make matters worse, Bush and Mosteller's approach amounts to an unintentional formalization of Hull's effect approach to macro-theory and many psychologists mistakenly regard it as an explicit attempt to formalize Hull's macro-learning theory. The micro-models of Audley and Jonckheere, designed primarily to account for individual behavior, are also math-originated statistical models. Probably the primary math-oriented micro-modeler, who does not treat learning strictly as a probabilistic or statistical process, is Luce, who developed his learning models from underlying math axioms about choice behavior.

Physical machines. By physical machines are meant such things as robots, computers, tracking devices, etc. (Modeling the human brain as a computer obviously comes under this classification.) With respect to learning, it is not the physical machine per se which serves as the source of the model; rather it is the system underlying the activity exhibited by the machine – i.e., electrical, mechanical, servomechanical, etc. These types of models are not typically used to generate the transition from S_1 to S_2; rather, they are employed by psychologists who are primarily interested in the "steady-state," asymptotic, or adaptive performance exhibited by the organism subsequent to achieving the S_2 state. Tracking behavior, behavior in repetitive manual or motor tasks, the ultimate adaptive behavior in the context of uniform reinforcement conditions (schedules) are examples of the kinds of behavior to which mechanical, electrical, servomechanical, etc. models have been applied.

Psychologists have constructed "machines" (i.e., electrical or mechanical systems) which can learn – i.e., their activity changes systematically as a function of prior experience. The form of these "machines" is irrelevant – some are just complicated relay systems tacked to a baseboard; others are wrapped in a nice package to look like a turtle, rat, etc.; others are merely programs on a computer. While these machines constitute an actual physical representation of a model, they are not predictive in any sense. They are merely illustrative or descriptive. In effect they justify using physical machines as a source of models in the first place.

Physiology. While it has always been fashionable to appeal to underlying physiology to account for observed behavior – recall the use of reductive constructs in the context of macro-learning theory – the use of physiology as the source of a model implies a more sophisticated interpretation of the notion of physiology. The macro-learning theories which made use of reductive constructs were certainly never empirically evaluated on the basis of the assumed properties of their physiological constructs and were regarded as merely illustrative of what a sophisticated physiologically based learning approach might consist of. On the other hand, micro-learning models are based on the specific chemical, biochemical, and neuronal processes which are believed to underlie learning. For instance, learning models are based on the relationship between DNA and RNA and learning, the mechanics of synaptic transmission, assumed neuronal consolidation processes, cortical arousal mechanisms, the existence of reinforcing centers in the brain, etc. The two primary areas of learning which have been "physiologically modeled" are classical conditioning and (human) memory (retention).

The majority of the physiologically based models do not yield as specific behavioral predictions as the other kinds of models; their behavioral predictions are quite similar to those of macro-learning theory. It is currently impossible to set up a direct one-to-one correspondence between a physiological state or event and the probability of learned or correct response occurrence. But, unlike macro-theory, the majority of the physiologically based models are also empirically evaluated in terms of the truth value of the underlying target physiological processes.

Micro-psychological content stages. This approach to models on the surface at least appears as the macro-theoretical approach in miniature. It is currently the dominant and most creative approach to micro-model construction. In the context of a specific learning task or experiment, what the modeler essentially does is to postulate the minimum number of stages or processes and their interactions which can reasonably be regarded as necessary to generate the response data. In addition, these stages or processes are given psychological content. For instance, in order to model a paired-associate learning experiment, using a 15-item list composed of S-R pairs of medium difficulty, the psychologist might assume that two interacting underlying processes are necessary: (1) an all-or-none conditioning process and (2) a temporary short-term memory store (storage process).

The reason this approach can be classified as "modeling" is as follows. The organism is interpreted as operating as a machine which has been designed to perform certain functions or possess certain capacities (i.e., conditioning, short-term memory). What the modeler simply does is to originate the deductive system underlying the machine.

Most models of this type have been designed to generate human learning situations: verbal learning, concept formation, memory, information processing, problem solving, etc. The titles of the models often derive from the dominant or most important stage assumed by the model — for instance, a decision-making, short-term memory, information-processing, problem-solving, etc. model. Many of the so-called computer or simulation models that are written in some kind of computer language and are typically evaluated on the computer are actually models of this type.

OTHER APPROACHES TO LEARNING THEORY:
MACRO-MODELS AND MICRO-THEORIES

Introduction

The dimension of what learning theory is supposed to generate has been analyzed in terms of micro versus macro; and the dimension of how it actually goes about accomplishing this has been expressed in terms of theory versus model. Macro was attached to theory and micro was appended to model because they represent the two significant historical periods of learning theory. But, it would be a gross oversimplification to assume that every specific generation attempt in learning is uniquely assignable to only one of these two categories. Two other categories are immediately created by rearranging the above pairings: (1) macro-model and (2) micro-theory. Let us briefly analyze how meaningful each of these categories would be.

Macro-Models

It has already been argued that, in the strict sense, it is impossible to model the underlying learning process itself because there simply is no one reference task or phenomenon which can be used to represent all learning situations. While this is true, various models differ with respect to their degree of generality. For instance, the stimulus sampling approach of Estes is certainly more general than a micro-psychological content stage model designed to cover a specific paired-associate learning experiment. In general, it can be argued that any learning model derived from an underlying macro-theory possesses a higher degree of generality than any of the other four types and if the term "macro-model" can be legitimately applied to any type of learning model at all it can be applied to a model which has a macro-theory as its source.

There are many psychologists who would classify the Estes (Guthrie), Restle (Tolman), and Bush and Mosteller (Hull) approaches as macro-models from which specific micro-models are derived depending upon which of many alternative assumptions are made and which values are assigned to specific parameters. These psychologists would interpret the modeling involved as the mere formalization (quantification) of the underlying informal, loosely stated macro-theory.

Micro-Theory

The notion of micro-theory is perfectly meaningful as an approach to the generation of learning data. It is a hybrid of macro-theory and micro-models. It served as an intellectual (symbolic) and historical (actual) transition between the macro-theoretical era and the micro-model era. It still remains because the typical contemporary learning theorist who eschews the mathematical specificity or philosophical assumptions of micro-models is a micro-theorist.

A micro-theory can be defined as a learning theory which applies the theoretical constructs and assumptions of traditional macro-theory to the learning process which underlies a specific or related set of learning or extinction task(s) or learning phenomenon(a) — but without generating the quantitative details of the transition process from S_1 to S_2. A micro-theory possesses all the characteristics of a macro-theory, but is much more limited in its scope. While there is no clear-cut criterion on the generality dimension which separates macro-theory from micro-theory, a micro-theory is not as micro as a micro-model. In a sense, multiprocess macro-learning theorists are micro-theorists because for them the nature of the underlying learning process varies with the learning task, etc. The traditional term for a micro-theory is "miniature theory" or "miniature system."

There are countless examples of miniature systems in learning psychology: Hull's theory of rote learning, Miller's account of conflict behavior, Osgood's transfer surface for transfer of training phenomena, Amsel's frustrative reward approach to extinction, Underwood's two-process theory of paired-associate learning, Postman's interference theory of forgetting and retention phenomena, Festinger's cognitive dissonance approach to partial reinforcement, Muenzinger's vicarious trial-and-error account of choice behavior in a T maze, etc.

Summary Perspective

So, although the concepts of macro-learning theory and micro-learning models constitute the dominant trends in theoretical learning psychology and serve as convenient reference or definitional devices, the concepts of macro-learning models and micro-learning theories also constitute valid approaches to the generation process. The distinction between theory and model is clear-cut. The distinction between macro and micro is not — it basically depends upon some amorphous point along the generality continuum in the context of theory and it is merely a semantic matter in the context of modeling. At any rate, these four generation categories exhaust the many different individual ways in which learning psychologists have attempted to structure the theoretical level of analysis.

A REVISED OVERVIEW OF THE
MACRO-THEORETICAL LEARNING SITUATION

Since the initial two generation categories have since been expanded to four, the brief historical introduction to learning theory appearing at the beginning of the chapter should now be more refined so as to include four explicit phases.

1. The macro-theoretical approach dominated experimental learning psychology from approximately 1920 to 1950. This was the era of the general, systematic theories of Hull, Tolman, Guthrie, Lewin, et al. which on the surface at least were strictly deductive theoretical approaches.

2. Micro-theory commenced in the 1930s and still exists today. Micro-theorists devise constrained theories limited to specific subareas of learning – namely, verbal learning, conditioning, maze learning, conflict, etc. It tends to have an informal or "functional" flavor.

3. Macro-models originated with the work of Estes and Bush and Mosteller during the early 1950s and dominated learning psychology for just one decade. In this approach the preferred form of generation is mathematical. In many respects the only difference between Estes' general stimulus sampling approach and the macro-theoretical approaches of Hull et al. is in the explicitness afforded by strictly mathematical or quantitative predictions.

4. Micro-models commenced during the early 1960s and constitutes the current preferred form of explanation and prediction. In this approach a model, usually mathematical in nature, is explicitly formulated just to cover a very restricted learning operation or phenomenon. A micro-model is much more specific and limited than a micro-theory.

To put these four historical phases in greater perspective, some additional terminology must be introduced. The dimension of what learning theory is supposed to generate will henceforth be referred to as the "generality" dimension; and the dimension of how learning theory actually goes about accomplishing its objectives will henceforth be referred to as the "formality" dimension. Thus, macro equals high on the generality continuum; micro equals low on the generality continuum. Theory equals low on the formality continuum, while model equals high on the formality continuum.

In the context of this new set of terminology, the history of American learning theory can be viewed as a sequence of interrelated formality and generality cycles. Basically, American learning theory has passed through two broad formality cycles. The first cycle (1920-1950) was characterized by low formality; the second cycle (1950-current) emphasizes high formality. Within the context of each formality cycle there exist two generality subcycles. The initial phase of each formality cycle is characterized by general or comprehensive theoretical efforts after which a transition to more limited or less comprehensive theoretical efforts occurs. This transition is sharp and abrupt (i.e., no overlap) in the second formality cycle; it is much less so in the first formality cycle – macro-theory and micro-theory coexisted for a good 20 years. The micro-theoretical approach has never really ceased; it continues to exist by default. Any learning theorist who eschews strict mathematicalizing or modeling must operate in the micro-theoretical framework, since macro-theory is dead.

THE RELATIONSHIP BETWEEN CONDITIONING AND LEARNING AT THE THEORETICAL LEVEL AND THE RELATIONSHIP BETWEEN CLASSICAL AND INSTRUMENTAL CONDITIONING AT THE THEORETICAL LEVEL: A CLASSIFICATION SYSTEM

INTRODUCTION

Chapter 4 briefly discussed classical conditioning and instrumental conditioning operationally as specific kinds of learning procedures or tasks. At the theoretical level, both procedures were described as simple forms of learning. Since the structure of the theoretical situation in learning psychology has since been introduced, it is now both necessary and appropriate to present a sophisticated discussion of the many different theoretical ways in which conditioning can be related to learning. A classification system of the basic types of relationships constitutes the most worthwhile method of presentation. It is not meaningful to consider the question of the theoretical relationship between conditioning and learning independent of the theoretical relationship between the two subvarieties of conditioning, so the classification system will involve two dimensions. Based on previous discussion, it should be apparent that these two questions are only meaningful in the context of macro-learning theory or any model derived from macro-learning theory.

THE CLASSIFICATION SYSTEM

Introduction

Each dimension will be treated as ternary-valued. Combining the two dimensions yields a 3 x 3 table, consisting of nine individual cells (See Fig. 7-4).

The Relationship Between Conditioning and
Learning at the Theoretical Level

		1	2	3
The Relationship Between Classical and Instrumental Conditioning at the Theoretical Level	A		Hull	Guthrie Estes
	B	Tolman	Spence Mowrer (Old) Thorndike Miller	Skinner
	C			

Fig. 7-4. A Classification System for the Macro-Theoretical Relationships Between Classical Conditioning, Instrumental Conditioning, and Learning

The horizontal dimension represents the relationship between conditioning and learning and the three interpretive columnar categories are labeled 1, 2, and 3. The vertical dimension represents the relationship between classical and instrumental conditioning and the three interpretive row categories are denoted by A, B, and C. Both sets of categories are strictly nominal in nature and no significance can be attached to the order in which they are presented. The content of the classification system depends upon the exact meaning and significance assigned to each category, so let us go over the specific denotative meaning associated with each category, starting with the conditioning, learning dimension.

The Conditioning, Learning Dimension

Interpretation 1. Conditioning is the simplest form of learning only and is completely unrelated to the more complex forms of learning. Conditioning, as a simple form of learning, is completely discontinuous with the more complex forms of learning. Completely different learning principles are needed to explain conditioning and the forms of learning to the right of it on the underlying operational learning continuum. It is impossible to explain complex learning by appealing to the same learning principles which explain conditioning. This interpretation implies that there is a qualitative, besides a quantitative difference between conditioning and learning.

Interpretation 2. Conditioning is the simplest form of learning, but can be generalized to more complex forms of learning through deduction and analogy. Conditioning, as a simple form of learning, is entirely continuous with the more complex forms of learning. The same learning principles which explain conditioning can be generalized to generate the complex forms of learning. This interpretation implies that there is a qualitative, besides a quantitative, difference between conditioning and learning.

Interpretation 3. Conditioning is the only form of learning and ipso facto can account for all kinds of learning. At the theoretical level, all learning is conditioning. Even though different learning tasks vary in their degree of operational complexity, all are forms of conditioning and can be explained by the same essential set of learning principles. This interpretation implies that there is neither a qualitative nor a quantitative difference between conditioning and learning.

The Classical, Instrumental Conditioning Dimension

Interpretation A. There are no differences between classical and instrumental conditioning at a theoretical level. They are essentially the same form of learning (whatever learning is). The same set of underlying learning principles can account for the operational differences between classical and instrumental conditioning.

Interpretation B. There is a theoretical difference between classical and instrumental conditioning. They are not the same form of learning. Different sets of underlying learning principles are needed to account for the operational differences between classical and instrumental conditioning.

Interpretation C. There is no theoretical difference between classical and instrumental conditioning, but one is the basis of and explains the other. Either the instrumental conditioning procedure is a form of classical conditioning at the theoretical level or the classical conditioning procedure is a form of instrumental conditioning at the theoretical level. This interpretation differs from interpretation A in that the learning principles involved are specifically equated with those that underlie either classical or instrumental conditioning.

Integration of the Two Dimensions: The Meaning of the Nine Individual Cells

1A. Classical and instrumental conditioning are the same form of learning, analyzable in terms of the same underlying learning principles, but are completely discontinuous with any other types of learning.

2A. Classical and instrumental conditioning are the same form of learning, analyzable in terms of the same underlying learning principles, and the principles can be extended through analogy and deduction to account for complex forms of learning.

3A. Only one form of learning exists in the sense that any learning task or phenomena, no matter how procedurally simple or complex, is generatable by the same basic set of learning principles.

1B. In effect, there are at least three forms of learning: classical conditioning, instrumental conditioning, and a broad class of complex learning, each of which requires a different underlying set of learning principles.

2B. Classical and instrumental conditioning are not the same form of learning and require different sets of underlying learning principles, but the different sets of underlying learning principles are each individually generalizable to more complex forms of learning through deduction and analogy.

3B. There are only two forms of learning: classical conditioning and instrumental conditioning, each of which is associated with its own set of underlying learning principles. Any learning task at the theoretical level is a form of classical conditioning or a form of instrumental conditioning.

1C. Classical and instrumental conditioning are the same form of learning, either classical or instrumental at the theoretical level, but this form is completely discontinuous with any other type of learning.

2C. Classical and instrumental conditioning are the same form of learning, either classical or instrumental at the theoretical level, and this form can be extended through analogy and deduction to account for complex forms of learning.

3C. Only one form of learning exists. It is either classical conditioning or instrumental conditioning. All learning is either classical conditioning or instrumental conditioning at the theoretical level.

The Macro-Theoretical Content of each Cell: A Sampling of the Major Macro-Learning Theorists Associated with each Cell

Figure 7-4 presents the major macro-learning theorists associated with each cell. The names of some macro-theorists and their approaches are missing because they are nonexplicit concerning the theoretical relationship between classical and instrumental conditioning. For instance, the Gestalt approach of Wertheimer, Koffka, and Köhler and the field theory approach of Lewin are not included, although they would definitely fall in the interpretation 1 category on the conditioning, learning dimension. The row associated with interpretation C on the classical, instrumental conditioning dimension has been left unfilled because no macro-theorist has as yet explicitly stated that classical is the basis of instrumental or instrumental is the basis of classical without specifying further what the learning principles are that underlie conditioning. It is a viable interpretation because it would be possible for a future inductively or purely descriptively oriented learning theorist to be so classified. Cell 1A is empty because to the best of the author's knowledge no macro-learning theorist makes this particular interpretation.

Every other cell is filled with at least one theorist and should be noted individually:

2A.   Hull
3A.   Guthrie, Estes
1B.   Tolman
2B.   Spence, Mowrer (old), Thorndike, Miller
3B.   Skinner

If any one of these cells can be regarded as the standard or focal interpretation of macro-learning theory, it would be 2A, associated with Hull's effect approach. Uniprocess contiguity theorists, such as Guthrie and Estes, tend to make the 3A interpretation; likewise, cognitive theorists, such as Tolman, tend to make the 1B interpretation. (Remember the Gestalt and field theory approaches were also listed in category 1.) All the theorists listed in 2B are Hullians, except for Thorndike. They differ from Hull in one respect with reference to this classification system: they are multi-(two)-process theorists. Although Skinner is not a traditional macro-theorist, he is included because his inductive, descriptive approach does make the 3B interpretation without specifying what the underlying theoretical learning principles are.

SUMMARY

The various approaches to higher order interpretation in the context of learning psychology (i.e., the topic of "learning theory") can be analyzed in terms of two orthogonal binary-valued classificatory dimensions: (1) a generality dimension specifying what the underlying theoretical learning constructs are supposed to generate and (2) a formality dimension determining how the generation objectives are actually accomplished. Generality can be high (macro: the underlying theoretical learning process is the focus of concern) or low (micro: performance in a specific learning task or the behavior associated with a specific learning phenomenon is the focus of concern). Formality can be high (model: within-group fine grain prediction of behavioral data, primarily through mathematical equations) or low (theory: between-group ordinal prediction of summary statistics).

The history of American learning theory can be viewed as a sequence of interrelated formality and generality cycles. Basically, it has passed through two broad formality cycles (low-high), each of which is composed of two generality subcycles (high-low). The macro-theoretical approach (Hull, Tolman, Guthrie, Lewin, et al.) dominated from approximately 1920 to 1950. Micro-theory (Miller, Osgood, Amsel, Postman, et al.) commenced in the 1930s and still exists today. Macro-models (Estes, Bush, Mosteller) started in the early 1950s and lasted for just one decade. Micro-models (Bower, Crothers, Suppes, et al.) commenced during the early 1960s and is the current preferred form of higher order interpretation.

The relationship between conditioning and learning constituted a key theoretical question in the context of macro-learning theory (remnants of it still persist) and it is possible to distinguish between three classic approaches to the issue.

1. Cognitive theorists, Gestalt psychologists, and field theorists view conditioning as the simplest form of learning and unrelated to more complex forms of learning.

2. The Hullian effect approach, its adherents, and two-process theorists treat conditioning as the simplest form of learning, but generalizable to more complex forms of learning through deduction and analogy.

3. Contiguity theorists and Skinner regard conditioning as the only form of learning — i.e., all learning is conditioning.

8
Measurement of the Learning Process: Three conceptual problems

INTRODUCTION

To continue the conceptual analysis of learning psychology, it is necessary to discuss the basic conceptual problems associated with measuring the learning process. This topic is quite didactic because it necessarily relates and ties together many of the crucial distinctions already presented.

Recall from Chapter 4 that learning, as a process, is an unobservable, inferred entity, which, as a property of the individual organism, intervenes between the external input (S) and output (R) situations. So, the learning process can only be measured indirectly through the analysis of the values of the measurable characteristics of a response class in the context of reinforced practice. Inferences are made about the intervening learning process from the change in the measurable characteristics of a learned response class as quantified across time or trials.

The conceptual problems associated with quantifying the learning process derive from this inferential requirement. More specifically, the basic conceptual problems are related to a series of decisions or assumptions which must be made in order to infer something about the learning process from obtained learned response data. There is a series of three basic decisions or assumptions which must be made. The next subsection previews the three conceptual problems and indicates the significance of each. Following subsections analyze the conceptual problems in detail and relate them to specific response measurement consequences and practices.

THE THREE CONCEPTUAL PROBLEMS

The first conceptual problem involves the nature of the underlying learning function residing in the individual subject. The experimenter must make an assumption about the form of the mathematical function which describes how learning accumulates in the organism across time or trials. There are three classic solutions to this problem and the specific solution which an experimenter adopts primarily determines whether or not the actual time at which or trial during which learning occurs can be discovered for the individual subject.

The second conceptual problem concerns the question of response equivalency. Chapter 3 introduced the analogical response characteristics of a unitary response and the digital characteristic of response occurrence. The question of response equivalency applies to the former, not to the latter, and exists on two dimensions. (1) Are the four independent analogical response characteristics (latency or interresponse time, magnitude, duration, and shape) equivalent to each other? Do they equally represent the underlying learning process? Does it make a difference which analogical characteristic is used to quantify the learned response in a specific learning situation? (2) Within the context of any one of the four analogical response characteristics, are the many different values which a response instance can take equivalent to each other? Is it valid to combine many differently valued response instances to quantify the underlying learning process?

The first dimension of response equivalency will henceforth be referred to as response characteristic equivalency and the second dimension will be described as response instance equivalency. These are essentially binary-valued dimensions which, when made orthogonal to each other, set up a 2 x 2 classification system. How an experimenter responds to the response equivalency question (i.e., where he fits in the classification system) primarily delimits his choice of appropriate response measures or dependent variables by which to quantify the underlying learning process.

The third conceptual problem relates to how adequately an average, group, or mean empirical learning curve represents the individual subject's empirical learning curve and, ipso facto, the underlying learning process in the individual. How legitimate is it to combine response data obtained from N individual subjects to form a mean learning curve? Given a mean empirical learning curve, is the form, etc. of the individual learning curve uniquely specified? The question of the appropriateness of representing the underlying learning process in an individual by means of an average learning curve admits of many approaches and the specific approach which an experimenter takes in large part determines his basic research methodology.

THE NATURE OF THE UNDERLYING INDIVIDUAL LEARNING FUNCTION

INTRODUCTION

In order to get specific about how learning accumulates in an individual subject across time or trials, some preliminary distinctions must be made. We assume that a subject starts in an initial unlearned state (S_1) with respect to some motor response, verbal item, concept rule, or the like and eventually the subject reaches a learned or completely learned state (S_2) with respect to the substance of learning. The underlying learning function describes how learning proceeds across time or trials by specifying the nature of the transition between S_1 and S_2.

The nature of the learning function is completely independent of the substantive content of the learning process – the question of how learning proceeds is completely independent of the question of what is learned. It is irrelevant for our analysis whether the substantive content of the learning process is an S-R association (habit), an S-S association (expectancy), a generation or concept rule, a reinforcement or environmental contingency, etc. But the nature of the learning function has been historically discussed almost exclusively in the context of acquiring an S-R association or habit. We shall follow that pattern here simply because it facilitates exposition. So, at a substantive level, what is involved in the transition from S_1 to S_2 is a transition from a zero or minimal degree of associative habit strength joining the S and R to an asymptotic or maximal degree of associative habit strength joining the S and R (a full bond or complete association). So, we are assuming that the learning function is one which describes how the habit strength underlying a specific S-R association accumulates across time or trials.

We are now in a position to introduce alternative conceptions of the learning function.

APPROACHES TO THE NATURE OF THE LEARNING FUNCTION

There are three more or less mutually exclusive views of the learning function: (1) the incremental approach, (2) the all-or-none approach, and (3) the multistate, multistage approach. Let us characterize each of these in turn.

The Incremental Approach

This approach postulates the existence of a physical continuum of habit strength joining the S_1 and S_2 states – the states are merely the two end points of the continuum. This view assumes that infinitely many degrees of partial learning or habit strength exist between the S_1 and S_2 states. The notion of partial degrees of habit strength makes the concept of partial association meaningful and the S_2 state must be interpreted as a complete learning state. The subject slowly proceeds over time or trials through these infinitely many habit strength values to reach S_2 — the habit strength curve increments slowly over time or trials. See Fig. 8-1, which presents three illustrative incremental curves: a, b, and c.

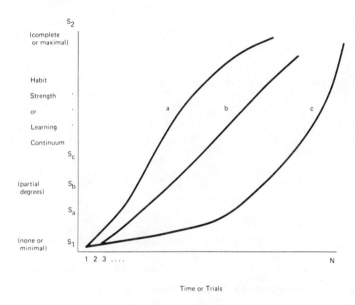

Fig. 8-1. A Representation of the Incremental Learning Function

This approach is often referred to as the gradual, continuous, linear, or multitrial approach. Here the learning process is essentially deterministic, in effect, mechanically accumulating during reinforced practice.

The All-Or-None Approach

This approach does not postulate the existence of a physical continuum of habit strength joining the S_1 and S_2 states — only the two states S_1 and S_2 are meaningful and the S_2 state need merely be termed the learned state. Partial degrees of habit strength or learning are not meaningful and the subject is either in the unlearned state or learned state with respect to the S-R association. The subject makes the transition from the S_1 state to the S_2 state suddenly, in an all-or-none manner, on some trial or at some moment in time — the habit strength curve is a discontinuous step function over trials or time. See Fig. 8-2, which presents three illustrative curves: a, b, and c, each of which essentially denotes a different transition trial or occasion. This approach is often called the sudden, discontinuous, or one-trial approach. Here the learning process is essentially random or probabilistic, a one-step jump occurring at some trial or time during reinforced practice.

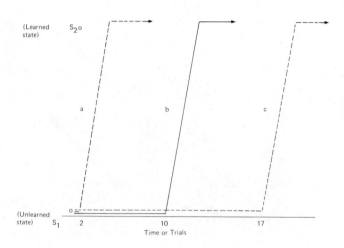

Fig. 8-2. A Representation of the All-Or-None Learning Function

The Multistate, Multistage Approach

This approach is a hybrid of the incremental and all-or-none approaches, although it is conceptually closer to the latter. It postulates the existence of a finite number of discontinuous states intervening between the S_1 and S_2 states. These intermediate states do not necessarily represent partial states of learning or habit strength and the S_2 state again need only be termed the learned state. (Their functional significance is related to the use of differential response rule axioms and has consequences for the occurrence of response instances from the learned response class in the overt response data.) Acceptable terminology for these intermediate states would be pre-solution or pre-learning states. In most interpretations the number of intermediate states does not exceed five; and we shall assume two intermediate states for illustrative purposes. The transition from one state to the next one is called a stage and the total number of stages is always one less than the total number of states. The subject proceeds through the successive stages in an all-or-none manner across time or trials — the habit strength curve is a discontinuous multiple step function over trials or time. Figure 8-3 presents three illustrative curves: a, b, and c, each of which essentially denotes a different transition pattern.

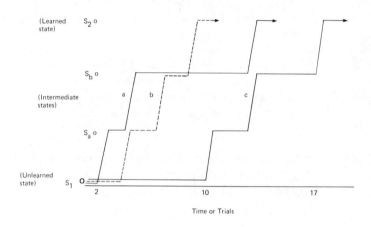

Fig. 8-3. A Representation of the Four-State, Three-Stage Learning Function

Here the learning process is a combination of a series of random or probabilistic events occurring during reinforced practice.

THE NATURE OF THE LEARNING FUNCTION IN RELATION TO
(a) MACRO-THEORY AND MICRO-MODELS AND
(b) EMPIRICAL EVALUATION

The incremental approach is the traditional one in the sense that it is characteristic of most macro-theoretical approaches to learning, Hull's effect approach constituting the primary example. It is also the prototypical approach because any macro-theorist who is mute concerning the nature of the underlying learning function is regarded as implicitly assuming the incremental approach. Actually, the nature of the underlying learning function is not an empirical question in the context of macro-theory because it does not possess the predictive methodological techniques by which to evaluate the alternative approaches.

The all-or-none interpretation, although rooted in Guthrie and Krech's macro-theoretical approaches, is primarily characteristic of the micro-model approach to learning, especially Estes and Bower's small sample models. The micro-model approach does possess the requisite predictive methodological techniques by which to assess the alternative approaches to the nature of the learning function. One of the primary empirical findings of the 1960s was that the all-or-none learning function is indeed appropriate for predicting overt response data in certain simple learning situations.

The multistate, multistage interpretation is a logical outgrowth of the empirical evaluation of the all-or-none approach. Micro-model investigation of certain learning situations, which were too complex to admit of the all-or-none learning function interpretation, demonstrated them to be adequately describable by discontinuous, multiple step learning functions.

METHODOLOGICAL SIGNIFICANCE OF THE NATURE OF THE LEARNING FUNCTION: THE DETERMINATION OF THE INDIVIDUAL SUBJECT'S TRIAL OR MOMENT OF LEARNING

Introduction

At a measurement level, it is desirable to determine just when an individual subject has learned the response in question (i.e., has formed the S-R association). It is desirable to specify on which particular trial or at what moment in time the subject actually does enter the S_2 state. But this determination is only possible in the context of one of the three conceptions of the learning function — the all-or-none approach, and only then under a restricted set of learning and response rule assumptions or axioms. Let us see why.

The Incremental Approach

In this approach, the "trial or moment of learning" must be rephrased the "trial or moment of complete learning" because of the existence of partial degrees of association. But it is never possible to infer from the subject's actual response data protocol just when the final S_2 state is reached. This is because any pattern of overt responding is predictable from any series of adjacent points along the underlying learning function once appropriate response rule assumptions are postulated. Even if the subject exhibits N response instances from the learned response class in a row, it is no guarantee he has entered the S_2 state. Partial degrees of learning in conjunction with various response rules allow instances from the learned response class to be made consistently.

The All-or-None Approach

It is possible to infer from the subject's actual response data protocol just when the S_2 state is reached if it is assumed that the transition from S_1 to S_2 can only happen on a trial during which the subject makes an error response – i.e., exhibits a response instance which is not a member of the learned response class. In this context, the trial of learning or moment of learning is the trial of last error or moment of last error.

If it is assumed that the transition from S_1 to S_2 can only happen on a trial during which the subject makes a correct response – i.e., exhibits a response instance which is a member of the learned response class – or if it is assumed that the transition from S_1 to S_2 can occur on any kind of trial (error or correct), then the trial of learning or moment of learning is indeterminate from the subject's actual response data protocol. In the former case, the occurrence of N response instances from the learned response class in a row can be generated while the subject is in the unlearned state S_1 if appropriate response rule assumptions are made. Even if the subject actually jumps from the S_1 state to the S_2 state during the string of correct responses, the actual trial of transition is indeterminate. Analogous comments apply to the latter case of jumping from S_1 to S_2 on any kind of trial (error or correct).

The Multistate, Multistage Approach

It is never possible to infer from the subject's actual response data protocol just when the S_2 state is reached. This is because any pattern of overt responding is predictable while the subject is in any one of the pre-solution or pre-learning states. Even if the subject exhibits N response instances from the learned response class in a row, it is no guarantee that he has achieved the S_2 state. The intermediate pre-solution states in conjunction with various response rules allow instances from the learned response class to be made consistently. Even if the assumption is made that successive state transitions can only occur on error responses, there is no guarantee that the final error response in the subject's actual response data protocol involves a transition to the final S_2 state. Unlike the all-or-none or one-stage case, the eventual lack of error responding could occur while the subject is in one of the pre-solution, intermediate states.

Illustration of the General Indeterminacy of the Trial or Moment of Learning in the All-or-None Case

Since the prior discussion is quite abstract and presumes familiarity with the notion of response data protocols, let us present some illustrative data protocols and evaluate them with respect to the possibility of determining the trial of learning. Also, because the attainment of the S_2 state is only determinable in one variant of the all-or-none approach, only the all-or-none interpretation of the learning function will be applied to the data.

In Fig. 8-4, response data protocols for five illustrative subjects are presented. Interpret 0 as an error response and 1 as a correct response. For instance, subject 4 exhibits a response instance of the learned response class on every trial; subject 5 never exhibits a response instance from the learned response class on any trial.

	Response Protocols											All-or-None Approaches		
					Trials							Learning only on error assumption	Learning only on correct response assumption	Learning on any kind of trial assumption
Subject #	1	2	3	4	5	6	7	8	9	10	... N			
1	0	1	0	1	1	0	0	1	1	1	... 1	TL = 7	TL = 8 → N	TL = 7 → N
2	0	0	0	1	1	1	1	1	1	1	... 1	TL = 3	TL = 4 → N	TL = 3 → N
3	0	1	1	1	1	1	1	1	1	0	... 1	TL = 10	TL = 11 → N	TL = 10 → N
4	1	1	1	1	1	1	1	1	1	1	... 1	Subject never has learned	TL = 1 → N	TL = 1 → N
5	0	0	0	0	0	0	0	0	0	0	... 0	Subject never has learned	Subject never has learned	Subject never has learned

Fig. 8-4. Illustration of the General Indeterminacy of the Trial of Learning in the All-or-None Case

TL stands for trial of learning. Note that only in the "learning only on error assumption" column is the TL for a subject determinate. In the "learning only on correct response assumption" column and in the "learning on any kind of trial assumption" column the TL for a subject is indeterminate and this is symbolized by an arrow indicating the range of possible trials on which transition to S_2 could have occurred. The content of the "learning on any kind of trial assumption" column is the conceptual combination of the contents of the columns of the other two all-or-none variants.

Interpretation of the response protocols of subjects 4 and 5 requires special comment. Subject 4 could never have jumped to the S_2 state in the context of the "learning only on error assumption" because he never committed an error. Subject 5 could never have jumped to the S_2 state according to any of the three subassumptions. He could not have learned according to the "learning only on correct response assumption" because he never exhibits a correct response. He could not have learned according to the "learning only on error response assumption" because he exhibits no trial of last error. He could not have learned according to the "learning on any kind of trial assumption" because there is both no correct response occurrence and no trial of last error.

METHODOLOGICAL CONSEQUENCE OF THE GENERAL INDETERMINACY OF THE TRIAL OR MOMENT OF LEARNING: THE USE OF A LEARNING CRITERION

Introduction and Definition

The general indeterminacy of the trial or moment of learning leads to the fundamental response measurement consequence associated with the nature of the underlying learning function — namely, the use of a learning criterion. In practice, the learning experimenter does not concern himself with measuring the exact moment or trial of learning because of its general indeterminacy. Instead, he uses a more functional approach to the measurement of the learning process. He concerns himself with the trial or moment by which learning (achieving of S_2) must have occurred. This moment or trial by which learning has occurred is determined by a somewhat arbitrary trials or responses to criterion learning measure. The trials or responses to criterion in effect serves as the experimenter's operational measure of learning (S_2 attainment). Let us illustrate the notion of trials to criterion in the context of the two kinds of response measurement — digital and analogical.

The Digital Measurement of the Characteristic of Response Occurrence

Assume a subject is exhibiting either response class A or response class B on every trial of a learning experiment and that response class A is the correct or learned response. The learning criterion could be the occurrence of X number of A responses in a row. Once the subject exhibits X number of A responses in a row, he is regarded as having attained S_2. If X = 2, we are using an easy or lax criterion; if X = 5, we are using a medium or average criterion; if X = 10 or more, we are using a difficult or strict criterion. The stricter the criterion, the higher is the probability the subject has in fact learned or achieved S_2 instead of exhibiting X correct responses in a row at random or by chance. For instance, if the probability of an A or B response on any trial is one-half by chance, regardless of the subject's underlying learning function, the probability of X occurrences of the A response class in a row is $(\frac{1}{2})^X$. This is an incredibly small number once $X \geq 10$.

The Analogical Measurement of a Unitary Response Characteristic (Latency)

Assume a subject is exhibiting response class C on most trials of a learning experiment and that this constitutes the response class to be learned. Each occurrence of a response instance from response class C has a latency reading associated with it. If we establish ahead of time what minimal value of latency constitutes the baseline latency, we have in effect set up a baseline for determination of the full strength of the learned response. The notion of baseline latency divides the latency value continuum into two subparts: (1) latency readings above the baseline value and (2) latency readings at or below the baseline value. Response instance latency readings in the latter part of the continuum are interpreted as indicating that the learned response class C is occurring at full strength. The learning criterion can then be defined in terms of these sub-baseline latency response instances. The learning criterion could be the occurrence of X number of response instances in a row at or below the baseline latency. Once the subject exhibits X number of response instances in a row at or below the baseline latency, he is regarded as having achieved S_2. The comments relating to the value of X above also apply here. The higher X is, the lower the probability that the baseline latency readings occur by chance and are in fact due to the subject's being in the learned state. See Fig. 8-5 for an illustration of the concept of criterion latency.

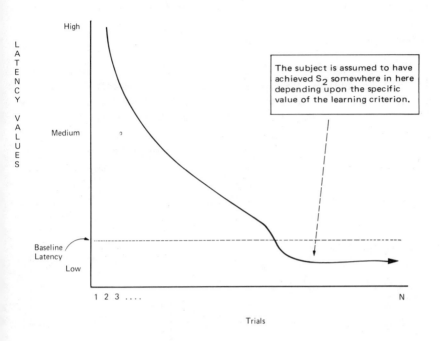

Fig. 8-5. An Illustration of the Concept of Criterion Latency

THE QUESTION OF RESPONSE EQUIVALENCY

INTRODUCTION

When the experimenter does not use the digital characteristic of response occurrence to indirectly measure the course of the learning process over time or trials, he must use one or more of the analogical response characteristics of a response and is faced with the conceptual problem of response equivalency. More specifically, he is forced to take a position with respect to the questions of response characteristic equivalency and response instance equivalency. Recall from prior discussion that these two questions operate as binary-valued dimensions which, when made orthogonal to each other, generate a 2 x 2 (four-cell) classification system. This system, in effect, generates the viable approaches to the response equivalency question. The purpose of this subsection is to describe these approaches in such a way as to present their methodological significance and/or relevance.

APPROACHES TO THE RESPONSE EQUIVALENCY QUESTION

Introduction

The classificatory scheme for generating the approaches is produced in Fig. 8-6. The assumptions of response characteristic equivalency and response instance equivalency serve as the horizontal and vertical dimensions respectively. The categories of acceptance and rejection constitute the binary values of each dimension.

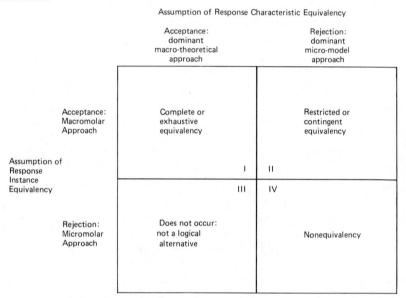

Fig. 8-6. A Classification System for Generating the Approaches to the Response Equivalency Question

We shall initially treat each of the four categories as independent of each other, provide each with some substantive interpretation, and then discuss their orthogonal use and significance.

Analysis of the Four Categories

Acceptance of response characteristic equivalency. This category is the traditional interpretation of the dimension. It is the position that is characteristic of the macro-theoretical approach to learning. The typical macro-theorist regards the different response measures discussed in Chapter 3 as being equivalent —

because learned changes in the different measurable characteristics of a response are treated as derivable from the same basic set of macro-theoretical statements. Hull is the most explicit advocate of this view although it is also held by others such as Tolman. The category is also the prototypical interpretation in the sense that any macro-theorist who is mute on this dimension is regarded as implicitly accepting response characteristic equivalency.

Rejection of response characteristic equivalency. This category is the more contemporary interpretation of the dimension. Although Skinner and a few macro-theorists, such as Spence and Logan, reject the assumption of response characteristic equivalency, this position is particularly characteristic of the micro-model approach to learning. The micro-model approach does not treat the different response measures discussed in Chapter 3 as ipso facto equivalent — because learned changes in the different measurable characteristics of a response are ordinarily not derivable from the specific deductive system underlying the model.

Digression: The distinction between a macromolar response class and a micromolar response class. It is necessary to digress for a moment to a crucial distinction initially presented in Chapter 3 so that the two categories of the response instance dimension can be formally interpreted. Chapter 3 established the fact that any functionally specified response class is a macromolar response class and is composed of an infinite number of different sets of mutually exclusive and exhaustive analogically specified micromolar response classes. (Refer back to pages 58 and 59 for a complete discussion and examples of this basic point.) The categories of the response instance dimension conceptualize the relationship between a macromolar response class and its constituent micromolar response classes quite differently.

Acceptance of response instance equivalency. This category is the traditional interpretation of the dimension. The different values that a response instance can take with respect to an analogical characteristic are equivalent to each other. Most learning theorists, both macro-theorists and micro-modelers, accept response instance equivalency. In effect, this position assumes that the individual micromolar response classes composing a macromolar response class are equivalent to each other; they are qualitatively the same response and only differ with respect to quantitative value. In other words, the individual micromolar response classes do not constitute different macromolar response classes — they are simply variants of the same general macromolar class. The technical label for this position is the macromolar approach. So, most learning theorists are macromolar in their orientation.

Rejection of response instance equivalency. This category is a more contemporary interpretation of the dimension. The different values that a response instance can take with respect to an analogical characteristic are not equivalent to each other. This position assumes that the individual micromolar response classes composing a macromolar response class are not equivalent to each other — the fact that they differ with respect to quantitative value also makes them qualitatively different. In other words, the individual micromolar response classes constitute individual macromolar response classes in and of themselves — they are not simply variants of the same general macromolar response class. The technical label for this position is the micromolar approach.

The prime example of a macro-theorist who accepts this position is Logan, who has made the micromolar orientation the cornerstone of his approach to learning. Operant psychologists in general and Skinner in particular could also be regarded as micromolar psychologists because the particular reinforcement criterion (band) which is operating in the experiment helps define which of the micromolar response classes of the general macromolar response class is being conditioned (i.e., is effective). The other micromolar response classes composing the general macromolar response class are extinguished (i.e., are not effective) and thus are not equivalent.

Orthogonal Use of the Four Categories: The Approaches to The Response Equivalency Question and Their Methodological Significance

Introduction. A number of interesting questions arise once the two dimensions are made orthogonal to each other. Two will be stressed here: (1) Are the two dimensions conceptually independent of each other or is one logically prior to the other? (2) Is each cell of the matrix filled — i.e., does each cell constitute a viable approach to the response equivalency question? Both questions can be resolved in the context of the following empirical fact. There is no learning theorist in existence who rejects response instance equivalency unless he also rejects response characteristic equivalency. Or, alternatively, there is no learning theorist in existence who accepts response characteristic equivalency unless he also accepts response instance equivalency. So, with reference to (1), it appears that the two dimensions are conceptually independent of each other and one is not logically prior to the other. In effect, how one responds to one of the dimensions is only partially determined by how one responds to the other dimension. Regarding (2), cell III of the matrix is unfilled — it does not constitute a viable approach to the response equivalency problem. So, with this as a background, let us label the three remaining cells of the matrix and indicate their methodological significance.

Acceptance of both kinds of response equivalency: Cell I. This could be termed the complete or exhaustive response equivalency approach. It is primarily held by macromolar macro-theorists. There is mutual substitutability with respect to which analogical characteristic is used to quantify the underlying learning process and the micromolar response classes composing the macromolar response class are equivalent and therefore combinable for calculating an empirical learning curve.

Rejection of response characteristic equivalency but acceptance of response instance equivalency: Cell II. This could be termed the restricted or contingent response equivalency approach. It is primarily held by macromolar micro-model learning psychologists, but it is also assumed by some macromolar macro-theorists. There is no mutual substitutability with respect to which analogical characteristic is used to quantify the underlying learning process; but once the specific analogical response characteristic is chosen, the analogical micromolar response classes composing the macromolar response class are treated as equivalent and therefore combinable for calculating an empirical learning curve.

Rejection of both kinds of response equivalency: Cell IV. This could be termed the nonequivalency approach. It is held by both Logan and Skinner. Neither is there mutual substitutability with respect to the analogical characteristic used to quantify the underlying learning process nor is there equivalency among the individual micromolar classes composing the macromolar response class so that they are not combinable for calculating an empirical learning curve.

THE APPROPRIATENESS OF REPRESENTING THE INDIVIDUAL LEARNING FUNCTION BY MEANS OF AN AVERAGE, MEAN, OR GROUP LEARNING CURVE

INTRODUCTION

We have already introduced the notion of an underlying individual learning function which describes how learning accumulates in the subject across time or trials. The point has also been made that this function can only be measured indirectly by noting systematic response changes during reinforced practice. It has also been demonstrated that, except under a set of very restrictive assumptions, it is impossible to unambiguously infer from overt response data just when the learned or completely learned state S_2 has been achieved; consequently, the subject's attainment of S_2 is operationally determined by the use of some minimal learning criterion.

The individual response data protocol generated by the typical subject prior to meeting the criterion is so variable that many learning experimenters bypass calculating the individual empirical learning curve and directly calculate a mean, average, or group empirical learning curve by combining N individual response data protocols. The degree of variability in the individual response data protocol is in part a function of how the learned response is measured. Usually the digital measurement of the characteristic of response occurrence is more variable than the measurement of one or more of the analogical response characteristics of a response.

The substance of the third conceptual problem relates to the appropriateness of the practice of not actually calculating the individual subject's empirical learning curve but rather combining N individual response protocols to generate an empirical mean or group learning curve. Does the average learning curve adequately represent the individual learning curve and, ipso facto, the underlying learning process in the individual? Is it legitimate to combine response data obtained from N individual subjects to form a mean learning curve? Given a mean learning curve, is the form, etc. of the individual learning curve uniquely specified?

To get a handle on this conceptual problem, it is necessary to operationalize the issue. Instead of using the absolute YES or NO form of the question as stated above, let us transform it into a relative one. Thus, the substance of the third conceptual problem functionally concerns the conditions under which the mean learning curve can be used to adequately represent the individual learning curve and the underlying individual learning function. So the basic question becomes "Under what conditions does the mean learning curve adequately represent the individual learning curve?"

APPROACHES TO THE REPRESENTATION OF THE INDIVIDUAL LEARNING CURVE BY THE USE OF AN AVERAGE CURVE AND THEIR METHODOLOGICAL SIGNIFICANCE

Introduction

The above question essentially establishes a three-category dimension: (1) under no condition, (2) under some conditions, and (3) under any or all conditions. Thus, there are three general approaches to the average curve representativeness problem; and each of them will be considered in turn.

Under No Condition Approach

Operant psychologists in general and Skinner in particular categorically refuse to assign any empirical significance to a mean learning curve. They do not expose an organism to reinforced practice unless the specific experimental situation affords a stable and interpretable individual learning curve. It is no coincidence that the cumulative recording of the digital characteristic of response occurrence over time (i.e., the rate of responding) in the operant conditioning situation meets the Skinnerian measurement stricture. Recall from Chapter 6 that the operant conditioning situation affords a peremptory degree of control over the subject's behavior. The individual subject's rate curve is both stable enough and sensitive enough to different environmental conditions and reinforcement contingencies that it can be used to reliably assess the effects of reinforced practice. Note that the above statement does not contain "that it can be reliably used to infer the state of the underlying learning process." For Skinner, the so-called "learning curve" is strictly a "performance curve." Recall from Chapter 4 that Skinner eschews any mysterious underlying intervening learning constructs. Overt behavior is all there is in relation to the environmental contingency in effect. The effect of the reinforcement operation must reside at the level of the individual's overt responding itself. If the individual response data protocol is garbage, the experimental manipulation is garbage. No amount of averaging or statisticulating with individual response data protocols will remedy the situation.

Under Some Conditions Approach

Introduction. In many respects this is the most sophisticated approach to the average curve representativeness problem — because various interpretations of "some" are possible. There are many alternative fomulations of just what constitutes the conditions under which the average learning curve adequately represents the individual learning curve. Two will be detailed here: (1) Spence's homogeneous subjects approach and (2) Estes' mathematical criterion approach.

Spence's homogeneous subjects approach. For Spence, the mean learning curve is representative of the individual learning function if it is calculated from response data generated by a set of homogeneous subjects. Actually this merely amounts to a statistical pre-selection of response data and has no conceptual significance beyond this fact. The representativeness is guaranteed because it is statistically built in. The crucial matter is what constitutes a set of homogeneous subjects. Many operational criteria of homogeneity exist:

1) how the subjects perform in a prior learning task;
2) how the subjects perform in the first X trials of the learning task;
3) how the subjects perform during the middle portion of the learning trials;
4) the proximity of the subjects in attaining the learning criterion;
5) etc.

Spence's homogeneous subjects approach is really a compromise between the strict Skinnerian view and the third (under any or all conditions) approach. For Skinner, the notion of representative is only meaningful for one subject's data; in the third approach, the notion of representative has meaning in the context of all the subjects in the learning experiment. For Spence, the notion of representative is meaningful for a selected subset of the subjects, with the size of the subset being greater than one but less than all (the universal set). In effect, Spence's approach puts constraints on which particular subjects are allowed to contribute to the mean learning curve.

Estes' mathematical criterion approach. Estes interprets the average curve representativeness problem as a mathematical one. Although every approach to this issue is informally mathematical or quasi-mathematical, Estes' approach is the only formal mathematical one in the sense that the ultimate arbiter of representativeness is the specific mathematical nature of the individual learning curve (underlying function). Estes distinguishes between three kinds of (individual) mathematical functions: (1) functions that are unmodified by averaging, (2) functions for which averaging complicates the interpretation of parameters but leaves the form unchanged, and (3) functions that are modified both in form and parameter values by averaging. Let us analyze each type.

1. The mean curve for the group has the same form as the individual function and the parameters of the mean curve are simply the arithmetical means of the corresponding individual parameters. The generating condition for this kind of function is as follows. Each parameter in the function either appears alone or is a coefficient multiplying the independent variable or a quantity which depends upon the independent variable. Examples of this kind of function include: $Y = a + bX$, $Y = a \log X$, and $Y = a/X$, where X and Y symbolize the independent and dependent variable, respectively, and a and b are parameters. The distinguishing mathematical feature of this class is the fact that all the second and higher order partial derivatives of the function, when evaluated by the Taylor series development, are equal to zero.

2. The mean curve for the group has the same form as the individual function but the parameters of the mean curve are some kind of mathematical transformation of the corresponding individual parameters other than the simple arithmetical mean. The generating condition for this kind of function is as follows. Each parameter in the function does not appear alone and is in a multiplicative relationship with the independent variable such that the product is either mathematically transformed or acted upon by some other quantity. Examples of this kind of function include: $Y = \log bX$ and $Y = 1/a + b/ax$. The distinguishing mathematical feature of this class is the fact that all the second and higher order partial derivatives of a certain linear transformation of the original function, when evaluated by the Taylor series development, are equal to zero.

3. The mean curve for the group does not have the same form as the individual function and the parameters of the mean curve are some kind of mathematical transformation of the corresponding individual parameters other than the simple arithmetical mean. The generating condition for this kind of function is as follows. It contains terms involving the independent variable which do not factor out when the values of Y are summed over a group of subjects for a constant value of the independent variable. The prime example of this kind of function is the exponential growth function: $Y = a + be^{-cX}$. The distinguishing mathematical feature of this class is the fact that some of the second and higher order partial derivatives of the function or a linear transformation of it, when evaluated by the Taylor series development, are not equal to zero.

So, the form of the average curve is representative of the individual curve in two of the three types of functions. But remember that Estes is a micro-modeler. He is not so much interested in whether the form of the mean learning curve represents the form of the individual curve as he is interested in using the form of the individual curve as a predictive device. Specifically, he is interested in deriving the properties that should hold for the average curve when the individual curve is hypothesized as having a certain form and then comparing the predicted mean learning curve with the empirical mean learning curve derived from a set of learning data. In the micro-model approach it is possible to predict the exact form of the mean learning curve from the underlying deductive structure and this can be compared with the obtained mean learning curve.

Under Any or All Conditions Approach

This is the traditional or implicit approach. It is primarily characteristic of the macro-theoretical approach to learning, especially of Hull. Hull naively assumed that the form of the mean learning curve faithfully represents the form of the individual curves regardless of the specific experimental circumstances in effect. Actually, with technical mathematical considerations aside, since Hull conceptualized the underlying learning process as being slow, gradual, smooth, incremental, etc., the group or average learning curve must have the same form (i.e., look the same): slow, gradual, smooth, incremental, etc. At a technical mathematical level, Hull assumed the underlying incremental habit strength function to be exponential in nature, which of course makes it belong to the third class of Estes' functions.

This approach is not as naive as it appears on the surface. Most learning psychologists employing this approach realize that, at the operational level, the use of an arbitrary trials to criterion measure for each subject can indeed distort the calculated mean learning curve — because different subjects meet criterion on different trials and therefore contribute disproportionately to the obtained mean learning curve. Various ways have been proposed to at least partially solve this statistical problem — for instance, the use of a Vincent mean learning curve and the use of a Hayes backward mean learning curve.

RELABELING THE THREE APPROACHES

For reasons that will become apparent in the next subsection, it is convenient to relabel the three approaches to the average curve representativeness problem. The "under no condition" approach will become the "no representation" approach; the "under some conditions" approach will be called the "contingent representation" approach; and the "under any or all conditions" approach will be renamed the "universal representation" approach.

THE THREE CONCEPTUAL PROBLEMS IN PERSPECTIVE: SOME INTERRELATIONSHIPS

INTRODUCTION

The three conceptual measurement problems are not independent of each other. How a specific learning psychologist responds to one of the problems is by and large related to how he responds to the other problems. A specific approach to one problem is associated with a specific approach to the other problems. Specifically, there are three rather obvious sets of correspondences among the approaches to the individual conceptual problems. These can be denoted by simply selecting the corresponding approach associated with each conceptual problem and conjoining them.

THE THREE SETS OF CORRESPONDENCES

Set I: Universal Average Curve Representation — Complete Response Equivalency — Incremental Underlying Learning Function

Collectively, this set characterizes the macro-theoretical approach to the measurement of the learning process. It could be termed an absolutistic approach to the measurement of the learning process.

Set II: Contingent Average Curve Representation – Contingent Response Equivalency – Nonincremental Underlying Learning Function

Collectively, this set specifies the micro-model approach to the measurement of the learning process. It could be termed a relativistic approach to the measurement of the learning process.

Set III: No Average Curve Representation – No Response Equivalency

This set is mute with respect to the first conceptual measurement problem in that no specific interpretation of the underlying learning function is associated with it. Collectively, this set describes how operant psychologists, such as Skinner, and the micromolar theorist, Logan, approach the measurement of the learning process. It could be termed an individualistic approach to the measurement of the learning process.

SIGNIFICANCE OF THE THREE SETS OF MEASUREMENT APPROACHES

The chapter began by reiterating that the learning process is an inferred construct and therefore can only be indirectly measured. Three conceptual problems associated with the measurement of the learning process were introduced and alternative approaches to these problems were presented. It just so happens that when the individual measurement approaches are grouped and classified they yield the primary theoretical approaches to learning introduced in prior chapters: the macro-theoretical approach, the micro-model approach, and the "nontheoretical" inductive approach. So how a specific learning psychologist measures the learning process is primarily determined by his theoretical conception of learning.

1. The macro-theorists regard the learning process as virtually an absolute property of the universe independent of specific learning tasks, procedures, etc. and, as such, they use an absolutistic measurement approach.

2. The micro-modelers treat the nature of the learning process as at least partially contingent upon the specific task or procedure used to investigate it and also strictly as a predictive device to account for obtained response data and, as such, they use a relativistic or contingent measurement approach.

3. The "nontheoretical" inductive approach characteristic of the Skinnerians does not impute independent nondescriptive reality to the learning process and, as such, uses an individualistic measurement approach in the context of which no kind of equivalence or representation is meaningful.

SUMMARY

There are three basic conceptual problems associated with measuring the learning process.

1. The first conceptual problem involves the nature of the underlying learning function residing in the individual subject. There are three classic solutions to this problem: (a) the incremental approach, (b) the all-or-none approach, and (c) the multistate, multistage approach.

2. The second conceptual problem concerns the question of response equivalency. This question only applies to the analogical characteristics of a response and exists on two dimensions: (a) response characteristic equivalency and (b) response instance equivalency. It is possible for a learning theorist to accept both kinds of equivalency (complete response equivalency approach), reject characteristic equivalency and accept instance equivalency (contingent response equivalency approach), or reject both kinds of equivalency (non-equivalency approach).

3. The third conceptual problem relates to how adequately an average, group, or mean learning curve represents the individual subject's empirical learning curve and, ipso facto, the underlying learning process in the individual. Operationalizing this issue yields three approaches: (a) under no condition (no representation approach), (b) under some conditions (contingent representation approach), and (c) under any or all conditions (universal representation approach).

The three conceptual measurement problems are not independent of each other — how a specific learning psychologist responds to one of the problems is related to how he responds to the other problems and three overall approaches can be distinguished: (1) the absolutistic approach, characteristic of macro-theory, (2) the relativistic approach, characteristic of micro-models, and (3) the individualistic approach, representative of operant psychologists and micromolar theorists. These three overall approaches are indicative of the three classic conceptions of the nature of the learning process: (a) an absolute property of the universe, (b) contingent upon the specific experimental situation in which it is investigated, and (c) possessing no independent nondescriptive reality.

9
Analysis of the Concept of Reinforcement

INTRODUCTION

We already know from Chapters 1 and 4 that the concept of reinforcement serves as the primary independent variable in learning psychology at the definitional level. Chapter 2 identified the notion of reinforcer with a certain kind of stimulus event and distinguished between two kinds of reinforcement operations: the S-S or experimenter-contingent operation and the S-R-S or response-contingent operation. Chapter 5 presented a classification system for the primary learning tasks based in part on the two different reinforcement operations. Chapter 7 established the fact that the nature and role of reinforcement at a theoretical level constitute key theoretical problems in the context of the macro-theoretical approach to learning.

To complete the conceptual analysis of learning psychology, it is necessary to assign more substantive content to the two reinforcement operations, to describe the nature of reinforced practice in some of the primary learning tasks, and to present some specific macro-theoretical interpretations of the nature and role of reinforcement. But the discussion of these topics will be embedded in a larger conceptual framework, the basic outline of which is indicated in the next subsection.

At this point, two focuses of our analysis must be made explicit. (1) Our conceptual discussion of reinforcement will stress the S-R-S reinforcement operation. This type of reinforcement operation will be analyzed as the prototypical case and the conclusions derived from it will be applied to the S-S reinforcement operation. This can be justified on at least two bases. Initially, recall from Chapter 2 that the S-R-S operation constitutes the superordinate operation and the S-S operation is merely a subset of it. Secondly, only the S-R-S operation actually makes reference to the subject's prior behavior, as a consequence of which only this operation can be definitionally related to the subject's responding. (2) Consideration of the nature and role of reinforcement at the theoretical level will primarily be done in the context of primary positive reinforcement, which is just one of the four existent operational types of reinforcement. The reason for this is strictly historical. The primary theoretical interpretations of the nature and role of reinforcement have almost exclusively been formulated in the context of this type of reinforcement.

So, with this as a background, let us list the specific aspects of reinforcement to be formally discussed in the chapter.

PREVIEW OF THE CONCEPTUAL ANALYSIS OF REINFORCEMENT

Our analysis of the concept of reinforcement will be organized around the following seven aspects of reinforcement.

1. The structure of the reinforcement situation. This section structures the reinforcement situation by distinguishing between such terms as reinforcer, reinforcing event, reinforcing stimulus, reinforcement, reinforcing operation, and reinforced practice.

2. Descriptive types of response-contingent reinforcing events. This section introduces the four basic operational kinds of reinforcers in the context of the response-contingent reinforcement situation.

3. Descriptive types of experimenter-contingent reinforcing events. This section analyzes to what extent the distinctions made in the context of the response-contingent reinforcement situation can be applied to the experimenter-contingent reinforcement situation.

4. Reinforcement in complex human learning: The concept of knowledge of results or feedback versus the concept of physical reward. This section examines the issue of whether reinforcement in complex human learning or cognitive situations is essentially different from reinforcement in simple animal learning and/or conditioning.

5. The nature of reinforced practice in some common learning tasks. This section describes the nature of reinforced practice found in some of the primary learning tasks used by learning psychologists.

6. Theoretical interpretations of the nature and role of primary positive reinforcement. This section distinguishes between the weak and strong laws of effect, relates the theoretical analysis of reinforcement to other learning issues, and presents both traditional and contemporary theoretical approaches to primary positive reinforcement.

7. Philosophical criticisms of the law of effect. This section describes the circumstances under which the law of effect can be interpreted as circular and teleological, two conditions which any construct or explanation should avoid according to the dictums of the philosophy of science.

THE STRUCTURE OF THE REINFORCEMENT SITUATION

Up to now the following terms have been used more-or-less equivalently: "reinforcer," "reinforcing event," and "reinforcing stimulus." Also the terms "reinforcement operation," "reinforcement," and "reinforced practice" have been used at various points in the text. Because we are now attempting a formal analysis of the reinforcement situation, subtle differences in the uses of the terms must be introduced.

We shall regard the terms "reinforcer" and "reinforcing event" to be synonomous and primitive – i.e., logically prior or at the first level of analysis. A reinforcer or reinforcing event at the next level of analysis is a stimulus or stimulus event – thus, the term "reinforcing stimulus."

Now recall from Chapter 2 that a stimulus is a change in the environment (either an onset, cessation, or modulation in amount). But up to now we have implicitly assumed that a reinforcing event was always the onset of an environmental event. From this point on, it must be realized that a reinforcing event can also be the termination of an environmental event. So there are two kinds of reinforcing events: the onset of an environmental event or the cessation of an environmental event. As a pragmatic matter, the learning psychologist informally uses the term "reinforcing stimulus" in both the onset and cessation sense – but the distinction is crucial for deriving the operational types of reinforcing events or response-contingent reinforcement operations. Henceforth, we shall use the term "reinforcing event" where we simply used the term "reinforcing stimulus" in the past.

At the next level of analysis, a specific reinforcing event appears as the second stimulus term in either the S-S or S-R-S reinforcement operation. A reinforcement operation is simply a sequence of two stimulus events (S-S) or of two stimulus events with a response intervening (S-R-S), in which the second stimulus event serves as a reinforcing event. Customarily, the subject is said to be receiving a "reinforcement" whenever he is exposed to a reinforcing event as part and parcel of being subjected to a reinforcement operation.

Finally, at the highest level of analysis, reinforced practice consists of exposure to a series of N successive reinforcement operations (where $0 < N < \infty$) either in the discrete-trial or continuous-time procedure.

The above distinctions are diagramed in Fig. 9-1. The content of the diagram is self-explanatory, especially since it is analogous to the figures representing the input (Chapter 2) and output (Chapter 3) situations respectively.

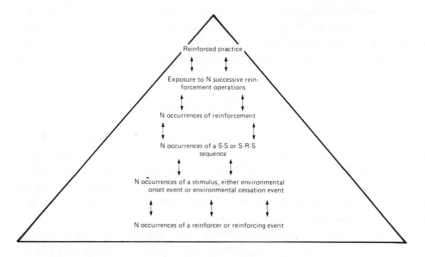

Fig. 9-1. The Structure of the Reinforcement Situation

DESCRIPTIVE TYPES OF RESPONSE-CONTINGENT REINFORCING EVENTS

INTRODUCTION

No substantial content has as yet been assigned to the response-contingent reinforcement operation other than the denotational property of the reinforcing event being contingent upon the prior occurrence of a response instance from the specific response class of interest and thus often being interpreted as the effect operation. Further denotational interpretation must now be given to the reinforcing event of the S-R-S operation. Ultimately, we shall see that it can be assigned to one of four cells of a 2 x 2 classification scheme, which in effect generates the four types of response-contingent reinforcing events.

DERIVATION OF THE DESCRIPTIVE KINDS OF RESPONSE-CONTINGENT REINFORCING EVENTS

Introduction

To generate the different kinds of operational reinforcers, it is necessary to introduce two key analytical dimensions. The first dimension relates to which aspect (onset or cessation) of the environmental event serves as the reinforcing event. The second dimension relates to the ultimate source of the reinforcing event: (1) innate or biologically sourced or (2) derived or learned. The first dimension is a behavioral, definitional, or operational dimension which is used to find out whether a stimulus event X taken at random from the environment can actually serve as a reinforcer. The second dimension is a theoretical or interpretive one, in the sense that it specifies why an already known reinforcer X possesses reinforcing properties. When these two binary-valued dimensions are made orthogonal to each other, they generate a four-cell classification scheme yielding the four operational types of reinforcers.

The Classification System Generating the Four Operational Types of Reinforcers

In Fig. 9-2, the stimulus aspect dimension and the source dimension constitute the horizontal and vertical dimensions, respectively. The binary categories of the horizontal dimension are labeled "onset" and "cessation"; and the category values of the vertical dimension are characterized as "biological" and "learned." Each of the four categories can be given a technical specification.

		Aspect of the Environmental Event Serving as the Reinforcing Stimulus	
		Onset (Positive)	Cessation (Negative)
Source of the Reinforcing Event	Biological (Primary)	I $+S^R$ Primary positive reinforcer food water sexual contact	II $-S^R$ Primary negative reinforcer shock intense illumination strong air blast
	Learned (Secondary)	III $+S^r$ Secondary positive reinforcer money recognition award	IV $-S^r$ Secondary negative reinforcer parking fine F exam grade tornado warning signal

Fig. 9-2. A Classification System for the Four Operational Types of Reinforcers

Technical Equivalents of the Four Categories

The technical names for the four categories are as follows:

1. The onset category establishes the notion of a positive reinforcer. If the onset of an environmental event serves as the reinforcing event, that stimulus operates as a positive reinforcer.

2. The cessation category establishes the notion of a negative reinforcer. If the cessation of an environmental event serves as the reinforcing event, that stimulus operates as a negative reinforcer.

3. The biological category sets up the concept of a primary reinforcer. If the origin of a reinforcing event is biological, it is called a primary reinforcer.

4. The learned category sets up the concept of a secondary reinforcer. If the origin of a reinforcing event can be traced back to past learning experience, it is called a secondary reinforcer.

Orthogonal Use of the Four Categories

Any reinforcing event X is a pairwise combination of a category value from each dimension — i.e., it is assignable to one of the four cells. Thus, the four cells generate the operational types of reinforcers as follows:

Cell I — primary positive reinforcer;
Cell II — primary negative reinforcer;
Cell III — secondary positive reinforcer;
Cell IV — secondary negative reinforcer.

The traditional symbolic notation for each type of reinforcer is included in the figure in such a way that the meaning of each subsymbol can be easily induced. To make the distinctions just introduced less abstract, three informal examples of each kind of reinforcer are also presented in the figure.

The Proper Interpretation of the Classification System

Although it is not necessary to assess the general descriptive significance of this classification scheme, its limits of applicability (resolvability) should be discussed. The reinforcing event for any specific learning task or experimental manipulation is uniquely assignable to one of the four cells; but, the scheme does not establish four mutually exclusive lists of reinforcers. The same identical qualitative, but not necessarily quantitative, stimulus event can be assigned to different cells depending upon the specific experimental circumstances in effect. Consider the following examples.

Shock is located in cell II because it usually serves as a primary negative reinforcer; but, if shock is used to signal the impending occurrence of some appetitive stimulus event, such as food, sexual contact, money, etc., it can develop secondary positive reinforcing properties. Likewise, food is located in cell I because it usually serves as a primary positive reinforcer; but, if food is used to signal the impending occurrence of some aversive stimulus event, such as shock, intense heat, intense noise, etc., it can develop secondary negative reinforcing properties. One final example: Light is a reinforcer under certain circumstances. Whether it is a positive or negative reinforcer depends upon the initial intensity or illumination level at which it is administered to the organism: if mild or low, it operates as a positive reinforcer; if intense or high, it operates as a negative reinforcer.

So, the scheme generates every operational type of reinforcer, but it does not in and of itself assign a particular reinforcing event to a specific cell. This is done by extraclassificational factors such as the specific experimental contingency in effect, the type of learned response, etc.

STRUCTURAL PREVIEW

It is procedurally inconvenient to analyze the four operational types of reinforcers (the cells themselves) because they are essentially conjunctive concepts. It is much easier to analyze each of the possible attributes of a reinforcer individually — i.e., to analyze the nature and characteristics of the dimensional input categories themselves. We shall process the two categories of the stimulus aspect dimension first and then process the two categories of the source dimension, starting with the leftmost and uppermost category in each case. (We shall not be dealing with the four basic operational reinforcers at the conjunctive level per se until later.) There is only one problem associated with the unidimensional approach to the analysis of reinforcing events — namely, it is difficult to present examples of reinforcing events in each category independent of the other dimension.

THE NOTION OF A POSITIVE REINFORCING EVENT

Alternative Conceptions or Definitions

To put the notion of positive reinforcer in proper perspective, let us analyze the two historically significant definitional approaches to the concept: (1) the classic, nonbehavioral, Thorndikian approach and (2) the contemporary, behavioral, Skinnerian approach.

Thorndike's approach. According to Thorndike, a stimulus event is a positive reinforcer if its onset results in a stamping in or strengthening of an S-R association preceding it immediately in time and also results in a state of satisfaction, pleasure, or the like on the part of the organism. More specifically, the satisfying state of affairs is the actual causal agent for the incrementing in the strength of the S-R association. The reinforcing event is not the literal external stimulus event itself but the subjective state to which it leads. The reason this definition is described as nonbehavioral is due to its reference to the subjective satisfying state. The use of the phrase "S-R association," although not residing at the level of overt behavior itself, offers no real problem because a stamping in or strengthening of an S-R association is ordinarily reflected in an increase in the frequency of occurrence of the response element of the association if the appropriate S element is present.

Skinner's approach. According to Skinner, a stimulus event is a positive reinforcer if its onset results in an increase in the frequency of occurrence of a response which immediately precedes it in time. Note that this conception of a positive reinforcer was used in the prior classification system for generating the different operational reinforcing events. Skinner's definition is labeled as behavioral because it only makes reference to external behavior and the reinforcing event exists at the level of the external stimulus event itself.

Comparison of the Two Approaches and a Resolution

There are many superficial differences between the two conceptions of a positive reinforcer. Thorndike never actually used the term "positive reinforcer" and described the relationship between a satisfying state of affairs and its effect on a preceding S-R connection in the general instrumental conditioning context. Skinner did use the word "positive reinforcer" and described the relationship between a stimulus event and its effect on a preceding response in the operant conditioning context (a subkind of instrumental conditioning – see Chapter 4). But the only real difference between the two approaches to a positive reinforcer relates to the appeal or nonappeal to a certain kind of subjective state. Contemporary learning psychologists have by and large resolved this one crucial difference between the two definitions by refusing to appeal to the notion of a subjective satisfying state of affairs. Once the reference to this state is deleted, the two approaches to defining a positive reinforcer become functionally equivalent to each other. So, contemporarily, the reason a stimulus event serves as a positive reinforcer is because its onset conditions the actual behavior preceding it in time and not because of any subjective side effects it might set up in the organism.

Examples of a Positive Reinforcer

The list of positive reinforcers is descriptively infinite. A few examples will be presented to develop a better "feel" for this category. (Note that all the examples below are restricted to the primary reinforcer category on the source dimension.) Positive (primary) reinforcers include the following: food, water, sexual contact, air (oxygen), novel stimulation, opportunity to manipulate some object or puzzle, opportunity to explore the environment, opportunity to engage in some highly complex cognitive activity, physical activity per se, physical contact of a nonaversive variety (e.g., maternal or affectional), light or tone onset, saccharin (nonnutritive foodstuff), etc.

A Caution: The Notion of Reward Versus the Notion of Positive Reinforcer

The term "reward" is a nontechnical one which the typical layman and even some psychologists use as a full equivalent for the term "positive reinforcer." Society, as a whole, has never heard of the concept of positive reinforcer. At best, they are merely partially overlapping terms in the response-contingent reinforcement situation. While we shall attempt no formal definition of reward here, it can be noted that a positive reinforcer in the response-contingent reinforcement situation in certain contexts possesses certain properties characteristic of a reward — i.e., it is earned or deserved, a certain behavior is necessary for its attainment, it is used to control and regulate behavior, etc. Likewise, a reward in certain contexts can functionally operate as a response-contingent positive reinforcer — i.e., condition a desirable response. But the notions of positive reinforcer and reward have no overlap whatsoever in the experimenter-contingent reinforcement situation where the specific reinforcing properties of a stimulus event cannot be defined or isolated in terms of its effect on prior behavior at all. For these two reasons, any further consideration of the concept of reward would not contribute substantially to the analysis of the reinforcement situation.

THE NOTION OF A NEGATIVE REINFORCING EVENT

Alternative Conceptions or Definitions

Again let us analyze the two historically significant definitional approaches to the concept: (1) the classic, nonbehavioral, Thorndikian approach, and (2) the contemporary, behavioral, Skinnerian approach.

Thorndike's approach. According to Thorndike, a stimulus event is a negative reinforcer if its onset results in a stamping out or weakening of an S-R association preceding it in time and also results in a state of dissatisfaction, displeasure, or the like on the part of the organism. More specifically, the dissatisfying state of affairs is the actual causal agent for the decrementing in the strength of the S-R association. The reinforcing event is not the literal external stimulus event itself but the subjective state to which it leads. Again, the reason this definition is termed nonbehavioral is due to its reference to the subjective dissatisfying state. The use of the phrase "S-R association" in this approach to a negative reinforcer does lead to problems because a stamping out or weakening of an S-R connection does not necessarily result in a decrease in the frequency of occurrence of the response element of the association when the appropriate S element is present.

Skinner's approach. According to Skinner, a stimulus event is a negative reinforcer if its termination results in an increase in the frequency of occurrence of a response which immediately precedes it in time. Note that this conception of a negative reinforcer was used in the prior classification system for generating the different operational reinforcing events. Again, Skinner's definition is described as behavioral because it only makes reference to external behavior and the reinforcing event exists at the level of the external stimulus itself. The problem of observing a decrease in the frequency of occurrence of a response is avoided in the Skinnerian approach to a negative reinforcer. The possible negative reinforcing properties of a stimulus event are still assessed in the context of a response increase because the crucial definitional aspect of a negative reinforcing event has been switched from a stimulus onset event to a stimulus termination event.

Comparison of the Two Approaches and a Resolution

As implied in the above discussion, the differences between these two conceptions of a negative reinforcer are significant and not superficial. To facilitate the comparison, the key corresponding phrases from the two definitions are contiguously presented below.

Thorndike: onset of a stimulus event — weakening of an S-R bond — dissatisfying state of affairs.

Skinner: termination of a stimulus event — increase in behavior occurrence — no corresponding analogue.

Even if we were to drop the reference to the dissatisfying subjective state, the two approaches would not be equivalent (i.e., resolved). We are still left with two fundamentally different operations or concepts.

The way most contemporary learning psychologists resolve this problem is by treating the two approaches as actually defining two entirely different operations or concepts. The Skinnerian approach is regarded as the acceptable characterization of a negative reinforcer; and a variant of the Thorndikian approach is treated by many learning psychologists as an acceptable characterization of a punishing event. A stimulus event is a punishing event if its onset results in a decrease in the frequency of occurrence of a response which immediately precedes it in time. (Both the subjective state reference and the S-R bond language have been eliminated in this variant of the original Thorndikian statement.)

Thorndike himself never used the term "negative reinforcer" and he would not be averse to having his statement labeled a punishing operation. In his later years, primarily as a result of active research, Thorndike had doubts about a dissatisfying state of affairs as actually resulting in a weakening or stamping out of an S-R bond. This doubt has become "institutionalized" in Skinner's contemporary definition of a punishing event. For Skinner and many contemporary psychologists, a punishing event is defined merely as the onset of a negative reinforcer without any reference at all to its possible effects on behavior. For Skinner, a piece of behavior is being punished if its occurrence is followed by the onset of a negative reinforcer. The typical research finding with the use of mild to moderate punishment is that the presentation of a negative reinforcer does not lead to any weakening (unlearning) of the punished response — it merely results in the temporary suppression of the response.

So, in summary, contemporarily, the reason a stimulus event serves as a negative reinforcer is because its cessation conditions the actual behavior preceding it in time and not because of any dissatisfying subjective side effects it might set up in the organism; and any operation involving the onset of a known negative reinforcer is definitionally treated as a punishing event whose effect on behavior is extradefinitional.

Consolidation on the Nature of the Resolution: The Concept of an Aversive Stimulus Event

The above discussion was really a roundabout way of introducing the notion of an aversive stimulus event. Let us assume that aversive stimulus events exist without formally defining them. For example, shock, intense heat, pain, etc. The point is that an aversive stimulus event can be used two ways. If the organism's behavior occasions the termination of an aversive stimulus event, the stimulus event is operating as a negative reinforcer. If the organism's behavior occasions the onset of an aversive stimulus event, the stimulus event is operating as a punisher. The former use of an aversive stimulus event invariably results in the acquisition of a learned response; the latter use of an aversive stimulus event typically results in a mere temporary suppression of the ongoing punished response class.

The Concept of an Appetitive Stimulus Event and the Generation of Another Type of Punishing Operation or Event

To complement the notion of an aversive stimulus event, let us assume that the notion of an appetitive stimulus event is meaningful, but without formally defining it. Examples of appetitive stimulus events would include food, water, sexual contact, etc. An appetitive stimulus event can be used to ways. If the organism's behavior occasions the onset of an appetitive stimulus event, the stimulus event is operating as a positive reinforcer. If the organism's behavior occasions the termination of an appetitive stimulus event, the stimulus event is operating as a punisher. The former use of an appetitive stimulus event invariably results in the acquisition of a learned response; the latter use of an appetitive stimulus event is a matter of current experimental concern and the provisional conclusion is that it possesses "true" aversive properties and suppresses the behavior to which it is applied.

Examples of a Negative Reinforcer

The list of negative reinforcers is descriptively infinite. A few examples will be presented to develop a better "feel" for this category. (Note that all the examples below are restricted to the primary reinforcer category on the source dimension.) Negative (primary) reinforcers include the following: shock, strong air blast, extreme heat, extreme cold, any kind of painful stimulus, intense illumination, intense noise, aversive odors, aversive tastes, aggressive physical contact, water immersion for a nonswimmer, etc.

A Caution: The Notion of Punishment Versus the Notion of Negative Reinforcer

Our prior discussion has established the fact that both terms have technical significance in learning, are denotatively distinct, and refer to the two ways in which an aversive stimulus event can be applied to behavior. Unfortunately, the typical layman and even some psychologists use the terms synonymously in such a way as to make punishment the dominant concept. As in the case of the relationship between reward and positive reinforcer, society, as a whole, has never heard of the concept of negative reinforcer and is only cognizant of the fact that an aversive stimulus event can be used as a punishing event to control behavior.

A Digression: Why Does a Psychologist Expose a Subject to Aversive Stimulation – i.e., Why Does an Experimenter Shock a Rat or a College Sophomore?

Introduction. For various moral, ethical, theological, or general humanistic reasons, some individuals are against the practice of using aversive stimulation either in the context of the everyday environment or in the lab or both, although most everyday complex human behavior is controlled by aversive contingencies rather than by appetitive contingencies (i.e., positive reinforcement). In fact, the whole fabric and structure of society seems to be built around the actual use or threat of use of aversive stimulation.

We are not going to evaluate this antagonism to the use of aversive contingencies on any moral or ethical grounds or even on any pragmatic, utilitarian grounds (i.e., whether aversive stimului efficiently control and/or manipulate behavior). Rather we are going to present two classes of reasons why the experimental learning psychologist employs aversive stimulation in the lab, specifically as a negative reinforcing event. The experimental learning psychologist can justify using shock or some other aversive stimulus event to condition a response on either of two grounds: (1) procedural or motivational or (2) theoretical or conceptual. We shall discuss each of these in turn.

Procedural, motivational advantages of negative reinforcement. It is procedurally more efficient and motivationally easier to use a negative reinforcer to condition a response than to use a positive reinforcer for the same purpose. Whenever a positively reinforcing substance is employed, the subject must be deprived of that substance for X hours before the learning session even begins. For instance, food serves as a positive reinforcer only if the organism has been previously deprived of food. Also, the motivational level or drive level of the subject decreases during the course of the learning session under typical reinforcement conditions and this affects the performance of the learned response. For instance, continued use of food as a positive reinforcer during the session causes the subject to satiate and eventually the subject stops responding – i.e., food no longer acts as a positive reinforcer because the subject is no longer deprived.

Neither of these problems arises in the context of negative reinforcement. Prior deprivation is not necessary and there are no satiation effects. For instance, shock can serve as a negative reinforcer with no prior deprivation of any kind; also the subject never satiates on shock and does not stop responding – within the temporal limits of the typical learning session.

These two procedural or motivational differences between positive and negative reinforcement can be stated quite succinctly. A negative reinforcer possesses automatic, built-in motivational properties, whereas a positive reinforcer has no automatic, built-in motivational properties. As a cautionary note, it must be emphasized that we are only discussing the relationship between reinforcement and motivation at a procedural level, not at a theoretical level, and these "motivational properties" are purely operational or descriptive entities.

Theoretical, conceptual superiority of negative reinforcement. Negative reinforcement is conceptually or theoretically "cleaner" than positive reinforcement. This relates to what actually constitutes the reinforcing event for the subject or to what moment in time the reinforcing event occurs for the subject. The basic point is that, at a low level of analysis, we know what the reinforcing event is and at what time it occurs in the context of negative reinforcement; but we are ignorant of these two things in the context of positive reinforcement. The reason for this is very simple. Negative reinforcement is identified with a stimulus termination event in the environment. Negative reinforcement, as the cessation of something, is a discrete event which occurs at a discrete moment in time. For instance, if shock is serving as the negative reinforcer, the content of the reinforcement is the actual shock termination and we know essentially at what moment in time it occurs.

On the other hand, positive reinforcement is identified with a stimulus onset event in the environment. The onset of a stimulus event is just the beginning of an extended chain of events which continues over time. For instance, if food is serving as the positive reinforcer, the presentation of a food object to the subject starts a whole series of events — it literally opens up a Pandora's box of goodies. Food presentation results in sight, smell of food object; touching, manipulation of food object; licking, chewing, tasting of food object; swallowing or esophageal passage of the food object; ingestion activity in the stomach; further biochemical processing of the food stuff; some hunger drive reduction; some ultimate physiological need reduction; etc. Any one or more of these can serve as the actual content of the positively reinforcing event; likewise, at which particular moment in time the reinforcing event occurs is indeterminate.

So, the vagueness and indeterminacy associated with the actual content and temporal moment of occurrence of a positively reinforcing event bothers many hard-core experimental learning psychologists and they prefer to use negative reinforcement exclusively in order to remain relatively conceptually "clean." Again, as a note of caution, it must be emphasized that the current use of the terms "conceptual" and "theoretical" is very low-level and this subsection has not discussed actual high-level theoretical or conceptual approaches to or interpretations of reinforcement.

THE NOTION OF A PRIMARY REINFORCING EVENT

Other Terms for a Primary Reinforcer

Since this category of reinforcing events comes from the theoretical source dimension, a listing of some of the alternative labels for the category can serve the purpose of providing some of the denotational properties of a primary reinforcer. These other terms include the following: biological, unlearned, innate, automatic, given, physical, natural, etc. So, fundamentally, a primary reinforcer is a physical or structural reinforcer dependent upon the underlying physiology of the organism; as such, its reinforcing properties are unlearned, innate, given, automatic, etc. Examples of primary reinforcers have already been presented in the context of the positive and negative reinforcer categories (e.g., food, water, shock, strong air blast, etc.).

Alternative Conceptions of a Primary Reinforcer

Introduction. Virtually no contemporary learning psychologist worries about defining a primary reinforcing event. Often it is only implicitly defined; when it is explicitly defined, some casual reference is made to its biological base or innateness. In fact, the term "primary reinforcer" itself is going out of style; instead this category of reinforcers is typically straightway described as biological or innate. This is not to intimate that there is no current controversy concerning the how or why of a primary reinforcing event. At a theoretical level, the specific mechanism underlying the effects of a primary reinforcer on behavior constitutes a classic and continuing conceptual problem. The point is that learning psychology has arrived at a stage in its development where it accepts a class of innate or biological reinforcers at face value. Historically, this was not always the case. There was a time during the heyday of macro-theories when the learning psychologist felt obliged to assign some fundamental property to a primary reinforcer other than the fact that it was biologically based. It was in this kind of atmosphere that the label "primary" was originally assigned to this category of reinforcers.

We are going to analyze three different approaches to characterizing a primary reinforcing event, one of which is the already informally stated general biological approach. The other two approaches implicitly assume an underlying biological base, so they really constitute subsets of the general biological approach. In effect, these other two approaches are successively more restrictive than the general biological approach and, as such, they reduce the size of the list of stimulus events which can act as primary reinforcing events. The reinforcing events successively excluded from the primary reinforcer category are still reinforcers, but they have to be assigned to the other category on the source dimension, the learned or derived category. In essence, these alternative conceptions of a primary reinforcing event differ with respect to where the cutoff point dividing reinforcing events into primary and secondary is located on the underlying dimension.

The general biological approach. In this approach, an already known reinforcing event X is a primary reinforcing event if it is biologically based — i.e., if it is a reinforcing event by virtue of the nature of the organism's underlying physiology. All the examples of reinforcing events presented while analyzing the stimulus aspect dimension are primary reinforcers in the context of this approach. These examples are reproduced in Fig. 9-3 as members of a universal set of biologically based reinforcers.

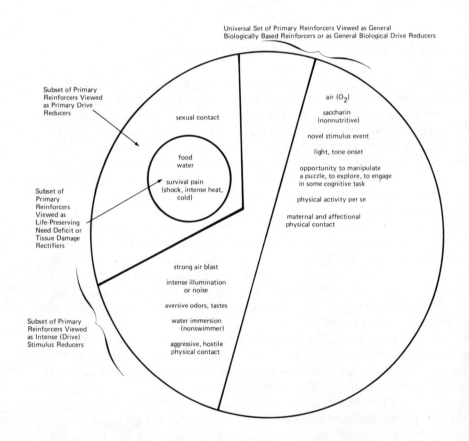

Fig. 9-3. Alternative Conceptions of Primary Reinforcing Events

The Biological Drive Reduction Approach

Introduction. In this approach, an already known reinforcing event X is a primary reinforcing event if it allows or causes reduction in some biological drive. Unfortunately, there are many alternative approaches to what constitutes a biological drive. We shall discuss three conceptions of biological drive and their consequences for what constitutes a primary reinforcing event.

Hull, Spence, Tolman, et al.'s interpretation of drive as a specific deprivation operation or restriction condition. In this approach to biological drive, a drive is established in a subject by virtue of his being deprived of some stimulus substance or of his being prevented from engaging in some activity, etc. Food, water, and sexual deprivation establish hunger, thirst, and sexual drives. Exposure to a restricted environment enhances the reinforcing properties of a novel stimulus or a tone, light onset. Restricting physical activity, positive physical contact, and the various types of opportunities enhances their reinforcing properties. The so-called negatively reinforcing events are inherently drive inducing in this approach to biological drive. Their onset in the laboratory situation automatically or operationally sets up a drive in the organism without prior deprivation or restriction. The functional consequence of this conception of biological drive is that virtually any biologically based reinforcer can also act as a biological drive reducer and thus serve as a primary reinforcing stimulus; and this approach does not appreciably constrict the universal set of primary reinforcing events.

Neal Miller (and later Hull's) interpretation of biological drive as an intense stimulus event. For Neal Miller, any stimulus event serves as a drive or has drive properties if it is made intense enough. Food, water, and sexual deprivation establish intense stimulation in the organism. The onset of any negatively reinforcing event also acts as intense stimulation for the organism. But, the deprivation or restriction of novel stimulus events, lights, tones, the various opportunities, physical activity per se, and positive physical contact do not serve as sources of intense stimulation for the organism. In this interpretation of biological drive, these biologically based reinforcers cannot reduce intense (drive) stimuli and therefore they cannot be primary reinforcing events and must be assigned to the secondary reinforcing event category. This consequence is indicated in Fig. 9-3 by separating these reinforcers from the others by means of a diagonal slice.

Hull's interpretation of drive as a specific need deficit or tissue damage. In this approach, a biological drive is established whenever some underlying need deficit or tissue damage arises. The organism is assumed to possess certain biological needs which, when they depart from optimal (homeostatic) levels (i.e., deficit), create biological drive states in the organism; likewise, excessive physical stimulation is assumed to cause physical tissue damage and this creates a biological drive state in the organism. This conception of drive severely constricts the set of primary reinforcing events. Hull only admits of four need-based or tissue-based biological drives: hunger, thirst, sex, and escape from pain. He calls these the four primary drives. Thus, the origin of the term "PRIMARY reinforcing stimulus event." There is no demonstrable biological need (and thus drive) for light onset, saccharin, physical activity, puzzle manipulation, exploration, positive physical contact, and the like; and not all negative reinforcers create tissue damage. These reinforcing events must be assigned to the secondary reinforcing event category. This consequence is indicated in Fig. 9-3 by separating the four primary drive related reinforcing events from the others by a pie slice.

The life preservative or physiological survival approach. Hull's need deficit and tissue damage approach to biological drives is often interpreted along physical survival or life preservative lines. Reduction in the need deficit or tissue damage is viewed as essential for survival of the individual. In this approach, an already known reinforcing event X is a primary reinforcing event if it allows or causes rectification of some survival need deficit or tissue damage. Only three of the four Hullian primary drives survive this more restrictive criterion; sexual contact is not really necessary for physical survival (although I am told it contributes to the quality of life) and must be assigned to the secondary reinforcer category. This further constriction is indicated in Fig. 9-3 by a circle enclosing the three appropriate survival items located in the pie slice.

The Notion of Primary Reinforcer in Perspective

Introduction. It might seem that too much attention has been paid to the concept of a primary reinforcer. After all, a primary reinforcer is a simple biological reinforcing event, which even most learning psychologists take at face value, and it does not seem to have much relevance for human learning — not one significant reinforcer for human learning appears in Fig. 9-3 and, by inference, the significant reinforcers for human learning almost exclusively fall in the secondary reinforcing event category. While this is not the place to interpret biological reinforcers at a theoretical level or discuss the differences between the reinforcement situations in animal and human learning, the above reservations can be adequately disposed of by considering the following two interrelated aspects of a biological reinforcer: (1) its species relativity and (2) its general relativity.

The species relativity of a biological reinforcer. There is no such thing as an absolute list of biological reinforcers applicable to every kind of living organism. Biological reinforcers are species relative. There are significant differences between the physiological structure and capacities of different species at virtually all levels of phylogeny. For instance, some insects have no heat (temperature) receptors. Cats cannot respond to (taste) sugar. Humans cannot respond to (hear) sound frequencies above 20,000 cycles per second while dogs, bats, etc. can. Water would not be an effective reinforcer for a camel except under unusual circumstances. Food deprivation is a meaningless operation for a bear nutritionally prepared for hibernation. The opportunity to run would really not be all that reinforcing for a pigeon, but the opportunity to fly is another matter. Shocking the "skin" of a rhinocerous would be a fruitless task for reinforcement purposes. Countless other examples could also be presented.

Since biological reinforcers are species relative, the determination of what stimulus events in the environment can and cannot serve as biological reinforcers for a specific species is really an empirical matter. In other words, it is not possible to simply assume that a class of biological reinforcers exists for a specific type of organism and leave it at that. Physicalization of the notion of a biological reinforcer for a specific subject type in an actual learning experiment involves all sorts of problems, assumptions, calibration procedures, etc. which simply cannot be glossed over by appeal to the word "biology."

The general relativity of a biological reinforcer. The relativity of a biological reinforcer extends far beyond the interspecies dimension. We already know that certain stimulus events cannot serve as biological reinforcers in an all-or-none sense unless prior deprivation or restriction operations are applied to the organism. As an extension of this, the specific graded reinforcing value or incentive value of a biological reinforcer depends upon a whole host of other factors associated with the subject and the experimental situation. The general principle implied by the prior two statements is that nothing is really accomplished by labeling a class of reinforcing events "biological" or "biologically based." The label does not explain anything or predict anything. At best, the term "biological" serves as a structural description of the reinforcer, but it has no relevance for the dynamic aspects of a reinforcer and its effects on behavior.

It is in this context that the relevance of biological reinforcement for human learning can be most meaningfully discussed. It is simply not true that biological reinforcement is never relevant for human learning. The relevance of biological reinforcement for human learning depends upon many factors, some of which are social, cultural, economic, or developmental in nature. For instance, the typical middle-class American adult is not starving, thirsty, cold (hot), or sexually deprived, etc. Food, water, warmth (cold), or sexual contact, etc. could not serve as effective reinforcers for conditioning learned responses. But this is not the case among primitive tribes in the jungles of New Guinea or Brazil, or for refugees living on the hillsides of Hong Kong, or for the inhabitants of a New Delhi slum, etc.

Note that the phrase "typical adult" is used in the above example. We shall now independently change each aspect of the'phrase. An untypical adult (e.g., a member of the abnormal population — mental retardate, schizophrenic, etc.) often does not respond to secondary reinforcers — biological reinforcers must be used to condition new responses. The typical nonadult (i.e., human infant) is essentially a pre-social, pre-verbal, pre-symbolic organism. The infant is only responsive to biologically sourced reinforcers, but even more significantly the specific reinforcing value or incentive value of a specific biological reinforcer is contingent upon the specific stage of maturational development. At birth, the only operating physiological systems are those that allow or mediate classical conditioning. Within three or four months after birth, maturation has proceeded to a point such that the physiological systems mediating some of the (instrumental, operant) motor responses become operative. It is one to two years before auditorily presented stimuli (i.e., speech sounds) can operate as symbolic, secondary reinforcers; it is four to five years before written language as visual stimuli can operate as symbolic, secondary reinforcers.

Conceptual Significance of a Primary Reinforcer and a Transition

The notion of a primary reinforcer possesses conceptual significance on at least three levels. (1) As has already been inferred many times, primary (positive) reinforcement is viewed as the prototypical type of reinforcement by the learning psychologist and it has served as the object of most of the theoretical formulations about reinforcement. (2) As will become apparent once the notion of secondary reinforcement is discussed, the acquired reinforcing properties of a stimulus event do not accrue in a vacuum but are explicitly based on the organism's prior exposure to primary reinforcement. So, the notion of primary reinforcement is conceptually and logically prior to that of secondary reinforcement. (3) As a transition to the next subsection, the most significant structural experimental work on reinforcement in the last 10 to 15 years involves primary reinforcement, not externally applied, but internally applied, the primary example of which is direct brain stimulation. Primary reinforcement by direct brain stimulation has opened up a whole new box of conceptual problems.

The Use of Internally Applied Primary Reinforcing Events

Introduction. Up to now we have implicitly assumed that a primary reinforcer is an external or peripherally applied event — that is, it is processed by any one or more of the organism's peripheral sensory systems or processed by any one or more of the organism's peripheral consummatory or manipulatory motor systems. Reinforcing events in the context of the everyday environment are exclusively external or peripherally applied; but, in the confines of the laboratory, the peripheral sensory and motor systems of the organism can be bypassed through the use of sophisticated delivery systems such that primary reinforcing events can be internal or centrally applied.

Examples of centrally applied primary reinforcing events in the response-contingent reinforcement situation include the following: direct stomach injection, direct injection into the blood stream, and direct electrical (sometimes chemical) stimulation of the brain. Water or a nutritive liquid, like milk, delivered directly into the mouth cavity is an ambiguous event — possessing elements of both peripheral and central stimulation. (Note: Examples of centrally applied primary reinforcing events in the experimenter-contingent reinforcement situation are far more numerous because the purpose of administering the second stimulus event to the organism is usually to activate some internal response or response system — e.g., stomach secretion, blood pressure level, heart rate, respiratory rate, a specific type of brain wave, autonomic activity, etc.)

The most significant class of response-contingent centrally applied primary reinforcement, both historically and conceptually, is that of electrical brain stimulation, commonly referred to as ESB, and our further comments are confined to this kind of central primary reinforcer. The shock stimulation from electrodes chronically implanted in the brain of an animal — typically rat, cat, or monkey — can have positive or negative reinforcing effects, depending upon such factors as specific location of stimulation, shock intensity, shock duration, and drug, deprivation, or ablation conditions in effect, etc. "Primary" (most reinforcing), "secondary" (less reinforcing), "neutral" (nonreinforcing), and "ambivalent" (sometimes positive reinforcing, sometimes negative reinforcing) brain centers of the rat, cat, and monkey have been extensively mapped through experimental investigation and have come to be regarded as structural entities independent of their actual stimulation.

ESB in Conceptual Perspective

Introduction. As indicated in the above transition, the use of ESB has opened up a whole new box of conceptual problems. Three will be briefly discussed here to indicate the general impact of ESB on the nature of the reinforcement situation: (1) whether ESB and conventionally applied reinforcement are continuous or discontinuous reinforcing events, (2) the nature of negative reinforcement in ESB, and (3) to what extent the reinforcing brain centers constitute an essentially independent reinforcement system.

The Continuity-Discontinuity Issue

Introduction. The first conceptual problem concerns whether or not the behavioral (i.e., reinforcing) effects of ESB are the same as the behavioral (i.e., reinforcing) effects of conventional, peripherally applied primary reinforcers like food, water, etc. Are they two distinct, dichotomous classes of reinforcing events or do they merely occupy different positions on some underlying continuum? (Note: We are only assuming the positive reinforcing category here.) This conceptual problem can be analyzed on both the experimental level and the theoretical level.

The Experimental Level

The discontinuity view. The argument for this interpretation goes as follows. There are a number of salient behavioral differences resulting from the use of ESB as opposed to conventional reinforcement, two examples of which are presented below. (1) A rat never satiates on ESB and will maintain a very high level of responding on a continuous reinforcement schedule in the operant conditioning situation to the point of ultimate physiological exhaustion; the same type of subject satiates on water or food reinforcement in the same experimental context. (But recall that such is not the case for a peripherally applied negative reinforcer.) (2) The rat ceases responding after only a few responses, when responding is no longer reinforced by ESB, after training on a continuous reinforcement schedule in the operant conditioning situation; the rat exhibits appreciable resistance to extinction, including an "emotional" outburst of responses, following a continuous schedule of conventional water or food reinforcement during acquisition. Because of the existence of a number of salient behavioral differences, many learning psychologists argue that ESB and conventional reinforcement do constitute two distinct classes of reinforcing events.

The continuity view. The argument for this interpretation runs as follows. It must be realized that the salient behavioral differences resulting from the use of ESB and conventional reinforcers arise when the different physical characteristics of ESB and a conventional reinforcer are not provided for or taken into account. For instance, the onset of ESB is immediate with respect to the learned response occurrence; its duration, intensity, etc. are uniform over successive responses; and its aftereffects or stimulus traces are quite transient. Conversely, the onset of a conventional food or water stimulus is delayed by an "apparatus minimum" with respect to the learned response occurrence; its duration, amount, etc. can vary from one response to the other because of the way the subject processes the external stimulus event on each occasion; and its after-effects or stimulus traces are fairly long-lasting. (Recall the sequence of events set off by the presentation of a food object described in a prior subsection of this chapter.) Incidentally, the rewarding (incentive) effect of one food pellet and one ESB occurrence are rarely if ever calibrated or provided for – i.e., what constitutes an equivalent amount of physical reward in these two presentation modalities is usually not taken into consideration. Analogously, the same is true when a lick or a drop of water constitutes the reinforcing event.

It also must be realized that the specific experimental procedures associated with the use of ESB and conventional reinforcement usually differ and are not provided for. For instance, ESB is usually applied to a satiated organism. Conventional reinforcement is usually applied to an organism in a high drive state (initially).

If these different physical characteristics and procedural differences associated with the usual use of these two classes of reinforcing events are provided for, no behavioral differences should result. This providing for takes the direction of making ESB as characteristically and procedurally similar to conventional reinforcement as possible since it is impossible to make conventional reinforcing stimuli centrally applied. Recent experimentation, which takes these characteristic and procedural differences into account, has removed or resolved most of these salient behavioral differences. (The remaining ones simply have not been experimentally assessed as yet in this "providing for" framework.)

Actually only one salient difference between the two classes of reinforcers can never be resolved – namely, that of insatiation versus satiation – example (1) above. The organism never satiates on ESB even though the specific experimental procedure in effect makes it an analogue to conventional reinforcement. Ultimately, this might be the only significant feature distinguishing between a central reinforcer like ESB and a peripheral reinforcer like food or water, a difference which in and of itself does not justify placing them into two distinct classes. So, it is possible to achieve analogous conditions in the use of ESB and conventional reinforcement such that they have the same effect on behavior and it can be argued that ESB and conventional reinforcement are continuous with each other on an underlying reinforcement continuum.

The theoretical level. The discontinuity and continuity views also occur at the theoretical level. The original theoretical interpretations of the effect of ESB on behavior – i.e., Deutsch and Howarth's drive decay theory, Ball's aversive aftereffect theory, and Grossman's conflict theory – all assume that ESB and conventional reinforcement are fundamentally different classes of reinforcement. The more current theoretical interpretations of the effect of ESB on behavior – i.e., Trowill and Pankrepp's incentive approach and Lenzer's associative or stimulus control theory – do not accept any fundamental difference between ESB and conventional reinforcement. In fact, these contemporary approaches predict the circumstances under which ESB and conventional reinforcement should have the same or a different effect on behavior. Specific aspects of two of these theoretical interpretations of ESB (drive decay and associative) will be discussed later when the concept of primary positive reinforcement is analyzed at the theoretical level in detail.

The nature of negative reinforcement in ESB. The second conceptual problem concerns the nature of negative reinforcement in ESB. Three aspects of the problem will be detailed here.

1. In the context of conventional reinforcement a reinforcing event is one whose onset or termination results in an increase in the frequency of occurrence of a response immediately preceding it in time. A negatively reinforcing ESB brain center is not originally isolated this way. Rather it is initially isolated by operations conventionally labeled as the punishing operation. If the electrical stimulation of brain center X elicits a withdrawal response from the organism or if it results in the cessation of ongoing behavior, the brain center is classified as a negative reinforcing area. It is only later used in the escape or avoidance conditioning paradigm to actually condition a learned response.

2. There is the associated problem of the same brain center operating either as a positively reinforcing or as a negatively reinforcing (ambivalent) center depending upon the duration and intensity of the shock stimulus. Is it literally the same area serving both functions or do intense or extended shock stimulations "branch out" and affect other adjacent areas?

3. Treating a positively reinforcing brain center as the conceptual given, it is not at all clear whether a brain center exhibiting negatively reinforcing properties operates as a "true" independent center or merely is inhibiting or depressing the activity of some adjacent positively reinforcing center.

In general, the sharp differences between positive and negative reinforcement in conventional reinforcement become blurred in the context of ESB. (1) In conventional stimulation, positive reinforcement serves as the prototypical operational category; in ESB, negative reinforcement seems to serve as the prototypical operational category. (2) In conventional stimulation, negative reinforcement does not satiate and requires no prior organismic deprivation; in ESB, positive reinforcement, in addition to negative, does not satiate and requires no prior organismic deprivation. (3) In conventional stimulation, negative reinforcement results in agitated and vicious behavior on the part of the subject; in ESB, positive reinforcement, in addition to negative, results in agitated and vicious behavior on the part of the subject.

ESB as an independent reinforcement system. The third conceptual problem relates to what extent the reinforcing brain centers constitute an essentially independent reinforcement system — i.e., to what degree do they overlap other systems known to affect or be related to conventional reinforcement, such as general motivational, activation, or energizing systems, specific emotional approach —avoidance systems, and sensory systems mediating the incentive value of a peripherally applied reinforcer, etc. No attempt will be made to consider this question in depth. Suffice it to point out two things. (1) In terms of pure anatomical overlap, most of the positive and negative reinforcing brain centers correspond to brain areas involved in the motivational and emotional, but not sensory, systems of the organism. (2) Although ESB requires no motivational state or activation condition to be effective, the graded or incentive reinforcing effect of a specific ESB location is affected by the specific type and degree of drive deprivation of the subject, the application of a specific activation or depressant drug, the ablation of an adjacent brain area, etc.

What is really being argued here at an informal level is that it is certainly possible to bypass the peripheral route into the organism's internal biological reinforcement system (whatever it is) and activate it directly; but, the effect of this direct, central activation is not independent of the essential operations involved in activating the system by the conventional peripheral route. It is just that these operations switch from necessity to optionality when bypassing the peripheral route.

THE NOTION OF A SECONDARY REINFORCING EVENT

Other Terms for a Secondary Reinforcer

Since this category of reinforcing events comes from the theoretical source dimension, a listing of some of the alternative labels for the category can serve the purpose of providing some of the denotational properties of a secondary reinforcer. These other terms include the following: conditioned, learned, derived, acquired, symbolic, etc. So, fundamentally, a secondary reinforcer is a stimulus event whose reinforcing properties are symbolic (nonphysical), having been derived or acquired through the process of learning or conditioning. At the animal level, "symbolic" simply means "ultimately exchangeable for some actual physical reward or predictive that some primary reinforcer is eventually going to follow." At the human level, "symbolic" in addition to the above can also mean "possessing verbal and/or social significance or meaning without the eventual exchange for reward or the eventual accompanying primary reinforcing event."

The terminological situation for this category of reinforcement is analogous to that for the primary reinforcer category; the term "secondary" is not actually used that much any more, having been replaced by the term "conditioned." This reflects the fact that the significant contemporary experimental research on secondary reinforcers is performed by operant psychologists who manipulate "tertiary," "quartenary," etc. reinforcing events. The basic conceptual problem associated with secondary reinforcement naturally pertains to the substance of the learning process involved in the creation of a secondary reinforcing event, a topic to which we now turn.

Alternative Approaches to the Generating Conditions for a Secondary Reinforcer

Introduction. The generating conditions can be treated on the operational level and the theoretical level. Unlike the case of primary reinforcement, it will be more didactic to analyze both the operational and theoretical aspects of secondary reinforcement together in the same subsection. It is easy to discuss the operational level because the two alternative classic operations for creating a secondary reinforcer correspond to the two types of reinforcing operations, as originally defined in Chapter 2. The theoretical level will pose some problems and we shall merely attempt a low-level resolution of the issue and present a glimpse of the basic contemporary theoretical framework from which secondary reinforcement phenomena are currently derived. The alternative operational approaches will be described first.

Alternative Approaches to the Operational Specification of a Secondary Reinforcer

Introduction. It is the aim of this subsection to present the sufficient operational conditions under which a secondary reinforcing stimulus is established, not the necessary and sufficient conditions. The latter set of conditions constitutes a theoretical specification and it is too early in the presentation to be concerned with theory. Another note of caution must be added. Although this section on the descriptive types of reinforcers is being presented in the context of the response-contingent reinforcement situation, it is absolutely necessary to sub-cycle through the experimenter-contingent reinforcement situation during the operational analysis of secondary reinforcement. So, with this as a background, it is now possible to state the two sufficient operational conditions under which an original neutral or nonreinforcing stimulus event can become a secondary reinforcer: (1) use it as the initial stimulus in the S-S reinforcement operation or (2) use it as the initial stimulus in the S-R-S reinforcement operation.

The S-S operational condition. In this operational condition, the original neutral stimulus is contiguously paired with a primary reinforcing event, either appetitive or aversive. If appetitive, the secondary reinforcer is positive; if aversive, the secondary reinforcer is negative. We are implicitly assuming here that the crucial pairing aspect of the second stimulus is its onset, not its termination. Pairing with the termination leads to a whole host of other distinctions and problems which are best left dormant.

The primary example of a learning situation consisting of a series of exposures to the S-S reinforcement operation, which has already been described in the text (Chapter 4), is that of classical conditioning. So if we interpret the initial S as a CS and the second S as a UCS, the S-S operational condition for generating a secondary reinforcer devolves into classical conditioning. As stated by many introductory learning texts, the way to make an original neutral stimulus into a secondary reinforcer is by using it as a CS in classical conditioning.

The S-R-S operational condition. In this operational condition, the original neutral stimulus is followed by the occurrence of a response which in turn leads to a primary reinforcing event. Or, alternatively, a response occurring in the presence of the neutral stimulus must be primarily reinforced. The primary reinforcer must be appetitive; and the secondary reinforcer generated is positive. (It is impossible to create a secondary negative reinforcer by the use of the S-R-S operational condition.) Again we are implicitly assuming here that the crucial aspect of the second stimulus event is its onset, not its termination.

The primary example of a learning situation consisting of a series of exposures to the S-R-S (appetitive) reinforcement operation, which has already been described in the text (Chapter 4), is that of operant conditioning (as a subset of instrumental conditioning), although previously the initial S was left implicit. So if we interpret the initial S as an S^D (S-dee) and the second S as a primary positive reinforcer ($+S^R$), the S-R-S (appetitive) operational condition for generating a secondary reinforcer devolves into operant conditioning. As stated by many introductory learning texts, the way to make an original neutral stimulus into a secondary reinforcer is by using it as an S^D or discriminative stimulus in operant conditioning. (Our use of the term S^D or discriminative stimulus here is fairly loose, but the situation will be tightened up shortly.)

Perhaps it should be briefly indicated why the S-R-S operational condition cannot generate a secondary negative reinforcer. If the second stimulus term were the onset of a biological aversive stimulus event, the S-R-S sequence devolves into the response-contingent punishment operation and the R term "disappears" eventually. Thus, secondary negative reinforcers can only be generated by the S-S operational condition, either explicitly or implicitly.

The use of a previously generated secondary reinforcer in either operational condition. Up to this point, the second S of each operational condition for generating a secondary reinforcer has been explicitly referred to as a primary reinforcer; but there is nothing to preclude the second S from being a previously generated secondary reinforcer — i.e., it is possible to generate a secondary reinforcer operationally on the basis of association with a previously generated secondary reinforcer. In the S-S operation, there is a technical label for this situation — namely, "higher order conditioning." In the S-R-S operation, there is no one name for this manipulation, although the term "chaining" is sufficient for many cases. The significance of the content of this paragraph will become apparent later.

Variations of the Prototypical Sufficient Conditions
for Generating a Secondary Reinforcer

Introduction. What have been described so far are the two prototypical sufficient operational conditions for generating a secondary reinforcer. Two variations will now be considered which enhance the reinforcing properties of the resultant secondary reinforcer relative to the reinforcing properties established by the prototypical operational conditions. These variations are called (1) discrimination training and (2) intermittent training, respectively. They can be performed in the context of either the S-S or S-R-S operation, but will only be defined and analyzed in the context of the S-R-S (appetitive) operation.

Discrimination training. The S-R-S (appetitive) operation was interpreted as the S^D-R-(+)S^R sequence of operant conditioning. The secondary reinforcing properties of the S^D are enhanced if a "true" discrimination training session is conducted. Specifically, periods of the S^D-R-(+)S^R operation are alternated with periods of the S^Δ-R-nothing operation, with each period of random length to prevent an alternation of two types of constant intervals. The S^Δ(S-delta) is called a nondiscriminative stimulus and, when this stimulus is in effect, responding is not reinforced. An R occurring in the presence of an S^Δ is an unreinforced response. In other words, S^Δ-R-nothing periods are applications of the S-R extinction operation, initially introduced in Chapter 2, where the S term is interpreted as an S^Δ and the R term is an unreinforced response. Thus, the discrimination training procedure, as a combination of the reinforcement operation and the extinction operation, constitutes a complex procedure and sets up a learning phenomenon to be measured, according to the distinctions made in Chapter 5.

Intermittent training. In the prototypical S-R-S operation, the sequence is deterministic. The R is always followed by the second S and the S-S pairing always occurs when an R is made. The S-R-S operation can also be used probabilistically. The initial S is only probabilistically associated with the second S. The S-R sequence is not always followed by the second S. On these occasions, of course, the S-R sequence operates as an extinction operation. This differs from discrimination training in that it is always the S^D which occurs in both operations. (There is no S^Δ event here.) Also the $S^D\text{-R-}(+)S^R$ and $S^D\text{-R}$ operations occur randomly over time − they do not constitute alternating random length time periods. So some responses are reinforced in the presence of S^D; some are not. Technically, this amounts to the use of some partial reinforcement schedule and the probabilistic occurrence of the $+S^R$ is done on a response-by-response basis. A partial reinforcement schedule, as a combination of the reinforcement operation and the extinction operation, constitutes a complex procedure and sets up a learning phenomenon to be measured, as discussed in Chapter 5.

Combined discrimination, intermittent training. The combination of the above two procedures is meaningful, but will be described only briefly. Basically, the combination procedure is implemented by using the probabilistic $S^D\text{-R-}(+)$ S^R operation in conjunction with the deterministic $S^\Delta\text{-R-nothing}$ operation. Technically, the subject is exposed to a complex multiple reinforcement schedule with two components. The S^D is the cue for the partial reinforcement schedule component and the S^Δ is the cue for the extinction component. Naturally, a multiple reinforcement schedule constitutes a learning phenomenon to be measured.

Alternative Theoretical Approaches to the Generation of a Secondary Reinforcer

Introduction. We are going to present the traditional theoretical interpretation of the generating conditions for a secondary reinforcer and more contemporary view of the theoretical nature of a secondary reinforcing event. The traditional approach involves a low-level comparison and resolution of the two sufficient operational conditions for generating a secondary reinforcer, while the contemporary approach puts the notion of a secondary reinforcer in an information theory or uncertainty reduction framework. Associated with the transition from operational to theoretical is a change in the reference point for generating conditions. Specifically, the reference point changes from one of "operationally sufficient" to "theoretically necessary and sufficient" − i.e., at the theoretical level what is the crucial event determining whether or not an original neutral stimulus event accrues secondary reinforcing properties?

A comparison and resolution of the two operational approaches to generating a secondary reinforcer. The obvious event which both operations have in common is the succession or contiguous pairing of two stimulus events. This is explicit in the S-S operation; it is implicit in the S-R-S operation. As a consequence of this, many nonoperantly oriented psychologists argue that the sole generating condition for a secondary reinforcer is classical conditioning. More technically, the sole necessary and sufficient condition for generating a secondary reinforcer at a theoretical level is that of classical conditioning. Even in the operant conditioning paradigm, successive stimulus events are being paired in a classical conditioning manner; so the ultimate learning principles involved in creating a secondary reinforcer at a theoretical level are the same learning principles which lead to the acquisition of a classically conditioned response, or CR (whatever they are).

A Contemporary Information Theory or Uncertainty Reduction Approach to Secondary Reinforcement

Introduction. The traditional view that the learning principles underlying classical conditioning are responsible for creating a secondary reinforcer is perfectly acceptable in the context of the two simple reinforcement operations, S-S and S-R-S. But, current experimentation on secondary reinforcement transcends the mere use of the S-S and S-R-S operations. We shall present, as an example of this, a procedural extension of the S-S operation. This extension is not a complex operation, as defined in Chapter 2, because the extinction operation is not employed. The terminological difficulties involved in presenting an extension of the S-R-S operation are so great that no derivative interpretation will be attempted in that context; but the conclusions derived from the S-S extension example will be applied to the S-R-S case.

An example of an extended S-S operation: The S-S-S operation. In this operation the third stimulus event is a primary reinforcing stimulus (appetitive) and can be interpreted as a UCS in classical conditioning. Both the first and second stimuli are original neutral stimulus events. Both occur in a paired contiguous manner with the UCS. But only the first S, and not the second S, develops secondary reinforcing properties — i.e., only the first S acts like a CS. Consequently, in this expanded operation, the pairing of two stimulus events (one neutral, the other a primary reinforcer) does not serve as a necessary and sufficient condition for generating a secondary reinforcer. Something else must also be operating in the situation. A natural theoretical specification of this something else can be given in terms of information theory or uncertainty reduction language. The initial S is informative, reduces uncertainty of what is going to follow, is nonredundant. The second S is not informative, does not reduce uncertainty of what is going to follow, is redundant.

So, in summary, once you go beyond the simple S-S operation, pure contiguous pairing is not enough to generate a secondary reinforcer. Only a stimulus, involved in a contiguous pairing, in such a way as to be informational or nonredundant, accrues secondary reinforcing properties. Only an original neutral stimulus event which becomes a reliable predictor that a reinforcing event is going to follow becomes a secondary reinforcer.

Application of information theory language to the S-R-S operational condition. Let us assume the strict interpretation of an S^D here and use the discrimination training procedure for illustrative pruposes. Recall that in the discrimination training paradigm responses occurring in the presence of an S^D are reinforced and responses occurring in the presence of an S^Δ are not reinforced; and this procedure enhances the secondary reinforcing value of the S^D.

It can be argued that the S^D and S^Δ stimulus events are informative to the organism. Whichever stimulus is in effect specifies the appropriate course of action to take — i.e., responding in the presence of the S^D because it is reinforced and not responding in the presence of the S^Δ because it is not reinforced. Either stimulus reduces uncertainty about what course of action to take. Each stimulus is a reliable predictor of what course of action to follow.

Actually, the above example is too restrictive to be very meaningful. Assume the existence of N or multiple S^Ds, each one indicating that a different reinforcement contingency (i.e., schedule) is in effect. The extinction operation need not be one of the reinforcement contingencies — there is no "true" S^Δ in this situation. Thus, S^D_1 might indicate that every other response is reinforced; S^D_2 might indicate that every tenth response is reinforced; S^D_N might indicate that every response is reinforced. (In essence, each S^D_i is indicating which reinforcement schedule — some variant of a fixed ratio — is in effect.) In this situation, each S^D_i becomes a secondary reinforcer. Each S^D_i is informative, reduces uncertainty, etc. with respect to the appropriate course of action (specific response rate) to take.

Note that the strict operational specification that a stimulus event only becomes a S^D (and thus a $+S^r$) if another stimulus event becomes an S^Δ in the same context is no longer applicable here. This multiple S^D situation involves no S^Δ at all. So making a stimulus event a "true" S^D in the operant situation is not a necessary and sufficient condition for generating a secondary reinforcer. In the information theory or uncertainty reduction context, the necessary and sufficient condition for making a stimulus event a secondary reinforcer in the S-R-S operational condition is to transform it into an informative stimulus — i.e., a stimulus controlling which course of action to follow.

The Evaluation and Use of a Secondary Reinforcer

Introduction. Once an original neutral stimulus event has been used as the initial stimulus in the S-S reinforcement operation or S-R-S reinforcement operation — i.e., once the acquisition phase of secondary reinforcement is completed — the stimulus is commonly inserted in another operation. This other operation has two purposes. One purpose is that of evaluation; the other purpose is that of use. These purposes are neither conceptually distinct nor often procedurally distinct. Each purpose logically implies the other and what the experimenter is doing at any moment in time is largely a function of his intentions.

The evaluation of a secondary reinforcer. Once the secondary reinforcement acquisition phase is over, the original neutral stimulus event has presumably accrued secondary reinforcing properties; but, it is not actually known at that time whether the stimulus event has indeed become a secondary reinforcer. This is especially true when the original training conditions did not involve either operationally sufficient condition. The presumed secondary reinforcing properties of the stimulus must actually be evaluated — its presumed secondary reinforcing properties must actually be demonstrated in the context of overt behavior.

Definitionally, this evaluation is accomplished by using the presumed secondary reinforcer as the second stimulus in the S-S reinforcement operation or in the S-R-S reinforcement operation. Because of the different response eliciting properties of a UCS in classical conditioning and a $+S^R$ in operant conditioning, typically the same type of reinforcement operation is used in the evaluation phase as was used in the acquisition phase, although there are no conceptual difficulties precluding a switch in reinforcement operation type between acquisition and evaluation. When successive S-S reinforcement operations are employed for acquisition and evaluation, the higher order classical conditioning procedure is being used; when successive S-R-S reinforcement operations are employed for acquisition and evaluation, no one label applies, although often the combined procedure is equivalent to what is termed "chaining."

The logic underlying this testing procedure should be self-evident. If a neutral stimulus has in fact achieved secondary reinforcing properties, it should act like a reinforcer. Functionally, this means inserting it in a position in a reinforcement operation which is usually occupied by a primary reinforcer. The original neutral stimulus is not switched from the initial stimulus position to the second stimulus position in the old reinforcement operation; it is used as the second stimulus event in an entirely new reinforcement operation. The presumed secondary reinforcing properties of the stimulus are being evaluated in a context which potentially allows the conditioning or learning of an entirely new or different response. If the response associated with the new reinforcement operation is learned, the original neutral stimulus is interpreted as having accrued secondary reinforcing properties. If the response associated with the new reinforcement operation is not learned, the original neutral stimulus is interpreted as not having accrued secondary reinforcing properties.

It should be noted that only the definitional way of evaluating a presumed secondary reinforcer has been described. Other properties of a reinforcing stimulus — e.g., increasing resistance to extinction (of an already learned response), maintaining (as opposed to original learning) response rate according to the dictates of a certain partial reinforcement schedule, eliciting approach responses (i.e., acting as an incentive stimulus) — can also be used to assess the presumed secondary reinforcing properties of an original neutral stimulus.

The use of a secondary reinforcer. Once an original neutral stimulus has accrued secondary reinforcing properties, it can be used in lieu of a primary reinforcer in virtually every context in which the use of a primary reinforcer is meaningful. It also can be employed in situations in which a primary reinforcer is not applicable or not meaningful — i.e., in the definitional extinction procedure to retard extinction.

When the experimenter is using a secondary reinforcer instead of merely testing the secondary reinforcing properties of an original neutral stimulus, the focus of interest changes from an all-or-none assessment to an analogical or graded assessment of how much instrumental reward or incentive value the secondary reinforcer actually possesses. At the operational level, this usually reduces to how long the secondary reinforcer can be used as the second stimulus event in the S-S reinforcement operation or S-R-S reinforcement operation before it loses its acquired reinforcing properties. Technically, this can be termed the durability of a secondary reinforcer. The durability of a $+S^r$ is a function of the potency of the secondary reinforcer as established during the initial acquisition session and the specific manner in which it is applied to behavior (S-R-S) or to the organism (S-S) during the use phase.

What is being argued here at a conceptual level is that the notion of a secondary reinforcer implies an input (creation) phase and an output (use) phase. The input phase is a function of certain input variables. The output phase is a function of certain output variables, but also is a function of the input variables. Potency is a function solely of acquisition variables; durability is a function of both potency and output variables.

It might seem that there is no operational distinction between potency and durability; but, the potency of a secondary reinforcer can be measured independently of its durability. For instance, the relative potency of a secondary reinforcer can be assessed by using a choice technique (i.e., assessing the relative preference for the secondary reinforcer) prior to assessing its durability during later use.

The consequence of the above discussion is that the experimenter can optimize the durability of a secondary reinforcer by maximizing potency and optimizing the schedule of use. As inferred previously, the operational way of maximizing potency is by using a combination discrimination — intermittent training procedure. The optimal schedule of use involves intermittent application (S-R-S) or exposure (S-S) so that the acquired reinforcing properties can be conserved.

Actually, potency and durability can be maximized by varying a whole host of input and output variables. The most significant nondefinitional factor of which potency is a function is the number of different primary reinforcers the neutral stimulus was associated with during acquisition. More will be written about this later in another context. The most effective nondefinitional way of increasing the durability of a secondary reinforcer is to insert the original S-R-S or S-S reinforcement operation periodically during the use phase (i.e., periodically re-pair the secondary reinforcer with the original primary reinforcer during the use phase while it is conditioning or maintaining the new response). Intermittent application or exposure in conjunction with periodic re-pairing can extend the "life" of a secondary reinforcer almost indefinitely.

Conceptual perspective on the relationship between evaluation and use. The mere all-or-none evaluation of a secondary reinforcer is equivalent to assessing its potency in a context which minimizes durability. The mere act of testing whether or not an original neutral stimulus has acquired secondary reinforcing properties by determining whether or not it conditions a new response demonstrates its potency at the expense of durability.

As a general rule, the learning psychologist who emphasizes the testing aspect of the output phase is just interested in the potency of the secondary reinforcer anyway; likewise, the learning psychologist who emphasizes the use aspect of the output phase is just interested in the durability or instrumental reinforcing value of the secondary reinforcer. When the experimenter is interested in assessing or maximizing both the potency and durability of a secondary reinforcer, then special assessment techniques must be employed to independently assess these two aspects of a secondary reinforcer. In the current sophisticated operant conditioning research on secondary reinforcement the input and output phases are conceptually and procedurally indistinct, yet potency and durability can be independently assessed when desired.

Examples of Secondary Reinforcers

Introduction. So far we have actively avoided presenting any examples of secondary reinforcers for a number of reasons. (1) In principle, virtually any neutral stimulus event can be transformed into a secondary reinforcer by pairing it with a biological or conditioned reinforcer. (2) Whether the neutral stimulus event becomes a conditioned incentive $(+S^r)$ or a conditioned aversive stimulus $(-S^r)$ depends upon the type of primary or conditioned reinforcer with which it is associated (+ or −). (3) As in the case of primary reinforcement, secondary reinforcement is a relative concept on many different concurrent dimensions (space, time, organism, etc.). (4) Laboratory examples from simple animal learning and/or conditioning have already been implicitly given in the context of analyzing the operationally sufficient conditions for generating a secondary reinforcer and in the context of describing the evaluation and use of a secondary reinforcer. (5) The general point has already been made that the significant source of reinforcement in typical adult human learning is the secondary or symbolic category; and the nature of reinforced practice in some common human learning tasks constitutes a separate section of the chapter.

Thus, there follow some examples of secondary reinforcers from everyday life, with the proviso that they be taken with a grain of salt.

Examples of conditioned incentives ($+S^r$s). Conditioned incentives include approval, praise, agreement, a promise, prestige, power, submission (of someone else), noncontact affection, etc. On a less lofty level, the following serve as symbolic positive reinforcing events: gold stars, excellent grades, prizes, scholarships, diplomas, medals, citations, praiseworthy reference in a newspaper article, paid vacations, free trips, high sign from a receptive member of the opposite sex, etc.

Examples of conditioned aversive stimuli ($-S^r$s). Conditioned aversive events include insults, threats, repression, confinement, demotions, layoffs, failure, disagreement, etc. On a less lofty level, the following serve as symbolic negative reinforcing events: parking fines, overdue bills, obscene phone calls, wrong numbers, bad grades, lost ball games, infant's cry at 3 A.M., etc.

Example of a generalized conditioned incentive. The term "generalized" is appended to a "conditioned incentive" if its potency has been significantly increased through association with many different biological reinforcers or other conditioned reinforcers. Functionally, in our culture, money (cash, coin, checks, etc.) serves as the primary example of this class of symbolic reinforcing events. Money is exchangeable for virtually any biological reinforcer or for virtually any lower order conditioned incentive (valued object).

Examples of ambivalent symbolic reinforcers. The relativity of secondary reinforcers can on occasion serve as a source of trouble. For instance, there is a class of ambivalent secondary reinforcing events (i.e., they are conditioned incentives for some people and conditioned aversive stimuli for others) in our culture which serves as a constant source of problems, examples of which include the American flag, the voice of the President, the concept of God, the Pope, a hiring quota system, the M-2 rifle, etc. These examples are associated with the institutional structures of our society: political, religious, economic, military, etc.

The Theoretical Significance and Use of Secondary Reinforcement

Introduction. The concept of a secondary reinforcer does not constitute the primary theoretical construct in anybody's theory of learning with the possible exception of Spence's concept of incentive motivation or fractional anticipatory goal response ($r_g - s_g$). This is because reinforcement is definitionally related to learning and the effect of reinforcement itself on behavior must be explained — i.e., reinforcement is not itself an explainer, rather it is a concept to be explained. But, the concept of secondary reinforcement does possess some theoretical significance because there are contexts in which it can be used as an explanatory theoretical construct. The key issue associated with its theoretical use is that of legitimacy. There are situations in which the use of a secondary reinforcer as an explanatory construct is legitimate; there are other situations in which the indiscriminate use of a secondary reinforcer at the theoretical level is not legitimate.

The criterion for legitimate and illegitimate use of secondary reinforcement as a theoretical explanation. Whenever the experimenter conducts a learning experiment (regardless of whether or not it is a secondary reinforcement experiment), explicit (operational) and implicit (inferred) sources of secondary reinforcement are created simply because previously neutral stimulus events are associated with a primary reinforcer. These explicit and implicit sources of secondary reinforcement are often used as theoretical constructs to explain other aspects or phases of the original learning experiment itself or behavior in successive learning experiments. This use of secondary reinforcement as an explanatory concept is legitimate if the following two conditions are fulfilled: (1) the learning psychologist possesses specific knowledge of the past laboratory training experience and extralaboratory rearing experience of the subject such that it includes specific generating conditions for secondary reinforcement and (2) the specific experimental situation or behavior to which it is applied is conceptually or procedurally related to the past training or rearing experience of the subject according to the general theoretical framework in which the psychologist is operating. If either of these conditions is violated, the use of secondary reinforcement as an explanatory concept is not legitimate.

When secondary reinforcement is not legitimately used at the theoretical level, it amounts to a "garbage concept." The most common instance of the use of secondary reinforcement as a garbage concept arises when the learning psychologist, in complete ignorance of the past experience of a specific subject or set of subjects, appeals to the concept of secondary reinforcement after the fact to explain some puzzling or unexpected experimental-learning data.

THE ASSESSMENT OF THE RESPONSE-CONTINGENT REINFORCING PROPERTIES OF ANY STIMULUS X CHOSEN AT RANDOM FROM THE ENVIRONMENT

Introduction

So far we have assumed the existence of a given set of already known reinforcers and we have distinguished among the members of the set by assigning them to one or more cells of a four-cell classification system. The known reinforcer served as the input and its classification served as the output. At this point, it is didactic to use the classification system and characteristics distinguishing between the types of reinforcers as input and analyze the extent to which a specific stimulus X chosen randomly from the environment can be assessed with respect to its reinforcing properties as the output. Is it possible to find out whether or not a specific stimulus X chosen randomly from the environment is a reinforcer? This question is not independent of the subject type, so it must be reworded as follows. Is it possible to find out whether or not a specific stimulus X chosen at random from the environment is a reinforcer for a specific organism Y (itself chosen randomly from the environment)? The answer is an unqualified "yes." There are two different methodological approaches to assessing the reinforcing properties of a stimulus X: the direct way and the indirect way. They will be analyzed in turn.

The Direct Verification Technique

This way can be termed the definitional or operational method. It uses the operational dimension of the classification system and, more specifically, Skinner's operational definition of a reinforcing event. To assess whether or not a stimulus X is a reinforcer, you must determine whether or not it increases the frequency of occurrence of the members of the response class which immediately precede it in time. Or, alternately, you must determine whether or not the stimulus X conditions a response in the operant conditioning situation. By definition, if stimulus X does, it is a reinforcer; if stimulus X does not, it is not a reinforcer – it is simply a neutral stimulus event.

Because of the nature of Skinner's behavioral test, the act of assessing the reinforcing status of stimulus X also assigns it to the positive or negative reinforcer category. If its onset has the reinforcing effect, it is a positive reinforcer. If its termination has the reinforcing effect, it is a negative reinforcer.

It is impossible to unambiguously assign a directly verified reinforcing stimulus X to one of the categories on the source dimension. Whether a reinforcing stimulus X is a biological or learned reinforcing event for organism Y depends upon his specific past history with respect to stimulus X. The only context in which this past history is explicitly known is in the laboratory with respect to experimentally generated secondary reinforcing events.

The Indirect Verification Technique

The indirect way employs the previously introduced, but undefined, distinction between appetitive and aversive stimulus events. Recall that the onset of an appetitive stimulus by definition operates as a positive reinforcer, while the cessation of an aversive stimulus by definition operates as a negative reinforcer. Therefore, if there is a way to operationally define appetitive and aversive stimulus events, a procedure exists to indirectly assess the reinforcing properties of stimulus X.

The discussion of Thorndike's approach to positive and negative reinforcers precludes defining appetitive and aversive stimulus events in terms of respective satisfying and dissatisfying subjective states. Some behavioral referent is required. An appetitive stimulus event could be operationally defined as a stimulus event which the organism actively approaches or investigates. An aversive stimulus event could be operationally defined as a stimulus event which the organism actively attempts to escape or even avoid if possible. In this context, a neutral stimulus event can be defined by default – it is one which elicits neither approach nor attempts to escape or avoid. So, if stimulus X is assessed to be an appetitive stimulus, it is a positive reinforcer; if stimulus X is assessed to be an aversive stimulus, it is a negative reinforcer. If stimulus X is assessed to be neither appetitive nor aversive, it is not a reinforcing stimulus.

As in the direct assessment case, the operational assessment involved in the indirect method, ipso facto, assigns a reinforcing stimulus X to the positive or negative reinforcer category. Likewise, it is impossible to unambiguously assign an indirectly verified reinforcing stimulus X to one of the categories on the source dimension. Whether the appetitive or aversive properties of stimulus X for organism Y are biological or learned in origin depends upon his specific past history with respect to stimulus X. The only context in which this past history is explicitly known is in the laboratory with respect to experimentally generated appetitive or aversive stimuli (via secondary reinforcement generating con- ditions).

Assessment and Response Specificity and Relativity

The question of whether a specific stimulus X is a reinforcer for organism Y can be interpreted as incomplete. This question is not independent of the specific response class which is used in the test. The complete conceptual question is as follows. Is it possible to find out whether or not a specific stimulus X chosen at random from the environment is a reinforcer for a specific organism Y when applied to instances of a specific response class Z? At the operational level, this question can only be evaluated by the direct verification technique because the question states the specific response class to be used for assessing the reinforcing effects of stimulus X. Assessing whether stimulus X is appetitive or aversive with respect to response class Z is operationally meaningless and impossible. It could be argued that stimulus X is aversive for response class Z if its onset disrupts or suppresses the occurrence of instances from response class Z, but what operation could be performed to assess its appetitiveness with respect to instances from response class Z?

The significance of this more restrictive question lies in the fact that a nonreinforcing or neutral stimulus X assessment with respect to response class Z does not close the issue of the reinforcing status of stimulus X. The experi- menter is tempted to proceed to response class K. With the current stress on the relativity of a reinforcer, the learning psychologist is well aware that the assessed reinforcing status of a specific stimulus X is contingent upon the specific choice of response class Z used for assessment and cannot safely be generalized to other response classes. The issue of the response relativity of a reinforcing stimulus X will appear again during discussion of the theoretical interpretations of primary positive reinforcement.

DESCRIPTIVE TYPES OF EXPERIMENTER-CONTINGENT REINFORCING EVENTS

INTRODUCTION

This section analyzes to what extent the distinctions made in the context of the response-contingent reinforcement situation can be applied to the experi- menter-contingent reinforcement situation. There are two limiting conditions of our analysis: (1) the S-S reinforcement operation is a subset of the S-R-S reinforcement operation and (2) the reinforcing value of the second S in the S-S operation cannot be assessed in terms of prior ongoing behavior. These two strictures vastly reduce the extent of the analysis which must be performed as well as determine the dimensions of analysis to be used in comparing response-contingent reinforcers and experimenter-contingent reinforcers. More specifically, we shall analyze to what extent the four types of reinforcing events defined in the response-contingent context transfer to the experimenter-contingent situation and to what extent the response-contingent assessment procedures carry over to the experimenter-contingent situation.

THE DESCRIPTIVE KINDS OF EXPERIMENTER-CONTINGENT REINFORCING EVENTS

Since the S-S operation is a subset of the S-R-S operation, the four categories of reinforcers — primary, secondary, positive, negative — and the four operational types of reinforcers — primary positive, primary negative, secondary positive, secondary negative — as generated in the response-contingent reinforcement situation transfer in toto to the experimenter-contingent reinforcement situation. Note that the prior statement refers to categories and operational types of reinforcers only; it does not refer to specific reinforcing stimulus events — i.e., the content of the four cells of the response-contingent classification system. It is not assumed that just because a stimulus X is a response-contingent reinforcer it, ipso facto, can also function as an experimenter-contingent reinforcer. What is assumed is that once a specific stimulus event is isolated as a reinforcer in the experimenter-contingent situation it must be one of the four operational types as originally defined in the context of the response-contingent reinforcement situation.

So the crucial difference between the second S term in the S-S operation and the S-R-S operation is the matter of operational assessment. Let us now proceed to an analysis of the assessment techniques for the experimenter-contingent reinforcement situation.

THE EXPERIMENTER-CONTINGENT ASSESSMENT TECHNIQUES: THE ASSESSMENT OF THE EXPERIMENTER-CONTINGENT REINFORCING PROPERTIES OF ANY STIMULUS X CHOSEN AT RANDOM FROM THE ENVIRONMENT

Introduction

Since the S-S operation is devoid of any intervening response event, the direct verification method of the response-contingent reinforcement situation has no relevance for the experimenter-contingent reinforcement situation. The reinforcing value of the second S in the S-S operation cannot be assessed in terms of prior ongoing behavior. Just because a stimulus X has been demonstrated to possess reinforcing properties in the context of the S-R-S operation by the direct verification technique does not guarantee that it can also be used as a reinforcing stimulus in the S-S operation. The indirect verification method of the response-contingent reinforcement situation, employing the distinction between appetitive and aversive stimulus events, does have relevance for the experimenter-contingent reinforcement situation. This is because appetitiveness and aversiveness are defined in terms of the response eliciting properties of a stimulus event.

The Indirect Verification Technique in the Experimenter-Contingent Reinforcement Situation

The definitional rule can be set up that if a stimulus X possesses appetitive or aversive properties it can be used as a reinforcer (second stimulus) in the S-S reinforcement operation. So if a stimulus X in the environment elicits an approach or investigatory response, it is an appetitive stimulus and can be used as the second stimulus in the S-S operation; if a stimulus X in the environment elicits an escape or withdrawal response, it is an aversive stimulus and can be used as the second stimulus in the S-S operation; if a stimulus X in the environment is found to possess neither appetitive nor aversive properties, it cannot be used as the second stimulus in the S-S operation.

Since the onset of the second S in the S-S operation is the operational reinforcing event and since it is independent of prior behavior, the notions of positive and negative reinforcement apply to the experimenter-contingent reinforcement situation by analogy only. The onset of an appetitive S is assumed to act as a positive reinforcer; the onset of an aversive S is assumed to act as a negative reinforcer. As in the case of the response-contingent reinforcement situation, it is impossible to unambiguously assign an indirectly verified experimenter-contingent reinforcing stimulus X to one of the categories on the source dimension. Only stimuli whose appetitive or aversive properties have been acquired in the context of the laboratory are unambiguously classifiable as secondary. Likewise, the assessment of a specific stimulus X is only subject type specific and not response class specific because of the nature of the operational definition of appetitive and aversive stimuli.

Allusion to Classical Conditioning

In classical conditioning, the prototypical experimental realization of the S-S reinforcement operation, the second S is interpreted as an unconditioned stimulus or UCS. This is a biological elicitor of one or more response classes. How do we find out whether a stimulus X chosen at random from the environment can serve as a UCS for organism Y? The behavioral test is quite simple. If it elicits any kind of consistent reaction from organism Y, it is a UCS; if not, it is simply a neutral stimulus event. The consistent reaction elicited by the UCS is called the unconditioned response or UCR and it is the biological connection between the UCS and UCR which is exploited by the S-S reinforcement operation. Note that in this application of the S-S operation no appeal is made to approach or withdrawal responses in the behavioral test. In classical conditioning the response elicited by the UCS provides the substance of the learned response so that if stimulus X reflexively elicits anything it can be used as a UCS.

Whether the UCS is interpreted as a positive or negative reinforcer depends exclusively on analogy with the response-contingent reinforcement situation. If a stimulus event which acts as a UCS in classical conditioning possesses positively reinforcing properties in some response-contingent reinforcement situation, the UCS is assumed to be a positive reinforcer. If a stimulus event which acts as a UCS in classical conditioning possesses negatively reinforcing properties in some response-contingent reinforcement situation, the UCS is assumed to be a negative reinforcer. A stimulus X chosen randomly from the environment and serving as a UCS cannot be unambiguously assigned to a category on the source dimension. Only UCSs created in the laboratory through appropriate pairing conditions can be unambiguously assigned to the secondary category.

Finally, note that the original question is usually not constricted to "Does a specific stimulus X serve as a UCS for specific response class Z for organism Y?" because the restricted question delimits the acceptable consistent reactions necessarily elicited by stimulus X in order to be classified as a UCS. Only in the case where response class Z is chosen ahead of time as the desired response class does the response class restriction make any operational sense.

RESPONSE-CONTINGENT REINFORCEMENT IN COMPLEX HUMAN LEARNING: THE CONCEPT OF KNOWLEDGE OF RESULTS OR FEEDBACK VERSUS THE CONCEPT OF PHYSICAL REWARD

INTRODUCTION

Many learning psychologists regard the denotations of the term "reinforcement" in human and animal learning to be so different that the concept really refers to two distinct things. In human learning, the term "knowledge of results" or "feedback" is used in lieu of the term "reinforcement"; in animal learning, the notion of reinforcement is interpreted primarily along lines of physical reward. The same view is expressed by learning psychologists who verbalize the situation as follows: "Reinforcement in the animal learning sense is completely irrelevant for human learning; rather what is important in human learning is information or knowledge of results." The purpose of this section is to analyze how and to what extent the notion of reinforcement does actually differ in the animal and human learning situations.

From comments already made in Chapter 4, it should be apparent that the conceptual analysis assumes that the same term is appropriate for both animal and human learning. The content of this section will serve the additional purpose of justifying the current usage of the term "reinforcement." Unfortunately, we are faced with many analytical and terminological problems. When comparing human and animal learning, different psychologists use the same term to refer to different things and different terms to refer to the same thing. Thus, much of the debate is essentially semantic in nature. We are going to attempt the most neutral or unbiased approach possible and shall begin by listing the differential characteristics of reinforcement in human and animal learning.

DIFFERENTIAL CHARACTERISTICS OF REINFORCEMENT IN HUMAN AND ANIMAL LEARNING

Four classes of differences between reinforcement in human and animal learning are as follows:

1. In animal learning, primary reinforcement constitutes the predominant category; the use of negative reinforcement is on a par with the use of positive reinforcement in the sense that both serve as the source of common, codified learning tasks. In human learning, secondary reinforcement constitutes the predominant category; the use of positive reinforcement far exceeds the use of negative reinforcement. (It is difficult to implement the notion of secondary negative reinforcer in the context of human learning.)

2. In animal learning, reinforcement is predominantly physical. A primary reinforcer by definition is physical, but most secondary reinforcers in animal learning are also physical events: lights, tones, buzzers, colors, etc. In human learning, reinforcement is predominantly symbolic or verbal. The secondary reinforcing events in human learning involve language or other kinds of symbolic communication systems.

3. In animal learning, reinforcement is usually explicit or externally sourced. In animal learning, the reinforcing event is usually some external environmental event occasioned by the apparatus or the experimenter. In human learning, reinforcement is often implicit or internally sourced. In human learning, the reinforcing event is often some internal judgment made by the subject with respect to the appropriateness or correctness of his response based on a pre-set

criterion or standard (sometimes multiple criteria or equivalent standards) presented to him by the experimenter before the learning trials even begin.

4. In animal learning, the correct or learned response class is always defined by the reinforcing event. Only a response instance from the correct or learned response class is followed by reinforcement. A response instance from the incorrect or nonlearned response class is not followed by reinforcement. As such, both the appropriate response occurrence and the occurrence of reinforcement are all-or-none or digital events which covary with each other. In human learning, the correct or learned response class per se is often specified by the original instructions given to the subject. On a given trial of the experiment, the performed response differs from the appropriate or criterion response on one or more analogical dimensions (i.e., it is "off") and this is indicated to the subject by use of a graded or analogical reinforcing event specifying in what direction and to what extent his response is in error. As such, both the response occurrence and the reinforcing event are analogical or graded events which covary with each other.

The content of the preceding paragraph does not preclude the existence of correlated analogical responses and analogical reinforcing events in the context of animal learning. Logan's micromolar approach (see Chapter 7) in particular makes one or more of the analogical properties of a reinforcer (amount, delay, etc.) contingent upon one or more of the analogical properties of the learned response class (usually response speed in a runway). This situation is technically referred to as "correlated reinforcement" as opposed to the conventional reinforcement situation (uncorrelated reinforcement). But the use of correlated reinforcement in the context of animal learning experiments is the exception rather than the rule — the majority of animal learning experiments involve uncorrelated reinforcement. More importantly, in an animal learning study involving correlated reinforcement, the correct or appropriate response(s) is (are) still defined and specified by the digital occurrence or nonoccurrence of the reinforcing event. The analogical properties of the reinforcing event in no way define the correct or appropriate response(s) or inform the subject of the correct or appropriate response(s).

It is the third and fourth dimensions of difference which serve as the actual source of the conceptual difficulty involved in relating animal and human reinforcement. The all-or-none, digital, explicit, externally sourced reinforcing events of animal learning lead to the interpretation of reinforcement as an actual physical reward. The graded, analogical, implicit, internally sourced reinforcing events of human learning lead to the interpretation of reinforcement as knowledge of results or informative feedback.

THE THREE FUNCTIONS OF REINFORCEMENT

Introduction

To put the issue of the differential nature of reinforcement in human and animal learning in further perspective, it is necessary to consider the three functions commonly attributable to reinforcing events at the theoretical level. As a cautionary note, it should be mentioned that not every learning theorist assigns all three theoretical functions to a reinforcing event; since we are not evaluating different theoretical approaches to reinforcement at this point, we can take these functions at face value and use them as dimensions of comparison between animal and human reinforcement. The functions of reinforcement are as follows:

The Reward or Stamping in Function

Many psychologists assume at the theoretical level that reinforcement is absolutely necessary for learning. The reinforcing event actually stamps in the learned response or the association underlying the learned response. Without the reinforcing event, there could be no learning. This reward function of a reinforcer has been traditionally associated with animal reinforcement and it has had less appeal to those learning psychologists engaged only in human research. The human subject often knows the correct response from the instructions or prior knowledge of the structure of the task and, as such, all that a reinforcing event can do is aid the subject in the proper performance of the learned response. So, in the context of human learning, at the theoretical level, reinforcement is usually interpreted as a performance variable, not as a learning variable.

The Motivational or Incentive Function

Many psychologists assume at the theoretical level that reinforcement acts as a motivator or incentive. This motivational or incentive function of a reinforcer has been traditionally associated with animal reinforcement and it has had less appeal to those learning psychologists engaged only in human research. An animal must be previously deprived of the stimulus substance which is going to serve as the primary positive reinforcer in a learning experiment; likewise, the onset of a negatively reinforcing event, whether primary or secondary, is inherently motivating. Stated from a different angle, reinforcing events serve as incentives and incentives are necessary to get the animal subject to perform the response to be learned. In the context of human research, the reinforcing events do not constitute the sole source of motivation or incentive. The instructions, the aspiration or expectation level of the subject, social factors, specific payoff conditions, etc. all contribute to determining the motivational or incentive conditions for the human subject. Reinforcement per se is not necessary to get the subject to emit response instances from the learned response class.

The Information, Feedback, or Knowledge of Results Function

Many psychologists assume at the theoretical level that reinforcement is informative or corrective in nature — it is a source of feedback or knowledge of results informing the subject of the correctness or appropriateness of his responding. This function of reinforcement makes reinforcement a cognitive event. This information or cognitive aspect of reinforcement has been traditionally associated with human reinforcement and it has had less appeal to those learning psychologists engaged only in animal research.

The Three Functions in Perspective

The third function of a reinforcer is redundant with respect to the other two functions. The animal-oriented psychologist emphasizes the stamping in and incentive functions of a reinforcer and deemphasizes the cognitive function of a reinforcer; the human-oriented psychologist emphasizes the cognitive function of a reinforcer and de-emphasizes its stamping in or incentive function. In other words, what the animal learns is basically a chance function of his motivational state and the external incentive conditions available to interact with this state; what the human learns is basically a nonchance product of his cognitive, information processing capacities. Based on the discussion of the fourth differential characteristic above, this is an ironic situation because for the animal the reinforcing event is the only source of information about appropriate responding, while for the human the reinforcing event is only one source of information about appropriate responding.

HUMAN AND ANIMAL REINFORCEMENT IN PERSPECTIVE

Now that the differential characteristics of reinforcement in animal and human learning and the theoretical functions attributable to reinforcement in animal and human learning have been discussed, it is possible to argue for the view that the use of the term reinforcement in human learning is continuous with its use in animal learning.

1. Both animal and human reinforcement employ the same categories and operational types of reinforcers — they merely emphasize different categories and operational types.

2. Reinforcement is informational in both human and animal reinforcement — the physical form of the reinforcement differs because the human possesses the language function while the typical lower order animal does not. So, in animal learning information is transmitted by physical, external, digital events; in human learning information is transmitted by verbal or symbolic analogical events, many of which are internally sourced.

3. The definitional function of reinforcement is the same in both animal and human learning — namely, to permanently alter the organism's responding. This must be done in the animal context by altering the motivational and incentive conditions of the organism; this can be accomplished in the human context by varying the cognitive or informational structure of the environment.

THE NATURE OF REINFORCED PRACTICE
IN SOME COMMON LEARNING TASKS

INTRODUCTION

The prototypical tasks of learning psychology were originally generated in Chapter 5 and are listed in Fig. 5-1. We are not going to analyze the nature of reinforced practice for every task appearing on the list. Rather, six learning tasks are selected for detailed analysis: (1) forward classical conditioning, (2) operant conditioning, (3) escape conditioning, (4) perceptual-motor learning, (5) paired-associate learning, and (6) concept formation.

The first three tasks essentially sample from the left end of the learning task continuum and constitute a set of traditional conditioning tasks. Because of the operational characterization of classical and instrumental conditioning in Chapter 4, no background introduction is given for each of the conditioning tasks prior to analyzing the nature of reinforced practice associated with each of them.

The last three tasks essentially sample from the right end of the learning task continuum and constitute a set of representative human learning tasks. A brief introduction is presented for each of the human learning tasks prior to analyzing the nature of reinforced practice associated with each of them.

The basic purpose of this section is to demonstrate the validity of the reinforcement terminology and operations developed in the text so far and this can be adequately accomplished by considering this particular subset of six learning tasks.

THE NATURE OF REINFORCED PRACTICE IN FORWARD
CLASSICAL CONDITIONING

Basic Description

Reinforced practice in forward classical conditioning consists of exposing the subject to N successive trials of the S-S reinforcement operation, with the initial stimulus interpreted as a CS and the second (reinforcing) stimulus interpreted as the UCS. The label "forward" derives from the fact that CS onset precedes UCS onset. The UCS is usually a biological reinforcer, although the use of a conditioned reinforcer is not precluded. If the UCS is classified as a positive reinforcer by analogy, the conditioning procedure is referred to as appetitive conditioning; if the UCS is classified as a negative reinforcer by analogy, the conditioning procedure is referred to as aversive or defensive conditioning. Actually there is only one significant class of appetitive classical conditioning procedures – Pavlovian salivary conditioning with meat, meat powder, or bread as the UCS. Pavlovian salivary conditioning with acid or acid powder as the UCS and virtually every other class of classical conditioning procedures – eyelid, leg flexion, pupillary constriction, GSR (galvanic skin response), finger or hand withdrawal, etc. – are aversive procedures. Also, whenever the UCS is internally applied, conditioning is aversive. (Internal UCS application is one of the defining conditions for interoceptive classical conditioning.)

The Nature of the S-S Operation in Forward Classical Conditioning – i.e., the Nature of the CS-UCS Pairing

By definition, the CS-UCS presentation order is the physical representation of the abstract S-S operation in forward classical conditioning; but, this presentation order is arbitrary. It is just that other orders – e.g., UCS-CS and CS-UCS (CS, UCS onset simultaneously) – are regarded as generating other kinds of classical conditioning procedures – backward and simultaneous respectively. The CS-UCS presentation order is considered the prototypical form of classical conditioning because it generates the best level of conditioning of the CR; and it constitutes by far the most frequently occurring laboratory realization of the abstract S-S operation. Thus, the appellation "forward" – forward is assigned to the majority occurring case.

The optimal temporal relation between CS onset and UCS onset and the optimal UCS intensity are empirical matters. By optimal is meant that which generates the best level of conditioning. A CS-UCS interval of .5 seconds is optimal for short latency UCRs; there is no one optimal CS-UCS interval for

long latency UCRs. Medium to high intensity UCSs afford the best conditioning.
Implicit in the above discussion is the fact that a paired presentation of a CS
and UCS is necessary for creating a CR. But this paired presentation is not taken
for granted. In certain experimental contexts, various control conditions are
employed to demonstrate that it is the CS-UCS pairing per se which leads to the
acquisition of the CR. The most common control condition is called the
pseudoconditioning procedure and is listed in Fig. 5-1. Here either the CS and
UCS are presented to the subject at random, although a CS-UCS pairing can
occur by chance, or the UCS is presented alone over many trials following which
the CS is presented alone as a test trial. If either of these pseudoconditioning
procedures results in the acquisition of a CR, commonly called a pseudoconditioned CR, the CR generated by the strict forward conditioning procedure
must be taken with a grain of salt. Actually, the existential status of a
pseudoconditioned CR is a matter of theoretical dispute. Some learning
experimenters regard it as simply another kind of CR (i.e., continuous with a
"true" forward conditioned CR), while other learning experimenters consider it
as an entirely different type of response (i.e., discontinuous with a "true"
forward conditioned CR).

The Relation Between the UCS (Reinforcing Stimulus) and CR
(Learned Response)

In classical conditioning, there is a one-to-one or biological relation between
the reinforcing event and the learned response. The response class of the CR in
classical conditioning is determined by the biological nature of the UCS because
the CR is a derivative of the UCR elicited by the UCS. In order to change the
response class of the CR in classical conditioning, it is necessary to change the
specific UCS (reinforcer) employed. Or, alternatively, if the specific UCS
(reinforcer) is changed, the response class of the CR will also change. The above
comments apply strictly to the response class typology (e.g., salivation, eyelid
closure, etc.) of the CR. the analogical features (values of a specific response
class (CR) depend on many factors besides the nature of the UCS and the
response class of the UCR.

THE NATURE OF REINFORCED PRACTICE IN OPERANT CONDITIONING

Basic Description

Reinforced practice in operant conditioning consists of exposing the subject
to N successive continuous-time occurrences of the S-R-S reinforcement opera-

tion. The first stimulus is often left implicit; if specified, it is termed an S^D. The response is the operant response class of interest — i.e., the CR or learned response. The reinforcing stimulus must be a positive reinforcer, usually primary, although the use of a conditioned reinforcer is not precluded. The abbreviation for a primary positive reinforcer is $+S^R$. The use of internally applied $+S^R$ (brain stimulation) is common. So the physical realization of the abstract S-R-S operation in operant conditioning is $\langle S^D \rangle - CR - (+)S^R$, with the brackets indicating optionality. As such, operant conditioning amounts to the straightway application of Skinner's operational definition of a positive reinforcer.

The Nature of the S-R-S Operation in Operant Conditioning — i.e., the Nature of the CR — $(+)S^R$ Contingency

By definition, reinforcement is response-contingent in operant conditioning; but, this contingent relationship is arbitrary, functional, merely temporal. There is no biological or universal causal necessity that a reinforcing event in an all-or-none sense or a specific reinforcing event in a graded or analogical sense follow the occurrence of a response instance from the operant response class of interest. This arbitrariness or functionality exists on many dimensions: the amount of $+S^R$ per response, the quality of $+S^R$ per response, the delay in onset of $+S^R$ subsequent to response occurrence, the reinforcement criterion — i.e., what specific aspect of the CR onsets reinforcement (usually the all-or-none occurrence of the CR), the type of reinforcement (usually $+S^R$, but $+S^r$ is also possible), and the schedule of reinforcement — i.e., the generating rule determining which specific response instances are reinforced (a continuous reinforcement schedule is the exception rather than the prototypical case in contemporary operant conditioning research). In other words, the experimenter has a choice of values on each of these dimensions when conducting the operant conditioning session. More realistically, he must fix the value of each of these dimensions before the session even begins. The prototypical case of operant conditioning employs a small or unit amount of $+S^R$ per response, a neutral (hedonic) quality of $+S^R$ per response, an immediate (apparatus minimum) $+S^R$ onset subsequent to response occurrence, a digital reinforcement criterion, primary reinforcement, and a continuous reinforcement schedule during the initial stage of training.

Implicit in the above discussion is the fact that the onset of the reinforcing event is dependent upon the prior occurrence of a response instance from the response class of interest — i.e., the specific response occurrence itself actually leads to the delivery of the reinforcing event. So, although the characteristics of the CR - $(+)S^R$ contingency are arbitrary, functional, merely temporal, the CR is the specific factor in the environment leading to the occurrence of a reinforcing event.

It would be a mistake to infer that the CR - $(+)S^R$ co-occurrence is necessary for conditioning an operant CR. As a control situation, Skinner and his associates have applied positive reinforcement to an organism, specifically a pigeon, at various moments in time, independent and irrespective of what response class the organism was actually exhibiting. This contingency generates what is called adventitious reinforcement — there is absolutely no connection between what the organism is doing and the delivery of reinforcement. Eventually, the organism develops a rather elaborate set of ritualistic behaviors, which Skinner termed "superstitious," in deference to the everyday life phenomenon.

It should be noted that the conditioning of superstitious behavior is somewhat species relative. Pigeons are "constantly" in motion — some behavior is always occurring so it can be adventitiously reinforced. Rats, monkeys, humans, etc. are not constantly in motion and superstitious behavior is the exception rather than the rule. But the general principle underlying the development of superstitious behavior has widespread application. Many complex reinforcement contingencies in operant conditioning involve the purely adventitious co-occurrence of a response and a reinforcing event or stimulus event (e.g., S^D) and the same caution must be used in interpreting the behavioral results.

The Relation Between the $+S^R$ (Reinforcing Stimulus) and CR (Learned Response)

Since the relationship between the reinforcing event and the learned response is arbitrary, functional, merely temporal in operant conditioning, there is a many to many or N to N relation between the $+S^R$ and CR. Many different positive reinforcers can be used to condition the same response or alternately the same reinforcer can be used to condition many different response classes in the context of the same organism. In order to change the response class of the CR in operant conditioning, it is not necessary to change the specific $+S^R$ used; likewise, if the specific $+S^R$ is changed, the response class of the CR need not change. This many to many relationship between response and reinforcer is what gives operant conditioning its tremendous flexibility both as a laboratory technique and as a model for the learning and/or reinforcement contingencies occurring in everyday life.

THE NATURE OF REINFORCED PRACTICE IN ESCAPE CONDITIONING

Basic Description

Reinforced practice in escape conditioning consists of exposing the subject to N successive trials of the S-R-S reinforcement operation. The second stimulus must be a negative reinforcer, usually primary (such as shock), although the use of a conditioned aversive stimulus is not precluded. The abbreviation for a primary negative reinforcer is $-S^R$. Brain stimulation can be used as the $-S^R$. The response is the efficacious escape response — i.e., the CR or learned response. The initial stimulus can be given two interpretations: (1) It is irrelevant and has no representation in the application of the S-R-S sequence to the escape conditioning operation — i.e., there is no stimulus event in the situation other than the second stimulus event or shock. (2) The initial stimulus is relevant and does have representation in the application of the S-R-S sequence to the escape conditioning operation — the onset of the shock begins the trial and serves as a cue or S^D for the escape response. Assuming the second interpretation of the initial stimulus, the physical realization of the abstract S-R-S operation in escape conditioning is S^D or cue (shock onset) — CR (escape response $-(-)S^R$ (shock termination). As such, escape conditioning amounts to the straightway application of Skinner's operational definition of a negative reinforcer.

The Nature of the S-R-S Operation in Escape Conditioning — i.e., the Nature of the CR — $(-)S^R$ Contingency

By definition, reinforcement is response-contingent in escape conditioning; but, this contingent relationship is arbitrary, functional, merely temporal. There is no biological or universal causal necessity that a reinforcing event in an all-or-none sense or a specific reinforcing event in a graded, analogical sense follow the occurrence of a response instance from the escape response class of interest. This arbitrariness or functionality exists on many dimensions: the intensity of the $-S^R$ per response, the type of $-S^R$ termination (sudden versus gradual), the delay in $-S^R$ termination subsequent to response occurrence, the reinforcement criterion, the type of reinforcement ($-S^R$ or $-S^r$), and the schedule of reinforcement or $-S^R$ terminations. The experimenter has a choice of values on each of these dimensions when conducting the escape session; in fact, he must fix the value of each of these dimensions before the session even begins. The prototypical case of escape conditioning involves a medium to intense $-S^R$, a sudden $-S^R$ termination, an immediate (apparatus minimum) $-S^R$ termination following escape response occurrence, a digital reinforcement criterion, primary reinforcement, and a continuous reinforcement schedule.

Implicit in the above discussion is the fact that the occurrence of the reinforcing event is dependent upon the prior occurrence of a response instance from the response class of interest — i.e., the specific response occurrence itself actually leads to the delivery of the reinforcing event. So, although the characteristics of the CR — $(-)S^R$ contingency are arbitrary, functional, merely temporal, the CR is the specific factor in the environment leading to the occurrence of a reinforcing event.

It would be a mistake to infer that the CR — $(-)S^R$ co-occurrence is necessary for conditioning an escape CR without the appropriate control. But, to my knowledge, no one has ever conducted the appropriate control situation in the escape conditioning context. No one has ever used an adventitious reinforcement contingency. There are probably two reasons for this.

1. The organism is not engaged in random activity following the onset of the shock. Shock onset acts like a UCS in classical conditioning and biologically elicits certain respondents or UCRs from the organism. (For the rat, in the escape conditioning apparatus, these respondents include screaming, jumping, urinating, defecating, climbing the walls, etc.) In a way, escape conditioning amounts to replacing these immediate reflexive responses to shock onset with response instances from the instrumental escape response class. If the instrumental escape response class is absolutely incompatible with the reflexive UCRs elicited by shock onset, the escape response class cannot be conditioned. Adventitiously introducing shock termination while these UCRs are in progress would not make much sense — in effect, the initial UCRs to shock onset would operate as the functional instrumental escape response class and the experimenter would be reinforcing responses that are already in the organism's repertoire.

The above discussion introduces a point of semantic ambiguity. Many psychologists would argue that the initial UCRs or respondents elicited by shock onset in the escape conditioning situation would constitute superstitious responses if the shock were in fact randomly or adventitiously terminated during their occurrence. But the basic point is that these responses are explicitly elicited and controlled by the experimenter when onsetting the shock in the escape conditioning situation. In the operant conditioning situation, the responses which can potentially by adventitiously reinforced and thus serve as superstitious responses are not under the direct control of the experimenter — they are merely emitted by the organism just as the criterion operant response class itself is emitted.

2. Unlike prototypical operant conditioning, where reinforcement can only be received by performing the criterion operant response class, the escape training situation contains many potential undesired sources of reinforcement. There are potentially many ways of escaping from the shock in escape conditioning instead of performing the experimenter-selected criterion escape response — i.e., for the rat: jumping out of the apparatus, climbing the walls, rolling over on the back, placing feet between the shock grids, perching on the escape response manipulandum itself, etc. The experimenter must consciously design these potential escape responses out of the situation — i.e., set up the apparatus so that these undesired responses cannot serve as escape responses. Since the experimenter has to actively control out these undesired sources of reinforcement in order to conduct the prototypical escape conditioning situation in the first place, it is no wonder that the adventitious control situation has not been conducted, a la operant conditioning.

The Relation Between the -S^R (Reinforcing Stimulus) and CR (Learned Response)

Since the relationship between the reinforcing event and the learned response is arbitrary, functional, merely temporal in escape conditioning, there is a many to many or N to N relation between the -S^R and CR. Many different negative reinforcers can be used to condition the same response or alternately the same reinforcer can be used to condition many different response classes in the context of the same organism. In order to change the response class of the CR in escape conditioning, it is not necessary to change the specific -S^R used; likewise, if the specific -S^R is changed, the response class of the CR need not change.

THE NATURE OF REINFORCED PRACTICE IN PERCEPTUAL-MOTOR LEARNING

Introduction

Perceptual-motor learning, in many respects, serves as the model human learning task because it illustrates quite nicely the subtle stimulus and response discriminations of which the human subject is capable. It involves finely graded physical movements and the integration of many physical components into a complex act (motor skill); and it involves subtle, finely graded verbal or symbolic reinforcing events, often implicitly sourced (discriminative feedback).

Many learning psychologists regard perceptual-motor learning as a combination of stimulus discrimination and response discrimination (differentiation) and integration and, as such, descriptively, it is applied instrumental/operant conditioning. Other psychologists — human factor and human engineering specialists — have absorbed the area of perceptual-motor skills into the more inclusive areas of human engineering, human factors, or man-machine interaction systems. Although the latter stress the asymptotic performance as opposed to the original acquisition of a motor skill, feedback systems are still involved.

Because of the literally infinite number of ways in which a specific perceptual-motor learning experiment can be conducted, the following discussion is necessarily only a very rudimentary interpretation of the nature of reinforced practice in perceptual-motor learning.

Basic Description

Reinforced practice in perceptual-motor learning consists of exposing the organism to N successive trials or N continuous-time occurrences of the S-R-S operation.

The first stimulus event can be resolved at any level of abstractness as desired. It can refer to any one or all of the following events: the overall experimental setup, the original instructions given at the start of the session or any continuing instructions, the specific apparatus, specific components or response manipulanda comprising the apparatus, specific residual feedback displays or counters containing information from prior trials or responses, a specific warning signal or ready signal, etc.

The response term is usually either a finely graded or sophisticated muscular movement or positioning (steady state) response or a combination of discrete muscular movements and/or steady state responses occurring in a fixed temporal order. In the latter physical realization of the response term, it is perfectly legitimate to conceptualize the R as a complex r-s-r-s-r-s etc. chain in which the mediating stimului or feedback events are internal (kinesthetic; proprioceptive).

The second stimulus event is usually some form of secondary positive reinforcement which informs the subject of the appropriateness or correctness of his response. This information event can be resolved at any level of specificity desired: a specific absolute dial reading, a verbal report of quantitative deviation from the desired response, the experimenter mumbling "good," the subject's subjective judgment of the accuracy of the response, the actual sight of the response accomplishing its intended purpose, etc.

We shall not get into the issue of whether symbolic aversive events like "wrong" or "incorrect," lost points or penalties, negative deviations, etc. or physical aversive events such as mild shock serve as actual punishing events and retard learning. (Remember, by definition, they are not negative reinforcers – either primary or secondary.) The informational value of these so-called aversive events can far outweigh any so-called punishing properties associated with them. (It must be realized that in the context of the natural environment extreme or exaggerated physical movements often result in pain – i.e., the wrong way of doing something often results in pain – and the information or cue value of this pain can override its immediate biological effects.) What is being argued here at an abstract level is that as long as the content of the reinforcing event can be interpreted at a cognitive level by the subject the aversive or nonaversive properties of the event are irrelevant.

Types of Reinforcing Events in Perceptual-Motor Learning

Introduction. Granted that reinforcement in perceptual-motor learning is basically secondary and positive, it is still necessary to provide some formal structure to the notion of a perceptual-motor reinforcer by deriving some mutually exclusive types of perceptual-motor reinforcing events. There are many extant classification systems involving different analytical dimensions for generating the different types of reinforcing events in perceptual-motor learning.

The classification scheme presented in Fig. 9-4 contains three hierarchically related, binary-valued dimensions and generates five types of mutually exclusive reinforcing events. This classification system is similar in structure and dynamics to the one used to generate the different macro-theoretical approaches to learning in Chapter 7; so it need not be evaluated in great detail. This particular scheme was selected for analysis because it contains dimensions which refer to crucial distinctions already made by the text relative to describing a reinforcing event. We shall describe the content of the classification scheme and then apply it to a simple discrete-trial "target shooting" perceptual-motor task.

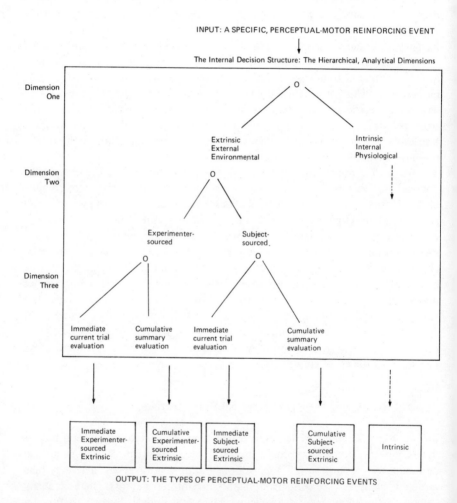

Fig. 9-4. A Classification Scheme for Generating the Types of Secondary Positive Reinforcing Events in Perceptual-Motor Learning

Description of the classification scheme. What follows is essentially a description of the internal decision structure of the generating system and a description of the output categories of reinforcing events.

The Internal Decision Structure

Dimension one. The initial dimension distinguishes between extrinsic or environmental reinforcing events and intrinsic or physiological reinforcing events. The intrinsic events are the internal, physiological kinesthetic/proprioceptive stimuli or feedback cues set up by performing the motor response during a trial — i.e., the particular stimuli associated with a specific level of muscle tension or state of bodily equilibrium, etc. This category is not subdivided further. (Note that the branching configuration in Fig. 9-4 terminates at this nodal value.) This class of reinforcing events gives the subject the "feel" of the correct or appropriate response and they cannot be prevented or removed from the situation by the experimenter. The extrinsic events are the externally sourced, cognitively based feedback cues occasioned by performing the motor response during a trial. This category constitutes the significant source of reinforcement in perceptual-motor learning because it is at least partially under the control of the experimenter and thus must be subdivided further (See Fig. 9-4).

Dimension two. This dimension divides the extrinsic reinforcer category into experimenter-sourced and subject-sourced reinforcing events. The latter category refers to the subject's own subjective judgment of how he is performing; the former category refers to the specific information provided to the subject by the experimenter relative to how he is performing. Naturally, experimenter-sourced feedback is under the direct control of the experimenter; subject-sourced feedback is only under indirect control of the experimenter. It is difficult, if not impossible, to remove all possible subject-sourced information from the perceptual-motor learning task situation; but, it is easy to create experimentally a discrepancy between experimenter-sourced and subject-sourced information because the experimenter explicitly controls the content of the experimenter-sourced category. But in the typical perceptual-motor learning task, the experimenter-sourced information is designed to be consistent with or verify the subject-sourced information.

Dimension three. This dimension divides the extrinsic reinforcer category into immediate and cumulative reinforcing events. Immediate reinforcing events refer to the information provided the subject concerning his response on the current trial — i.e., it evaluates the appropriateness of the current response.

Cumulative reinforcing events refer to the summary information provided the subject concerning all his past responses in the session – i.e., it provides the subject with a continual, updated evaluation of his cumulative performance as the session progresses.

The output categories. The five output categories of reinforcing events in perceptual-motor learning as generated by this scheme are: (1) immediate, experimenter-sourced, extrinsic; (2) cumulative, experimenter-sourced, extrinsic; (3) immediate, subject-sourced, extrinsic; (4) cumulative, subject-sourced, extrinsic; (5) intrinsic. The last three categories are largely indigenous to perceptual-motor learning. Intrinsic is such because the learned response is a physical/motor response requiring exertion, movement, etc. Subject-sourced is such because of the nature of perceptual-motor learning. In most experiments, the subject automatically knows how he is doing while performing the task. The first category corresponds to the prototypical reinforcing event in animal learning and other human learning tasks, such as verbal learning, concept formation, etc. It might be puzzling why the second category is used in a perceptual-motor learning task, since its incidence is rare in animal learning and other human learning tasks. It is employed to counteract the subject's often faulty subjective cumulative "memory" system – i.e., the fourth category of reinforcing events.

Application of the scheme to discrete-trial target shooting: Examples of the five types of reinforcers. In a discrete-trial target shooting task, the subject aims and shoots at one or more targets, either stationary or moving, during each trial. The target(s) is (are) usually subdivided into areas of differential significance or importance. The "shooting" is usually accomplished by some lightbeam gun or electronically controlled gun so that actual physical "ammunition type" contact can be avoided. The subject's task is to improve in performance (i.e., hit rate) over the course of the session, according to some experimenter-defined criterion of success. In this context, the physical representation of the five types of reinforcing events could be as follows.

  1. Immediate, experimenter-sourced, extrinsic reinforcing events: This category would include any verbal report from the experimenter or the visual feedback from appropriate dials or counters with respect to the correctness of the current response (shot).

  2. Cumulative, experimenter-sourced, extrinsic reinforcing events: This category would include summary information from the experimenter or visual feedback from appropriate cumulative counters or dials relative to the subject's mean or accumulated hit rate, etc.

  3. Immediate, subject-sourced, extrinsic reinforcing events: This category would refer to the subject's sight of hitting or not hitting the target during a

particular trial and his perception of any specific deviation of the shot from the crucial area of the target.

4. Cumulative, subject-sourced, extrinsic reinforcing events: This category would refer to the subject's subjective impression of his mean or accumulated hit rate.

5. Intrinsic reinforcing events: This category would include the "feel" of the trigger, the "feel" from the positioning of the arm, etc. Eventually the correct or appropriate physical aiming and shooting response would have a distinctive set of kinesthetic/proprioceptive cues associated with it.

Mechanisms Underlying the S-R-S Operation in Perceptual-Motor Learning — i.e., Mechanisms Underlying the Motor Skill Movement or Positioning-Symbolic Reinforcing Event Contingency

One of the drawbacks of perceptual-motor learning is that it can be described by everyday common sense terms which have intuitive appeal and general cultural validity. Every "Tips to the Golfer or Bowler" newspaper column and "How to Do It" book are replete with them. So it can justifiably be argued that the above description of reinforced practice in perceptual-motor learning has merely formalized the obvious.

Unfortunately, perceptual-motor skills learning is an area of learning psychology in which the theoretical mechanism(s) underlying the descriptive effects of reinforcement has (have) not been of crucial concern, probably because the second stimulus term is virtually infinitely resolvable at the physical level. Thus, the popularity of conceptualizing perceptual-motor learning as applied instrumental/operant conditioning. Historically, the abstract S-R-S operation in perceptual-motor skills learning has been given the following types of interpretations: motivational or incentive, biological strengthening or facilitation, cognitive or hypothesis testing, information processing, cybernetic or servomechanical, and strictly mathematical.

THE NATURE OF REINFORCED PRACTICE IN PAIRED-ASSOCIATE VERBAL LEARNING

Introduction to Verbal Learning

Verbal learning is a classic area of learning psychology, originated by Ebbinghaus in the late 19th century, in which the subject must learn a list of either individual verbal elements or associations between two or more verbal elements. Most investigations of human memory and retention phenomena are performed in the context of verbal learning (i.e., presuppose verbal learning in the original acquisition phase) because usually it is verbal or symbolic memory which is being measured.

Historical interest in verbal learning centered around (1) parametric studies of a relatively fixed list of variables (e.g., meaningfulness, association value, familiarity, frequency, pronunciation value, etc. of the verbal material; specific conditions of practice, like massed versus distributed practice, whole versus part learning, etc.) and (2) the interpretation of verbal learning as surrogate classical conditioning — i.e., verbal learning was simply the most convenient context in which to investigate association formation in the human being. Contemporary interest in verbal learning centers around (1) using specific verbal learning procedures to arbitrate between different micro-models of learning and (2) the interpretation of verbal learning as simply another kind of information processing or cognitive task, involving coding, mediation, integration, information transmission and reduction, etc.

Although there are literally an infinite number of verbal learning tasks or procedures, the area is codified enough so that a specific task or procedure can be assigned to at least one cell of a classification system. The generating dimensions of this classification scheme include the nature of the verbal item, the reinforcement operation, the testing operation, whether or not learning is run to a criterion, and the order of presentation of the items from trial to trial. Each of these dimensions is essentially binary valued. We are not going to formally present the classification system here because we are only going to analyze the nature of reinforced practice for the prototypical or most representative verbal learning task — namely, paired-associate learning. But, the elements of the classification scheme must be used to describe the nature of the paired-associate learning situation.

Introduction to Paired-Associate Learning

The subject in a paired-associate learning experiment learns a list of verbal material. The list is composed of N items, where N is usually some number between eight and 16. The individual verbal item is a paired associate (an association between two or more verbal elements), in which the first element is called the stimulus term and the second element is called the response term: for instance, COW - SIX; DXQ - KFT. Typically, only the formation of the association is of concern and amounts to the substantive learning event. To implement this, stimulus and response terms are usually kept relatively simple and the stimulus term is used as a cue for the response term when the association is tested. The exposure of the subject to the content of the list, usually on an item-by-item basis, is called a trial. There are three kinds of trials used in paired-associate learning: (1) a reinforcement trial, (2) a test trial, and (3) a combination trial in which both testing and reinforcement occur. The method of testing is usually straight recall or multiple choice recognition. The order of the items on a list must vary randomly from trial to trial to prevent a response from being associated with a specific position instead of solely to a specific stimulus. The subject can be run to a learning criterion or simply stopped after a predetermined fixed number of trials has been completed.

We are going to assume that the subject is run to a criterion and tested by the recall method; thus the nature of the paired-associate task need only be further analyzed with respect to the kinds of trials employed. It is at the level of trial that the abstract reinforcement operations are physically represented. The nature of reinforced practice in paired-associate learning is contingent upon the specific kinds of trials that are used.

Use of the Three Kinds of Trials: Derivation of the Two Traditional Paired-Associate Criterion Learning Procedures

Over the course of the paired-associate learning session, the experimenter must both reinforce and test the subject. This can either be done on a (1) trial-by-trial basis or on an (2) item-by-item basis.

The trial-by-trial basis involves reinforcing and testing the subject on different trials, usually alternately, but any logical sequence is possible. Reinforcement and testing do not occur in the context of the same trial. Thus, the trial-by-trial basis of reinforcing and testing employs two of the three types of trials: reinforcement trials and test trials. Diagrammatically, the trial-by-trial method, with alternating reinforcement and test trials, can be symbolized as follows:

$$R\,T\,R\,T\,R\,T\,R\,T\ldots\ldots R\,T_N.$$

A reinforcement trial must be first; the subject reaches criterion on a test trial so it is the last kind of trial in the sequence. This sequence of trials defines the nonanticipation or multiple R T paired-associate criterion learning procedure.

The item-by-item basis involves testing and reinforcing the subject in the context of each item. Both reinforcement and testing occur in the context of the same trial. Thus, the item-by-item basis of testing and reinforcing essentially employs one of the three types of trials, combination trials. Diagrammatically, the item-by-item method can be symbolized as follows:

$$R\,(TR)\,\,(TR)\,\,(TR)\,\,(TR)\ldots\ldots\ldots(TR)_N.$$

Note that the very first trial of the session is a pure reinforcement trial. Each successive trial is a combination trial. The T appears before the R in each ( ) because the individual item is tested before reinforcement occurs. This sequence of trials defines the anticipation paired-associate criterion learning procedure −

the subject must attempt to anticipate the correct response for a stimulus before the reinforcing event occurs.

The Two Physical Reinforcement Operations Used in Paired-Associate Learning

Abstracting from the above discussion, it can be deduced that two physical reinforcement operations are used in paired-associate learning: (1) the R trial operation and (2) the R item operation. The R trial operation simply exposes the subject to all the individual paired-associate items of the list with no testing. The multiple R T paired-associate procedure employs the R trial operation. The R item operation supplies the subject with immediate feedback of results after the individual item is tested. The anticipation paired-associate procedure employs the R item operation after the first trial.

The Physical Realization of the Abstract S-S Reinforcement Operation and the Abstract S-R-S Reinforcement Operation in Paired-Associate Learning: Interpretation of the R Trial and R Item Reinforcement Operations

The physical representation of the S-S reinforcement operation in paired-associate learning involves the R trial operation. More specifically, the exposure to the subject of each individual paired-associate item during an R trial is an instance of the S-S reinforcement operation. Or, alternately, an R trial exposes the subject to N successive S-S reinforcement operations, where N is the number of paired associates composing the list. So, the S-S reinforcement operation in paired-associate learning amounts to the contiguous presentation to the subject of the stimulus and response elements of an individual paired-associate item.

The physical representation of the S-R-S reinforcement operation in paired-associate learning is the R item operation. More specifically, the testing and reinforcing of an individual paired-associate item during a combined trial is an instance of the S-R-S operation. Or, alternately, an R item operation exposes the subject to an S-R-S reinforcement operation. A combined trial exposes the subject to N successive S-R-S reinforcement operations, where N is the number of paired associates composing the list. So, the S-R-S reinforcement operation in paired-associate learning amounts to the testing of an individual paired-associate item and the later contiguous presentation to the subject of the stimulus and response elements of that paired-associate item.

The Nature of Reinforced Practice in Multiple R T
Paired-Associate Criterion Learning

Reinforced practice in multiple R T paired-associate criterion learning consists of exposing the subject to K R trial operations, each of which is composed of N S-S reinforcement operations. Each S-S reinforcement operation is mapped into an individual paired-associate item such that the first stimulus is the stimulus term of the association and the second stimulus is the response term of the association. Thus, reinforced practice in multiple R T paired-associate criterion learning involves the contiguous presentation to the subject of the elements of the individual paired-associate items.

The Nature of Reinforced Practice in Anticipation
Paired-Associate Criterion Learning

Reinforced practice in anticipation paired-associate criterion learning consists of exposing the subject to K combined trials, each of which is composed of N S-R-S reinforcement operations. Each S-R-S reinforcement operation is mapped into an individual paired-associate item such that the first stimulus is the stimulus term of the association, the response term is the subject's response to the cuing stimulus term, and the second stimulus is the reinforcing event (the correct response term presentation) following the test. Thus, reinforced practice in anticipation paired-associate criterion learning involves the contiguous presentation to the subject of the elements of the individual paired-associate items, following intervening tests.

Interpretation of the S-S Reinforcement Operation
or R Trial Operation

Recall from Chapter 2 that the S-S reinforcement operation was termed the contiguity operation because it involves the contiguous presentation to the subject of two stimulus events. Its physical realization in the paired-associate R trial operation involves exposing the subject to the stimulus and response terms of a paired associate simultaneously. Do not get confused because the second term in a paired associate is called both a stimulus and a response. The second term in a paired associate is a stimulus to the subject on an R trial; the second term in a paired associate is a response to be supplied by the subject on a T trial.

The critical feature of the S-S reinforcement operation is that it supplies the subject with information. Note that the second stimulus of the S-S operation has not been explicitly labeled a reinforcing stimulus event. The whole S-S sequence constitutes the reinforcing event. This interpretation of the S-S operation differs from its prior applications (e.g., in forward classical conditioning).

Interpretation of the S-R-S Reinforcement Operation
or R Item Operation

Recall from Chapter 2 that the S-R-S reinforcement operation was termed the effect operation because it involves more than the contiguous presentation to the subject of two stimulus events; this something else was effect — i.e., the R leads to the second S event. Its physical realization in the paired-associate R item operation preserves this effect property. The correct response term of an individual paired-associate item is not presented, thus implementing a contiguous presentation of the stimulus and response elements of the paired-associate item, until after the subject attempts to correctly anticipate it. As in the above case, do not get confused because the second term in a paired associate is called both a stimulus and a response. The second term in a paired associate is a response during the test phase of the R item presentation when the stimulus term serves as a cue; the second term in a paired associate is a stimulus during the reinforcing phase of the R item presentation.

The critical feature of the S-R-S reinforcement operation is that it supplies the subject with information — but, unlike the above case, the information is corrective or confirmational — i.e., it possesses feedback properties. Note that the second stimulus of the S-R-S operation has been explicitly labeled a reinforcing or feedback event and this interpretation of the S-R-S operation is continuous with its prior applications (e.g., in various instrumental conditioning situations). The S-R-S operation also implicitly contains the S-S information operation because of the eventual contiguous presentation of the stimulus and response element of the paired-associate item during the R item operation.

The Type of Reinforcement Used in Paired-Associate Learning

The reinforcing events in paired-associate learning definitely fall into the secondary reinforcer category. Resolution in terms of the operational dimension is more difficult. The second stimulus event in the S-R-S operation can be assigned to the positive reinforcer category with much justification; although a correctional instance of feedback may be more aversive than a confirmational instance of feedback, the information value of the stimulus far surpasses any punishing properties associated with it. The reinforcing event contained in the S-S operation can only be assigned to an operational category by analogy; and by analogy we shall duly assign it to the positive reinforcer category.

THE NATURE OF REINFORCED PRACTICE IN CONCEPT FORMATION

Introduction to Concept Formation

Concept formation is probably the most pervasive form of human learning because every stimulus object in the natural environment is an instance of some concept. Actually, a given stimulus object is an instance of many different concepts simultaneously because of the many different ways in which it can be classified. For instance, an orange is an instance of the concepts of orange (color), round, ball, solid, fruit, consumable, etc. A concept can be defined as a classification system or generating rule which divides the world into two mutually exclusive sets: positive instances of the concept and negative instances of the concept. The incidence of concepts range from simple physical concepts defined in terms of external physical stimulus dimensions such as color, angularity, shape, size, etc. to complex abstract concepts such as truth, justice, beauty, etc. whose generating rules or critical defining properties are elusive.

The classic set of studies on concept formation were performed by Hull, Smoke, and Heidbreder. Contemporary research on concept formation includes the work of Hunt, Bruner, Bourne, Bower, Trabasso, and others. A shift in theoretical emphasis, paralleling that in verbal learning, has also happened in concept formation. From initial characterization as simple classical conditioning and stimulus generalization and/or discrimination, concept formation is now regarded as a complex cognitive, information-processing task.

Transition to the Laboratory: Some Preliminary Distinctions

Operationally, in the laboratory, the subject is exposed to positive and negative instances of an unknown concept and he has to induce the classification system or generating rule for the concept — i.e., he must induce what the concept is. To effect this, the experimenter has to control and delimit the particular stimulus dimensions and attributes (as input) used to generate the stimulus instances and use unambiguous, verbalizable generation or classification rules.

To create the stimulus input situation, the experimenter typically uses N k-valued stimulus dimensions (for instance four binary-valued stimulus dimensions) to generate a universal set of stimulus instances in terms of which various concepts can be defined. The number of stimulus instances in the universal set is doubled, tripled, etc. for each additional stimulus dimension used in the input when $k = 2, 3$, etc. For instance, eight stimulus instances are generated using the following three binary-valued dimensions as the input: (1) color (black, white); (2) shape (triangle, circle); (3) size (small, large) — see Fig. 9-5.

To establish an inducible concept rule, the experimenter typically uses one or more of the input stimulus dimensions as the defining attribute of the concept. If only one stimulus dimension is used to generate the concept, it is

Fig. 9-5. The Universe of Eight Stimulus Instances Generated by a Specific Set of Three Binary-Valued Stimulus Dimensions

called the "relevant" dimension and the remaining dimensions are termed "irrelevant" dimensions. A concept defined by one relevant dimension is a simple concept. For instance, the set of eight stimulus instances in Fig. 9-5 can be divided into two mutually exclusive subsets (positive and negative instances) by using either color, shape, or size as the relevant dimension. Thus, three different simple concepts are definable in the context of this set of eight stimulus instances. If the combination of two or more stimulus dimensions is used to generate the concept, the concept is called a "complex" concept. Most complex concepts are generated by using logical operations (combination rules): conjunction, disjunction, conditional, biconditional, etc. As an example of a complex concept, one possible conjunctive concept would be white triangle. Color and shape are the generating stimulus dimensions and members of the positive instance class are only stimulus instances which are both white and triangle. (As a didactic aside, most physical stimulus objects in the natural environment are conjunctive concepts in the sense that they are the conjunctive combination of stimulus attributes from N stimulus dimensions.)

The Four Basic Laboratory Procedures Used to Study Concept Formation

Introduction. There is an infinite number of ways to conduct a concept formation experiment. We shall generate four classes of procedures for studying concept formation. These four classes derive from how the individual stimulus instances are displayed to the subject and the manner in which the subject is informed of the positive and negative instances of the concept.

With respect to the means of display, (1) all stimulus instances of the universal set are always in view for the subject — and the processing of one stimulus instance from the display is regarded as a trial, or (2) only one stimulus instance from the universal set is ever viewed by the subject at a time — and the processing of all the stimulus instances of the universal set (individually, one by one) constitutes a trial. In (1), it is customary to allow the subject to choose which stimulus instance he wants to process on a given trial, although this is not necessary and the sequence of processing can be done according to an experimenter-predetermined fixed order. In (2), it is usually necessary to schedule the appearance of the individual stimulus instances according to an experimenter-predetermined fixed order.

With respect to how the subject is informed of positive and negative instances, (1) the subject is directly told by the experimenter about the significance or meaning of the stimulus instance (i.e., whether it is a positive or negative instance) or (2) the subject guesses the meaning or significance of the stimulus instance (positive or negative instance) and then the guess is corrected or confirmed by the experimenter.

Generation of the four classes of concept formation procedures. Henceforth, we shall assume that whenever all the members of the universal set of stimulus instances are on display, the subject always selects the processed stimulus instance and whenever only one member of the universal set of stimulus instances is on display at any one time, the stimulus instances appear according to some experimenter-predetermined order. This assumption establishes two independent binary-valued dimensions which, when made orthogonal to each other, generate four classes of concept formation procedures. The four classes (See Fig. 9-6) are as follows:

1) direct identification selection method (Cell I);
2) indirect identification selection method (Cell II);
3) paired-associate R trial method (Cell III);
4) paired-associate R item method (Cell IV).

Description of the Four Procedures

Selection procedures. Natural terminology for the procedures in which the subject selects the stimulus instance to be processed on a particular trial is that of "selection." This general class of procedures is employed by learning psychologists specifically interested in studying what strategies or hypotheses subjects use or how subjects process information, etc. This class does not put a premium on memory. The stimulus instances are always in sight; presumably, the subject can request a repeat processing of a specific stimulus instance (i.e., sample from the universal set with replacement). The two subsets of the general

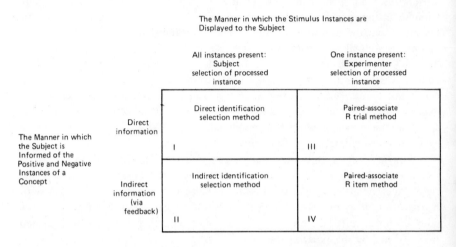

Fig. 9-6. A Classification Scheme for Generating the Four Classes of Concept Formation Procedures

selection class are referred to as the direct identification method and the indirect identification method, respectively, dependent upon how the subject is informed of the significance or meaning of the stimulus instance. Recall that, unlike the typical verbal learning task, the exposure to one stimulus instance and its significance is called a trial — i.e., an individual item is a trial. It is not even necessary to process every single stimulus instance before the generating rule can be learned. The subject is run to some kind of criterion — usually the self-report that he knows the concept.

Paired-associate procedures. Somewhat less obvious terminology for the procedures in which the subject is exposed to one experimenter-selected stimulus instance at a time is that of "paired associate." In actual practice, this class of procedures is conducted as a virtual paired-associate experiment. The individual stimulus instance serves as a stimulus of an individual S-R association, in which the response term is some verbal label or symbol related to the significance or meaning of the stimulus instance. Unlike the typical paired-associate verbal learning experiment in which all items of the list are composed of different and randomly connected stimulus and response terms, the paired-associate procedure of concept formation uses only two response terms (one representing the positive instance class and the other representing the negative instance class) and the two terms are systematically assigned to stimulus instances depending on their positive, negative instance class membership.

This general class of procedures is used by learning psychologists primarily interested in generating quantitative data for arbitrating between different micro-model approaches to concept formation. This class does put a premium on memory. Only one stimulus instance at a time is ever seen by the subject; the subject presumably must cycle through all stimulus instances once before any particular stimulus instance is repeated. The two subsets of the general paired-associate class are referred to as the R trial method and the R item method, respectively, by analogy to paired-associate verbal learning. The direct information approach is analogous to the use of the R trial operation in paired-associate verbal learning; the indirect information or feedback approach is analogous to the use of the R item operation in paired-associate verbal learning. Recall that, like the typical verbal learning task, the exposure to one stimulus instance and its significance is called an item and a trial consists of one exposure to all the items of the list. The subject is run to some kind of criterion – usually K successive trials of no error responding.

Testing for the acquisition of a concept (i.e., the generating rule). Regardless of the specific class of procedures used to study concept formation, the subject is usually given a behavioral test to actually determine whether or not he has learned the generating rule. Often this behavioral test is the simple, informal request to the subject to verbalize the generating rule. But, due to circumstances such as the use of pre-verbal subjects and the use of generating rules very difficult to verbalize, a formal behavioral test is sometimes administered to the subject. This consists of presenting the subject with an entirely new universe of stimulus instances in the context of which the subject must apply the acquired generating rule – i.e., he must divide its members into the positive and negative instance subsets. Operationally, this amounts to a test for stimulus generalization of the generating rule.

The Nature of Reinforced Practice in the Four Basic
Laboratory Procedures Used to Study Concept Formation

Cell I: The direct identification selection method. Reinforced practice in this method consists of exposing the subject to N successive trials of the S-S reinforcement operation. The first stimulus term is a stimulus instance from the universal set; the second stimulus term is the experimenter's report of the class membership (+,-) of the stimulus instance.

Cell II: The indirect identification selection method. Reinforced practice in this method consists of exposing the subject to N successive trials of the S-R-S reinforcement operation. The first stimulus term is a stimulus instance from the universal set; the response term is the subject's guess relative to the class membership of the stimulus instance; the second stimulus term is the experimenter's correctional or confirmational feedback response to the subject's guess.

Cell III: The paired-associate R trial method. Reinforced practice in this method consists of exposing the subject to K R trial operations, each of which is composed of N S-S reinforcement operations. Each S-S reinforcement operation is mapped into an individual paired-associate item such that the first stimulus term is a stimulus instance from the universal set and the second stimulus term is the verbal label or symbol indicating the class membership (+,-) of the stimulus instance.

Cell IV: The paired-associate R item method. Reinforced practice in this method consists of exposing the subject to K combined trials, each of which is composed of N S-R-S reinforcement operations. Each S-R-S reinforcement operation is mapped into an individual paired-associate item such that the first stimulus term is a stimulus instance from the universal set, the response term is the subject's emission of one of the two verbal labels or symbols indicating class membership, and the second stimulus term is the experimenter's correctional or confirmational feedback response to the subject's response.

Interpretation of the S-S Reinforcement Operation in the Direct Identification Selection and Paired-Associate R Trial Procedures

The S-S reinforcement operation was previously defined as the contiguity operation. The critical feature of the S-S reinforcement operation in this context is that it supplies the subject with information. Note that the second stimulus of the S-S operation has not been explicitly labeled as a reinforcing stimulus event. The whole S-S sequence constitutes the reinforcing event. This interpretation of the S-S operation is equivalent to the interpretation of the S-S operation presented in paired-associate verbal learning.

Interpretation of the S-R-S Reinforcement Operation in the Indirect Identification Selection and Paired-Associate R Item Procedures

The S-R-S reinforcement operation was previously defined as the effect operation. The critical feature of the S-R-S reinforcement operation in this context is that it supplies the subject with information — but, unlike the above case, the information is correctional or confirmational — i.e., it possesses feedback properties. Note that the second stimulus of the S-R-S operation does explicitly serve as a reinforcing or feedback event and this interpretation of the S-R-S operation is continuous with all of its prior applications. The S-R-S operation also implicitly contains the S-S information operation because of the eventual contiguous presentation of the stimulus instance and its proper class membership.

The Type of Reinforcement Used in Concept Formation

The reinforcing events in concept formation definitely fall in the secondary reinforcer category. Resolution in terms of the operational dimension is more difficult. The second stimulus event in the S-R-S operation can be assigned to the positive reinforcer category with much justification. Although a correctional instance of feedback may be more aversive than a confirmational instance of feedback, the information value of the stimulus far surpasses any punishing properties associated with it. The reinforcing event contained in the S-S operation can only be assigned to an operational category by analogy; and by analogy we shall duly assign it to the positive reinforcer category.

It should be noted that positive and negative instance specifications (the second stimulus term in both operations) as secondary positive reinforcers need not possess the same information value. The type of concept, the instructions, the proportion of positive and negative instances given to the subject, etc. all determine the respective information value of the two kinds of instance specifications. It is only in the simple concept case with bisymmetrical positive and negative instance classes that the information value of the two kinds of instance specifications are automatically equal.

THEORETICAL INTERPRETATIONS OF THE NATURE AND ROLE OF RESPONSE-CONTINGENT PRIMARY POSITIVE REINFORCEMENT

INTRODUCTION

Recall that a primary positive reinforcer in the response-contingent context is a stimulus event whose onset biologically increases the frequency of occurrence of response instances of the response class which immediately precedes it in time. This type of reinforcing event is the prototypical reinforcing event in the sense that it has served as the focus of analysis for most learning psychologists interested in giving reinforcement a theoretical interpretation. The theoretical analysis of primary positive reinforcement has primarily been conducted along two interrelated dimensions: its nature and its role in learning. Henceforth the term "reinforcer," unmodified, will be used in lieu of the phrase "response-contingent primary positive reinforcer."

THEORETICAL ANALYSIS OF THE NATURE OF REINFORCEMENT

Theoretical questions related to the nature of reinforcement include the following:

1. What is (are) the mechanism(s) underlying the procedural effects of reinforcement? Why does reinforced practice result in a permanent change in one or more of the measurable characteristics of a response class?

2. Is the concept of reinforcement absolute or relative? Is there a fixed list of reinforcers or is the list of stimulus events which can serve as reinforcers contingent upon other factors?

3. What are the theoretical criteria for determining whether or not a stimulus event is a member of the list of reinforcers?

4. How much should be subsumed by one's theory of reinforcement? This is the question of just what should be given in one's system of reinforcement and what has to be derived as secondary reinforcing events in one's system of reinforcement.

5. What is the anatomical site or physiological locus of reinforcement?

The initial question concerning the underlying mechanism(s) of reinforcement is the primary one, such that once this is explicitly answered by a particular theorist his answers to the other questions are by and large determined. So we are going to concentrate on the mechanism(s) issue in our analysis and only refer to the other subquestions where it is didactically necessary (primarily in the context of contemporary theoretical approaches to reinforcement).

The specific theoretical approach to the nature of reinforcement taken by one theorist is often translatable into the reinforcement system of another theorist and this can serve as the source of many conceptual problems. In effect, various learning psychologists, faced with the same essential set of empirical data, interpret the data situation differently, using different theoretical distinctions, labels, etc.; and no one interpretation serves as the canonical case.

THEORETICAL ANALYSIS OF THE ROLE OF REINFORCEMENT IN LEARNING

The two primary theoretical questions related to the role of reinforcement in learning can be expressed as follows. (1) Is the theoretical mechanism(s) underlying the procedural effects of reinforcement absolutely necessary for learning — i.e., is reinforcement a learning variable? (2) Is the theoretical mechanism(s) underlying the procedural effects of reinforcement necessary for the occurrence of the learned response — i.e., is reinforcement a performance variable?

All learning psychologists answer the second question in the affirmative, even if they postulate no underlying mechanism(s) for the procedural effects of reinforcement. So all learning psychologists assign reinforcement response performance properties, even purely descriptive learning psychologists such as Skinner. (Answering the question in the negative amounts to defining away the concept of learning at least to the extent that it is related to or dependent upon the concept of reinforcement.) Not every psychologist answers the first question in the affirmative — in fact treating reinforcement as a learning variable is a minority view.

Complicating the issue of what the mechanism(s) underlying the procedural effects of reinforcement are responsible for is the fact that it is not independent of the issues of the nature of the underlying learning process, the origin of the learned response, the fundamental laws of learning, and what is learned. Reference to these issues, especially the last one, must be made in our analysis wherever it is didactically necessary (primarily in the context of macro-theoretical approaches to reinforcement).

THE NATURE AND ROLE OF REINFORCEMENT IN HISTORICAL PERSPECTIVE: LAW OF EFFECT TERMINOLOGY

Introduction

The content of the prior discussion can be neatly summarized and put in historical perspective by distinguishing between what is technically called the weak or empirical law of effect and the strong or theoretical law of effect. The phrase "law of effect" is simply formal terminology for the fact that a response-contingent reinforcer increases the frequency of occurrence of a prior response.

The Weak or Empirical Law of Effect

This is the descriptive law of effect. It amounts to the statement that the reinforcing operation is procedurally necessary for the performance of a learned response. Reinforcement consists of a set of operations which raises the probability of response occurrence. As such, accepting this law of effect is equivalent to accepting the performance variable interpretation of the pro-cedural effects of reinforcement.

No learning psychologist denies the empirical law of effect; but it is the only law of effect accepted by those learning psychologists such as Skinner and Spence who postulate no underlying theoretical mechanism(s) for the procedural effects of reinforcement. Also, most contemporary micro-modelers operate solely in the context of the weak law of effect in the sense that the mathematical representation of reinforcement is for reinforcement operations only.

The Strong or Theoretical Law of Effect

This is the interpretive law of effect. It includes the weak or empirical law of effect, but in addition makes reference to the theoretical nature of reinforcement and the role of reinforcement in learning. Thus, a learning psychologist accepting the strong law of effect postulates an explicit underlying mechanism for the procedural effects of reinforcement and takes an explicit stand on whether reinforcement is necessary for learning.

Virtually all learning psychologists in the macro-theoretical tradition and their macro-model derivatives accept the theoretical law of effect — because they postulate underlying mechanism(s); but only those macro-theoretical learning psychologists operating in the general effect tradition, such as Hull and Thorndike, assume that reinforcement is a learning variable in addition to a performance variable. Current research by micro-theorists operating in the theoretical law of effect tradition is concentrated solely on the nature of the theoretical mechanism(s) underlying the operational effects of reinforcement on behavior.

TRADITIONAL THEORETICAL APPROACHES TO REINFORCEMENT VERSUS CONTEMPORARY THEORETICAL APPROACHES TO REINFORCEMENT: AN OVERVIEW

Before describing specific theoretical interpretations of reinforcement, it is necessary to characterize the two broad historical approaches to theorizing about reinforcement.

The Traditional Approach

The traditional approach coincided 100% with the macro-theoretical era of learning psychology. In effect, the traditional approach to reinforcement is the macro-theoretical approach to reinforcement. Virtually every macro-theorist listed in Chapter 7 had his own theory of reinforcement; or, alternately, an explicit formulation of the theoretical nature of reinforcement was a component of every macro-theory of learning.

Because of the absolutistic and all-inclusive nature of macro-theory (see Chapter 7), the traditional theoretical approach to reinforcement emphasized two things: the absolute nature of reinforcement and the mechanism(s) under- lying the procedural effects of reinforcement. In the traditional approach to reinforcement, there is a fixed list of reinforcers, quite delimited and restrictive according to present standards. Not only were the mechanisms underlying reinforcement spelled out, but they were postulated as a part of a total theoretical package which also included statements about the fundamental conditions of learning and the units of learning. As such, these macro-theoretical mechanisms were highly qualitative and embedded in larger symbolic systems. This feature made them largely mutually translatable approaches, which were beyond realistic empirical arbitration. Except for the theoretical mechanisms involved in the effect approach, they were exclusively performance, not learning, mechanisms — another factor which complicated their differential evaluation.

In summary, the macro-theoretical approach to reinforcement can be characterized as being basically concerned with interpreting the nature of the reinforcement operation (either S-S or S-R-S) at the theoretical level.

The Contemporary Approach

The contemporary approach overlaps historically with the micro-model and micro-theoretical approaches to learning; but, in no respect is there a characteris- tic micro-model or micro-theoretical interpretive approach to reinforcement. With the demise of macro-theory and fragmentation of theoretical learning psychology, the theoretical nature of reinforcement became a separate, indepen- dent issue in learning, an issue with which only a minority of micro-theorists is even concerned.

Current theoretical approaches to reinforcement are much more functional than the traditional approaches. They emphasize one or more of the following: the relativistic nature of reinforcement, the theoretical criteria for determining a reinforcing event, the givens associated with a biological reinforcer, or the physiological basis of reinforcement. Current theories of reinforcement do not come as part of total theoretical packages concerning the fundamental condi- tions of learning, units of learning, or reinforcement as a learning variable; they are more quantitative and easier to experimentally assess. Although reinforce- ment is a performance mechanism, it does not constitute the sole or even the most important performance variable.

In summary, the contemporary approach to reinforcement can be charac- terized as being primarily concerned with analyzing at the theoretical level the conditions under which a stimulus event serves as a reinforcer in the all-or-none, digital sense as well as the conditions which determine the specific graded or analogical reinforcing value of a reinforcer.

Preview

We are going to present five different macro-theoretical approaches to reinforcement; it is not meaningful to discuss these independent of the units of learning or what is learned issue (see Chapter 7). A sample of seven of the more functional, contemporary approaches to reinforcement will also be given. Finally, two theoretical interpretations of ESB (as an example of internally applied reinforcement) will also be presented.

FIVE TRADITIONAL, MACRO-THEORETICAL APPROACHES TO REINFORCEMENT

Introduction

Figure 9-7 lists the specific approaches to be considered as well as the analytical dimensions to be used. The first column nominalizes the five approaches. The first three approaches should be recognizable as the three primary categories of classical macro-theory derived in Chapter 7. The fourth and fifth approaches should also be recognizable as subsidiary categories derived in the same chapter. The second column presents the primary psychologists associated with each of the respective approaches. The third column represents the units of learning or the "what is learned" issue. The fourth and fifth columns represent the two interpretive dimensions of the theoretical law of effect: (1) the nature of reinforcement and (2) the role of reinforcement in learning.

To delimit the extent of the discussion, no formal analysis of the Gestalt and field theory approaches is going to be presented. They are only included in the figure for purposes of maintaining historical exhaustiveness.

The ideal course of action to follow with respect to analyzing the three primary macro-theoretical approaches to reinforcement would be to demonstrate just how they differentially interpret what is going on in a specific response-contingent primary positive reinforcement learning situation, such as operant conditioning or discrete-trial reward instrumental conditioning. But, the text has not developed other aspects of the three theoretical approaches (i.e., specific S.R. and intervening theoretical constructs, response rule assumptions, etc.) required to analyze what is going on in these situations so that such a presentation would be misleading and actually unrepresentative of the three approaches.

Specific Macro-Theoretical Approach	Primary Psychologists Associated with the Approach	Units of Learning; What is Learned	Theoretical Mechanism Underlying the Procedural Effects of Reinforcement	Is Activation of the Theoretical Mechanism Necessary for Learning
1. Effect	Hull Thorndike	Responses, as part of S-R associations or habits	Hull: Primary drive reduction Thorndike: Satisfaction Reinforcement physiologically stamps in the learned response or S-R association	Yes
2. Contiguity	Guthrie Estes	Responses, as part of S-R associations	Stimulus situation transformation Reinforcement prevents unlearning of S-R associations	No
3. Cognitive	Tolman	Performances, as defined by the stimulus situation; S-S associations or expectancies	Goal attainment or confirmation The reinforcing stimulus is merely the last stimulus in a chain of stimulus events	No
4. Gestalt	Wertheimer Koffka Köhler	Memory traces and structural reorganization of the perceptual field − but overt responses are defined by the stimulus situation	Closure	No
5. Field Theory	Lewin	Structural reorganization of the life space	Tension reduction or return to equilibrium	No

Fig. 9-7. Five Traditional, Macro-Theoretical Approaches to Reinforcement $(+S^R)$

As a compromise course of action, it is possible to adequately demonstrate just how the three approaches differentially interpret the nature of the S-R-S reinforcement operation underlying operant and discrete-trial reward instrumental conditioning. In effect, structural and not dynamic aspects of the three macro-theoretical approaches to reinforcement are going to be analyzed.

The Effect Interpretation of the S-R-S Reinforcement Operation

The initial stimulus term and response term of the operation constitute the units of learning and an association is formed between them. This associative bond is sometimes referred to as a habit and the degree of the bond is referred to as habit strength (see Chapter 8).

The second stimulus term is the reinforcing stimulus event and it possesses "true" effect properties. Hull gives the effect a primary drive reduction interpretation. Reinforcement at the theoretical mechanism level is primary drive reduction. (Recall from prior discussion that Hull used variants of the general drive reduction approach over the years, but that need not concern us here.) Thorndike gives the effect a satisfaction subjective state interpretation. Reinforcement at the theoretical mechanism level establishes satisfaction in the organism. (Recall from prior discussion that Thorndike used the concept of satisfaction to help define a positive reinforcer.)

In either interpretation of effect, the occurrence of reinforcement actually physiologically stamps in the associative bond connecting the S term and R term. As such, reinforcement at the theoretical level (effect) is absolutely necessary for learning (formation of the S-R association) – i.e., reinforcement at the theoretical level is a learning variable. As a corollary of this approach, usually many reinforcements are necessary to fully form the associative bond such that an incremental underlying learning function is assumed (see Chapter 8).

The Contiguity Interpretation of the S-R-S Reinforcement Operation

The initial stimulus term and response term of the operation constitute the units of learning and an association is formed between them. For reasons best left unstated at this point, this associative bond is usually not referred to as a habit and the degree of the bond is not referred to as habit strength. Rather the association is referred to as being in one of two states: not formed, unlearned, unconditioned or formed, learned, or conditioned.

The second stimulus term is the reinforcing stimulus event; but it possesses no effect properties. The contiguous occurrence of the S and R terms is sufficient to establish the association. Thus, the name of this approach. Reinforcement, in the contiguity approach, is not necessary for learning (formation of the S-R bond) and serves merely as a performance variable.

The theoretical mechanism underlying the performance effects of reinforcement, originally postulated by Guthrie and later taken over by Estes, is quite subtle. Reinforcement acts as a stimulus situation transformer. It takes the organism out of the original stimulus situation or changes the original stimulus situation (i.e., it terminates the physical realization of the S-R sequence) and thereby prevents unlearning or deconditioning of the S-R bond. Cessation of the S-R sequence prevents new responses from being conditioned to the initial stimulus by contiguity.

So, for contiguity theorists, reinforcement at the theoretical level is merely a procedural artifact which preserves original learning and/or prevents unlearning. As a corollary of this approach, one contiguous pairing of an S and R is presumed sufficient to achieve the conditioned state so that an all-or-none underlying learning function is usually assumed (see Chapter 8). Thus, the nonuse of the terms "habit" and "habit strength" in this approach.

The Cognitive Interpretation of the S-R-S Reinforcement Operation

The initial stimulus term and the second stimulus term of the operation constitute the units of learning and an association is formed between them. This is an S-S association and should not be confused with the notion of an S-R association used in the prior two approaches. This S-S association is given many labels by Tolman: means-end-readiness, cognitive map, cognition, expectancy, etc. depending upon the specific experimental situation in which it appears. The most general and convenient term is expectancy and we shall use that term exclusively.

The expectancy is formed solely on the basis of contiguity. The occurrence of the intervening response term of the S-R-S operation is only necessary to make the two stimulus events occur contiguously — i.e., the second stimulus does not occur unless the subject responds appropriately.

The initial stimulus term is interpreted by Tolman as a sign stimulus — as a stimulus informing the subject that the second stimulus is going to occur if the appropriate response is made. In other words, the subject eventually learns to expect the second stimulus following the occurrence of the S-R sequence.

The second stimulus term of the S-R-S operation is often referred to by Tolman as a goal. Performance of the proper response in the context of the appropriate sign stimulus achieves a certain goal. This goal is the reinforcing event; as such, the reinforcing event is simply the last stimulus event in the chain. (Only a simple chain of two stimulus events is used here.) After the expectancy has been formed, performance of the response is necessary to implement the expectancy — i.e., to make the second stimulus event occur and obtain the goal.

At the theoretical level, reinforcement performs a confirmation function. It confirms the continued appropriateness of the response in the context of the sign stimulus or, more loosely, it confirms the appropriateness of the expectancy. As such, reinforcement is a performance variable. As a corollary of this approach, one contiguous pairing of the two S terms is not necessarily regarded as sufficient to form the S-S association so that an incremental underlying learning function is not precluded.

SOME CONTEMPORARY, FUNCTIONAL APPROACHES TO REINFORCEMENT

Introduction

We are going to discuss the following seven theoretical approaches: (1) stimulational, (2) drive induction or incentive, (3) consummatory response, (4) prepotent response or differential response hierarchy, (5) adaptation level, (6) facilitation of species specific neuronal motor patterns, and (7) consolidation. The first four approaches and to some degree the last two approaches are representative of the current concern with the digital criteria for a reinforcing event — e.g., "Why is stimulus X a reinforcer or under what conditions is stimulus X a reinforcer"? The first four approaches are not mutually exclusive and do not be surprised if the discussion of them reminds you of the chain of events set off by the presentation of a positive reinforcer referred to earlier in the chapter. The fifth approach is related to the analogical aspects of reinforcement — e.g., "What determines the specific degree of reinforcing value of a reinforcer X"? The fourth approach and to some degree the fifth approach illustrate quite nicely the contemporary emphasis on the relativity of a reinforcing event. The last two approaches are examples of current theorizing about the physiological basis of reinforcement. We are going to repress the issue of how much should be subsumed by one's theory of $+S^R$ reinforcement because the text has not developed the necessary conceptual machinery to do it justice.

The Stimulation Approach (Pfaffman)

In this approach, object X serves as a reinforcer because it possesses theoretical stimulus properties. The prototypical reinforcer in this approach is food, especially nonnutritive, but sweet tasting substances like saccharin. The presentation of such a food object to the organism sets up certain stimulus properties that trigger the sense of taste or smell in the organism in some special way, even in a way which is innately "pleasant." These theoretical stimulus properties are used here as the criteria distinguishing between a reinforcer and nonreinforcer. An object X possessing theoretical stimulus properties can serve as a reinforcer. There might be some confusion concerning the notion of theoretical stimulus properties — but recall that Chapter 6 introduced the notion of theoretical stimulus constructs. The stimulational approach to reinforcement simply makes reinforcement a constructive stimulus construct at the theoretical level.

The Drive Induction or Incentive Approach (Sheffield)

In this approach, stimulus X serves as a reinforcer because it operates as a highly valued incentive object or induces drive or heightens the general activity level of the organism. There is no one prototypical reinforcer in this approach, although the presentation of a food object to the organism can be interpreted as an incentive or drive inducing. These incentive or drive-inducing properties are used here as the criteria distinguishing between a reinforcer and a nonreinforcer. An object X possessing theoretical incentive or drive-inducing properties can serve as a reinforcer. The incentive or drive-inducing approach to reinforcement makes reinforcement a constructive stimulus construct at the theoretical level — just like the stimulational approach, except that it is more specific because it supplies denotative reference to the stimulus properties — namely, that they are incentives or drive inducers.

The Consummatory Response Approach (Sheffield)

In this approach, stimulus X serves as a reinforcer because it elicits consummatory responses. Consummatory responding is that behavior which is necessary to achieve or process stimulus X. For instance, if stimulus X is food, the consummatory activity is licking, tasting, swallowing, in short, eating; if stimulus X is water, the consummatory activity is drinking; if stimulus X is a sexual object, consummatory activity is all the foreplay sexual activity short of the actual physiological occurrence of ejaculation or orgasm. The consummatory activity is used here as the criterion for distinguishing between a reinforcer or nonreinforcer. An object X eliciting theoretical consummatory activity can serve as a reinforcer. The consummatory activity approach to reinforcement makes reinforcement a constructive response construct at the theoretical level (see Chapter 6).

The Prepotent Response or Differential Response
Hierarchy Approach (Premack)

To describe this approach, a shift in terminological emphasis is necessary. Up to now, the procedural reinforcing event has always been specified as a stimulus event, either physical or symbolic. In this approach, the procedural reinforcing event is the opportunity to engage in a certain response. Naturally, the opportunity to engage in a certain response is the onset of a new physical stimulus situation; but semantically it is easier to denote the reinforcing event as a response event.

This approach constitutes the example par excellence of a situational or relational, as opposed to transsituational or absolute, conception of reinforcement. In this approach it is impossible to determine whether a response class X can serve as a reinforcing event independent of the specific response class Y upon whose occurrence response class X is contingent. (Recall the prior discussion about the operational determination of the reinforcing properties of a stimulus X taken randomly from the environment.) Response X can serve as a reinforcer for response Y if in a free choice or preference situation the organism prefers response X to response Y. The determination of the specific preference relation existing between response X and response Y involves of course an operational assessment independent of the reinforcement (learning) situation itself. Assuming X is preferred over Y, it can be termed the prepotent or dominant response of the X-Y response hierarchy. In general, a response hierarchy can include N individual response classes (e.g., A, B, C, D, E, etc.) arranged in preference order from least to most preferred. A specific response class taken at random from the hierarchy can only serve as a reinforcer for response classes to the left of it and cannot reinforce response classes to the right of it.

So, the prepotent or differential response hierarchy approach to reinforcement makes reinforcement a constructive response construct preference relation at the theoretical level. It includes the consummatory response approach as a subset, because typically in most dual response hierarchies the dominant or prepotent response is a consummatory one.

Some Perspective

Under the usual conditions of conducting a response-contingent reinforcement learning task (operant or discrete-trial reward instrumental conditioning), all four theoretical sources of reinforcement operate. For example, with the use of food as the reinforcer $(+S^R)$, the following events occur.

1. The food, possessing theoretical stimulus properties, activates the olfactory and gustatory, etc. sensory modalities of the organism.

2. The food acts as an incentive reward object or drive inducer.

3. The food elicits consummatory activity from the organism — tasting, chewing, in short, eating.

4. The consummatory activity elicited by food presentation is the dominant response of the operant and/or instrumental response-consummatory response hierarchy.

The Adaptation Level Approach (Helson, Bevan)

We are using this approach as one example of how the trial-to-trial analogical variation in reinforcing properties of a stimulus object or the situational dependent analogical reinforcing properties of a stimulus object can be explained at the theoretical level. Any adaptation level theory involves a standard or frame of reference. Helson and Bevan's adaptation level approach is a perceptual one, so the standard or frame of reference is defined in terms of physical, external stimuli. Helson postulated that the adaptation level in a specific experimental situation is the weighted log mean of all the stimuli affecting the organsim — i.e., relevant focal stimuli, background stimuli, residual stimuli from prior responses, and constitutionally or organically based stimuli. Every time the subject is reinforced, he compares the reinforcing event (on some implicit dimension, usually amount or intensity) to the current standard or adaptation level. The reinforcing properties of the stimulus object can be postulated as a function of both the degree and direction of discrepancy or of the degree of discrepancy alone. This approach can explain or predict interexperimental session changes in reinforcing properties of stimulus events, intraexperimental session changes in reinforcing properties of stimulus events, changes in reinforcing properties due to altered deprivational or motivational conditions, altered differential response hierarchies or preference relations, etc.

The Facilitation of Brain Stem Neuronal Motor Patterns Approach (Glickman and Schiff)

In this approach, stimulus X serves as a reinforcer because it facilitates (elicits) at the neuronal level, in the lower brain stem, the motor patterns underlying overt approach or withdrawal responses — i.e., overt consummatory responses. For instance, the presentation of a food object to the organism, successive to performing the instrumental response, activates the underlying neural motor pattern mechanism required for the emission of an approach response. (Do not be surprised with the classification of a withdrawal response as a consummatory response — this refers to behavior in the context of a primary negative reinforcement situation.)

This approach to reinforcement is equivalent to Sheffield's consummatory response approach, except that the reinforcing event is given reductive or physiological reality as the neural events which organize and produce the overt consummatory responses. Glickman and Schiff regard the neural organization responsible for the activation of the overt consummatory responses to be species specific and evolutionary in origin. These theoretical neural facilitation properties are used here as the criteria distinguishing between a reinforcer and a nonreinforcer. An object X possessing these reductive facilitating properties can serve as a reinforcer. This approach to reinforcement makes reinforcement a reductive or physiological response construct at the theoretical level.

The Consolidation Approach (Landauer)

The general consolidation approach to learning postulates that the occurrence of the learned response in a stimulus context sets up neuronal structural traces or reverberating circuits in the organism. These internal trace representations of the overt behavior persist over time but at a decreasing rate. This decremental persistence of traces/circuits over time is referred to as consolidation. If the consolidation process is interrupted, the response cannot be learned.

Landauer simply postulates that a reinforcing event reactivates the decrementing consolidation process to its original level at the moment of learned response occurrence. Thus, reinforcement generates additional consolidation (i.e., prolongs it). In this approach, stimulus X can serve as a reinforcer if it re-excites the consolidation process. For instance, the presentation of food, successive to instrumental response occurrence, reactivates the consolidation process originally set up by the response occurrence itself. These theoretical consolidation reactivation properties are used here as the criteria for distinguishing between a reinforcer and a nonreinforcer. An object X possessing these reductive reactivating consolidation properties can serve as a reinforcer. This approach to reinforcement makes reinforcement a reductive or physiological construct at the theoretical level.

TWO THEORETICAL APPROACHES TO ESB

Introduction

We are going to discuss (1) Deutsch and Howarth's drive decay approach to ESB and (2) Lenzer's associative or stimulus control approach to ESB. Both approaches were alluded to previously during the discussion of ESB versus conventional reinforcement — Deutsch and Howarth presume that ESB and conventional reinforcement are discontinuous and Lenzer presumes that ESB and conventional reinforcement are continuous. Our current focus will be on the types of events, set up in the organism as the result of an ESB occurrence, that are postulated by each approach. Although the approaches use denotationally different theoretical constructs to describe the aftereffects of an ESB, it will become evident that the two approaches are far more similar than different.

The Drive Decay Approach

According to Deutsch and Howarth, an ESB occurrence has two aftereffects for the organism. It reinforces the response upon whose occurrence it is contingent. It does this by activating specific reinforcing or reward anatomical pathways. Also, it activates a separate set of motivational anatomical pathways. As such, the ESB occurrence establishes the necessary elicitation conditions for the occurrence of the next response. The amount of drive created depends on many parameters and decays with time. (Thus, the name of the approach.) So, the occurrence of an ESB has reward properties for the prior response and motivational or elicitational properties for the succeeding response. This motivational or elicitation mechanism explains why high rates of acquisition operant responding occur with ESB, why acquisition operant responding does not cease with ESB, why operant responding ceases quite rapidly once the extinction operation is instituted (ESB discontinued), why long intertrial intervals depress instrumental responding maintained by ESB (the drive has completely decayed between trials), etc. There is no counterpart in conventional reinforcement to this automatic ESB motivational or elicitation mechanism; and it is on this basis that Deutsch and Howarth essentially differentiate between ESB and conventional reinforcement.

The Associative, Stimulus Control Approach

According to Lenzer, an ESB occurrence sets up a biphasic stimulus trace in the organism. The initial phase of the stimulus trace acts as the reinforcing event for the prior response. The second phase serves as an internal CS to which the instrumental response can potentially get conditioned. (Thus, the name of the approach.) The instrumental response (CR) must get conditioned to the second phase of the stimulus trace through associative processes before the trace can operate as an internal CS and have actual stimulus control over the overt learned response. Unlike the drive decay approach, the elicitation function of ESB must be acquired — it is not innate or automatic. Lenzer also assumes that the stimulus trace of the second phase decays rapidly, like drive does in the other approach. So, this approach can also account for the typical behavioral effects of ESB mentioned in the prior paragraph (high rate, no satiation, swift extinction, performance decrement during long intertrial intervals, etc).

Lenzer's associative mechanism allows her to relate ESB maintained behavior and behavior maintained by conventional reinforcement. There is a counterpart in conventional reinforcement to the conditioned elicitation or associative control mechanism of ESB — namely, external physical stimulus control. In conventional reinforcement, the instrumental response (CR) gets conditioned only to external, physical stimulus events. These external stimulus events are regarded by Lenzer as more diffuse and less specific than the ESB stimulus trace aftereffect, but also as more persistent over time (i.e., they do not decay). Thus in any given experimental situation in which ESB is used, the behavior initially maintained by ESB can eventually take on the characteristics of behavior exclusively maintained by conventional reinforcement to the degree that both the conditioned elicitation properties of the internal CS can be reduced in the situation and the overt instrumental learned response gets conditioned to the external, physical stimulus cues as elicitors.

PHILOSOPHICAL CRITICISMS OF THE LAW OF EFFECT

INTRODUCTION

The general law of effect has often been criticized on philosophical grounds. These philosophical criticisms fall into two classes, circularity and teleology, each one of which is essentially associated with a particular interpretation of the law of effect. A brief discussion of these two concepts is necessary before presenting their specific tieups to the law of effect.

According to the dictates of the philosophy of science, circularity, both with respect to definition and explanation, should be avoided and teleological explanations should be avoided. Presumably, a psychological concept should not be circularly defined, nor should its explanatory use be circular or teleological. Circular definition is usually avoided by defining a psychological concept in terms of primitives or previously derived terms existing at some other level of reality. Circular explanation is usually avoided by making sure that the situation in which the explanation for a piece of behavior arises is independent of the situation in which evidence for the existence of that piece of behavior arises. Teleological explanation is usually avoided by making sure that the postulated causes of a specific piece of behavior do not occur after the behavior in time — i.e., causes cannot have retrograde effects.

Many philosophers consider the empirical law of effect to be circularly defined and circularly used as an explanation; and many philosophers regard the theoretical law of effect to be a teleological explanation. It is the purpose of this section to dispel these two criticisms of the law of effect. It is possible for the empirical law of effect to be circularly defined and circularly used as an explanation under certain circumstances. So the focus of the presentation concerns how the effects of circularity can be reduced if not outrightly avoided. The theoretical law of effect simply is not a teleological explanation; but why it is not has to be discussed.

CIRCULAR DEFINITION OF THE EMPIRICAL LAW OF EFFECT

Basic Description

Remember that the empirical law of effect simply states that a reinforcing event is procedurally necessary for the performance of a learned response — i.e., reinforcement consists of a set of operations which raises the probability of response occurrence. What is meant by the circular definition of the empirical law of effect is the circular definition of a positive reinforcer. The typical operational definition of a positive reinforcer (e.g., Skinner's) specifies that a positive reinforcer is a stimulus event whose onset raises the probability of response occurrence or conditions a response. Now, if this definition of a positive reinforcer is substituted in the above law of effect statement we have the following expression: "A stimulus event whose onset raises the probability of response occurrence or conditions a response is procedurally necessary for the performance of a learned response." This statement is circular. It is circular because the law of effect – which states the typical result of a positive reinforcer on behavior– is used to operationally isolate a specific positive reinforcer. So, the law of effect is certainly circular with respect to the learning of response class Y in relation to reinforcing stimulus X when response class Y is also used to experimentally assess the reinforcing properties of stimulus X.

Resolution of the Circularity

Most psychologists do not worry about the above definitional circularity of the law of effect. Circularity only exists for the specific response class Y-stimulus X contingency used to assess the original, digital reinforcing properties of stimulus X. The general empirical law of effect statement has empirical content, generality, or noncircular definitional use with respect to the learning of any other response class (non-Y) in a contingent relationship with reinforcing stimulus X. In other words, the law of effect statement is transsituational. Positive reinforcers are assumed to possess transsituational reinforcing properties. The reinforcing properties of stimulus X defined or isolated in the context of response class Y can be tested on response classes A, B, C, or D, etc. . . . the reinforcing properties of stimulus X can be used to condition non-Y response classes. Even if a psychologist takes the relative (nontranssituational) approach of Premack, the question of the rank order of a series of reinforcing events M, N, R, etc. is an empircal question. Thus, if N is found to reinforce R and M is found to reinforce N by the definitional use of the law of effect, it is predictable that M should reinforce R.

Avoidance of the Circular Definition of the Law of Effect

It is possible to define or operationally isolate a positive reinforcing stimulus without reference to the empirical law of effect entirely and thus avoid the circular definition of the empirical law of effect. One way of doing this was given previously. Simply define a positive reinforcer as a stimulus event whose onset elicits approach responses. If this definition of a positive reinforcer is substituted in the law of effect statement we have the following expression: "A stimulus event whose onset elicits approach responses is procedurally necessary for the performance of a learned response." This statement is not circular. It is not circular because the law of effect — which states the typical result of a positive reinforcer on behavior — is not used to operationally isolate the specific positive reinforcer. Once a particular positive reinforcing stimulus X has been operationally isolated by using the approach response criterion, it can be used as a reinforcer to condition any response class Y in the context of the law of effect.

CIRCULAR EXPLANATORY USE OF THE EMPIRICAL LAW OF EFFECT

Basic Description

The empirical law of effect is strictly descriptive. The empirical law of effect is not a higher order explanatory statement from which lower order empirical relationships are derivable. It cannot be used to explain anything, especially the acquisition of a learned response. When it is incorrectly used to explain the acquisition of a learned response, its explanatory use is circular. The logic underlying the circular explanatory use of the empirical law of effect is the same as the logic underlying the circular definition of the empirical law of effect and which philosophical error the psychologist commits is basically a matter of intention.

As an illustration of its circular explanatory use, consider the conjunction of the following two statements.

1. The thing to be explained or empirical observation: A learned response is currently being performed as a function or result of reinforcement.
2. Why? The explanation: A reinforcement is procedurally necessary for the performance of a learned response.

The second or explanatory statement is simply the empirical law of effect as stated in the prior subsection. Both statements refer to the same thing but in reverse order; so the second one cannot be used to explain the first.

Avoidance of the Circularity

The above circularity can be avoided by not using the empirical law of effect in an explanatory manner; but, more functionally, the circularity can be avoided by using a variant of the theoretical law of effect in the above conjunction. The theoretical law of effect involves some higher order explanatory mechanism for the performance or learning (or both) effects of reinforcement.

For illustrative purposes, let us assume the consummatory response interpretation of reinforcement. Using the consummatory response variant of the theoretical law of effect, the above conjunction is transformed into the following combination of statements.

1. The thing to be explained or empirical observation: A learned response is currently being performed as a function or result of reinforcement.
2. Why? The explanation: The elicitation of consummatory responses by reinforcing events is procedurally necessary for the performance of a learned response.

Since the second or explanatory statement is one variant of the theoretical law of effect, both statements do not refer to the same thing in reverse order. The second one can be legitimately used to explain the first — i.e., the first one is derivable from the second one.

THE THEORETICAL LAW OF EFFECT AS A TELEOLOGICAL EXPLANATION

Basic Description

The theoretical law of effect (i.e., a variant of it) postulates a mechanism to account for the procedural effects of reinforcement on the learning or performance of a learned response. As the law is worded, the reinforcing mechanism is assumed to increase the probability of occurrence of the prior response — i.e., the response upon whose occurrence the activation of the reinforcement mechanism is contingent. So, regardless of the specific reinforcement mechanism involved — drive reduction, consummatory response, stimulus properties, incentive or drive induction, prepotent response, etc. — the reinforcing stimulus event comes after the learned response in time and ostensibly the reinforcement mechanism works retroactively in time. Thus, for many philosophers, the theoretical law of effect constitutes a teleological explanation.

Resolution of the Teleology

Introduction. Most psychologists do not consider the theoretical law of effect to be teleological. The reinforcement mechanism is not generally viewed as interacting with the literal physical response occurrence itself. Rather the reinforcement mechanism is viewed as interacting with some theoretical structure or construct. Rarely is a specific variant of the theoretical law of effect proposed in a theoretical vacuum. More specifically, the theoretical law of effect is just one aspect of a learning theorist's overall theoretical approach to learning and/or reinforcement. Activation of the theoretical reinforcement mechanism is just one of a number of theoretical events, many of which co-occur with or succeed the reinforcement in time.

Viewed from this perspective, there are two conceptual approaches to resolving the indictment of teleology: the co-occurrence approach and the succession approach. The co-occurrence approach assumes that the reinforcement mechanism interacts with theoretical events that have their effect during the same trial or response upon whose occurrence the reinforcing event was contingent. The succession approach specifies that the reinforcement mechanism interacts with theoretical events that have their effect on the next trial or the next response occurrence.

The co-occurrence approach. This is by far the most frequently used approach. Two subvariants of it exist: (1) Some theoretical representation of the actual physical response must persist through time and co-occur with the activation of the theoretical reinforcement mechanism. (2) Some theoretical representation of the actual theoretical reinforcement mechanism must co-occur with the actual physical response. Nonmutually exclusive examples of the type (1) mechanism include general or specific consolidation processes set up by the response occurrence, general or specific neural events or reverberatory circuits set up by the response occurrence, response-produced stimulus trace(s), etc. Nonmutually exclusive examples of the type (2) mechanism include theoretical external secondary reinforcing events, theoretical internal response-produced secondary reinforcing events, fractional anticipatory goal responses, etc.

Many learning psychologists prefer the type (1) mechanism over the type (2) mechanism because it is biologically based and automatically occurs during every trial of the experiment or on every response during the experiment. The type (2) mechanism is a learned, acquired mechanism and, as such, can never occur during the first reinforcement of the session and also requires an appreciable number of training trials or responses before it occurs on a regular basis or is effective.

The succession approach. This approach is almost invariably physicalized in terms of a changed stimulus situation on the next trial or during the next response occurrence; but, specific postulated stimulus mechanisms do not abound in the literature.

As an example of this approach, we can present Estes' concept of a stimulus population, the elements of which get conditioned to the correct or learned response on a trial-by-trial (sample-by-sample) basis. The elements of the stimulus sample present on a trial are contiguous with the occurrence of the learned or correct response on that trial and thus get conditioned to the response. Reinforcement at the theoretical level consists of terminating the stimulus sample so that the conditioning events which occurred on that trial are preserved. The stimulus population from which the subject samples on the next trial is different from the one that appeared on the prior trial because of the additional elements conditioned to the correct or learned response.

SUMMARY

The concept of reinforcement is the canonical aspect of learning and is multidimensional in nature. When the term appears unmodified in the technical literature, it is usually primary positive reinforcement in the response-contingent context which constitutes the specific physical realization of the notion. The following review concentrates on the two types of reinforcement operations, the four descriptive kinds of reinforcing stimuli, the assessment of the possible reinforcing properties of a stimulus, the three classic theoretical interpretations of the S-R-S reinforcement operation, contemporary theoretical views of a primary positive reinforcer, animal versus human reinforcement, the nature of reinforcement in some common learning tasks, and philosophical criticisms of the law of effect.

A given reinforcing stimulus can be applied to an organism independent of its behavior or contingent upon its behavior. The former option establishes the notion of an experimenter-contingent reinforcement operation (the S-S operation), while the latter one generates the response-contingent reinforcement operation (the S-R-S operation) — with the second S of each symbolic sequence denoting the reinforcing event. The conceptual analysis treats the S-R-S operation as the superordinate one, the S-S operation merely constituting a subset of it, with the consequence that the critical reinforcement distinctions are invariably made in the response-contingent context.

A given response-contingent reinforcing event can be classified according to two analytical dimensions. It is either primary (biologically based) or secondary (its reinforcing properties are learned/acquired); and it is either positive (onset is reinforcing) or negative (termination is reinforcing). Thus, there are four descriptive kinds of response-contingent reinforcing events: primary positive, primary negative, secondary positive, and secondary negative. These four categories are assumed to transfer in toto to the experimenter-contingent reinforcement situation, although the notions of positive and negative do so only by analogy.

The assessment of the possible response-contingent reinforcing properties of a stimulus can be done directly or indirectly. The direct verification technique exploits Skinner's operational definition of a reinforcer and the indirect verification technique involves an extension of the distinction between an appetitive and an aversive stimulus event. The assessment of the possible experimenter-contingent reinforcing properties of a stimulus can only be done indirectly.

Each of the three major types of classical macro-theory has its own differential interpretation of the S-R-S reinforcement operation. The effect approach assumes that an S-R association is physiologically stamped in via reinforcement (satisfaction for Thorndike; drive reduction for Hull). The contiguity approach postulates that an S-R association is formed by mere temporal contiguity with reinforcement simply preventing unlearning through stimulus situation transformation. The cognitive approach assumes that an S-S association is formed by mere temporal contiguity with reinforcement (the last S in the chain) simply serving a confirmation or goal function.

Most contemporary theoretical interpretations of a primary positive reinforcer make it either a theoretical stimulus construct or a theoretical response construct. Pfaffman's stimulational approach and Sheffield's drive induction or incentive approach impute constructive theoretical stimulus properties to a primary positive reinforcer. Sheffield's consummatory response approach and Premack's prepotent response or differential response hierarchy approach make a primary positive reinforcer a constructive theoretical response construct. Glickman and Schiff's facilitation of brain stem neuronal motor patterns approach imputes reductive theoretical response properties to a primary positive reinforcer.

In animal learning, reinforcement typically consists of all-or-none, digital, explicit, externally sourced physical events from the primary positive or primary negative category. In human learning, reinforcement often consists of graded, analogical, implicit, internally sourced symbolic events from the secondary positive category. The operational characteristics of animal reinforcement are usually interpreted in a combined "stamping in-incentive" conceptual framework, while those of human reinforcement are usually interpreted in an information or feedback conceptual framework.

It is possible to resolve the nature of reinforced practice for each of the learning tasks derived in Chapter 5 in terms of the two types of reinforcement operations and the four descriptive kinds of reinforcing events. This was explicitly demonstrated for a set of traditional conditioning tasks (forward classical conditioning, operant conditioning, escape conditioning) and for a set of representative human learning tasks (perceptual-motor learning, paired-associate learning, concept formation). Classical conditioning constitutes the prototypical experimental realization of the S-S operation — with any descriptive kind of reinforcer substitutable for the second S (UCS). Operant conditioning involves the S-R-S operation and amounts to the straightway application of Skinner's operational definition of a positive reinforcer. Escape conditioning also involves the S-R-S operation, but amounts to the straightway application of Skinner's operational definition of a negative reinforcer. Perceptual-motor learning is ultimately reducible to the S-R-S operation with reinforcement basically being secondary and positive. Both the S-S and S-R-S operations can be employed in the context of paired-associate learning and concept formation; and the reinforcing events in both tasks are basically secondary and positive.

The general law of effect has often been criticized on philosophical grounds. Many philosophers consider the empirical law of effect to be circularly defined and circularly used as an explanation; and they regard the theoretical law of effect to be a teleological explanation. While it is true that the empirical law of effect is circularly defined when it is used to isolate the possible reinforcing properties of a stimulus X in the context of response Y, the law possesses empirical content with respect to any other response non-Y. But, more significantly, it is demonstrable that the circular definition and use of the law can be outrightly avoided. The theoretical law of effect simply is not teleological — but this is not evident until it is realized that the law is not proposed in a theoretical vacuum and the postulated underlying theoretical reinforcement mechanism is not assumed to be interacting with the literal physical learned response itself.

References

Adams, J.A. *Human memory.* New York: McGraw-Hill, 1967.

Adams, J.A. A closed-loop theory of motor learning. *Journal of Motor Behavior,* 1971, **3**, 111-149.

Adams, J.A., Goetz, E.T., & Marshall, P.H. Response feedback and motor learning. *Journal of Experimental Psychology,* 1972, **92**, 391-397.

Anderson, J.R., & Bower, G.H. *Human associative memory.* Washington, D.C.: Winston, 1973.

Atkinson, R.C. A stochastic model for rote serial learning. *Psychometrika,* 1957, **22**, 87-96.

Atkinson, R.C., Bower, G.H., & Crothers, E.J. *An introduction to mathematical learning theory.* New York: Wiley, 1965.

Atkinson, R.C., & Estes, W.K. Stimulus sampling theory. In R.D. Luce, R.R. Bush, & E. Galanter (Eds.), *Handbook of mathematical psychology.* Vol. 2. New York: Wiley, 1963.

Atkinson, R.C., & Shiffrin, R.M. Human memory: A proposed system and its control processes. In K.W. Spence & J.T. Spence (Eds.), *The psychology of learning and motivation.* Vol. 2. New York: Academic Press, 1968.

Audley, R.J. A stochastic description of the learning behavior of an individual subject. *Quarterly Journal of Experimental Psychology,* 1957, **9**, 12-20.

Audley, R.J., & Jonckheere, A.R. The statistical analysis of the learning process. *British Journal of Statistical Psychology,* 1956, **9**, 87-94.

Azrin, N.H., & Holz, W.C. Punishment. In W.K. Honig (Ed.), *Operant behavior: Areas of research and application.* New York: Appleton Century Crofts, 1966.

Ball, G.G., & Adams, D.W. Intracranial stimulation as an avoidance or escape response. *Psychonomic Science,* 1965, **3**, 39-40.

Bandura, A. (Ed.) *Psychological modeling: Conflicting theories.* New York: Lieber-Atherton, 1974.

Batchelder, W.H. An all-or-none theory for learning on both the paired-associate and concept levels. *Journal of Mathematical Psychology,* 1970, **7**, 97-117.

Battig, W.F. Procedural problems in paired-associate learning research. *Psychonomic Monograph Supplements,* 1965, **1**, 1-12.

Battig, W.F. Paired associate learning. In T.R. Dixon & D.L. Horton (Eds.), *Verbal behavior and general behavior theory.* Englewood Cliffs, New Jersey: Prentice-Hall, 1968.

Beecroft, R.S. *Classical conditioning.* Goleta, California: Psychonomic Press, 1966.

Bergmann, G., & Spence, K.W. Operationism and theory in psychology. *Psychological Review,* 1941, **48**, 1-14.

Berlyne, D.E. Arousal and reinforcement. In D. Levine (Ed.), *Nebraska symposium on motivation.* Vol. 15. Lincoln: University of Nebraska Press, 1967.

Bernbach, H.A. A forgetting model for paired-associate learning. *Journal of Mathematical Psychology,* 1965, **2**, 128-144.

Best, R.M. Encoding of memory in the neuron. *Psychological Reports,* 1968, **22**, 107-115.

Bilodeau, E.A. (Ed.) *Acquisition of skill.* New York: Academic Press, 1966.

Bindra, D. A motivational view of learning: Performance and behavior modification. *Psychological Review,* 1974, **81**, 199-213.

Bitterman, M.E. Techniques for the study of learning in animals: Analysis and classification. *Psychological Bulletin,* 1962, **59**, 81-93.

Bitterman, M.E., & Schoel, W.M. Instrumental learning in animals: Parameters of reinforcement. *Annual Review of Psychology,* 1970, **21**, 367-436.

Bjork, R.A. Why mathematical models? *American Psychologist,* 1973, **28**, 426-433.

Black, A.H., & Prokasy, W.F. (Eds.) *Classical conditioning: II. Current theory and research.* New York: Appleton Century Crofts, 1972.

Black, R.W. Incentive motivation and the parameters of reward in instrumental conditioning. In D. Levine (Ed.), *Nebraska symposium on motivation.* Vol. 17. Lincoln: University of Nebraska Press, 1969.

Boe, E.E., & Church, R.M. *Punishment: Issues and experiments.* New York: Appleton Century Crofts, 1968.

Bolles, R.C. Reinforcement, expectancy, and learning. *Psychological Review,* 1972, **79**, 394-409.

Booth, D.A. Vertebrate brain nucleic acids and memory retention. *Psychological Bulletin,* 1967, **68**, 149-177.

Boucher, J.L. Higher processes in motor learning. *Journal of Motor Behavior,* 1974, **6**, 131-138.

Bourne, L.E., Jr. *Human conceptual behavior.* Boston: Allyn & Bacon, 1965.

Bourne, L.E., Jr. Learning and utilization of conceptual rules. In B. Kleinmuntz (Ed.), *Concepts and the structure of memory.* New York: Wiley, 1967.

Bourne, L.E., Jr. Knowing and using concepts. *Psychological Review,* 1970, **77**, 546-566.

Bourne, L.E., Jr., Ekstrand, B.R., & Dominowski, R.L. *The psychology of thinking.* Englewood Cliffs, New Jersey: Prentice-Hall, 1971.

Bourne, L.E., Jr., & Restle, F. Mathematical theory of concept identification. *Psychological Review,* 1959, **66**, 278-296.

Bower, G.H. An association model for response and training variables in paired-associate learning. *Psychological Review,* 1962, **69**, 34-53.

Bower, G.H. A multicomponent theory of the memory trace. In K.W. Spence & J.T. Spence (Eds.), *The psychology of learning and motivation.* Vol. 1. New York: Academic Press, 1967.

Bower, G.H., & Trabasso, T. Concept identification. In R.C. Atkinson (Ed.), *Studies of mathematical psychology.* Stanford: Stanford University Press, 1964.

Broadbent, D.E. A mechanical model for human attention and immediate memory. *Psychological Review,* 1957, **64**, 205-215.

Bruner, J.S., Goodnow, J.J., & Austin, G.A. *A study of thinking.* New York: Wiley, 1956.

Brush, F.R. (Ed.) *Aversive conditioning and learning.* New York: Academic Press, 1971.

Burke, C.J. Measurement scales and statistical models. In M.H. Marx (Ed.), *Theories in contemporary psychology.* New York: Macmillan, 1963.

Bush, R.R., & Mosteller, F. A mathematical model for simple learning. *Psychological Review,* 1951, **58**, 313-322.

Bush, R.R., & Mosteller, F. *Stochastic models for learning.* New York: Wiley, 1955.

Calfee, R.C., & Atkinson, R.C. Paired-associate models and the effects of list length. *Journal of Mathematical Psychology,* 1965, **2**, 254-265.

Campbell, B.A., & Church, R.M. (Eds.) *Punishment and aversive behavior.* New York: Appleton Century Crofts, 1969.

Catania, A.C. (Ed.) *Contemporary research in operant behavior.* Glenview, Illinois: Scott Foresman, 1968.

Catania, A.C. On the vocabulary and the grammar of behavior. *Journal of the Experimental Analysis of Behavior,* 1969, **12**, 845-846.

Catania, A.C. Elicitation, reinforcement, and stimulus control. In R. Glaser (Ed.), *The nature of reinforcement.* New York: Academic Press, 1971.

Chapanis, A. Men, machines, and models. *American Psychologist,* 1961, **16**, 113-131.

Chumbley, J.L. A duoprocess theory of concept learning. *Journal of Mathematical Psychology,* 1972, **9**, 17-35.

Church, R.M. The varied effects of punishment on behavior. *Psychological Review,* 1963, **70,** 369-402.

Coan, R.W. Dimensions of psychological theory. *American Psychologist,* 1968, **23,** 715-722.

Coombs, C.H., Dawes, R.M., & Tversky, A. *Mathematical psychology.* Englewood Cliffs, New Jersey: Prentice-Hall, 1970.

Cotton, J.W. Theory construction and instrumental learning. In M.H. Marx (Ed.), *Theories in contemporary psychology.* New York: Macmillan, 1963.

Cowan, T.M. A Markov model for order of emission in free recall. *Journal of Mathematical Psychology,* 1966, **3,** 470-483.

Deutsch, J.A. The cholinergic synapse and the site of memory. *Science,* 1971, **174,** 788-794.

Deutsch, J.A. (Ed.) *The physiological basis of memory.* New York: Academic Press, 1972.

Deutsch, J.A., & Howarth, C.I. Some tests of a theory of intracranial self-stimulation. *Psychological Review,* 1963, **70,** 444-460.

Dixon, T.R., & Horton, D.L. (Eds.) *Verbal behavior and general behavior theory.* Englewood Cliffs, New Jersey: Prentice-Hall, 1968.

Doty, R.W. Electrical stimulation of the brain in behavioral context. *Annual Review of Psychology,* 1969, **20,** 289-320.

Dunham, P.J. Punishment: Method and theory. *Psychological Review,* 1971, **78,** 58-70.

Dykman, R.A. On the nature of classical conditioning. In C. Brown (Ed.), *Methods in psychophysiology.* Baltimore: Williams & Wilkins, 1967.

Egger, M.D., & Miller, N.E. Secondary reinforcement in rats as a function of information value and reliability of the stimulus. *Journal of Experimental Psychology,* 1962, **64,** 97-104.

Egger, M.D., & Miller, N.E. When is a reward reinforcing? An experimental study of the information hypothesis. *Journal of Comparative and Physiological Psychology,* 1963, **56,** 132-137.

Eisenberger, R. Explanation of rewards that do not reduce tissue needs. *Psychological Bulletin,* 1972, **77,** 319-339.

Ellis, H.C. *The transfer of learning.* New York: Macmillan, 1965.

Estes, W.K. Toward a statistical theory of learning. *Psychological Review,* 1950, **57,** 94-107.

Estes, W.K. The problem of inference from curves based on group data. *Psychological Bulletin,* 1956, **53,** 134-140.

Estes, W.K. The statistical approach to learning theory. In S. Koch (Ed.), *Psychology: A study of science.* Vol. 2. New York: McGraw-Hill, 1959.

Estes, W.K. Learning theory and the new mental chemistry. *Psychological Review,* 1960, **67,** 207-223.

Estes, W.K. Probability learning. In A.W. Melton (Ed.), *Categories of human learning.* New York: Academic Press, 1964.

Estes, W.K. Reinforcement in human learning. In J. Tapp (Ed.), *Reinforcement and behavior.* New York: Academic Press, 1969.

Estes, W.K., Koch, S., MacCorquodale, K., Meehl, P.E., Mueller, Jr., C.G., Schoenfeld, W.N., & Verplanck, W.S. (Eds.), *Modern learning theory.* New York: Appleton Century Crofts, 1954.

Estes, W.K., Hopkins, B.L., & Crothers, E.J. All-or-none conservation effects in the learning and retention of paired associates. *Journal of Experimental Psychology,* 1960, **60**, 329-339.

Falmagne, R. Construction of a hypothesis model for concept identification. *Journal of Mathematical Psychology,* 1970, **7**, 60-96.

Feigenbaum, E.A. Information processing and memory. In D.A. Norman (Ed.), *Models of human memory.* New York: Academic Press, 1970.

Feigl, H. The "orthodox" view of theories: Remarks in defense as well as critique. In M. Radner and S. Winokur (Eds.), *Analyses of theories and methods of physics and psychology.* Vol. 4. Minneapolis: University of Minnesota Press, 1970.

Fitts, P.M. Perceptual-motor skill learning. In A.W. Melton (Ed.), *Categories of human learning.* New York: Academic Press, 1964.

Frijda, N.H. Simulation of human long-term memory. *Psychological Bulletin,* 1972, **77**, 1-32.

Gaito, J. DNA and RNA as memory molecules. *Psychological Review,* 1963, **70**, 471-480.

Gardner, R.A., & Gardner, B.T. Teaching sign language to a chimpanzee. *Science,* 1969, **165**, 664-672.

Gibbon, J., Berryman, R., & Thompson, R.L. Contingency spaces and measures in classical and instrumental conditioning. *Journal of the Experimental Analysis of Behavior,* 1974, **21**, 585-605.

Gibson, E.J. *Principles of perceptual learning and development.* New York: Appleton Century Crofts, 1969.

Gibson, J.J. The concept of stimulus in psychology. *American Psychologist.* 1960, **15**, 694-703.

Gibson, J.J. *The senses considered as perceptual systems.* Boston: Houghton Mifflin. 1966.

Gibson, J.J. On the proper meaning of the term "stimulus." *Psychological Review,* 1967, **74**, 533-534.

Gilbert, R.M., & Millenson, J.R. (Eds.) *Reinforcement: Behavioral analysis.* New York: Academic Press, 1972.

Glaser, R. (Ed.) *The nature of reinforcement.* New York: Academic Press, 1971.

Glassman, E. The biochemistry of learning: An evaluation of the role of RNA and protein. *Annual Review of Biochemistry,* 1969, **38**, 605-646.

Glickman, S.E., & Schiff, B.B. A biological theory of reinforcement. *Psychological Review,* 1967, **74**, 81-109.

Gormezano, I. Classical conditioning. In J.B. Sidowski (Ed.), *Experimental methods and instrumentation in psychology.* New York: McGraw-Hill, 1966.

Goss, A.E., & Nodine, C.F. *Paired-associates learning: The role of meaningfulness, similarity, and familiarization.* New York: Academic Press, 1965.

Grant, D.A. Classical and operant conditioning. In A.W. Melton (Ed.), *Categories of human learning.* New York: Academic Press, 1964.

Greeno, J.G. Paired-associate learning with short-term retention: Mathematical analysis and data regarding identification of parameters. *Journal of Mathematical Psychology,* 1967, **4,** 430-472.

Greeno, J.G., & Bjork, R.A. Mathematical learning theory and the new "mental forestry." *Annual Review of Psychology,* 1973, **24,** 81-116.

Gregg, L.W. (Ed.) *Cognition in learning and memory.* New York: Wiley, 1972.

Gregg, L.W., & Simon, H.A. Process models and stochastic theories of simple concept formation. *Journal of Mathematical Psychology,* 1967, **4,** 246-276.

Gurowitz, E.M. *The molecular basis of memory.* Englewood Cliffs, New Jersey: Prentice-Hall, 1969.

Guthrie, E.R. Conditioning as a principle of learning. *Psychological Review,* 1930, **37,** 412-428.

Guthrie, E.R. *The psychology of learning.* New York: Harper & Row, 1935.

Guthrie, E.R. Association and the law of effect. *Psychological Review,* 1940, **47,** 127-148.

Guthrie, E.R. Association by contiguity. In S. Koch (Ed.), *Psychology: A study of a science.* Vol. 2. New York: McGraw-Hill, 1959.

Guthrie, E.R., & Horton, G.P. *Cats in a puzzle box.* New York: Rinehart, 1946.

Hall, J.F. *Verbal learning and retention.* New York: Lippincott, 1971.

Harlow, H.F. The formation of learning sets. *Psychological Review,* 1949, **56,** 51-65.

Harlow, H.F. Learning set and error factor theory. In S. Koch (Ed.), *Psychology: A study of a science.* Vol. 2. New York: McGraw-Hill, 1959.

Hayes, J.R. (Ed.) *Cognition and the development of language.* New York: Wiley, 1970.

Hayes, K.J. The backward learning curve: A method for the study of learning. *Psychological Review,* 1953, **60,** 269-275.

Hebb, D.O. *The organization of behavior.* New York: Wiley, 1949.

Helson, H. *Adaptation-level theory.* New York: Harper & Row, 1964.

Hendry, D.P. (Ed.) *Conditioned reinforcement.* Homewood, Illinois: Dorsey, 1969.

Herrnstein, R.J. Superstition. In W.K. Honig (Ed.), *Operant behavior: Areas of research and application.* New York: Appleton Century Crofts, 1966.

Herrnstein, R.J. Method and theory in the study of avoidance. *Psychological Review,* 1969, **76,** 49-69.

Herrnstein, R.J. On the law of effect. *Journal of the Experimental Analysis of Behavior,* 1970, **13**, 243-266.

Hilgard, E.R., & Bower, G.H. *Theories of learning.* 4th Ed. New York: Appleton Century Crofts, 1974.

Hilgard, E.R., & Marquis, D.G. *Conditioning and learning.* (Revised by G.A. Kimble, 1961) New York: Appleton Century Crofts, 1940.

Hoffman, H.S. The analysis of discriminated avoidance. In W.K. Honig (Ed.), *Operant behavior: Areas of research and application.* New York: Appleton Century Crofts, 1966.

Honig, W.K. (Ed.) *Operant behavior: Areas of research and application.* New York: Appleton Century Crofts, 1966.

Honig, W.K., & Mackintosh, N.J. (Eds.) *Fundamental issues in associative learning.* Halifax, Nova Scotia: Dalhousie University Press, 1969.

Hull, C.L. Quantitative aspects of the evolution of concepts. *Psychological Monographs,* 1920, **28** (123).

Hull, C.L. A functional interpretation of the conditioned reflex. *Psychological Review,* 1929, **36**, 498-511.

Hull, C.L. Knowledge and purpose as habit mechanisms. *Psychological Review,* 1930, **37**, 511-525.

Hull, C.L. *Principles of behavior.* New York: Appleton Century Crofts, 1943.

Hull, C.L. Behavior postulates and corollaries. *Psychological Review*, 1950, **57**, 173-180.

Hull, C.L. *Essentials of behavior.* New Haven: Yale University Press, 1951.

Hull, C.L. *A behavior system.* New Haven: Yale University Press, 1952.

Hull, C.L., Hovland, C.I., Ross, R.T., Hall, M., Perkins, D.T., & Fitch, F.B. *Mathematico-deductive theory of rote learning.* New Haven: Yale University Press, 1940.

Hunt, E.B. *Concept learning: An information processing problem.* New York: Wiley, 1962.

Hunt, E.B., Marin, J., & Stone, P.J. *Experiments in induction.* New York: Academic Press, 1966.

John, E.R. *Mechanisms of memory.* New York: Academic Press, 1967.

Jones, J.E. All-or-none versus incremental learning. *Psychological Review,* 1962, **69**, 156-160.

Jung, J. *Verbal learning.* New York: Holt, Rinehart & Winston, 1968.

Kausler, D.H. *The psychology of verbal learning and memory.* New York: Academic Press, 1974.

Kelleher, R.T., & Gollub, L.R. A review of positive conditioned reinforcement. *Journal of the Experimental Analysis of Behavior,* 1962, **5**, 543-597.

Keppel, G. Retroactive and proactive inhibition. In T.R. Dixon & D.L. Horton (Eds.), *Verbal behavior and general behavior theory.* Englewood Cliffs, New Jersey: Prentice-Hall, 1968.

Kimble, G.A. Categories of learning and the problem of definition: Comments on Professor Grant's paper. In A.W. Melton (Ed.), *Categories of human learning.* New York: Academic Press, 1964.

Kimble, G.A. (Ed.) *Foundations of conditioning and learning.* New York: Appleton Century Crofts, 1967.

Kintsch, W. *Learning, memory, and conceptual processes.* New York: Wiley, 1970.

Klausmeier, H.J., & Harris, C.W. (Eds.) *Analyses of concept learning.* New York: Academic Press, 1966.

Koffka, K. *Principles of Gestalt psychology.* New York: Harcourt & Brace, 1963.

Köhler, W. *Gestalt psychology.* New York: Liveright, 1947.

Konorski, J. *Conditioned reflexes and neuron organization.* London: Cambridge University Press, 1948.

Krechevsky, I. (Krech, D.) "Hypotheses" in rats. *Psychological Review,* 1932, **39**, 516-532.

Lachman, R. The model in theory construction. *Psychological Review,* 1960, **67**, 113-129.

Landauer, T.K. Two hypotheses concerning the biochemical basis of memory. *Psychological Review,* 1964, **71**, 167-179.

Landauer, T.K. Reinforcement as consolidation. *Psychological Review,* 1969, **76**, 82-96.

Laughery, K.R. Computer simulation of short-term memory: A component decay model. In G.H. Bower & J.T. Spence (Eds.), *The psychology of learning and motivation.* Vol. 5. New York: Academic Press, 1971.

Laughery, K.R., & Pinkus, A.L. A simulation model of short-term memory: Parameter sensitivity studies and implications for two current issues. *Journal of Mathematical Psychology,* 1970, **7**, 554-571.

Lawrence, D.H. The nature of a stimulus: Some relationships between learning and perception. In S. Koch (Ed.), *Psychology: A study of a science.* Vol. 5. New York: McGraw-Hill, 1963.

Lenzer, I.I. Differences between behavior reinforced by electrical stimulation of the brain and conventionally reinforced behavior. *Psychological Bulletin,* 1972, **78**, 103-118.

Lewin, K. *Field theory in social science.* New York: Harper & Row, 1951.

Lewin, K. *Principles of topological psychology.* New York: McGraw-Hill, 1966.

Logan, F.A. A micromolar approach to behavior theory. *Psychological Review,* 1956, **63**, 63-73.

Logan, F.A. The Hull-Spence approach. In S. Koch (Ed.), *Psychology: A study of a science.* Vol. 2. New York: McGraw-Hill, 1959.

Logan, F.A. *Incentive: How the conditions of reinforcement affect the performance of rats.* New Haven: Yale University Press, 1960.

Logan, F.A. Incentive theory and changes in reward. In K.W. Spence & J.T. Spence (Eds.), *The psychology of learning and motivation.* Vol. 2. New York: Academic Press, 1968.

Logan, F.A. The negative incentive value of punishment. In B.A. Campbell & R.M. Church (Eds.), *Punishment and aversive behavior.* New York: Appleton Century Crofts, 1969.

Logan, F.A., & Ferraro, D.P. From free responding to discrete trials. In W.N. Schoenfeld (Ed.), *The theory of reinforcement schedules.* New York: Appleton Century Crofts, 1970.

Logan, F.A., & Wagner, A.R. *Reward and punishment.* Boston: Allyn & Bacon, 1965.

Luce, R.D. *Individual choice behavior.* New York: Wiley, 1959.

MacCorquodale, K., & Meehl, P.E. On a distinction between hypothetical constructs and intervening variables. *Psychological Review,* 1948, **55,** 95-107.

MacCorquodale, K., & Meehl, P.E. Edward C. Tolman. In W.K. Estes et al. (Eds.), *Modern learning theory.* New York: Appleton Century Crofts, 1954.

Macintosh, N.J. *The psychology of animal learning.* London: Academic Press, 1974.

Marx, M.H. Intervening variable or hypothetical construct. *Psychological Review,* 1951, **58,** 235-247.

Marx, M.H. (Ed.) *Learning: Processes.* New York: Macmillan, 1969.

Marx, M.H. (Ed.) *Learning: Interactions.* New York: Macmillan, 1970.

Marx, M.H. (Ed.) *Learning: Theories.* New York: Macmillan, 1970.

Marx, M.H. Theory construction and evaluation: Formal modes. In M.H. Marx (Ed.), *Learning: Theories.* New York: Macmillan, 1970.

Massaro, D.W. A three state Markov model for discrimination learning. *Journal of Mathematical Psychology,* 1969, **6,** 62-80.

McGuigan, F.J., & Lumsden, D.B. (Eds.) *Contemporary approaches to conditioning and learning.* Washington, D.C.: Winston, 1973.

McNeill, D. *The acquisition of language: The study of developmental psycholinguistics.* New York: Harper & Row, 1970.

Meehl, P.E. On the circularity of the law of effect. *Psychological Bulletin,* 1950, **47,** 52-75.

Melton, A.W., & Martin, E. (Eds.) *Coding processes in human memory.* Washington, D.C.: Winston, 1972.

Menyuk, P. *The acquisition and development of language.* Englewood Cliffs, New Jersey: Prentice-Hall, 1971.

Miller, N.E. Experimental studies of conflict. In J.M.V. Hunt (Ed.), *Personality and the behavior disorders.* New York: Ronald Press, 1944.

Miller, N.E. Liberalization of basic S-R concepts: Extensions to conflict behavior, motivation, and social learning. In S. Koch (Ed.), *Psychology: A study of a science.* Vol. 2. New York: McGraw-Hill, 1959.

Miller, N.E. Learning of visceral and glandular responses. *Science,* 1969, **163,** 434-445.

Morgan, M.J. Negative reinforcement. In L. Weiskrantz (Ed.), *Analysis of behavioral change.* New York: Harper & Row, 1968.

Mostofsky, D. (Ed.) *Stimulus generalization.* Stanford: Stanford University Press, 1965.

Mowrer, O.H. On the dual nature of learning: A reinterpretation of "conditioning" and "problem solving." *Harvard Educational Review,* 1947, **17,** 102-148.

Mowrer, O.H. *Learning theory and behavior.* New York: Wiley, 1960.

Muenzinger, K.F. On the origin and early use of the term vicarious trial and error (VTE). *Psychological Bulletin,* 1956, **53,** 493-494.

Murdock, B.B. *Human memory: Theory and data.* New York: Wiley, 1974.

Neimark, E.D., & Estes, W.K. (Eds.) *Stimulus sampling theory.* San Francisco: Holden-Day, 1967.

Neisser, U. *Cognitive psychology.* New York: Appleton Century Crofts, 1967.

Newell, A., & Simon, H.A. Computer simulation of human thinking. *Science,* 1961, **134,** 2011-2017.

Newell, A., & Simon, H.A. *Human problem solving.* Englewood Cliffs, New Jersey: Prentice-Hall, 1972.

Nodine, C.F. Temporal variables in paired-associate learning: The law of contiguity revisited. *Psychological Review,* 1969, **76,** 351-362.

Norman, D.A. (Ed.) *Models of human memory.* New York: Academic Press, 1970.

Notterman, J.M., & Mintz, D.E. *Dynamics of response.* New York: Wiley, 1965.

Nuttin, J., & Greenwald, A.G. *Reward and punishment in human learning.* New York: Academic Press, 1968.

Olds, J. Physiological mechanisms of reward. In M.R. Jones (Ed.), *Nebraska symposium on motivation.* Vol. 3. Lincoln: University of Nebraska Press, 1955.

Olds, J., & Milner, P. Positive reinforcement produced by electrical stimulation of septal area and other regions of the rat brain. *Journal of Comparative and Physiological Psychology,* 1954, **47,** 419-427.

Pavlov, I.P. *Conditioned reflexes.* (Trans. by G.V. Anrep.) London: Oxford University Press, 1927.

Pavlov, I.P. *Lectures on conditioned reflexes.* 2 Vols. (Trans. by W.H. Gantt.) New York: International Publishers, 1928, 1941.

Perkins, C.C., Jr. An analysis of the concept of reinforcement. *Psychological Review,* 1968, **75,** 155-172.

Peterson, L.R. Immediate memory: Data and theory. In C.N. Cofer & B.S.

Musgrave (Eds.), *Verbal behavior and learning.* New York: McGraw-Hill, 1963.

Pfaffman, C. Taste preference and reinforcement. In J.T. Tapp (Ed.), *Reinforcement and behavior.* New York: Academic Press, 1969.

Pollio, H.R. *The psychology of symbolic activity.* Reading, Mass.: Addison-Wesley, 1974.

Polson, M., Restle, F., & Polson, P.G. Association and discrimination in paired-associates learning. *Journal of Experimental Psychology,* 1965, **69**, 47-55.

Popper, K. *The logic of scientific discovery.* New York: Basic Books, 1959.

Postman, L. The history and present status of the law of effect. *Psychological Bulletin,* 1947, **44**, 489-563.

Postman, L. The present status of interference theory. In C.N. Cofer (Ed.), *Verbal learning and verbal behavior.* New York: McGraw-Hill, 1961.

Postman, L. Rewards and punishments in human learning. In L. Postman (Ed.), *Psychology in the making.* New York: Knopf, 1962.

Postman, L., & Underwood, B.J. Critical issues in interference theory. *Memory and Cognition,* 1973, **1**, 19-40.

Premack, D. Toward empirical behavioral laws: I. Positive reinforcement. *Psychological Review,* 1959, **66**, 219-233.

Premack, D. Reversibility of the reinforcement relation. *Science,* 1962, **136**, 255-257.

Premack, D. Prediction of the comparative reinforcement values of running and drinking. *Science,* 1963, **139**, 1062-1063.

Premack, D. Reinforcement theory. In D. Levine (Ed.), *Nebraska symposium on motivation.* Vol. 13. Lincoln: University of Nebraska Press, 1965.

Premack, D. A functional analysis of language. *Journal of the Experimental Analysis of Behavior,* 1970, **14**, 107-125.

Premack, D. Catching up with common sense on two sides of a generalization: Reinforcement and punishment. In R. Glaser (Ed.), *The nature of reinforcement.* New York: Academic Press, 1971.

Premack, D. Language in chimpanzees? *Science,* 1971, **172**, 808-822.

Pribram, K.H., & Broadbent, D.E. (Eds.) *Biology of memory.* New York: Academic Press, 1970.

Prokasy, W.F. (Ed.) *Classical conditioning: A symposium.* New York: Appleton Century Crofts, 1965.

Reitman, W.R. *Cognition and thought: An information processing approach.* New York: Wiley, 1965.

Rescorla, R.A., & Solomon, R.L. Two-process learning theory: Relationships between Pavlovian conditioning and instrumental learning. *Psychological Review,* 1967, **74**, 151-182.

Restle, F. A survey and classification of learning models. In R.R. Bush & W.K.

Estes (Eds.), *Studies in mathematical learning theory.* Stanford: Stanford University Press, 1959.

Restle, F. The selection of strategies in cue learning. *Psychological Review,* 1962, **69**, 329-343.

Restle, F. Significance of all-or-none learning. *Psychological Bulletin,* 1965, **64**, 313-325.

Restle, F. *Mathematical models in psychology: An introduction.* Baltimore: Penguin, 1971.

Restle, F., & Greeno, J.G. *Introduction to mathematical psychology.* Reading, Mass.: Addison-Wesley, 1970.

Riley, D.A. *Discrimination learning.* Boston: Allyn & Bacon, 1968.

Rock, I. The role of repetition in associative learning. *American Journal of Psychology,* 1957, **70**, 186-193.

Rock, I., & Heimer, W. Further evidence of one-trial associative learning. *American Journal of Psychology,* 1959, **72**, 1-16.

Rosenzweig, M.R., Møllgaard, K., Diamond, M.C., & Bennett, E.L. Negative as well as positive synaptic changes may store memory. *Psychological Review,* 1972, **79**, 93-96.

Saltz, E. *The cognitive bases of human learning.* Homewood, Illinois: Dorsey, 1971.

Schick, K. Operants. *Journal of the Experimental Analysis of Behavior,* 1971, **15**, 413-423.

Seligman, M.E.P. On the generality of the laws of learning. *Psychological Review,* 1970, **77**, 406-418.

Sheffield, F.D. A drive-induction theory of reinforcement. In R.N. Haber (Ed.), *Current research in motivation.* New York: Holt, Rinehart & Winston, 1966.

Sheffield, F.D. New evidence on the drive-induction theory of reinforcement. In R.N. Haber (Ed.), *Current research in motivation.* New York: Holt, Rinehart & Winston, 1966.

Sheffield, F.D., & Roby, T.B. Reward value of a non-nutritive sweet taste. *Journal of Comparative and Physiological Psychology,* 1950, **43**, 471-481.

Sheffield, F.D., Roby, T.B., & Campbell, B.A. Drive reduction versus consummatory behavior as determinants of reinforcement. *Journal of Comparative and Physiological Psychology,* 1954, **47**, 349-354.

Shiffrin, R.M., & Atkinson, R.C. Storage and retrieval processes in long-term memory. *Psychological Review,* 1969, **76**, 179-193.

Sidman, M. Avoidance behavior. In W.K. Honig (Ed.), *Operant behavior: Areas of research and application.* New York: Appleton Century Crofts, 1966.

Skinner, B.F. The concept of the reflex in the description of behavior. *Journal of Genetic Psychology,* 1931, **5**, 427-458.

Skinner, B.F. The generic nature of the concepts of stimulus and response. *Journal of Genetic Psychology,* 1935, **12**, 40-65.

Skinner, B.F. *The behavior of organisms.* New York: Appleton Century Crofts, 1938.

Skinner, B.F. "Superstition" in the pigeon. *Journal of Experimental Psychology,* 1948, **38**, 168-172.

Skinner, B.F. Are theories of learning necessary? *Psychological Review,* 1950, **57**, 193-216.

Skinner, B.F. *Science and human behavior.* New York: Macmillan, 1953.

Skinner, B.F. *Verbal behavior.* New York: Appleton Century Crofts, 1957.

Skinner, B.F. *Contingencies of reinforcement: A theoretical analysis.* New York: Appleton Century Crofts, 1969.

Skinner, B.F. *Cumulative record.* 3rd Ed. New York: Appleton Century Crofts, 1972.

Skinner, B.F. *About behaviorism.* New York: Knopf, 1974.

Solomon, R.L. Punishment. *American Psychologist,* 1964, **19**, 239-253.

Spence, K.W. The nature of theory construction in contemporary psychology. *Psychological Review,* 1944, **51**, 47-68.

Spence, K.W. The postulates and methods of behaviorism. *Psychological Review,* 1948, **55**, 67-68.

Spence, K.W. Cognitive versus stimulus-response theories of learning. *Psychological Review,* 1950, **57**, 159-172.

Spence, K.W. Theoretical interpretations of learning. In S.S. Stevens (Ed.), *Handbook of experimental psychology.* New York: Wiley, 1951.

Spence, K.W. The relation of response latency and speed to the intervening variables and N in S-R theory. *Psychological Review,* 1954, **61**, 209-216.

Spence, K.W. *Behavior theory and conditioning.* New Haven: Yale University Press, 1956.

Spence, K.W. *Behavior theory and learning.* Englewood Cliffs, New Jersey: Prentice-Hall, 1960.

Spooner, A., & Kellogg, W.N. The backward conditioning curve. *American Journal of Psychology,* 1947, **60**, 321-334.

Staddon, J.E.R. Asymptotic behavior: The concept of the operant. *Psychological Review,* 1967, **74**, 377-391.

Stevens, S.S. (Ed.) *Handbook of experimental psychology.* New York: Wiley, 1951.

Stevens, S.S. Mathematics, measurement, and psychophysics. In S.S. Stevens (Ed.), *Handbook of experimental psychology.* New York: Wiley, 1951.

Stubbs, D.A. Second-order schedules and the problem of conditioned reinforcement. *Journal of the Experimental Analysis of Behavior,* 1971, **16**, 289-313.

Suppes, P., Groen, G., & Schlag-Rey, M. A model for response latency in paired-associate learning. *Journal of Mathematical Psychology,* 1966, **3**, 99-128.

Terrace, H.S. Stimulus control. In W.K. Honig (Ed.), *Operant behavior: Areas of research and application.* New York: Appleton Cent

Theios, J. Simple conditioning as two-stage all-or-non *Review,* 1963, **70**, 403-417.

Theios, J., & Brelsford, J. Theoretical interpretation avoidance conditioning. *Journal of Mathemati* 140-162.

Thorndike, E.L. Animal intelligence: An experimer processes in animals. *Psychological Review Monograph Suppl.* **2** (8).

Thorndike, E.L. *Animal intelligence.* New York: Macmillan, 1911.

Thorndike, E.L. The law of effect. *American Journal of Psychology,* 1927, **39**, 212-222.

Thorndike, E.L. *The fundamentals of learning.* New York: Teachers College, Columbia University, 1932.

Thorndike, E.L. *The psychology of wants, interests, and attitudes.* New York: Appleton Century Crofts, 1935.

Timberlake, W., & Allison, J. Response deprivation: An empirical approach to instrumental performance. *Psychological Review,* 1974, **81**, 146-164.

Tolman, E.C. *Purposive behavior in animals and men.* New York: Appleton Century Crofts, 1932.

Tolman, E.C. Cognitive maps in rats and men. *Psychological Review,* 1948, **55**, 189-208.

Tolman, E.C. There is more than one kind of learning. *Psychological Review,* 1949, **56**, 144-155.

Tolman, E.C. Principles of performance. *Psychological Review,* 1955, **62**, 315-326.

Tolman, E.C. Principles of purposive behavior. In S. Koch (Ed.), *Psychology: A study of a science.* Vol. 2. New York: McGraw-Hill, 1959.

Tolman, E.C., & Brunswik, E. The organism and the causal texture of the environment. *Psychological Review,* 1935, **42**, 43-77.

Trabasso, T.R. Stimulus emphasis and all-or-none learning in concept identification. *Journal of Experimental Psychology,* 1963, **65**, 398-406.

Trowill, J.A., Panksepp, J., & Gandelman, R. An incentive model of rewarding brain stimulation. *Psychological Review,* 1969, **76**, 264-281.

Tulving, E., & Madigan, S.A. Memory and verbal learning. *Annual Review of Psychology,* 1970, **21**, 437-484.

Turner, M.B. *Philosophy and the science of behavior.* New York: Appleton Century Crofts, 1967.

Turner, M.B. *Realism and the explanation of behavior.* New York: Appleton Century Crofts, 1971.

Underwood, B.J. *Experimental psychology.* 2nd Ed. Englewood Cliffs, New Jersey: Prentice-Hall, 1966.

wood, B.J., & Schulz, R.W. *Meaningfulness and verbal learning.* New York: Lippincott, 1960.

ngar, G. (Ed.) *Molecular mechanisms in memory and learning.* New York: Plenum Press, 1970.

Vinacke, W.E. *The psychology of thinking.* New York: McGraw-Hill, 1974.

Vincent, S.B. The function of the vibrissae in the behavior of the white rat. *Behavioral Monograph,* 1912, 1(81).

Watson, J.B. Psychology as the behaviorist views it. *Psychological Review,* 1913, 20, 158-177.

Watson, J.B. The place of the conditioned reflex in psychology. *Psychological Review,* 1916, 23, 89-116.

Watson, J.B. *Behaviorism.* New York: Norton, 1925.

Waugh, N.C., & Norman, D.A. Primary memory. *Psychological Review,* 1965, 72, 89-104.

Wertheimer, M. *Productive thinking.* New York: Harper, 1959.

Wike, E.L. *Secondary reinforcement.* New York: Harper & Row, 1966.

Wike, E.L. Secondary reinforcement: Some research and theoretical issues. In W.J. Arnold & D. Levine (Eds.), *Nebraska symposium on motivation.* Vol. 19. Lincoln: University of Nebraska Press, 1971.

Winograd, T. *Understanding natural language.* New York: Academic Press, 1972.

Woods, P.J. A taxonomy of instrumental conditioning. *American Psychologist,* 1974, 29, 584-597.

Zimmerman, D.W. Durable secondary reinforcement: Method and theory. *Psychological Review,* 1957, 64, 373-383.

Zimmerman, D.W. Sustained performance in rats based on secondary reinforcement. *Journal of Comparative and Physiological Psychology,* 1959, 52, 353-358.

Index

evaluation (testing) of, 224-225
evaluation of *versus* use of, 226
examples of, 197, 226-228
generation of, 197-198
as interpreted in information theory or
    uncertainty reduction context,
    222-223
interpreted as reliable predictors,
    222-223
methods of creation of, 218-221
other terms for, 217-218
prototypical operational generating
    conditions for, 218-220
potency of, 225-226
theoretical significance and use of,
    228-229
use (application) of, 225-226
Simple experimental procedures, 30
Simple learning, denotative properties of,
    82-83
Simplicity of a theory, in relation to
    heuristic evaluation, 129
Single (unitary) response characteristics,
    analogical measurement of, 54-55,
    56
Single (unitary) response occurrence,
    digital measurement of, 56
Single (unitary) response situations, 50-51
Standard input situation, notion of, 30-31
Standard input situation, as related to
    learning task, 31
Statistical analysis, in learning macro-theory,
    135-136
Statistical analysis, in learning micro-models,
    153-154
Stimulational approach to response-
    contingent primary positive
    reinforcement, 272
Stimulus, 20-23, 82-83, 203-204
    definition of, 20
    initial characterization of, 20-22
    nature of, in complex learning, 82-83
    nature of, in simple learning, 82-83
    properties of, 22-23
    types of, 22-23, 203-204
Stimulus-response relationship, 15. *See
    also* Functional relationship,
    nature of.
Strong law of effect. *See* Theoretical law
    of effect
Summarization, as function of theory, 99-100
Symbolic responses, definition of, 46

Symbolic responses, measurement charac-
    teristics of, 57

Theoretical approaches to ESB, 276-277
Theoretical construct, 101-104
    characteristics of, 101-104
    definition of, 101
    nature of, 101-104
Theoretical intervening situation, genera-
    tion of, 94-95
Theoretical intervening situation, nature
    of, 94-130
Theoretical law of effect, 266
Theoretical law of effect, as teleological
    explanation, 281-283
    co-occurrence approach to resolution
        of, 282
    definition of, 281
    resolution of, 281-283
    succession approach to resolution of,
        282-283
Theory, 96-100
    construction of, 105-117
    definition of, 97
    evaluation of, 117-129
    functions of, 97-100
    "goal" function of, 100
    "means" function of, 100
    origin of, 104-105
    types of, 105-117
Theory evaluation, types of, 100, 117
Traditional macro-theoretical approaches
    to response-contingent primary
    positive reinforcement, 268-271
Traditional macro-theoretical approaches
    to "What is learned?" or "units
    of learning" issue, 269

Validity, as a property of measuring
    device, 39-40
Verbal learning, nature of, 251-252
Verbal responses. *See* Symbolic responses,
    definition of

Weak law of effect. *See* Empirical law of
    effect
"What is learned?" (units of learning)
    issue, 137, 268-269

TITLES IN THE PERGAMON GENERAL PSYCHOLOGY SERIES (Continued)